Saskatewan   Quebec   Ontario   Prince Edward   New Brunswick   Nova Scotia

Baffin Island

Frobisher Bay

Hudson Strait

James Bay

Hudson Bay

Canada A to Z

Schefferville

Goose Bay

NEWFOUNDLAND

Labrador

QUEBEC

Gulf of St. Lawrence

Bonavista

St. John's

Corner Brook
Stephenville

Placentia

Sept-Îles

NEW BRUNSWICK

Port-aux-Basques

Gaspé

St. Lawrence River

Matane

Moncton

Charlottetown

PRINCE EDWARD ISLAND
Cape Breton Highlands N.P.

Sydney

Chicoutimi

La Malbaie

Edmundston

Antigonish

NOVA SCOTIA

Ste. Anne
de Beaupré

Amherst

Quebec

Fredericton

Halifax

Cap de la Madeleine

Saint John

Lunenburg

Trois Rivières

St. Agathe

Montreal

Sherbrooke

Hull

Granby

Yarmouth

Bay of Fundy

Timmins

North Bay

Ottawa

Atlantic Ocean

Midland

Kingston

Hamilton

Lake Ontario

Boston

Niagara Falls

Albany

Buffalo

New York

Jefferson

CANADA *A to Z*

Robert S. Kane's A to Z World Travel Guides

Canada A to Z
Hawaii A to Z
London A to Z
Paris A to Z
Grand Tour A to Z: The Capitals of Europe
Eastern Europe A to Z
South Pacific A to Z
Asia A to Z
South America A to Z
Africa A to Z

CANADA
A to Z

REVISED EDITION

ROBERT S. KANE

DOUBLEDAY & COMPANY, INC.   Garden City, New York
DOUBLEDAY CANADA LTD.   Toronto

Library of Congress Cataloging in Publication Data

Kane, Robert S.
  Canada A to Z, Revised Edition

  Includes index.
  1. Canada—Description and travel—Guidebooks. I. Title
  ISBN: 0-385-09947-9 (Trade)
         0-385-09948-7 (Paperbound)
  Library of Congress Catalog Card Number 75-36630

For DeWitt Davidson

Contents

Foreword	ix
Canada Alphabetically	xi
Canada: The Background	1
Canada: Tourist Territory	21
Alberta	39
British Columbia	66
Manitoba	100
New Brunswick	125
Newfoundland	143
Northwest Territories	160
Nova Scotia	171
Ontario	199
Prince Edward Island	246
Quebec	260
Saskatchewan	307
Yukon Territory	324
Acknowledgments	336
Index	338

Maps
   Introducing each Province and Territory
   Preceding Chapter 1

Foreword

Americans are not out to conquer Canada. But an army of some 35 million of us descend upon it each year. (That figure does not include the many additional millions who go back and forth across the border for a day's visit, as they might walk across the street.)

Falsely modest though we may attempt to be, there's no doubt about it: The United States *is* the North American Big Brother. The Canadian recognizes this fact of life (though he is noticeably more critical about it than he used to be), and he is fantastically well-informed about the United States. He keeps himself up to date on his own neighborhood, his province, his country nationally, *and* the United States. Indeed, his orientation is that of a *North American,* a term infrequently used in the United States. He is as interested in what the Washington columnist reports in his newspaper as he is in that paper's dispatches from Ottawa.

Those of us in the United States are as unconcerned, by and large, with the affairs of the world's second largest country as we are with those of Finnish Lapland. Our press has but a handful of permanent correspondents stationed in the Canadian capital. We consider ourselves *au courant* if we know the name of the Prime Minister. Provincial premiers? Come on, now. The Governor-General's identity? Don't be silly. Geography? We know that Montreal is in the east, Vancouver in the west, Toronto and Banff (not necessarily—but possibly—in that order) somewhere in between. Not a few of us believe the Yukon is a part of our forty-ninth state, and we're frequently surprised to learn that the Trans-Canada Highway is not the Alaska Highway. We know Saskatoon, Saskatchewan, as the catchy title of a once-popular song—and then only if we're old enough.

But it would appear, too, that there are Canadians who are not as familiar with distant parts of their own country as they are with regions of the United States near where they live, or with other lands. The Montrealer can be more interested in Paris than in Winnipeg, the British Columbian looks toward the Pacific and Washington state rather than the prairies on the other side of the Continental Divide, while the New Brunswicker can tell you a lot about Boston—and possibly even wicked New York. I cannot produce statistics, but I remain incredulous at the number of Canadians I have met—loyal as the day is long to their Queen—who bristle with umbrage when one comments that Canada is a monarchy. Not a *colony,* mind you—even we Americans know it is completely sovereign—but a monarchy, with the Queen of Canada its Head of State.

Canada A to Z, though, is not a political science lecture, a history primer, or a refresher course in geography—although at times it may appear to be. It is the attempt of a neighbor—admittedly presumptuous but, by and large, enthusiastic—to appraise province by province (and not excluding the territories) the touristic highlights of a country so remarkable that too often it is taken for granted not only by its neighbors to the south, but by its own people, not a few of whom never get around to traversing that portion of the continent which is theirs—and which they have made great.

Robert S. Kane

Canada Alphabetically

Province or Territory	Capital	Area (Square Miles)	Population[1]
Alberta	Edmonton	255,285	1,747,000
British Columbia	Victoria	366,255	2,441,000
Manitoba	Winnipeg	251,000	1,014,000
New Brunswick	Fredericton	28,354	670,000
Newfoundland	St. John's	156,185	546,000
Northwest Territories	Yellowknife	1,304,903	40,000
Nova Scotia	Halifax	21,425	818,000
Ontario	Toronto	412,582	8,171,000
Prince Edward Island	Charlottetown	2,184	118,000
Quebec	Quebec City	594,860	6,165,000
Saskatchewan	Regina	251,700	912,000
Yukon Territory	Whitehorse	207,076	20,000
Total		3,851,809	22,659,000

[1] 1975 estimates.

0 100 200 300 400 500 miles

Baffin Bay

Baffin I.

Frobisher Bay

Hudson Strait

Hudson Bay

Schefferville

Labrador

Goose Bay

NEWFOUNDLAND

Gander

St. John's

Corner Brook

Placentia

Stephenville

QUEBEC

Gulf of St. Lawrence

Port-aux-Basques

Sept-Îles

NEW BRUNSWICK

Gaspé

ONTARIO

Matane

Moncton

Charlottetown

PRINCE EDWARD ISLAND

Sydney

Chicoutimi

La Malbaie

Edmundston

Antigonish

Amherst

NOVA SCOTIA

Ste. Anne de Beaupré

Fredericton

Halifax

Timmins

Quebec

Saint John

Cap de la Madeleine

Trois Rivières

Lunenburg

Trans-Canada Highway

Ste. Agathe

Sherbrooke

Yarmouth

North Bay

Montreal

Granby

Atlantic Ocean

Superior

Hull

Sault Ste. Marie

Ottawa

Sault Ste. Marie

Lake Huron

Midland

Kingston

Boston

Lake Michigan

Toronto

Lake Ontario

Albany

Hamilton

Niagara Falls

London

Buffalo

Detroit

Windsor

Lake Erie

New York

Canada
A to Z

Canada: The Background

The history of Canada is a study in political survival.

—EDGAR MCINNIS, *Canada: A Political and Social History*

There is no virtue in mere size. . . . In Canada's case, it can raise many different problems in a country's development. And Canada above all has been affected by its geography; there is so much of it.

—J. M. S. CARELESS, *Canada: A Story of Challenge*

NUMBER TWO

Canadians, of which there are more than 22 million, become accustomed to the disproportionate size of their country by the time they've studied its geography in school. Newcomers to the Canadian scene—if they know nothing else about Canada—know that it is capacious. But most, nonetheless, cannot help but be impressed with even the most basic statistics on our planet's second-biggest nation, which is exceeded in area only by the Soviet Union. Occupying over 3.8 million square miles, Canada extends from the Northwest Territories' Cape Columbia on Ellesmere Island—a relative hop and a skip from the North Pole—to Pelee Island, in Ontario's portion of Lake Erie—and with the same latitude as central

Spain. That's a north–south distance of 2,850 miles. The east to west span is 5,780 miles—from Cape Spear, Newfoundland, to Mount St. Elias in the Yukon Territory—a distance considerable enough to necessitate seven distinct time zones—three more than in the U.S. (The added trio: Yukon Time, Atlantic Time—in three of the Maritime provinces—and Newfoundland Time—for the fourth of that group.)

In between these points are twelve principal political subdivisions—ten provinces and the two territories that embrace most of the vast north, accounting for 38 per cent of Canada's area and an infinitesimal fraction of its population.

Canada's shores are washed by three great oceans—the Atlantic, the Pacific, and the Arctic. It occupies about a third of the world's known fresh-water area, which constitutes about 6 per cent of the country. All but one of the Great Lakes (Michigan) are partially Canadian. But, of course, enormous Hudson Bay is exclusively Canadian, as are such massive but relatively little-known inland seas as Great Bear Lake (12,275 square miles), Great Slave Lake —just a bit smaller—and Lake Winnipeg, which is bigger than Lake Ontario. Other liquid assets? Well, it is by and through Canada that the St. Lawrence Seaway flows some 2,300 miles—making possible big-scale shipping from Atlantic ports all the way to harbors on the Great Lakes in the heart of the continent. Canada's longest river system, the Mackenzie, drains into the Arctic Ocean. The Columbia and Fraser rivers flow into the Pacific; the Nelson and Churchill connect with Hudson Bay; the Yukon drains into the Bering Sea; and the Saskatchewan empties into Lake Winnipeg.

Geographically, there are five principal Canadian regions. The *Appalachian,* in the east, takes in a quartet of relatively small Atlantic Provinces and a portion of southeastern Quebec; this is a land of lovely hills and gentle plains, much of it devoted to farming and forestry. The *St. Lawrence Lowlands,* between the St. Lawrence River and the Great Lakes, in Ontario and southern Quebec, is a fertile area of dairy farms, fruit orchards, and tobacco plantations, rich in industry which is made possible by extensive and inexpensive hydroelectric power. The *Canadian,* or *pre-Cambrian, Shield* is far and away the country's largest geographic unit—covering some 1.6 million square miles, or almost half of Canada. This horseshoe-shaped area of ancient terrain is a mass of rock, of many lakes and of endless swampland, or muskeg, as it is called. It is sparsely populated but exceedingly rich not only in timber but in nickel, gold, platinum, cobalt, uranium, silver, copper, and iron ore.

Still other riches come from the *Interior Plains,* which sweep across southern Manitoba, Saskatchewan, and Alberta north through the Mackenzie River Valley to the Arctic coast. The southern part of the plains—the prairies—are, more often than not, flat as a pancake, but they are fertile and they constitute Canada's magnificent wheatlands. In recent decades they have yielded, besides the golden wheat, liquid gold—oil from beneath the surface, and natural gas as well. They are bordered on the north by thick forest lands.

West of the Plains lies the Continental Divide and what is known as the *Canadian Cordillera.* This is the region of western Alberta, British Columbia, and the Yukon, which comprises the glorious Canadian Rockies as well as the Mackenzie and Stikine Mountains and the peaks of the St. Elias and Coast ranges. It is in this area that one finds Mount Logan, in the Yukon—Canada's highest peak, climbing some 19,850 feet skyward. Not all of this region is mountainous, though. The interior of British Columbia is a land of plateaus and valleys prosperous with orchards and cattle ranches. The forests of the west are among the most productive in the world, and the Pacific coast, like the Atlantic, helps make Canada a major fishing nation.

Canada's border with the United States is not only one of the friendliest extant, but one of the longest: it extends 3,986 miles, and is broken by scores upon scores of entry-exit points between the two nations. It is near this frontier that some 85 per cent of the Canadian populace is clustered. Much of the massive north is attractive only to Eskimos and Indians and a relative handful of whites. Indeed, in this country where less than a tenth of the land is occupied by farms, some two thirds of the total area is not developed. The Canadians have a great deal of room to roam, and they have only begun to exploit the tremendous mineral wealth of their largely uninhabited areas.

CABOT TO CONFEDERATION

Canada's history—detailed in the chapters following, dealing with the various provinces and territories—can hardly be surpassed for sheer excitement and adventure, faith and courage, guts and derring-do. It is, in other words, a New World success story of the kind that Americans—whose own history was similar in a number of ways and which, indeed, has long been interlinked with that of Canada—can understand and appreciate. Similarities of background the two countries do possess, but only certain similarities. The differences are, perhaps, even more important.

Canada was, of course, before newcomers came, the domain of a relatively small number of Indians, and of Eskimos above the tree line in the Arctic. If we accept the legendary accounts, the first visitors from abroad were the Vikings of Leif Ericson fame. They came—if indeed they did come—a millennium ago and set up a trio of colonies on the east coast. But it was centuries later until there was additional activity. In 1497 John Cabot, a Genoese out of Bristol who, like Columbus, was looking for a short cut to the Orient, came upon the Canadian coast. A few decades later, the Breton Jacques Cartier sailed from the old France to what became the new.

When, in 1534, Cartier erected a fleur-de-lis-embellished cross at Gaspé in what is now Quebec, he established the colony of New France. And on later voyages, he sailed the St. Lawrence as far as Montreal. But the intrepid Samuel de Champlain was not yet on the scene. He was not to arrive until 1604 when he founded Port Royal, in what is now Nova Scotia, as the first permanent settlement and followed that up four years later with Quebec. This fortress-city was to become the core of French power—politically autocratic, commercially daring, and aggressive—on the continent, and from which the French, competing with the English, pushed into the wilderness, enriching themselves on the fur trade with the Indians, charting vast new territory—to James and Hudson bays in the north, and to the Mississippi, New Orleans, and the Gulf of Mexico in the west and south, thereby enclosing the English colonies in a massive arc running through the Great Lakes and down the Mississippi.

The English, though, wanted their share of the gold that the furs brought in Europe. In 1670 they established the Hudson's Bay Company; it, and the French-controlled North West Company were fierce rivals until the former absorbed the latter in the early nineteenth century. Long before that time, however, New France had its demise. In 1759, on the Plains of Abraham in Quebec, England's Wolfe defeated France's Montcalm in a battle that took both leaders' lives. The French possessions joined their neighbors to the south as segments of British North America. During the American Revolution, though, they remained loyal to the Crown (indeed, many American colonists, as United Empire Loyalists, emigrated north during that period to play an important role in young Canada's maturity).

The colonies that were to become Canada were alone in the Americas in that they did not revolt against their motherland for freedom. The original severance from France was the result of an essentially Anglo-French political settlement. With Britain, thereafter, the colonies remained politically separate, going about their development in their own separate ways—absorbing new immigrants from Europe and the United States, creating new communities, building roads, earning their livings by the sea, by the land, by trapping and lumbering and shipbuilding.

The War of 1812 against the United States—resulting in a victory for neither side, but with no loss for the British in Canada—impeded progress but was a factor in the movement for intercolonial unity, which followed some decades later. For the colonies of British North America began to appreciate the advantages of joint defense against possible attacks from the United States. (It was not, indeed, until the third quarter of the nineteenth century that the Canadians were able to finally allay fears of U.S. annexation.) There were other important reasons for unity: a desire for the joining of the territories in the west with those of the east, a desire to co-operate on building a railroad from the Atlantic coast to the central provinces, and a conviction that political union would promote economic development. In 1867 the Confederation of Canada was created as a result of the British North America Act, and with Sir John A. Macdonald as the first Prime

Minister. Its initial members—Quebec, Ontario, Nova Scotia, and New Brunswick—combined under a federal parliamentary system along the lines already practiced in each province, and with a provision allowing for new members from among the other territories and provinces. Manitoba joined in 1870, British Columbia (after being assured that a transcontinental railroad would be built to link it with the east) in 1871, Prince Edward Island in 1873, Alberta and Saskatchewan in 1905, and—decades later—Newfoundland, in 1949.

The transcontinental railroad, which British Columbia insisted upon in its agreement to join the confederation, was completed in 1885 and opened the west for expansion. The first decade of the twentieth century saw nearly two million immigrants—many from central Europe—come to Canada, many of them settling in the prairies and the west. With this development came the desire for Canadian self-government. Prime Minister Sir Wilfrid Laurier said in 1900, that "in the future Canada shall be at liberty to act or not to act . . . and that she shall reserve to herself the right to judge whether or not there is cause for her to act."

In 1909 the government's Department of External Affairs was founded, but it was World War I that lifted Canada into the international scene. Besides a substantial contribution of manpower, Canada shipped more than a billion dollars' worth of war matériel overseas. As a result, Canada was represented at the Versailles Peace Conference, and later it joined the League of Nations as a separate member, independent of Britain. In 1923 Canada signed its first bilateral treaty (with the United States). In 1926 an Imperial Conference determined that the nations of the British Commonwealth were "equal in status and in no way subordinate one to another in any aspect of their domestic or external affairs, though united by a common allegiance to the Crown and *freely* associated as members of the British Commonwealth of Nations" (italics mine). Half a decade later these principles were incorporated in the Statute of Westminster, and Canada—increasingly each year—was on its own. In 1927 it opened its first legation abroad—at Washington. Now, of course, it has embassies and diplomatic and consular representatives around the world. (Its representatives to other Commonwealth countries are called high commissioners, rather than ambassadors. For long the only Commonwealth member in the Western Hemisphere, Canada has been joined in recent years by such former West Indian colonies as Barbados, Jamaica, and Trinidad-Tobago.)

Canada entered World War II by its own declaration of war, in September 1939; four out of ten Canadian men between the ages of eighteen and forty-five saw service, and there were nearly a hundred thousand war casualties. It stepped up industrial production almost miraculously during this period and was second among the exporting Allied nations; four fifths of its exports were war goods for the Allies, and these it gave to its comrades as gifts, in the amount of some four billion dollars. And be it remembered that Canada alone of the Allies did not accept American Lend-Lease assistance, instead paying cash for what it received from the United States. World War II cost Canada nineteen billion dollars.

The postwar period saw Canada gain new international prestige as well as a healthier internal economy. Added to fish, furs, timber, and agriculture were the mineral industries resulting from the airplane's penetration of the great north, and tremendously accelerated manufacturing activity.

Canada was, of course, a charter member of the United Nations. She joined the North Atlantic Treaty Organization when that body was formed in 1949. Canada was one of the founders in 1950 of the Colombo Plan for aid to Asian countries, and its post-World War II foreign aid program has run into the billions and is the fourth largest in the non-Communist world. For a country that was an unfederated group of colonies less than a century ago, that —despite its small population—spans a continent but has been served by modern transport for even less time, that has been completely sovereign only since the First World War, and that still has not fully resolved the internal conflicts created by its peculiar Anglo-French heritage, one understates by terming Canada one of the most remarkable countries the world has known.

CANADA'S MUCH-MISUNDERSTOOD FORM OF GOVERNMENT

Here is what Canada is *not:* It is *not* a colony or a possession of Great Britain. It is *not* a republic. And to call it a "dominion" (which it at one time officially styled itself and which some people, Canadian and otherwise, still call it) is to term it nothing more— according to Webster's Collegiate Dictionary and other authorities —than a "territory governed" or a "self-governing colony."

What, then, is Canada? It is a sovereign state—completely sovereign, free, and independent, with a democratic, parliamentary form of government. And it is, at the same time, a monarchy, for the Chief of State is the Queen of Canada or, to use the official title: "Elizabeth the Second, by the grace of God of the United Kingdom, Canada and her other realms and territories, Queen, Head of the Commonwealth, Defender of the Faith."

Now, make no mistake about it: the Queen's role as Head of State is titular, and largely ceremonial. She wields no political power or authority in the affairs of Canada and her role is limited to participation, either by herself or her representative, at the opening of Parliament, the awarding of honors, and the assent to bills. (Queen Elizabeth II was the first monarch to officiate at an opening of Parliament when she read the Speech from the Throne —prepared for her by the Canadian Government—in 1957; she has since visited Canada regularly. The visit of her parents, King George VI and Queen Elizabeth—later the Queen Mother—in 1939 was the first to Canada of a reigning British monarch, but there had been a number of other royal visits.)

More than anything else, the Queen today symbolizes the unity and continuity of the British Commonwealth. Her chief representative in Canada is the Governor-General, who in recent years has been appointed by her on the recommendation of the Canadian Government. Major General Georges P. Vanier (in office 1959–67) was the first French-speaking Canadian to hold the post. Governor-General Vanier's immediate predecessor, Vincent Massey, was unusual in that he was the first *Canadian* to be Governor-General; earlier Governors-General—and there had been seventeen of them since confederation in 1867—were all British.

Jules Léger, who took office in 1974, succeeding Roland Michener, is the second French Canadian to hold the office. The Governor-General's official residence is Government House, Ottawa, although for part of each summer he lives at the historic Citadel in Quebec City. His duties are primarily ceremonial. He receives the credentials of foreign ambassadors, acts as host to visiting chiefs of state, and entertains officially. But he does have rarely used powers and can dismiss a government for unconstitutional or unlawful action. The Crown, aside from being represented at Ottawa, also has representation in each of the ten Canadian provinces through the Lieutenant (often pronounced *leff*-tenant) Governors, who are appointed and paid by the federal government and perform on a provincial scale, much like the Governor-General does on a national basis. In most provincial capitals, there is an official Lieutenant Governor's residence, known as Government House.

The business of actually governing Canada is entrusted to the Prime Minister—the country's chief executive, and the bicameral Parliament, which has a Senate consisting of 102 members appointed by the government for life, and a House of Commons, whose 265 members are elected. The number of members from each province is determined by population and subject to readjustment following the national census which is conducted once every decade.

The Prime Minister represents, of course, the political party in power, and selects to run the ministries of the government's Cabinet personnel from among the members of the majority party in the House of Commons. M.P.s are elected for terms not to exceed five years, but the Prime Minister may "advise the Governor-General" to dissolve the House at any time and call for a new election. This usually occurs when the government loses majority support of the House on an issue of consequence.

It happened in February 1963, during the administration of Prime Minister John Diefenbaker of the Progressive Conservative Party (Conservatives, for short). In the election that followed, the then opposition party—the Liberals—came through with 130 seats in contrast to the Conservatives' 94. As a result Mr. Diefenbaker, a son of the prairie province of Saskatchewan, resigned, to become Leader of the Opposition. Governor-General Vanier called upon the Liberals' leader, Lester B. Pearson—bilingual native of Ontario, ex-University of Toronto professor, ex-Canadian External Affairs Minister, one-time ambassador to Washington, former President of the United Nations General Assembly, and 1957 Nobel Peace Prize laureate—to become Canada's fourteenth Prime Minister. Pearson stepped down in 1968, to be succeeded by

Pierre Elliott Trudeau, a Québecois bilingual in English and French, dynamic, attractive, controversial—and the most internationally talked-about Canadian Prime Minister of modern times.

Though the Prime Ministership has been held through the years by members of either the Liberal or Progressive Conservative parties—neither of which could be considered worlds apart from the other on most issues—there are two other parties currently represented in Parliament: the New Democratic Party, a socialist group; and the Social Credit Party.

CANADA TODAY

There is not, in either the developed or developing parts of the world, a country without problems and Canada—whose population consists of mortal beings—is no exception. Recent governments have encouraged economic development to continue while at the same time assuaging the fears of nationalist-minded Canadians that their country is being inundated—to their detriment—by U.S. capital and the influence it may (or may not) wield.

There have been problems regarding the relatively slow development of the Atlantic Provinces (New Brunswick, Newfoundland, Nova Scotia, Prince Edward Island) where wages and living standards still lag behind the rest of the country.

A legacy of Anglo-Saxon influence which is evident in the United States as well as Canada—racial and ethnic prejudice—bugs Canada as well as its southern neighbor, if on a smaller scale. The Canadian Indian, though the recipient of government aid while resident in reservations, continues to be discriminated against and is still at the bottom of the educational, social, and professional barrel. But organizations like the Indian-Eskimo Association of Canada are spurring the native peoples to fight for more enlightened legislation so that they may participate more fully in the Canadian community. The Eskimo—beloved for his good humor, his smile, and his peaceful, live-and-let-live way of life—is considered by expert observers as being in danger of facing cultural extinction, thanks to increasing contact with the white man, his diseases, and the conflicts resulting from education for the technological, temperate-zone world, despite continued Arctic residence. The blacks of Canada face no legislated color bar. Still, though relatively few in number, they encounter racial, occupational, and social prejudices not unlike those of the United States. Ontario elected a black to its legislature in 1963—the first in Canada; and in 1968 Lincoln Alexander of Hamilton, Ontario, became the first black elected to the Federal Parliament; he was re-elected in 1972.

Far and away Canada's biggest problem lies in the relations of the federal government with the provinces. Of the provinces, the most concerned with federal relations are British Columbia and Quebec. Indeed, Quebec is the major thorn in the fabric of Canadian unity. The largest province in area, the second largest in population, and dominantly French-speaking and Roman Catholic, Quebec has always been a reluctant partner in confederation. It has never considered that the rest of Canada has appreciated the role of the French in founding Canada, and it has never quite gotten over the British conquest of 1763. It resents, and well it might, the contempt which many Canadians feel toward its magnificent language—even though it is the language of about a third of the Canadian populace. In an attempt to give the French language more national prestige, and to assure the French-speaking Canadian that he or she may deal in French with all agencies of the Federal Government, Parliament passed the Official Languages Act in 1969. It stipulates that English and French enjoy equal status and are the official languages of Canada for all—note the "all"—purposes of the parliament and government of Canada.

After World War II Quebec, for long lagging in technology, sprang forth as a great industrial complex. It began to feel that its national pride was not commensurate with its importance. By the mid-1960s knowledgeable observers began to realize that Quebec's secession from the confederation was a distinct possibility unless its demands for more autonomy were satisfied.

A 1963-appointed national commission on biculturalism was a start, and ever since there has been considerable accommodation of Anglo-Canada toward Quebec. Even so, in 1974 the Quebec legislature enacted the so-called Law 22, which made French the sole official language of the province for purposes of education, commerce, and government. Fears exist that if Quebec secedes, heavily French-speaking New Brunswick and parts of eastern Ontario might join it, and that eventually the other provinces would become states of the Big Brother to the south.

THE CANADIAN FLAG

In the spring of 1964 Prime Minister Pearson proposed a new, entirely Canadian flag to replace the long-used Red Ensign which included the British Union Jack, was often confused with the similar flags of Australia and New Zealand, and was unpopular in Quebec. The new colors were adopted in 1965—an instant international success, thanks to the simplicity of the design and the wise use of the maple leaf symbol; a red maple leaf occupies the center of the flag, with a white background framed on left and right by blocks of red. "O Canada" is the national anthem, sung in both English and French. And the national motto is *A Mari Usque ad Mare*—From Sea to Sea.

CULTURAL CANADA

Canada is not, Mr. Newcomer, the exclusive domain of the backwoodsman or the hockey player. It has evolved a culture that, even if derivative in part of the United States, Britain, and France, is still distinctively Canadian—dynamic and, very often, exciting. Canadians have long been interpreting their country and its people through the arts, but since World War II they have been doing so with added self-assurance, maturity, and style. And since 1957, to help "foster and promote the study and enjoyment of, and the production of works in the arts, humanities and social sciences," the government-sponsored Canada Council has been aiding the arts and their practitioners by means of grants and scholarships.

Canada is sadly underappreciated, beyond its frontiers at least, as regards its striking accomplishments in the field of *painting*. Early Canadian greats—out of the nineteenth century—to look for in art museums throughout the country are Cornelius Krieghoff, Paul Kane, and Homer Watson. Later, in the years leading up to World War I, the work of Tom Thomson and David Milne rose to the forefront, and can now be seen in museums throughout the land. Simultaneously, the paintings of Emily Carr graphically interpreted the Indian culture and the wilderness of Canada's Far West. (There are more than four hundred Milne works in Ottawa's National Gallery, while Thomson is honored with the Tom Thomson Memorial Gallery in Owen Sound, Ontario, near where he was born; Miss Carr's work—or at least two hundred of her finest paintings—are a major asset of the Vancouver Art Gallery, just across the water from Victoria, where she was born and where her home is today a museum.)

Thomson and Milne's work—brisk, strong, full of color, movingly personal—set the scene for the post-World War I canvases of the Group of Seven. Again, works of each of the gifted members of this group are to be seen in museums coast to coast, and their names are worth noting. Alphabetically, the Group of Seven consisted of Franklin Carmichael, Lawren Harris, A. Y. Jackson, Frank F. "Franz" Johnston, Arthur Lismer, J. E. H. MacDonald, and F. H. Varley. Note, also, the names of A. J. Casson and Edwin Holgate, later members. Of the lot, A. Y. Jackson and Lawren Harris are probably the most popular today, although that is a subjective opinion.

Contemporary painting plays as vital a role on the domestic art scene in Canada as in the United States or Europe. An interesting summation of the contemporary art scene was a traveling exhibition called "The Canadian Canvas," with 85 works by 46 artists selected by curators of five museums (Vancouver Art Gallery—for the west coast, Edmonton Art Gallery—for the Prairies, Art Gallery of Ontario—for Ontario, Musée d'Art Contemporain in Montreal—for Quebec, and Anna Leonowens Gallery in Halifax—for the Maritimes). The show crossed the country (I happened across it at the Vancouver Art Gallery) and indicated that Canadian painting runs a refreshingly wide gamut, from the traditional through abstract into experimental works. More conventional painters in the show included Dorothy Knowles of Saskatchewan, William Kurelek and Clark McDougall of Ontario, and Christopher Pratt of Newfoundland. Abstractionists included British Columbia's Jack Shadbolt and Brian Fisher, Manitoba's Don Reichert, Alberta's Harold Feist, Ontario's Gershon Iskowitz, Quebec's Rita Letendre, Claude Tousignant, and Jacques Hurtibise, and Nova Scotia's Gerald Ferguson and Bruceg Parsons.

Canada has achieved remarkable success with *ballet.* Canada's most noted company—and the only group in the Commonwealth, outside of London's Royal Ballet, accorded by the Crown the honor of terming itself "royal"—is the Royal Winnipeg Ballet. There are, as well, the National Ballet of Canada, which head-quarters in Toronto, and Les Grands Ballets Canadiens, of Montreal. Other troupes include the Toronto Dance Theatre, Winnipeg's Contemporary Dancers, and La Groupe de la Place Royale from Quebec City. A number of cities have fine *symphony orchestras;* Toronto's is outstanding, but they range from Vancouver in the west to Montreal in the east. Toronto, in addition, has an opera company with a regular repertoire of more than twenty operas, and there are the newer Opéra du Québec as well as companies in the bigger western cities. Many Canadian soloists, both singers and instrumentalists, are gaining international reputations —pianist Glenn Gould, singers Maureen Forester and Jon Vickers, and composer Healy Willian are but a handful. Composers like Robert Fleming, Eldon Rathburn, and Maurice Blackburn have introduced a Canadian idiom to their works.

Press and literature: Canadians are articulate both verbally and on paper. Canada supports 118 daily newspapers, with a total daily circulation of more than four million copies; a dozen of these are published in French, and a half dozen in other languages. There are, as well, 923 weeklies, 212 of these in French. There are over a hundred foreign-language publications in more than a score of languages. Still, Canada is plagued, not unlike the U.S., with one-newspaper towns. In all Canada there are only five cities of any size in which competing newspapers exist. The dailies collectively support Canadian Press—the major news-gathering agency—and the wires of United Press International are also used by Canadian papers. *Maclean's Magazine* (with separate English and French editions), a mass-circulation general-readership bi-monthly, might well be emulated in the United States; it is literate, intelligent, and with a stimulating point of view. *Canada Month, Saturday Night,* and *Quest* (aimed at men) are among the other interesting national magazines, and there are sprightly regional and local ones, too. Of the English-language papers, the *Globe and Mail* of Toronto is considered the most authoritative, on a national basis. The *Toronto Star* and the *Gazette* of Montreal are outstanding papers. Among

French-language papers, standouts include Montreal's *La Presse,* that same city's intellectually oriented *Le Devoir,* and Quebec City's *Le Soleil.*

Canadian novelists—writing in both French and English—are preoccupying themselves increasingly with the Canadian scene; among them are Margaret Alwood, Robertson Davies, Margaret Laurence, Roger Lemelin, W. O. Mitchell, Al Purdy, Thomas Raddall, Hugh MacLennan, Mordecai Richeler, Morley Callaghan, Gabrielle Roy, and Robert Elie, not to mention old-established names like Mazo de la Roche, Stephen Leacock, and Louis Hémon, whose *Maria Chapdelaine* was for many Americans, myself included, a memorable introduction to Canadian writing.

Non-fiction is a field in which Canadians shine. Pierre Berton is probably the country's most noted contemporary commentator, by means of essays, columns, articles, and books. And there have been many original, thoughtful works on the country and its background—mostly unknown in the United States—by such men as A. R. M. Lowrer, Donald Creighton, J. M. S. Careless, Peter C. Newmark, and Fernand Oudlette.

Bliss Carman is probably the best known of Canadian poets, at least abroad, but there have been a number of others—Charles G. D. Roberts, Duncan Campbell Scott of earlier years, and more recently, E. J. Pratt, A. M. Klein, Earle Birney, Rina Lasnier, D. V. Le Pan, and Gaston Miron.

Canada's most coveted prize for writing is the Governor-General's Literary Award, given in several categories.

In *theatre,* Canada may hold its head high. Its Stratford Festival (dealt with in the chapter on Ontario) is one of the Western Hemisphere's most brilliant contributions to the drama. Halifax's Neptune Theatre, a professional repertory group organized in 1963, and covered in the chapter on Nova Scotia, is also outstanding and should make much larger North American cities hide their heads in shame. And there are other annual drama festivals, such as the Shaw Festival in lovely Niagara-on-the-Lake, Ontario, and the Charlottetown Festival on Prince Edward Island. French-language theatre thrives in Montreal, and though skipped by most English-speaking visitors, reflects the vigor of the theatre in that sparkling city. The Théâtre du Nouveau Monde, la Comédie Canadienne, and Gratien Golinas' repertory theatre are among Montreal's standouts, but there is fine English-language theatre, too, and the multilingual productions of the Poudrière Théâtre are a delight. Winnipeg and Vancouver are theatre-minded, too, and the annual Theatre Canada is a worthy nationwide project, as are the productions of regional professional theatres and amateur groups in many Canadian communities.

Not a few Americans are devotees of the short subjects produced by the National Film Board of Canada, dealing with phases of Canadian life and social problems, including mental health and problems of the aging; the Board's films have taken more than a hundred prizes in the recent decades, and beginning in the mid-1960s, Canada entered the feature-length field, with the French-language films of Claude Jutra (*Mon Oncle Antoine* and *Kamouraska*) and the English-language films of Don Shehib (*The Rowdy Man* and *Going Down the Road*) are outstanding.

In *radio and television* Canada, like the United Kingdom, has both government and private stations. The Canadian Broadcasting Corporation dates from 1936, and its radio and TV services—both English-language and the French-language Radio Canada—commissions and produces original drama, opera, and music by Canadians, as well as the works of such writers as Jean Anouilh, Arnold Wesker, Harold Pinter, and Molière. Its competitor is CTV, the privately operated network.

Architecture remains perhaps the most unashamedly derivative of Canadian arts. But it is practiced with a refreshing quantity of good taste. One can find exceptional traditional-design buildings from St. John's, Newfoundland (the old legislative building), to Victoria, British Columbia (the still-used legislative building), and not excluding the splendid Gothic Parliament buildings in Ottawa. Modern design? Consider The Habitat apartment house and Place Ville-Marie in Montreal and the city halls in Toronto and Edmonton, as examples.

Handicrafts are dealt with in the chapters on each province. Suffice it to say at this point that the outstanding work in this field is the traditional soapstone sculpture of those original Canadians, the Eskimos. Some good work is being done in ceramics (Quebec, the Maritimes, and British Columbia) and weaving—in a number of provinces. The work of the Canadian Indians, some in British Columbia excepted, is less interesting.

THE MOUNTIES AND "THE BAY"

The Royal Canadian Mounted Police and the Hudson's Bay Company are both world symbols of Canada, both created and developed as a result of Canada's own peculiar destiny—one a force of government, the other an enormous private enterprise which, in earlier days, had been, at once trader, landlord, and government administrator. Indeed, one took over where the other left off.

The Royal Canadian Mounted Police is the modern-day descendant of the earlier North-West Mounted Police, established by Act of Parliament in 1873, just a few years after Confederation when much of the west had only recently been transferred from the jurisdiction of the Hudson's Bay Company to the government. Originally designated the North-West Rifles, the name was changed by a stroke of the pen of the first Prime Minister, Sir John A. Macdonald. The force's original functions were semi-military—to break up liquor traffic among settlers and Indians in the then raw west, to gain the respect of the Indians, to collect customs dues, and, at the same time, perform the more conventional duties of a police force. By the turn of the century the Mounties had received Crown recognition from Edward VII, with the prefix "royal" added to their official title. As the country grew, so did the scarlet-jacketed Mounties, who worked co-operatively with the governments of the provinces. (To this day, the RCMP acts as the police force of every province except the Big Two—Ontario and Quebec—which have their own provincial police.) Primarily, though, the modern-day RCMP is a Federal force representing the law-enforcement medium of the Canadian Government, under the control of the Minister of Justice, and divided into a dozen scattered divisions and with nationwide jurisdiction in the enforcement of Federal laws. The Mounties are the sole police force in the Northwest Territories and the Yukon Territory. In their contemporary work, they run a wide gamut—from criminal investigation to the patrol of highways. They still train with horses (training barracks are open to visitors, at Regina, Saskatchewan), but can be seen today in patrol boats, airplanes, and behind dog sleds in the Far North. And please note: the red tunic is now reserved for ceremonial occasions and the wide-brimmed hat is frequently replaced by visored caps. The most frequently seen work uniform is easily distinguished by the wide yellow trouser stripe and the sleeve identification patches in both English and French; the latter, for your information is: *Gendarmerie Royale Nationale.*

The Hudson's Bay Company's history is intertwined with that of Canada to the extent that "The Bay's" early activity is dealt with in almost every chapter of this book. Incorporated on May 2, 1670, as "The Governor and Company of Adventurers of England Trading Into Hudson's Bay" (and still possessed of what is unquestionably the most glamorous corporate title extant) "The Bay," following on the heels of the French-founded North West Company (which it later absorbed) opened up much of Canada, through its traders, trappers, and administrators. To this day one finds old Bay posts and forts at many points throughout the country, and the development of many areas is inexorably interwoven with that of the Hudson's Bay Company. The Bay keeps right in step with modern Canada. Indeed, one is never far from a Bay operation. For the company has great department stores in many cities, smaller stores in suburbs and minor communities, trading posts in the Far North, fur auction houses, a wholesale department, even, indeed, a Scotch whisky division. General headquarters are in London, as they have been for almost three centuries, although the Canadian operations are directed from Hudson's Bay House in Winnipeg. But The Bay has not forsaken its past. It still operates under the Royal Charter of 1670, still flies its ensign at every one of its operations, still is administered by a governor, deputy governor, and "committee."

YOUR HOSTS, THE CANADIANS

The American visitor in Canada can have a difficult time discerning his hosts from his fellow countrymen. Canadians are 97 per cent literate. They are well-scrubbed and quite as well dressed as their American cousins—and in much the same types of clothing. Their standard of living is high—about as high as Americans, sometimes lower, sometimes higher. They go to similar churches (the Anglican Church is Episcopalian; the United Church is a merger of the Methodists, Congregationalists, and some Presbyterians; 47 per cent of the Canadians are Roman Catholics). They dote on sports, join organizations quite as avidly as their southern neighbors, are quite as materialistic and as interested in making money, living well, and enjoying themselves. Many have relatives in the United States, where several million Canadians make their home.

Well, then, no difference? In Quebec, the French-speaking areas of New Brunswick, Nova Scotia, Manitoba, and Ontario, language is an immediate difference, of course; and there still are country folks in Quebec who lead traditionally old-fashioned existences. However, many more French-speaking Canadians are bilingual than are English-speaking Canadians. Expect to meet Canadians with French names who speak only English, and with Anglo-Saxon names whose mother tongue is French. In Newfoundland and Nova Scotia, there are delightful Scottish, Irish, and, occasionally, early Elizabethan influences in speech. All over Canada, from coast to coast, one finds English-speaking Canadians who pronounce words ending in "out" more like "oot" than "out." There are, of course, a certain number of Englishisms in Canadian English—perm for permanent wave, cairn, meaning plaque or marker; lieutenant is often pronounced *lefftenant*. Italian frequently is pronounced *eye*-talian, to the visitor's shock; hotel is often *ho*-tel; theatre is frequently thee-*ay*-tr; Detroit, *Dee*-troit. There are certain differences in spelling, due to British influence. Words like color are sometimes spelled with an "our" ending—colour; plateaus are plateaux, center is centre.

Four generalizations that I have no hesitation making: (1) Although hostility toward Americans is more evident than formerly—it took a long time to surface—Canadians, by and large, are exceeded by no people in the realm of politeness and courtesy. (2) Canada is the most spotless country I've ever seen, and I've been in more than a hundred. (3) Canadians—on virtually every issue except Quebec—tend to be less politically emotional than Americans. (4) Not every Canadian one meets is scintillating, heaven knows. Every nation has its share of dullards. But there's a high proportion of interesting, thoughtful, amusing, sensitive people— from the Atlantic to the Pacific, from the Northwest Territories to southern Ontario.

Canada: Tourist Territory

If the Canadian people are to find their soul, they must seek for it not in the English language or the French but in the little ports of the Atlantic provinces, in the flaming autumn maples of the St. Lawrence valley, in the portages and lakes of the Canadian Shield, in the sunsets and relentless cold of the prairies, in the foothill, mountain and sea of the West and in the unconquerable vastness of the North. From the land, Canada, must come the soul of Canada.

—A. R. M. LOWRER: *Colony to Nation*

VACATIONLAND FOR THE MILLIONS

Take a frontier nearly four thousand miles in length, intersperse it with an extensive chain of crossing stations, eliminate the need for visas, passports, and inoculations for the 200 million-plus residents of the countries separated by the invisible line—and you've a tourist industry whether you want it or not. It so happens that both countries involved *do* want tourists. And both get them. Canada, as a matter of fact, receives some 35 million annually.

And, mind you, those figures were only for visitors who had stayed in Canada twenty-four hours or longer. Millions of *additional* crossings are made from the United States to Canada each year for less than twenty-four hours. Tourism in Canada is Big Business. All told, tourists spend approximately $6 billion in Canada annually, according to *The Travel Agent,* authoritative U.S. travel industry journal. About $1.5 billion is spent by Americans.

No nation is more tourist-conscious than Canada. There is not a level of government without a tourist organization of some kind or other, from the Canadian Government Office of Tourism, whose function is to encourage visitors from abroad to enter Canada, through the travel departments of every one of the ten provinces and two territories, as well as municipal and regional travel and convention bureaus, from those of the great cities and resorts to the small towns, where chambers of commerce, boards of trade, and volunteer Jaycees put out the official welcome mats.

Name an area of tourist concern and you'll find that the Canadians have worked at it in recent years to bring it up to standard— and that they're not resting on their laurels. Federal and provincial governments are constantly improving roads; the pride and joy of the nation, the Trans-Canada Highway, makes traversing the continent by car not only possible, but pleasureable. One can drive all the way from British Columbia through the Yukon Territory to America's forty-ninth state on the Alaska Highway. And there are extensive networks of modern roads in every province. Railroads? The two great systems, Canadian National and Canadian Pacific, span the nation. Airways? Air Canada and CP Air, as well as a number of smaller lines, fly every nook and cranny of the country. Other air services link Canada with the United States and more distant points. The long-distance bus is a popular Canadian mode of transport. And in a country like Canada, with so many waterways and so much coastline, ship travel has been highly developed.

Every important Canadian city has improved its hotels. Older, well-established hotels—many of them operated by Canadian National and CP Hotels have been spruced up, redecorated, modernized, and often enlarged. New hotels and motor hotels are a feature of virtually every urban area. In small towns, along the highways and fringing the urban centers are countless modern motels. There are thousands of trailer parks, camp sites, and picnic grounds situated with great imagination at scenic locales. Hunting and fishing are excellent in every Canadian province and territory. The national parks—a chain of splendidly maintained reserves to be found in every province—are invariably choice travel destinations, as is the network of federally maintained historic parks and sites. Added to these are still more parks maintained by the various provinces. Almost everywhere one finds attractive eating places with inviting menus featuring well-prepared—often excellently prepared—foods of varying national pedigrees. Coupled with this has been a liberalization of archaic liquor laws in every province. Quebec's Montreal, long the unquestioned leader in the realms of food and drink, still retains the title, but places like Ontario's Toronto, Manitoba's Winnipeg, British Columbia's Vancouver, and Alberta's Calgary typify the excellence of the Canadian table. And there is, in many centers, a wealth of after-dark activity. Cleanliness is a commonplace—I have already expressed my incredulity at the all-pervasive spick-and-span quality of Canada. The Canadian is a pleasant, honest person to do business with. Courtesy, even in the larger cities, still is regarded as an essential in dealing with strangers.

OFFICIAL HELP

The Canadian Government Office of Tourism, with headquarters in Ottawa, exists to serve the foreigner interested in traveling to and through Canada. It is one of the most intelligently organized and operated government travel offices in the world, and I speak with experience, having dealt with scores of them on every continent. It can help you with general information—through a variety of excellent folders, pamphlets, and booklets, and it has a separate division whose travel counselors answer *specific* questions. Write to it directly, in Ottawa, or write to one of its branches. Here are the addresses:

Canadian Government Office of Tourism
Ottawa, Ontario, Canada

Eastern U.S.A.

Atlanta   260 Peachtree Street, N.W.
            Atlanta, Georgia

Boston	The Prudential Center Boston, Massachusetts
Buffalo	One Marine Midland Center Buffalo, New York
Cleveland	1250 Euclid Avenue Cleveland, Ohio
Detroit	1001 Woodward Avenue Detroit, Michigan
New York	1251 Avenue of the Americas New York, New York
Philadelphia	3 Benjamin Franklin Parkway Philadelphia, Pennsylvania
Pittsburgh	Four Gateway Center Pittsburgh, Pennsylvania
Washington	1771 N Street, N.W. Washington, D.C.
Washington	2450 Massachusetts Avenue, N.W. Washington, D.C.

Western U.S. and Pacific

Chicago	332 South Michigan Avenue Chicago, Illinois
Los Angeles	510 West Sixth Street Los Angeles, California
Mexico	Melchor Ocampo 463 Mexico 5, D.F., Mexico
Minneapolis	124 South Seventh Street Minneapolis, Minnesota
San Francisco	One Maritime Plaza San Francisco, California
Seattle	600 Stewart Street Seattle, Washington

Sydney	AMP Building, Circular Quay
	Sydney, Australia

Tokyo	AIU Akasaka Building
	Tokyo, Japan

Europe

London	1, Grosvenor Square
	London, England

Frankfurt	Biebergasse 6–10
	Frankfurt, Germany

Paris	4, Rue Scribe
	Paris, France

The Hague	Laan Van Meerdervoort 96
	The Hague, The Netherlands

Additionally, every one of the ten provinces and both of the territories maintain their own travel bureaus; these are noted in the chapters that follow dealing with those areas. Remember, too, that every province and territory, particularly during the summer season, has branch information offices operating at or near border crossings and places of major touristic interest. These are supplemented by municipal tourist and convention bureaus in many cities; and chambers of commerce and junior chambers of commerce operate information booths on the highways leading to their localities as well as in the town centers. Remember, too, that the entrance gates and headquarters of all the national parks and national historic parks double as information centers, with gratis material available; this is sometimes the case at provincial parks, too. Your own travel agent as well as hotel and motel desks and the proprietors of service stations are usually good bets, as are offices of Canadian National, Canadian Pacific, and Air Canada.

For material on Canada of a *non-touristic* nature, the Canadian Embassy in Washington is an important source, as are the information sections of the Canadian consulates in Atlanta, Boston, Buffalo, Chicago, Cleveland, Dallas, Detroit, Los Angeles, Minneapolis, New Orleans, New York, Philadelphia, San Francisco, San Juan, and Seattle.

Within Canada, the United States Government is represented by its embassy in Ottawa and by consulates in Montreal, Halifax, Toronto, Calgary, Quebec City, Vancouver, Winnipeg, and St. John's, Newfoundland.

ENTERING CANADA

For United States citizens: couldn't be simpler at any of the 138 border-crossing stations along the frontier. Neither passports nor visas are needed, simply a bona fide identity document such as a birth certificate, voter's card, driver's license, baptismal certificate —or any document of substance that asserts unequivocally that you're you. Naturalized citizens do well to carry documentary evidence of citizenship, such as a naturalization certificate, and alien permanent residents of the U.S. should have their Alien Registration Receipt Cards. Another bonus: no vaccination or health certificates required. Others—those *not* citizens of the United States—*do* need a valid passport and, usually, unless they're citizens of Western Hemisphere countries, a visa, as well. For further details, inquire of the Canadian Government Office of Tourism, the Canadian Embassy, or a Canadian consulate.

CUSTOMS—GOING AND COMING

Entering Canada, the visitor may take duty-free his clothing and personal effects, of course; a carton of cigarettes, fifty cigars, forty ounces of liquor, two pounds of tobacco, and gifts for friends or relatives in Canada (spiritous beverages excluded). Hunters and anglers may lug fishing tackle, non-automatic sporting rifles, and fifty rounds of ammunition; golfers may take their clubs; campers their tents and associated paraphernalia. The regulations say that "a reasonable amount" of film and flashbulbs may be admitted, and it's my experience that customs inspectors—invariably pleasant and courteous—are flexible in this respect, particularly if you convince them that you're not opening up a photo-supply shop. Pleasure boats? Yes, either by water or on the trailer—but they require permits from the Customs office at point of entry. Dogs? Again yes, but only if they have a rabies certificate. Cats may enter freely without documentation. Flying your own plane? First, write the Ministry of Transport, Ottawa, for regulations.

Returning to the United States, you'll find—by and large— American customs officers polite, personable, and reasonable. At certain airports—like Montreal and Toronto—U.S. customs officers are on duty to pre-clear passengers on flights bound for the United States. If you've been in Canada for forty-eight hours or more, you may take back home duty-free—and once every thirty-one days— one hundred dollars' worth of purchases, including a quart of liquor. You may also bring back one hundred cigars or a carton of cigarettes, but these not being bargains in Canada, present no problems. Remember, too, that *antiques*—duly certified to be at least 100 years old—are admitted duty-free, and do not count as part of the one-hundred-dollar quota. Neither do duly certified *original works of art,* including paintings, sculpture, and substantial wood carvings; important Eskimo soapstone carvings come within this category and the better gift shops and department stores will give you proper papers for such purchases. Printed matter—books and the like—are best mailed home; there rarely is any duty levied on them. Remember, too, that—unless the United States Government becomes even more stringent than it is now in the matter of duty-free purchases—you may ship, *duty-free,* without having to declare them, and *not* counting as part of your one-hundred-dollar allowance, parcels not exceeding ten dollars in value. Send *as many as you like* from wherever you like, but not more than one parcel per day to the same recipient. Mark each such parcel "GIFT—TOURIST PURCHASE—VALUE UNDER $10."

MAIL

There are times, it must be admitted, when Canada seems so un-foreign that American visitors are silly enough to use U.S. postage on their cards and letters. It should go without saying, but I will say it anyway: Canada is a sovereign country and one must use *its* stamps when using the mails. Generally, postal service between the two countries is reasonably efficient. If you are undertaking a fairly lengthy trip, with a pre-planned itinerary, have letters addressed to you in care of your hotels along the way. Mail sent to regions of Canada close to your home in the United States should arrive within a few days if sent air mail. Still, have your correspondents allow a good five or six days for letters to reach you, even via air mail. If they arrive sooner, no harm has been done, so long as they are marked, "Hold for Arrival." If you're moving along before expected mail has arrived, leave a forwarding address. You'll find well-designed stamp machines in convenient locations.

CURRENCY

The Canadian unit of currency is the dollar—divided into half dollars, quarters, nickels, dimes, and pennies—as is the United States dollar, and the coins are similar in size. Bills come in similar denominations as those of the U.S., except that the Canadians use their two-dollar bills frequently and regard Americans—who use them infrequently and consider them to be bad luck—as a little odd when they ask for two singles instead of a two-dollar bill! The value of the Canadian dollar is similar to that of the American, but it can fluctuate. Most places in Canada will accept American money, but the visitor from the U.S. is advised to convert American funds, as it is needed, into Canadian money at banks in Canada; dealing with the currency of the country is far more convenient. I suggest, too, that you take the bulk of your funds in traveler's checks. Take along a good batch in ten- and twenty-dollar denominations; they create rather a bulge, but they're the most convenient.

TIPPING

Canada is less tip-happy than the United States, especially in the smaller places. There are still Canadians who tip only for exceptional service—a commendable philosophy. The average should be 15 per cent. Service charges are *not* added to bills, as in some countries.

SHOPPING

The department stores of Canada—about which more in the chapters following—are a joy in which to browse, lunch, have tea— and make purchases. Every city of any size has good smaller shops as well. And the new shopping centers of Canada are quite as impressive as those of the United States. Supermarkets—splendid ones—are the rule for food purchases; pharmacies and five-and-tens are similar to those of the U.S. One can find just about anything one wants, but there are relatively few Canadian goods that are unique or a bargain. In the chapters that follow, therefore, I make mention principally of those Canadian handicrafts—and good sources for them—that constitute, in my view, the most interesting kind of souvenir or gift. British imports are frequently good buys—cashmere sweaters, woolen fabrics, men's and women's accessories, and last but hardly least, bone china, particularly teacups. Canada appears, at times, as a vast sea of teacups. You are on your own when you search for these, but I think you may have more difficulty finding stores that *don't* stock them than those that do.

CLIMATE

The weather, season by season, is dealt with in the chapters that follow, for each province and territory. Suffice it to say, at this point, that Canada—at least the most visited and most inhabited parts of it—has a climate similar to the northern United States, with four distinct seasons. Broadly speaking, summer runs from mid-May to mid-September; autumn, from mid-September to mid-November; winter from mid-November to mid-March; spring from mid-March to mid-May. There are, of course, variations in this respect, area by area. It is well to recognize that summers, except in mountain, forest, and coastal areas, can be quite as hot—and upon occasion as humid—as they frequently are in the United States. And winters can be considerably colder, although the cold is dry, generally, and far easier to take than the damp frigidity of many U.S. areas. The Far North, of course, is *really* cold in winter, with temperatures of thirty below—and colder—not uncommon.

PACKING

There is little point in outlining a suggested wardrobe for the Canada-bound traveler, for the length of Canada vacations vary greatly, and so much is dependent, in this respect, upon the season and mode of travel. Summer motorists, for example, will want casual clothes for long drives and daily sightseeing, but men will want jackets and ties for evenings in the cities and bigger resorts, and women, at such places, usually prefer after-dark changes somewhat dressier than daytime cottons. Especially warm clothing is, of course, the rule in winter, but even during the hot-weather months, sweaters and substantial wraps are a necessity for evenings in the mountains and along the coasts, and for the occasionally cool day. Skiers, anglers, and hunters require the special clothing and gear of their avocations, and do well to make specific inquiries in this regard in advance of departure. All travelers, at all seasons, are wise to take as much advantage as possible of drip-dry apparel. Laundry, in most hotels, is returned in the evening when sent before breakfast, but not on weekends. Pressing and dry cleaning are done rapidly and well. *Good things to have along on an extensive trip:* sunglasses, an extra pair of eyeglasses and/or a copy of the prescription; Band-Aids; a roll of Scotch tape (it has innumerable uses on a trip); a small envelope of paper clips and rubber bands (both valuable, too); a few of the cheapest ballpoint pens; several plastic bags (keep your bathing suit in one of its own so that it can be packed even when wet); a plastic bottle of aspirin; an anti-diarrhea preparation—just in case; a one-of-each supply of toilet articles is adequate, for all such items (often the same brands you buy at home) are easily replenishable, and there's no need to take soap if you're staying in hotels or motels (all of them supply it). Do, however, be prepared with insect repellent for woodsy areas.

SEEING CANADA

Planning your trip: go by car, go by plane, go by train, go by ship, go by bus; go by a combination of the foregoing. Transport to and through Canada is excellent. The country—so great in area, so relatively small in population—has from earliest times been preoccupied, of necessity, with the importance of good transportation. And today's tourist benefits. He may travel as he pleases. Many families pack the car and take off for a fortnight in a region of Canada near their home. Many cross the country by car. (Canada, incidentally, uses the Imperial gallon—a fifth larger than the U.S. gallon. Also, Canada has begun using metric measurements concurrently with the old units of measurement familiar to Americans.) Some motorists attach a trailer to their auto and spend each night in one of the country's vast number of trailer parks. Others with low budgets stay in modestly priced motels; or, with somewhat higher budgets, in luxury motels, motor hotels, city hotels, and fine resorts. Camping is extremely popular. Increasingly, Canada is visited by means of tours arranged by, or booked through, travel agents. It is important, of course, to select an agent who knows Canada—or who at least is familiar with the region you're interested in. Invariably, agents who are members of ASTA—the American Society of Travel Agents—are good bets. Generally speaking, there are four types of tours: (1) *independent* travel, in which you do all the work—purchase your transportation tickets, book your hotels, arrange for your own sightseeing—either in advance, or as you go along; (2) *group* travel on a packaged, escorted tour purchased in advance from a travel agency; (3) *unescorted tours*—pre-planned, but undertaken by individual travelers without professional escorts, and (4) *individual* travel, *but* by means of a travel agency's prearranged, custom-tailored-just-for-you itinerary, with some or all arrangements—transportation, hotels, sightseeing—made for you prior to your departure.

Regardless of how you go, you do well to procure all of the free literature obtainable from the Canadian Government Office of Tourism (addresses given earlier in this chapter) and the provincial and territorial travel bureaus, whose addresses are noted in

ensuing chapters. The Canadian Government Office of Tourism
also serves as an information source on the national parks. The
major transport companies have gratis material for you, too. Even
if you use a travel agency, it's not likely that it will have all of the
material available; pick up what you can get there, and write away
for the rest. The federal government and the provinces *want* you
as their guest; they go all out to be of assistance.

The transport giants: *Canadian National,* a government-owned
corporation, operates the largest railway system in North America
—embracing nearly thirty-five thousand miles of track. Though a
public enterprise, CN operates much like a large private corporation. The enormous CN railway operation gives the statistician a
field day. There are more than 7,000 bridges on its lines, and 70
tunnels—the largest of which exceeds three miles in length. In the
Montreal terminal alone, there are more than 525 miles of track.
Amtrak—the American passenger railroad organization—and CN
have an agreement that enables rail travelers from either Canada
or the U.S. to purchase transportation on both national rail lines
in a single transaction. But railroads are only a part of CN's business. It owns a nationwide chain of noted hotels, including Jasper
Park Lodge in Alberta, and the Queen Elizabeth in Montreal; two
of its hotels—the last-mentioned and the Hotel Vancouver—are operated for it by Hilton of Canada. Additionally, CN operates a
fleet of ships. Its steamers ply the coast of Newfoundland and
Labrador; connect Vancouver and other British Columbia ports
with Alaska; ferry passengers and cars between Maine and Nova
Scotia and between New Brunswick and Prince Edward Island.
CN runs one of Canada's two telegraph services, and maintains
truck lines, docks, stockyards, and warehouses.

Canadian Pacific is a private-enterprise giant that has played a
tremendous role in the history and development of Canada. CP
Rail is the granddaddy of the operation. It came about following
the establishment of the Canadian Confederation, after more than a
decade of unsuccessful governmental efforts to build the transcontinental railway which British Columbia had insisted upon
when it joined Canada. Such men as Sir William Van Horne, Lord
Shaughnessy, and Lord Mount Stephen were able to marshal the
resources—technical, financial, and otherwise—that made possible
the ingenious construction of the line, a half decade ahead of

schedule, in 1885. The first train left Montreal on June 28, 1886, and reached Port Moody, British Columbia, five and a half days later. CP's accomplishment not only kept British Columbia in the confederation—it might have joined the United States—but made possible the rapid development of central and western Canada. Today, *CP Rail*'s network totals nearly seventeen thousand miles of track. It has been fully diesel since 1961 and pioneered with dome-car service in Canada. But there's more. The company operates a chain of hotels—*CP Hotels*—ranging from the Empress in Victoria, British Columbia, to the Algonquin in New Brunswick and including the Banff Springs Hotel and Château Lake Louise, in the Alberta Rockies, as well as Toronto's Royal York and Quebec's Château Frontenac. *CP Air* flies a route that joins five continents; it is Canada's flag carrier in the Pacific, and flies domestically, as well, to U.S., South American, and European points.

Air Canada made its first flight in 1937 between Vancouver, British Columbia, and nearby Seattle, Washington, as Trans-Canada Air Lines. A quarter of a century later, it was one of the world's major airlines, serving Canadian communities from the Atlantic to the Pacific, and linking Canada to the United States, Europe, and the Caribbean. Other Canadian-flag airlines include *Eastern Provincial Airways, Québecair, Transair, Pacific Western Airlines, Norcanair,* and *Nordair.* Many foreign carriers—both U.S. and from other countries—serve Canada.

The Trans-Canada Highway, longest in the world, extends some five thousand miles, from St. John's, Newfoundland, to Victoria, British Columbia. Opened in 1962, it is the twentieth-century counterpart of the transcontinental railroad that joined the Atlantic and Pacific in 1885. Long envisioned by Canadians, it was authorized in 1949 by an Act of Parliament and opened almost a decade and a half later. The highway is a work of engineering art, and it traverses many of Canada's leading cities as well as any number of key national and provincial parks. The Trans-Canada Highway runs through all ten provinces of Canada. To drive to the Yukon Territory (and its next-door neighbor, the state of Alaska), the route is via the Alaska Highway, which begins in Dawson Creek, British Columbia. And to drive to the Northwest Territories, one takes the Mackenzie Highway from Grimshaw, Alberta,

to Yellowknife, on Great Slave Lake in the Territories. A Trans-
Canada Highway motor trip? Give it a month for a comfortable
journey—more, of course, for leisurely stopovers en route; much,
much less if you're really in a hurry. Succeeding chapters note the
route of the Trans-Canada Highway in each province. The Alaska
Highway is dealt with in the chapters on the Yukon Territory and
British Columbia, and the Mackenzie Highway is covered in the
Northwest Territories and Alberta chapters.

Car rental in Canada is quite as well-organized as in the U.S.
Major firms are Tilden—a Canadian company—Avis, and Hertz.

Itineraries and packaged tours: Your itinerary in Canada is dependent upon the time at your disposal, your budget, and your in-
clinations. I have already suggested how trans-Canada tours can
be effected by means of motor (the Trans-Canada Highway), air
(Air Canada and CP Air), and train (Canadian National and CP
Rail). The best public transport bargains are, of course, for long
distances. But seeing Canada region by region is extremely popular and quite advantageous. The Atlantic provinces—or the Maritimes, as they are also called—make for a convenient grouping, and
frequently are combined with Quebec and eastern Ontario. Central
and western Canada is another good mixture. British Columbia is
frequently teamed with the Yukon Territory and the state of
Alaska. And very often, visits are made to a single province or a
single region thereof. The eastern United States resident could not
do better, for example, than to visit Montreal and Quebec City.
British Columbia in itself is a vast vacationland, as is Alberta with
two fine cities and two great national parks in the Rockies. Nova
Scotia attracts many holidaymakers on its own, as well it might. So
does every province and region. To cross Canada from the Atlantic to the Pacific on a single journey is to undertake one of the
world's most exciting and memorable journeys. But I'm all for seeing however much you can, when you can.

HUNTING AND FISHING,
CAMPING AND CANOEING

Every one of the twelve Canadian provinces and territories
offers hunting and fishing, and each, of course, has its own special-

ties in these areas. For specifics not alluded to in the following chapters—on seasons, license fees, special equipment needed, arms and ammunition, and the like—the interested reader is referred to the Canadian Government Office of Tourism (whose addresses are given earlier in this chapter) and the official travel bureaus of the various provinces and territories (whose addresses are given in the chapters dealing with those areas). Campers and canoeists are likewise directed to the same sources for detailed material on those activities.

A CANADIAN CALENDAR

Herewith, a minimal selection of annual festivals, special events, and Canadian holidays.

January

New Year's Day (national holiday); Alpine ski jumping, Vancouver, British Columbia; curling bonspiels, all Canada; pro hockey, all Canada; Royal Winnipeg Ballet, Winnipeg, Manitoba; theatre, major cities; International Boat Show, Toronto, Ontario; Polar Bear Swim Meet, Vancouver.

February

Trappers' Festival, The Pas, Manitoba; pro hockey, all Canada; Winter Carnival, Vancouver, British Columbia; Winter Carnival, Quebec City; Bon Soo Winter Carnival, Sault Ste. Marie, Ontario; curling bonspiels, all Canada; Carnaval-Souvenir de Chicoutimi, Chicoutimi, Quebec; National Boat Show, Montreal, Quebec; National Ballet of Canada, Toronto; winter carnivals all over Canada; Sourdough Rendezvous, Whitehorse, Yukon Territory.

March

Newfoundland provincial holiday; ski competitions, British Columbia; curling bonspiels across Canada; Canadian National Sportsmen's Show, Toronto; Winnipeg Symphony concerts, Winnipeg; Quebec Winter Games, Quebec; Aurora Snow Festival,

Churchill, Manitoba; Alberta Winter Games and Banff Winter Festival, Banff, Alberta; Trappers' Rendezvous, Fort Nelson, British Columbia; Caribou Carnival, Yellowknife, Northwest Territories.

April

Manitoba Winter Fair, Brandon; Maritime Boat and Trailer Show, Moncton, New Brunswick; Festival of Music, Saint John, New Brunswick; Flower Show, Montreal; Black Creek Pioneer Village spring demonstrations, Toronto; Guelph Spring Festival, Guelph, Ontario; Light Horse Show, Saskatoon, Saskatchewan; Kobasa Kapers, Jasper, Alberta; Kiwanis Music Festival, Vancouver; Toonik Tyme, Frobisher Bay, Northwest Territories.

May

Victoria Day (national holiday); Music Festival, Charlottetown, Prince Edward Island; Blossom Times, Penticton, British Columbia; Festival of Spring, Ottawa, Ontario; Annapolis Valley Blossom Festival, Nova Scotia; harness racing, Charlottetown and Summerside, Prince Edward Island; sailing races, Conception Bay, Newfoundland; Loyalist Day celebrations, Moncton, New Brunswick; Shaw Festival, Niagara-on-the-Lake, Ontario (May–October); International Band Festival, Moose Jaw, Saskatchewan; International Horse Show, Calgary, Alberta; British Columbia Spring Festival of Sports, province-wide; Victorian Days, Victoria, British Columbia.

June

Shakespeare Festival, Stratford, Ontario (June–October); Potato Festival, Grand Falls, New Brunswick; Man and His World International Cultural Exhibition, Montreal (June–September); Theatre Arts Festival International, Wolfville, Nova Scotia; Mariposa Folk Festival, Toronto; Changing the Guard, Ottawa (June–September); International Freedom Festival, Windsor, Ontario; Red River Exhibition, Winnipeg; Fête Franco-Manitobaine, La Broqerie, Manitoba; Trout Festival, Flin Flon, Manitoba; Midnight Golf Tournament, Yellowknife, Northwest Territories;

Gaslight Follies and Klondike Nights, Dawson City, Yukon Territory; thoroughbred racing, Toronto (June–November).

July

Dominion Day, July 1 (national holiday); Gathering of the Clans, Pugwash, Nova Scotia; Orangemen's Day, July 12, Newfoundland; Stampede, Williams Lake, British Columbia; Calgary Exhibition and Stampede, Calgary, Alberta; Klondike Days, Edmonton, Alberta; Banff Indian Days, Banff, Alberta; Frontier Days, Swift Current, Saskatchewan; International Regatta, Valleyfield, Quebec; Lobster Festival, Summerside, Prince Edward Island; Summer Festival, Charlottetown, Prince Edward Island (July–August); Highland Games, Antigonish, Nova Scotia; Summer Theatre, Point-du-Chêne, New Brunswick; International Swimming relay race, La Tuque, Quebec; Festival Canada, Ottawa; Royal Canadian Henley Regatta, St. Catharines, Ontario; Stampede and Exhibition, Yorkton, Saskatchewan; Bathtub Race, Nanaimo, British Columbia; Lobster Festival, Shediac, Nova Scotia.

August

Canadian National Exhibition, Toronto; Discovery Day (Yukon Territory holiday); Theatre Under the Stars, Vancouver; Natal Day, Dartmouth, Nova Scotia; Gaelic Mod, St. Ann's, Nova Scotia; Old Home Week, Charlottetown, Prince Edward Island; Regatta, St. John's, Newfoundland; Nova Scotia Festival of the Arts, Halifax, Nova Scotia; Atlantic National Exhibition, Saint John, New Brunswick; Lake of the Woods sailing regatta, Kenora, Ontario; Central Canada Exhibition, Ottawa; Canadian Turtle Derby, Boissevain, Manitoba; Canadian Gladiolus Show, Saskatoon, Saskatchewan; International Air Show, Abbotsford, British Columbia.

September

Labor Day (national holiday); Pacific National Exhibition, Vancouver; Exhibition and Livestock show, Fredericton, New Brunswick; Nova Scotia Fishermen's Exhibition and Fishermen's Reunion, Lunenburg, Nova Scotia; Harvest Moon Golf Tournament, Brudenell, Prince Edward Island; International Tuna Cup Match, Wedgeport-Cape St. Mary, Nova Scotia; International Canoe Race, La Tuque-Trois Rivières, Quebec; Western Fair, London, Ontario; Grape and Wine Festival, St. Catharines, Ontario; Totem Pole Golf Tournament, Jasper, Alberta; Oktoberfest, Vancouver; Delta Daze, Inuvik, Northwest Territories.

October

Thanksgiving Day (national holiday); pro football across Canada; Fall Festival, Rimouski, Quebec; Snow Goose Festival, Montmagny, Quebec; Oktoberfest, Kitchener-Waterloo, Ontario; Atlantic Winter Fair, Halifax, Nova Scotia; Theatre of New Brunswick, New Brunswick; Manitoba Theatre Centre, Winnipeg; Oktoberfest, Saskatoon, Saskatchewan.

November

Santa Claus Parade, Toronto, Ontario; Remembrance Day, November 11 (national holiday); pro hockey across Canada; Royal Agricultural Winter Fair, Toronto; Neptune Theatre, Halifax, Nova Scotia; Moncton Curling Bonspiel and Donkey Barbecue, Moncton, New Brunswick; Auto-Sport Show, Montreal, Quebec.

December

Christmas Day (national holiday); pro hockey across Canada; Flower Show, Montreal; Winter Wonderland, London, Ontario; Royal Winnipeg Ballet, Winnipeg; Knights of Columbus Indoor Games, Saskatoon, Saskatchewan; Christmas Tree Golf Tournament, Victoria, British Columbia.

Alberta

L'ALBERTA

Best times for a visit: *Summers—June through September—are dry and sunny, with daytime temperatures averaging in the seventies and cooler evenings, especially in the mountains. Spring and autumn, both short seasons, are pleasant,*

*and winter—though frequently way, way below zero—is crisp,
surprisingly replete with sunny days, and attractive to the
vacationer interested in skiing and other winter sports, which
are well developed.* Provincial statisticians claim that Alberta
has more hours of sunshine—winter as well as summer—than
any other part of Canada, and I suspect they're correct.*
Transportation: *Alberta is well served by highways. Some
sixty-seven hundred miles are paved, and there are more than
eighty thousand additional miles of roads. It is from Alberta
that one may drive on an all-paved route (from Edmonton
northwest) to the terminal point of the Alaska Highway, in
Dawson Creek, British Columbia. It is in Alberta that one
finds the only road (the Mackenzie Highway) leading into
the Northwest Territories (see the Northwest Territories
chapter). The Trans-Canada Highway traverses the province
from just east of Medicine Hat, near the Saskatchewan border, through Calgary and Banff National Park, to British Columbia, west of Lake Louise. There is modern bus service via
Canadian Coachways, Greyhound, Brewster Transport, and
Lethbridge Northern Bus Lines. Both national railways—
Canadian National and Canadian Pacific—as well as Northern
Alberta Railways, serve this area. A number of airlines serve
Alberta, including Air Canada, CP Air, Pacific Western,
Western Airlines, Hughes Air West, Northwest Orient, Time
Air, and Bayview Air; there are charter lines, too.* **Having a
drink:** *Beverage rooms, cocktail lounges, dining lounges. Liq-
uor is sold in provincial stores; beer to take out may be ob-
tained in most hotels and in beverage rooms.* **Further in-
formation:** *Travel Alberta (the Provincial Tourism De-
partment), 10255 104th Street, Edmonton, Alberta; 501
Victoria Building, Ottawa, Ontario; 510 West Sixth Street,
Los Angeles, and Akasaka Tokyu Building, Tokyo; Agent-
General of Alberta, 37 Hill Street, London; Canadian Government Office of Tourism, Ottawa and branches.*

INTRODUCING ALBERTA

Alberta rates all three of the *a*'s that it takes to spell Canada. One because it is exhilarating—the Alberta air gives the impression of being the purest, cleanest, and crispest in North America. A second because it is beautiful—the wonderlands of Banff, Jasper, and Waterton Lakes are unsurpassed on this or any other continent. And a third because in many ways it typifies the West at its best—modern-minded and efficient, but hospitable and invariably with a smile on its sunny, well-scrubbed, prosperous face.

Alberta is big (among the provinces, only Quebec, Ontario, and British Columbia have greater areas), and Alberta is rich. Within its borders one finds the northernmost permanent agricultural settlements in Canada. Except for a tiny northeast corner which is part of the rocky Canadian Shield, almost all of the province is arable. Some seventy thousand square miles of land are under cultivation, and there is an equal amount of yet untilled territory that is suitable for farming. And from under the ground, in recent years, have come other riches—oil and natural gas are the most spectacular, but there is coal, too.

But Alberta was very much in business long before there were dreams of liquid gold beneath its soil. The first white man to visit Alberta was quite the opposite of a settler. He was Anthony Henday, an apparently optimistic (or naïve) Hudson's Bay Company emissary who was sent west in 1754 to coax the original Albertans —Indian trappers—to move east with their rich stores of furs. The Indians, Mr. Henday learned, were not about to go along, what with shiny beads and trinkets the only lures. And so the Hudson's Bay man went along—back east, and it was not until two decades later that the Indians had visitors of consequence.

Early trading posts: Hudson's Bay's great rival, the North West Company, concluded that *they* had better go to the source of the furs, rather than attempt again what their competitors had failed in. And so in ensuing years, they set up trading posts in Alberta, and before long the Hudson's Bay people joined them. By 1778 the winter trading post near Fort Cipewyan was the principal settlement of the region, and the two trading companies became increasingly competitive. They called a halt in 1821 when Hudson's Bay took over North West to become the government as well as the chief business of the region.

But in 1870, after Rupert's Land—the area which is now mainly Alberta and Saskatchewan—was sold to the Canadian Government for $1,350,000, Alberta became a part of the Northwest Territories and attracted settlers of varying types—the most interesting of which were whiskey traders out of the United States. They set up shop—albeit illegally—in a series of whimsically named trading forts (Whoop-up, Slideout, and Standoff were but three of them), and they carried on to the point where the Mounties had to come out from Manitoba to bring law and order to the plains.

Toward the middle of the nineteenth century, missionaries, both Protestant and Roman Catholic, went to Alberta to convert the Indians. In 1882 the region was separated from the rest of the Northwest Territories and created a district with the name Alberta after Princess Louise Caroline Alberta, wife of the then Governor-General of Canada, the Marquis of Lorne, and a daughter of Queen Victoria. In 1885 the Canadian Pacific Railroad arrived and made possible the westward trek to Alberta of many homesteaders from the East who took advantage of free government farmlands.

Full-fledged province: By 1905 the population had increased enough to warrant Alberta's transition from region to province. It was created a full-fledged partner in the Canadian Confederation in that year, to be governed from within its own borders, instead of from the then-capital of the Northwest Territories, Regina.

Through the years it continued to attract Canadians from the East, Europeans from across the Atlantic and from the Continent, particularly the Ukraine and Germany, as well as the British Isles, and even Americans from south of the border. The rich prairies, the great ranches brought the province a prosperity that disappeared with the Depression of the 1930s.

Albertans were looking for a miracle to ease them out of their poverty. The time could not have been more propitious for the emergence into the provincial political scene of William "Bible Bill" Aberhart, a hefty (250 pounds) Ontario teacher who had, prior to the Depression, migrated to Calgary, founded the Calgary Prophetic Bible Institute, and developed a considerable following among Albertans—possibly the most religious-minded English-speaking Canadians to this day—from his evangelical radio programs. Aberhart, no less aware than his fellow citizens of Alberta's plight, became interested in the theories of an English major, Clifford Hugh Douglas, known as the Social Credit philosophy. Social Credit held that unemployment was nothing more than the result of inadequate purchasing power, and that to alleviate hard times government had an obligation to make purchasing power—the ability of the consumer to buy things—equivalent to productive capacity. The most dramatic of Social Credit schemes, in this regard, was a system of passing out dividends to the citizenry, thereby redistributing purchasing power.

Enter Social Credit: Not even an affluent people likes to look a gift-horse in the mouth, and the Albertans of the early thirties were anything but prosperous. As they heard Aberhart extoll Social Credit over the radio, they, too, became interested. The Social Credit Party was founded in 1932, and in 1935 Aberhart, as its leader, swept the United Farmers Party out of office (it had held thirty-six of sixty-one seats in the legislature) and brought his party in, with fifty-six seats. The world's first Social Credit government was in office.

More than a dozen of its schemes—legislation outlawing debts, controlling the press, suspending mortgage foreclosures, among them—were outlawed by the federal government as unconstitutional. There was a widespread clamor—understandably enough—for Aberhart to follow through on his pledge of a twenty-five dollar dividend for every man, woman, and child resident in the province.

The "Socreds" lost some power in the 1940 election. But they remained at the helm into the early seventies, and there is little doubt that they were helped, at this period, in two ways: the advent of prosperity, which was a concomitant of World War II, and the accession to the provincial premiership in 1943 of Aberhart's first lieutenant and former Bible Institute protégé, Ernest Manning.

Preacher-premier: The Manning career was one of the most phenomenal in North American politics. Manning, like his predecessor, was a religious broadcaster and there is little doubt that his weekly "Back to the Bible" program did him little harm politically, particularly in as Bible-conscious a province as Alberta. Indeed, when Manning was re-elected in 1963 Canadian politicos were quick to realize that he would exceed the record of the late William Lyon Mackenzie King, who stayed in office as Prime Minister for a total of twenty-two years, and of John Bracken, who was premier of Manitoba for twenty years. But in 1971, after thirty-six years, the Progressive Conservatives, under Harvard-trained Peter Longheed, took over the Alberta government.

The current boom: Meanwhile, Alberta goes along its sprightly way. The government is rich. It builds excellent roads, puts up fine hospitals, supports a progressive school and university system, and has undertaken a wide range of other worthy projects. And, as things stand, about all it lacks is a seaport. There's the liquid gold which is oil, the golden wheat of the southern prairies, the natural gas, and coal. There are two handsome major cities and a number of smaller but no less prosperous towns; there are the splendid Rockies and the national parks within their confines, to say nothing of provincial parks throughout a province that abounds in spectacular beauty.

YOUR VISIT TO ALBERTA

If Manitoba and Saskatchewan are misnamed "prairie" provinces—and of course they are, for only a portion of their areas are treeless—Alberta deserves that designation even less so. Only a quarter of the area of this great plateau of a province is actually prairie. Great portions of the remainder of the province are anything but prairie, for here one finds the foothills of the Rockies and portions of the Rockies themselves. Central Alberta is parklike and wooded. The north is a region embracing great stretches of virgin forest and is drained by the Peace River, which flows into the western shores of Lake Athabasca and is flanked by a fertile valley well cultivated by hardy farmers. There are, in addition, major rivers like the Saskatchewan, the Red Deer, the St. Mary, and the Milk. And there are lakes—Lesser Slave and Cold are among them—as well as innumerable streams. Most Albertans live in the central and southern parts of the province, wherein are the most noteworthy of attractions for visitors. Even the briefest

Alberta visit should embrace Edmonton, the capital; Jasper and Banff national parks, and Calgary, which is not far from Banff. Waterton Lakes National Park should also rank high on itineraries.

Edmonton doesn't much think about the distinctiveness of its location, but it is the most northern city of any consequence on the North American continent. The capital of the Yukon and major cities of Alaska are even more to the north, to be sure, but they are smallish towns in contrast to this handsome, bustling metropolis with a metropolitan population exceeding half a million.

Edmonton is by no means young, as western cities go. It was born in 1795 as a Hudson's Bay Company post named Fort Edmonton, after an English river. And it remained just that—growing slowly—for the better part of a century. In 1873 the Village of Edmonton came into being when the Reverend George McDougall put up the first building outside of the stockade; several families followed him. The following decade saw the Canadian Pacific Railroad at Calgary to the south. Edmonton benefited indirectly at that time, for many rail workers decided to remain in the west, and some helped build up the little community. In 1891 the first spur of the railroad from Calgary reached Edmonton—then with a population of four hundred.

The town became a starting point for trekkers to the Klondike Gold Rush in the Yukon, and that added to its importance and size. In 1904 it was substantial enough to be incorporated as a city, and in 1906 it became capital of the then one-year-old Province of Alberta. In the years just before World War I it had amassed a population of some thirty thousand, and from then on there appeared to be no stopping it.

Its importance as the provincial seat of government increased as the province developed. And with improved transportation—rail, highway, air—it became the focal point of central Alberta and the gateway to the north with its important agriculture, lumber, and mining activity. In more recent years, oil refineries added tremendously to its wealth, and industry has had substantial beginnings. Buildings—industrial, business, residential, educational—go up at a furious rate; there are the Edmonton Symphony Orchestra, the Edmonton Opera, and a continuing program of presentations in the Jubilee Auditorium. Sports-minded Edmontonians see to it that facilities for their enjoyment—golf courses, tennis courts, bowling greens, swimming pools, skating rinks—are available to visitors. And in spectator sports, professional football (almost a mania in western Canada), hockey, and baseball are popular as is harness and stock-car racing in summer, and you can see cricket and British rugby, too. Edmonton is not without fine restaurants, night clubs, and places for dancing and a quiet drink or two.

There are a variety of organized sight-seeing tours by bus, but with one's own car, Edmonton can be seen independently without difficulty. Wide and welcoming Jasper Avenue—the main business intersection is Jasper Avenue and 101st Street—is perhaps the quickest indicator of the city's modernity and wealth. So is the view of the skyline from Mayfair Park, or of the whole town from the observation-floor telephone museum of the Alberta Telephone Tower. The core of town is the beautifully designed Civic Center. It embraces City Hall—modern and with a landmark sculpture entitled "Wild Geese" at its front entrance; the provincial Court House, of inverted pyramid design; the Edmonton Public Library (whose basement Children's Library doubles as a zoo, with live geese, ducks, rabbits, guinea pigs, chinchillas, turtles, and mourning doves—the better to lure juvenile readers!); the sleek twenty-nine-story CN Tower; Churchill Square—a public ice-skating rink in winter; and most important for the visitor, the Edmonton Art Gallery.

The art gallery moved into its present home in 1969. It is a striking poured-concrete building designed by local architects in consultation with the New York master, Philip Johnson, and embraces two exhibition floors and a lovely sculpture garden. It is not without a representative sampling of world art—one finds works by such diverse artists as Cranach, Degas, and Helen Frankenthaler, and there are frequently changing special shows. (An especially memorable one was "The Group of Seven in the Rockies," organized in co-operation with Banff's Peter Whyte Galleries in 1974.) But the Gallery's most distinctive asset—aside from its building—is the Ernest R. Poole Foundation Collection put together, painting by painting, over a period of many years by a native Prince Edward Islander who became an Alberta pioneer. It includes early Krieghoffs, goes on into the Group of Seven—Jackson, MacDonald, Harris, Lismer, Varley, Carmichael, Johnston—is strong on greats like Tom Thomson, David Milne, and Emily Carr, and even includes non-Canadian works, especially British, with an Epstein sculpture probably the finest piece among this grouping.

In Coronation Park is to be found the Queen Elizabeth Planetarium, dedicated to Her Majesty during a Royal visit to Edmonton in 1959. The George McDougall Memorial Shrine and Museum is the first building erected outside of the stockade walls, in 1873, and is now adorned with memorabilia of that era. The first log house built in Edmonton—that of John Walter—is now maintained as a tiny museum; it is still on its original site, on the south bank of the Saskatchewan River. The city of Edmonton tells its story in the Historical Exhibits Building, and if you have seen no others similar to it in western Canada, I suggest you visit the Ukrainian Church of St. Josephat, an elaborate Byzantine edifice, as well as the Ukrainian-Canadian Archives and Museum (9543 110th Avenue) chockablock full of the lore and history of the area's Ukrainian community. Worth noting, too, is what is perhaps Edmonton's most distinctive house of worship: the Mosque of Ali Raschid, North America's very first.

Even if you are not traveling with children, I most emphatically recommend that you do not leave Edmonton without a visit to Valley Zoo, an amusing youngsters' animal park which makes even the one in New York's Central Park pale in contrast. The architecturally innovative University of Alberta campus should be a requisite destination. Highlights of the campus include Rutherford Library, Student Union, the H.U.B. housing complex, the gym, and the University Museum and Art Gallery—little known beyond the campus but with some excellent exhibits, especially of Eskimo and Indian objects. Adjacent to the campus is Northern Alberta Jubilee Auditorium, built in 1955 by the provincial government as a fiftieth birthday gift to the people. It is identical with its counterpart in Calgary, and seats nearly three thousand.

I've saved for last two attractions as requisite as the Art Gallery and Legislative Building. The first is the Provincial Museum—a contemporary repository of Alberta historical and cultural materials that is especially strong on Indian exhibits, but not without interest in every gallery. (Adjacent is a mock-Tudor mansion that had been Government House—the Lieutenant Governor's official residence, now used for public meetings. Today's lieutenant governors live in a substantial but undistinguished ranch-style house at 58 St. George's Crescent, just down the street from the Premier's official residence.) The second of these attractions is Fort Edmonton Park, outside of town, on the North Saskatchewan River. The idea here is to provide the visitor with an idea of what this part of the world was like in earlier eras, starting with the fur trade in the mid-nineteenth century, by means of a diverse mix of structures—soldiers' barracks, an Indian settlement, shops and mills, turn-of-century habitations, the roaring twenties, the post-World War II oil boom, the current era. A final Edmonton note: If you can, time your visit for July, especially during the ten-day Klondike Days celebration, when the whole town turns on, with the citizenry decked out in Gold Rush-era togs, and special programs everywhere ranging from Exhibition Grounds shows through parades and barbecues.

Eight miles north of town is the little chapel built in 1861 by Father Lacombe, a Roman Catholic priest, and now a museum and memorial to one of the northwest's outstanding missionary pioneers. More distant—fifteen miles east of the city, but worth the excursion time—is the Alberta Game Farm, a largely wooded thousand-acre park with some of the most remarkable animal displays to be found on the continent, from Canadian moose and timber wolves to Tibetan yaks and North African camels.

Elk Island National Park, thirty miles east of Edmonton, is the site of one of the few herds of buffalo extant. Nearly fifteen hundred of the great beasts roam and graze in this protected refuge, which flanks Lake Asotin (and there are many other species of wildlife, too). There are camping facilities, a trailer park, restaurants, a nine-hole golf course, and swimming in the lake.

Calgary, while always effervescent and handsome, with the added fillip of a snowy Rockies backdrop, has only recently been able to compete with less ebullient albeit more secure Edmonton. At least as regards substantial attractions for the visitor. Oil-rich, with a substantial American colony, it has never concealed its Texas-in-Canada ambience, has long been known for good amenities and for its summer whoop-de-do—the ten-days-in-July Stampede celebrations. Now, though, there are other lures.

The basics are agreeable enough—Happy Valley's fun-and-games appeal for all the family, an especially diverse assortment of wildlife at the zoo; life-size reproductions of dinosaurs which roamed this part of Canada eons ago, at Dinosaur Park (adjoining the zoo); super views of the city from the sleek on-high campuses of Southern Alberta Tech and neighboring Alberta College of Art (which has a worth-visiting picture gallery); the exemplary plana-tarium and its building—an asymmetrical poured-concrete master-work; slim and soaring Calgary Tower with observation gallery and revolving restaurant 626-feet heavenward; the ever-expanding University of Calgary campus; and historical exhibits at places like the Horseman's Hall of Fame and Princess Patricia's Canadian Light Infantry Museum.

Then one gets to the Big Two. First of these is Heritage Park, one of the handful of top-drawer village museums in North America. The park, embracing ten acres southwest of town, por-trays western Canada from the period of the fur traders in the early nineteenth century through the First World War. There are more than three-score buildings, almost all carefully transported from other parts of the region as distant as Manitoba to the east and British Columbia to the west, with some purely local. But the park is a good deal more than quantity. The quality is what impresses. I have seen no more attention to detail, no finer authen-ticity, no more developed a sense of style in any similar museum. The interested visitor gives himself a minimum of half a day. (One can lunch well in Wainwright Hotel—out of the nineties.) Every-one has his favorites at Heritage Park; mine include the charming frame Thorpe House, and the three-story brick Prince House (an early Calgary mansion). Journalism students turn out a newspaper using an antique Alberta press; there's entertainment at Canmore Opera House; and gingerbread and peanut brittle on sale at the bakery. All in addition to a church and a cemetery, a blacksmith shop and miner's cabin, a horse-drawn trolley and venerable loco-motive.

Of equal import is the home, in the ultracontemporary Calgary Convention Center—one of the best equipped in North America—of the Glenbow-Alberta Museum and Art Gallery. These institu-tions, formerly in their own separate quarters, joined forces with the mid-'70s opening of the Convention Centre. The museum part of the operation concerns itself with Alberta history and lore, and its Indian exhibits are first-rate. (Don't miss the rare old photos.)

There are, as well, collections of Eskimo artifacts; room settings depicting early Alberta life—a parlor, a kitchen, a bedroom; a dramatic presentation of the RCMP when it was the North-West Mounted Police. The art gallery's emphasis is on Canadian works —as they relate to the west—nineteenth-century painters of the Indians like Irish-born Paul Kane and Ontario-born Frederick Arthur Verner, to name two outstanding examples. It stages special shows, both its own and imports.

Cultural Calgary extends to the performing arts. The Southern Alberta Opera has annual winter seasons, drawing on the shared resources of Opera West, a co-operative venture of companies in Winnipeg, Edmonton, and Vancouver. Theatre Calgary puts on a play series in winter; there is a winter season of the Calgary Philharmonic, and a variety of entertainments at the Jubilee Auditorium (a twin of the similarly named hall in Edmonton) and theatre in the earlier-described Planetarium complex.

If the truth be known, Calgary is not, except at Stampede time, the cowboy town it often pretends to be. It is, however, Canada's greatest Oilville—a far cry from 1875, when it was founded as a Mounty post (and named, by its first commander, after the Gaelic for "clear running water"). The Canadian Pacific arrived in 1883, the homesteaders started arriving thereafter, oil was discovered in 1912 in Turner Valley, and the city grew by leaps and bounds as petroleum hub, transport terminus, distribution center. Today, tourism plays no small part in its economy, for Calgary, on the Trans-Canada Highway, is but an hour and a half from Banff National Park, Alberta's greatest drawing card.

Banff National Park: I am not going to attempt to do Banff justice, any more than I will, later on in this chapter, with its northern neighbor, Jasper National Park. Writing as one who has seen a good bit of five continents, I would rank Banff as one of the seven scenic touristic wonders of the world. It is not Canada's largest national park (Jasper is a good bit bigger), but it is the oldest of the federally operated parks and is, understandably, a source of great national pride, from Victoria to St. John's. Even to Canadians who prefer vacationing in the United States, Europe, or the Caribbean, Banff has a special meaning. Albertans, so many of whom live within the shadow of the Rockies, rarely tire of excursions to Banff. And although British Columbians don't complain, I suspect many of them regret that Banff, which borders their province, is not just over the line on their side.

Banff owes its establishment as a federal recreation center for Canadian Pacific railroad workers who, while constructing the transcontinental railway, came across mineral hot springs on the slopes of Sulphur Mountain. They spread the word, not only about the springs (which have long since become a lesser Banff attraction) but about the grandeur of the area, and in 1885 the Canadian Government set aside a ten-square-mile area at Banff as a national park. Today, the park embraces more than twenty-five hundred square miles, and within it are a bevy of soaring Rockies peaks. Mount Assiniboine at 11,870 feet is the highest, and there are a number of others in excess of ten thousand feet. There are silvery glaciers, magnificent forested valleys, splendid lakes with surfaces so clear that the snowy peaks of nearby mountains are more often than not perfectly reflected on their surfaces. There are winding rivers and frothy streams strewn with boulders. And the amenities are superb. In no national park are they better, more diverse, or better maintained. Two of the continent's finest hotels are operated by Canadian Pacific within Banff. There are, as well, smaller hotels, motels, campsites, and trailer parks. The Trans-Canada Highway traverses Banff, but there are lesser roads, too, not to mention paths for trekkers, trails for serious climbers, and facilities for every kind of sport—from summer golf to winter skiing. (There is now first-rate skiing, with five facilities and lodges, at Mt. Norquay and Sunshine Village near Banff, as well as in the Lake Louise area. Sunshine Village has hotel facilities; it draws mostly intermediate and expert skiers, and has the longest season in the area—early November through late May, with some 350 inches of snow per year.)

A Banff visit is a tonic, and the longer one stays, the more efficacious. There are ingeniously contrived sight-seeing tours that occupy as little time as a few hours. The visitor with his own car has more choices before him than he'll know how to take advantage of. The tourist with sturdy legs and strong feet has a field day. Even the art student is drawn to Banff. The Banff School of Fine Arts, a unit of the University of Calgary, has been on the scene since 1933, has its own attractive campus—the Banff Centre—and sponsors the annual summer Banff Festival of the Arts, as well as offering summer courses in intensive French, music, drama, dance, painting, and photography.

The *town of Banff* is park headquarters, and is dotted with shops, places to stay, and places to eat and visit; there is nothing of the honky-tonk about it. I especially like its street names; with the exception of Banff Avenue—the main drag—they're mostly named for local fauna: Big Horn, Squirrel, Marten, Beaver, Muskrat, Otter, Grizzly, Buffalo, Caribou, Wolf, Elk, Moose, and Rabbit—streets, every one. From town one can see—hugging the Bow River Valley—such peaks as Rundle, Norquay, Stoney Saw, Sulphur, and Cascade. A drive around the area of the town might be made to such destinations as Bow Falls, Upper Hot Springs (where one can swim in a naturally heated springs pool), and the Buffalo Paddock.

To be undertaken as a requisite—no matter how short one's stay—is the ascent of Sulphur Mountain via its aerial cable-car "gondola" lift. The ride begins near Upper Hot Springs, and within minutes one is at an elevation of 7,495 feet, with what appears to be the entire universe below. The Mount Norquay lift—1,300 feet in ten minutes—is still another adventure. Within Banff town there are requisites, too. The Archives of the Canadian Rockies is a small but worthy museum-library-art gallery complex, placing emphasis on local history and culture. The federally operated Banff Natural History Museum is a turn-of-century repository of stuffed local animals and birds. And out of town is the exemplary Luxton Museum, a unit of Calgary's Glenbow-Alberta Institute. Luxton, built in the style of a log fortress, devotes itself to Indian themes exclusively, primarily by means of a series of dioramas—a buffalo hunt, a dog team in the snow, a ritual Sun Dance. Good murals and paintings, too.

Lake Louise is within the confines of Banff National Park some sixteen miles west of Banff. It is quite as lovely as you've heard—no mean praise—and the drives to and from it are experiences in themselves. En route, one does well to stop off at Johnston Canyon to see its falls. Lake Louise is backed up by the splendid Victoria Glacier. There are a number of places of accommodation, but the Château Lake Louise is the most noted. The lawns of its terrace front the lake, as do most public—and many guest—rooms. One can canoe or row on the waters, and there are a number of excursion points in the vicinity. One is the sedan lift, near Pipestone Bridge, which takes passengers to the summit of Mount Whitehorn, at 6,755 feet. Another might be the nine-mile trip to Moraine Lake in the rugged Valley of the Ten Peaks. And to the west of Lake Louise, thirty-one miles on the Trans-Canada Highway, is Yoho National Park, located in British Columbia, and dealt with in the chapter on that province. As you tour, look on the surface as well as skyward. The region is chock full of animals—black and grizzly bears (who may *appear* tame but who are not; feed or pet them at the risk of having a finger or hand bitten into); beautiful Rocky Mountain sheep with their tubalike horns; elk, deer, moose—and even beaver. The wildflowers are lovely (do *not* pick them as some are threatened with extermination), and you'll see more species of evergreen than you'll be able to identify.

The National Parks Service operates a many-faceted educational program for Banff visitors out of the park Administration Building (in which there's an interesting museum) in Banff town. There are nature courses, evening movies, and other services—all of them free.

The Ice-Field Highway connecting Banff and Jasper: Not all visitors are able to visit both Banff and Jasper parks. Many enter Banff from Calgary and exit the same way or by means of the Trans-Canada Highway leading into British Columbia. And Jasper is sometimes visited as an excursion destination from Edmonton, to the north. One's itinerary is the determining factor in respects like these, but if at all possible, I strongly suggest you visit *both* parks and that you get from one to the other by means of the day-long drive along the unique and dazzling Ice-Field Highway connecting the two. It runs through a series of valleys west of the main Rockies range, between Lake Louise in Banff park, north to Jasper. And I doubt whether you'll ever have had a more memorable ride. The highway skirts the Bow, Mistaya, North Saskatchewan, Sunwapta, and Athabasca rivers, traversing the Bow and Sunwapta passes. As you drive, you have only to look out the window for unbelievable views of glaciers on the Continental Divide—Waputik Ice Field (north of Lake Louise), Wapta Ice Field (west of Bow and Peyto lakes), and the fantastic Columbia Ice Field.

From the lookout point at Peyto (on a side road off the highway) one gains splendid vistas of Peyto Glacier, Peyto Lake, and peaks to the north. At another point, a side road will take you to the tongue of the Athabasca Glacier, part of which may be traversed by means of a specially designed vehicle known as a snowmobile. All along the Ice-Field Highway there are lookout points for the apparently interminable series of lakes, peaks, and glaciers. There are conveniently located picnic and camping areas en route; and some—not many—lodges and cabins may be found en route. The distance covered is only 142 miles, but there's no other 142 miles quite like it—anywhere.

Jasper National Park is almost twice as big as Banff in area, but because it does not have the advantage of being really close to a major city—as Banff is to Calgary—it does not have anything like the quantity of visitors that converge upon Banff. It is, as a result, a less lively place. Jasper townsite is smaller and quieter than Banff, public places of accommodation are fewer, and there are no requisite attractions in little Jasper town.

I suspect the difference in personality between the two parks could be nowhere more apparent than at the major hotels in each park. Canadian Pacific's Banff Springs Hotel is a towering sky-scraper in the Rockies (as is Château Lake Louise), while Canadian National's Jasper Park Lodge is a low-key, low-slung, bungalow-type hostelry—handsome, understated, and smaller than the giants at Banff. Jasper itself is, in many ways, less startlingly spectacular than Banff. While it has more than its share of peaks, it gives one the impression of being more horizontal and less vertical an area than its neighbor to the south.

Less vivid than Banff? Possibly. But Jasper has a gentle beauty which distinguishes it to the point that it demands of many of its visitors return trips, season in and season out. Not even the Edmonton people who return to it frequently ever see *all* of Jasper's forty-two hundred square miles, and the short-term visitor can count only on taking in the highlights. There are a variety of excellent bus tours from Jasper Park Lodge. There are tours, too, from Jasper town, the site of park headquarters. You should most certainly hie yourself to Maligne Lake, Tonquin Valley, and Mount Edith Cavell, perhaps the three most popular destinations in a brilliant galaxy. Shorter trips might be made, too, to Lac Beauvert, Pyramid Lake, Medicine Lake, and Maligne Canyon. Hikers, trekkers, and horseback riders have a wide choice of excursion points. And there's an aerial tramway at Whistler's Peak Mountain which ascends to a 7,500-foot elevation. Jasper, like Banff, is excellently equipped—if on a smaller scale—for winter sports, and perfectly beautiful to visit in winter, even if one is not a skier. (Skiing is centered on a trio of contiguous peaks—Whitehorn, Ptarmigan, and Temple.)

Waterton Lakes National Park requires introductory clarification. Occupying some two hundred square miles at the southern fringe of Alberta—on the Montana border—it constitutes a Canadian national park in its own right, but also is the Canadian sector of the unique Waterton-Glacier International Peace Park, whose American portion is Glacier National Park in Montana. From the United States, Waterton Lakes is gained by means of the scenic Chief Mountain International Highway, from Glacier National Park. The nearest major Alberta town is Lethbridge.

Though considerably smaller in area than either Jasper or Banff, and without the reputation of either of its bigger neighbors, Waterton Lakes can hold its own as a beauty spot. Its focal point is Waterton Lakes townsite, wherein are located park headquarters and places to stay and eat. From the townsite, bus and car tours can be made to many park areas—including Cameron Falls (at the edge of the townsite), Cameron Lake, and Red Rock Canyon. Unless one has come from Glacier Park, a trip to and through it (the area is much larger than Waterton Lakes) is indicated. What one most remembers of Waterton Lakes—and what distinguishes it from Banff and Jasper—is the distinctive coloring of its peaks. The Waterton Rockies are *really* rocky—and they are rocks of red, green, and purple. A nice way to see the park is from the passenger launch that plies upper Waterton Lake. There is swimming, fishing, golf, and any number of trails for hikers. Facilities range from the chalet-like Prince of Wales Hotel to campsites and trailer parks.

Lethbridge, Alberta's third city, is located on a river named—no kidding—Oldman. It has grown rich thanks to the agricultural and mineral wealth of the region it serves, runs a rodeo every July, is home to the Sir Alexander Galt Museum (pioneer lore), the University of Lethbridge and its Art Gallery, the perfectly lovely

Nikka Yuko Japanese Garden, and an out-of-town reproduction of early Fort Whoop-up.

Medicine Hat is Alberta's fourth city, and aside from its odd name (which derives from a long, complicated, and not terribly interesting Indian legend) it is distinguished because it lies atop natural gas reserves. There are some odd geologic formations in the area—fossils of prehistoric trees and animals from wa-a-ay back. There is a Stampede in July, patterned—on a much smaller scale—after Calgary's, and the Historical Museum displays local dinosaur bones—among other things.

Drumheller: If the replicas of dinosaurs at Calgary, and the bones at Medicine Hat interest you, then Drumheller will, too. Its Dinosaur Trail leads into a "valley of the dinosaurs" dotted with petrified remains of prehistoric animals and trees. And all about, covering a three-hundred-square-mile area, are fantastic—sometimes grotesque—rock and soil formations, the work of centuries of soil erosion. The Drumheller Museum tells the region's geologic history, and tells it well, and the Homestead Antique Museum is full of local lore from our own era.

Wood Buffalo National Park is an enormous (17,300 square miles) but undeveloped area that is primarily a refuge for deer, moose, elk, and a celebrated herd of some 12,000 buffalo—the largest on the continent. The park extends into the Northwest Territories and is easily reached via a road connecting it with Fort Smith, N.W.T.

SHOPPING

The two major cities and Banff offer the province's most interesting shopping. **Edmonton** provides several outlets for handicrafts, both Albertan and from throughout Canada. *Arctic Arts* (10064 104th Street) makes a specialty of Eskimo soapstone carvings as well as whalebone, ivory, and other Eskimo work. There is an Indian crafts section, too, and attention is paid to ceramics and weaving done by Edmonton artisans. *Canadiana Gifts, Ltd.* (10414 Jasper Avenue) has a collection of Indian and Eskimo artifacts, from totems and baskets to parkas and pots. There's an art gallery upstairs featuring work by Albertans. *Can-*

ada's Four Corners (Macdonald Hotel lobby) is one of a country-wide chain. The range is national, as the name implies. Traditional-style pine furniture is a basic commodity, but there are more portable and no less interesting wares, as well: pottery, hand-woven neckties, Canadian furs, quilts and rugs, smallish gifts like soap, candles, and maple sugar. And the level of style is high. *The Gallery Shop* (Edmonton Art Gallery) sells hand-woven wall hangings, hand-wrought jewelry, hand-painted water colors, hand-turned pottery—all Alberta origin, as well as crafts from other parts of the country, and of the planet. *McCauley Plaza,* under the AGT Building downtown is a shopping mall, with some half a hundred stores and services. The department stores are excellent. *Woodward's,* in the sleek *Edmonton Centre* (it houses another half a hundred shops) has a convenient grocery and delicatessen in its basement, an inexpensive cafeteria on three. *Eaton's* has a small Canadiana department for gifts and souvenirs in its basement, along with a big grocery and a sit-down restaurant. *Hudson's Bay* has a Canadiana department on the main floor, along with books; groceries are in the basement. And there's a smart *Holt, Renfrew* (men's, women's clothes), too.

Calgary: *Calgary Cabin,* in the Palliser Square shopping complex, is a first-rate source of mostly Albertan handicrafts—wooden-ware, ceramics, jewelry, leatherwork, local rocks and gems, Indian and Eskimo artifacts, even postcards and notepaper with locally created motifs. *Cottage Crafts* (Elbow Drive at Mayfair Shopping Centre) handles Canadian work only—Eskimo, Indian, and a variety of Alberta-made woven, carved, and other objects. *Canadiana House* (509 Second Street Southwest) specializes in Canadian antiques—prints and maps, china, silver, glass. The department stores are good. *Eaton's* main-floor book department is worth knowing about for its big selection of magazines and newspapers. There are a pharmacy and bakery in the basement, and a nice cafeteria and post office on four. *Hudson's Bay's* downtown store has a commendable Canadiana shop on main—both Eskimo and Indian wares—good places to eat, too. *Holt, Renfrew* is downtown, too, and so is the *Penny Lane* shopping complex—in a cluster of handsomely restored elderly buildings on Eighth Avenue between Fourth and Fifth streets, S.W. **Banff:** *The Quest,* on Banff Avenue (and its Victoria, B.C. branch) remains one of the better-quality

craft shops in the west. The work comes from all over Canada—
Eskimo and Indian wares, ceramics, weaving, jewelry, prints.
Whatever it is—and the stock changes from month to month—
quality is high, workmanship first-rate. *Banff Indian Trading Post*
(Corner of Birch and Cave avenues) features skins and pelts—a
wolf rug if you like, for many hundreds of dollars, or a rabbit skin
for a few bucks; hand-woven sweaters, miniature totem poles,
moccasins, parkas. There is nothing at all Canadian about *Fitz-
Gerald's,* on Banff Avenue opposite the Natural History Museum.
I mention it only because it's so full of lovely Irish imports that
you'll want to have a look. *Hudson's Bay Company* is on the
scene, in a smallish brownstone store.

CREATURE COMFORTS

Long one of the most tourist-trod of the provinces, Alberta has
a good idea of what hospitality is all about, and visitors can count
on being comfortable, especially in the major centers. Here is a selective sampling of places to stay and to eat. **Edmonton:** *Château
Lacombe*—named for a priest who was an Alberta pioneer—stands
out in downtown Edmonton, thanks to its soaring, circular-tower
design. This is a good-looker of 330-rooms and suites, with a revolving restaurant-lounge to top it off; it's CP Hotels' first Edmonton property. Worth noting are a middle group of rooms, so-called
studio suites—they're ideal for small families or the executive who
needs a small living room for entertaining or meetings. Besides the
roof-top restaurant, there are two off the lobby—the Chevalier Grill
with its adjacent Garrison Lounge, and a cafeteria as well. *The
Macdonald* is Canadian National's long-time Edmonton landmark.
There are 455 handsome rooms and suites, all recently
refurbished, a honey of a glass-walled indoor pool and adjacent
sauna, and rather special places to eat and drink, including the
Inglenook Restaurant, Izba Lounge for drinks, a dilly of a coffee
shop called the Peppercorn, and that rarity of rarities in northern
Canada, an outdoor summer restaurant-café. *Edmonton Plaza* is a
typically exemplary Western International hotel. Its façade—tall
and pencil-slim and elegant—is among the city's more innovative.
Within, there are 350 rooms and suites—at once functional and

luxurious. There are a pair of restaurants—the Terrace Grill, with a cocktail lounge leading from it overlooking the lobby proper, and a coffee shop. And there's a *boîte* called the Stage Door, not to mention a pool and sauna. Very classy. *Edmonton Inn,* near the in-town municipal airport, has an understated mod look—from lobby through to the comfortable accommodations. There are 200 rooms including two-level suites that executives will want to note, and restaurants and lounges; the latter range from a birch-furnished coffee shop to the lively—and delicious—Vintner Restaurant, with entertainment and dancing. *Sheraton-Caravan Hotel,* with 141 rooms, restaurant, cocktail lounge and coffee shop, is downtown, and has full facilities. *Holiday Inn* (192 rooms) with the usual conveniences of that chain—restaurant, cocktail lounge, coffee shop, pool. *Le Château Louise Motor Inn,* also near the municipal airport, is a leader among Edmonton's motels, at once managing the convenience of a motor hotel and a mock eighteenth-century décor. Rooms are pleasant and the amenities include an attractive restaurant, cocktail lounge, and coffee shop. **Calgary:** *Four Seasons Hotel* is one of the most beautiful in western Canada, as tasteful as it is sumptuous. And this is a combination not often encountered. There is convenience, too; this 387-room house adjoins Calgary Convention Centre. All of the accommodations—minimum-rate twins to luxury suites—are uncommonly attractive. The Wheatsheaf is about as classy as a coffee shop can get and still be a coffee shop. The fancy restaurant is called the Traders—and is posh indeed, as are its next-door cocktail lounge and the Scotch Room, for drinks and entertainment. Lovely pool, too. A part of the Four Seasons chain. *Palliser Hotel* is Canadian Pacific's long-admired Calgary property, a gracious traditional-design house with 415 rooms and suites, a big and busy lobby, a good restaurant—the high-ceilinged Rimrock, and its popular lounge. Palliser Square, with all of its amenities, adjoins, but it's the engaging ambience of the Palliser Hotel that is its biggest asset. *Calgary Inn* lacks the warmth and smiling charm of other Western International hotels in Canada, but is modern, central, and comfortable, with spacious rooms and a variety of places to eat and drink. *The International* is unusual in that its 255 units are suites, each with separate bedrooms, living-dining rooms, kitchens, and balconies, as well of course as baths. There are, as well, restaurant and cocktail lounge, indoor pool, and sauna. *Holiday Inn* is centrally placed downtown, with 200 modern rooms, restaurant, cocktail lounge and—to note if you come in summer—an elevated outdoor heated pool surrounded by a capacious sun deck. *Sheraton-Summit Hotel* is downtown-convenient, with 141 rooms and the expected Sheraton features, including restaurant, cocktail lounge, pool. *Highlander Motor Hotel* is on the Trans-Canada Highway opposite North Hill Shopping Centre and near Jubilee Auditorium. It's very attractive—rooms and suites as well as restaurant, coffee shop, and lounge. An outdoor pool is a summer lure. *Blackfoot Inn* is on Blackfoot Trail near the Stampede Grounds; 100 rooms, restaurant, coffee shop, lounge-cum-entertainment, and a sauna. Pool for summer. *Crowchild Inn,* on Crowchild Trail, en route to Banff, and just beyond the University of Calgary, is a handsome, low-slung complex embracing 40 attractive rooms, a good restaurant, cocktail lounge, coffee shop, pool, and sauna. *Trade Winds Motor Hotel,* at Chinook Ridge, is good-sized (175 rooms), and full-facility. **Banff:** Along with a couple of its fellow CP Hotels—Quebec's Château Frontenac and Victoria's Empress, the *Banff Springs Hotel* is among the more beloved of Canadian institutions. It goes back to 1887 when Canadian Pacific first planned a resort to be created in the Rockies at a place named after Banff, Scotland, by Lord Strathcona, an early CP director. The first Banff Springs Hotel was a five-story frame structure that went up in 1888. It was replaced by the nucleus of the present hotel in 1913, just before World War I. A decade and a half later—just before the Great Depression—north and south wings were added and the hotel's façade is not changed today. The idea of a skyscraping 550-room mock-French château in the Alberta wilderness may have been preposterous. But it has worked. From the hotel evolved a vacation center that became one of the planet's most popular, four seasons of the year. The hotel itself, traditional architecture and advanced age notwithstanding, keeps abreast of the times. The aging furniture in many of the guest rooms, to give you an idea of the hotel's contemporary flavor, has been decorated in light, whimsical designs by a student waitress who, the management learned by accident, was also a gifted artist. The suites are as elegant as ever, and the varying-size rooms are comfortable and well maintained. There are three restaurants—the traditional Alhambra, the Alberta for beef, and the Rob Roy. The Sundance is a basement disco. There are drinks and entertainment in a pair of lounges, afternoon tea in two other rooms (my choice: the Riverview, for the vistas). The 18-hole, 6,643-yard, par 71 golf course is one of the most magnificent to look upon—and to play—extant, with a bar-lounge-café in its own handsome clubhouse. There are two swimming pools, sauna, health club, tennis courts, game rooms, outdoor shuffleboard, winter ski packages. *Timberline Hotel,* away from the core of town en route to Mount Norquay, is smallish (just under 50 rooms) and charming, with a Tyrolean-chalet look to it, lovely rooms, a dining room to whose windows the neighborhood deer come for glances of the diners; a cozy cocktail lounge with entertainment, and gorgeous views from virtually any and every window; old-timers will recall that this was once a part of the CP chain. *Voyager Inn* has 88 modern rooms, and a range of facilities—restaurant-cocktail lounge, coffee shop, all-year heated pool, sauna, and winter ski packages. Décor tends toward the gaudy. *Banffshire Inn* has more than half a hundred pleasant rooms, and a heated pool; no restaurant or cocktail lounge, but the Voyager Inn is next door. *Red Carpet Inn* is another smallish (30 rooms) motel without restaurant or cocktail lounge, but with nice rooms, and a close-to-downtown location. *Ptarmigan Inn* is a striking, dark-frame structure wrapped around a central patio. Rooms are spacious and well equipped, and some have kitchens. No wine-dine facilities, but downtown is nearby. *Bighorn Motel* is a quadrangular complex with 35 well-equipped rooms and a licensed restaurant. *Sunshine Village Inn* is a charmer of a ski-resort, in the heart of the Sunshine Village ski complex, fourteen miles from town, and at a 7,200-foot elevation. Rooms (a total of 90), most with bath, are smallish and spare, in true ski-lodge style, but comfortable enough. There is a cocktail lounge with evening entertainment, and a restaurant with simple fare and smashing views. **Lake Louise:** Quieter than its cousin, CP's Banff Springs Hotel, *Château Lake Louise* is also smaller (360 rooms). The setting is sublime, with the lake itself at the base of the hilly front lawn, and Victoria Glacier as its smashing backdrop. This is the view you get from either the long, front-of-house lobby, the main restaurant, and the front rooms. But even those in the rear offer panoramas of the majestic

Pipestone peaks. In summer, Lake Louise is ideal for shortish walks, longer hikes, horseback riding, boating on the lake, fishing in nearby streams, and evening merriment in the cocktail lounge or pub. In winter, there's skiing at Lake Louise or at easily reached Mount Norway and Sunshine Village. Tiny Lake Louise village offers accommodation, too. The 73-room *King's Domain* features kitchens in all of its units; it's attractive. The log-sheathed *Post Hotel* and adjacent *Pipestone Lodge* are jointly operated. The former is a cozy place with but 14 rooms (only 7 of which have their own baths) and a trio of cabins. There's a welcoming cocktail lounge and restaurant, with a coffee shop in the basement, all shared by residents of 24 modern units (all with bath) in the Pipestone next door. *Moraine Lake Lodge* is an isolated summer retreat on the shores of beautiful Moraine Lake, embracing 14 cottages, each with bath, a main-house lounge and restaurant; not licensed, but you may bring your own booze for sunset cocktails on the little porch of your cabin. Note the view of lake and mountains from the lodge; you'll see it reproduced on the Canadian twenty-dollar bill. *Emerald Lake Chalet and Cottages,* under the same management as Moraine Lake Lodge, is also near Lake Louise, on still another mountain-fringed lake of especial beauty. There are rooms—with and without bath—in the main building, which houses an attractive, albeit unlicensed, restaurant, and in surrounding cottages. **Ice-Field Highway:** *Num-Ti-Jah Lodge* is a real old-fashioned mountain lodge, just the kind you hope you'll come across in the Rockies. There are chairs made of antlers and antlers are on the walls; a splendid setting with horses for riding just outside. Eighteen of the 28 rooms have baths; licensed restaurant. **Jasper:** Canadian National's *Jasper Park Lodge* opened in 1953 to replace its predecessor which burned. It combines considerable style with the informality of the Rockies, although one must be prepared for a cooler, lower-key kind of ambience than that of, say, the Banff Springs Hotel. The high-ceilinged central building houses the main lobby, main restaurant, and other public rooms. Almost all of the accommodations—there are 365 rooms, each with sitting room and porch or balcony—are in detached wings, and are very comfortable indeed. The situation—on the shores of mountain-backed Lac Beauvert—is one of the loveliest in Jasper. There is a range of activities—evening dancing and entertainment, a heated outdoor pool on a terrace overlooking the lake, golf, tennis, riding, boating and canoeing, fishing for half a dozen types of trout, trails for hikers and picnickers. Ski packages for winter guests. *Marmot Motor Lodge* is a handsome 106-unit house in Jasper town. The rooms are inviting and well equipped, and facilities include a heated indoor pool and sauna, a cocktail lounge, and one of the best restaurants in the area. *Andrew Motor Lodge* is a capacious complex of nearly 100 attractive rooms and suites, a bright and well-run restaurant, and a nice cocktail lounge. *Jasper Inn* has 50 distinctively designed units, with wood-burning fireplaces set in brick walls, full kitchens, and in some instances bedrooms up a flight from the living room-kitchen. Maid service is optional. There is neither restaurant nor bar, but groups may make use of a delightful lounge for their own merriment. *Athabasca Hotel* is a landmark of Jasper town. It's just opposite the rustic-style CN railroad station and the adjacent little park with its totem and flagpoles. Forty of its 60 rooms have baths; restaurant, coffee shop, cocktail lounge. *Becker's Bungalows*—there are 43 with from one to three rooms; all have bath and are kitchen-equipped. Location is three miles south of town at the edge of the Ice-Field Highway. There's a licensed restaurant, too. **Waterton Lakes National Park's** long-time leader is the *Prince of Wales Hotel,* a chalet-style house dedicated in 1928 by the late Duke of Windsor while he was Prince of Wales. All 82 rooms have private baths, there's a restaurant and cocktail lounge and a honey of a view from the huge lobby windows. Motels, none with restaurants or cocktail lounges, but some with some kitchen facilities, include the *Bayshore Motel* (44 units, lake front), *Emerald Bay Motel* (23 units), and *Windflower Motel* (23 units). **Lethbridge:** *Holiday Inn* has close to 140 fully equipped rooms, as well as a restaurant, cocktail lounge, coffee shop, and indoor pool. *Heidelberg Inn* has 66 rooms with bath, and a licensed restaurant. **Medicine Hat:** *Park Lane Motor Hotel*—77 rooms with bath, and a range of facilities including restaurant, cocktail lounge, coffee shop, and heated pool. *Westlander Inn*—40 rooms with bath, restaurant, cocktail lounge. *Travelodge Motor Inn*—51 rooms and suites with bath, heated pool, no restaurant or cocktail lounge. **Drumheller:** *Drumheller Motor Inn*—35 rooms with bath.

   Dining in Calgary, Banff, Edmonton, and Jasper: CALGARY: *The*

Trader's—very posh, haute cuisine—and the *Wheatsheaf*—western
Canada's most beautiful coffee shop—are both in the Four Seasons
Hotel, and both recommended. The *Rimrock* in the Palliser Hotel
is animated and delicious at both lunch and dinner. The *Panorama
Room,* atop the Calgary Tower and operated by CP Hotels, is fun
for lunch-cum-view. *Hy's* (316 Fourth Avenue, S.W.), like its
counterparts coast to coast, is handsome and clublike as regards
décor, with excellent steaks, professional service, and—especially
in the case of the Calgary Hy's—amusing at cocktail time. *Caesar's*
(512 Fourth Avenue, N.W.) is noted for its hearty steaks. *Inn on
Lake Bonavista* (747 Lake Bonavista Drive, S.W.) offers a pretty
view, tasty dinners. *Gasthaus* (2417 Fourth Street, S.W.) is Calgary at its most Teutonic delicious—sauerbraten, good beer.
Smuggler's Inn (6920 Macleod Trail) puts one in mind of northern California or B.C.—rocks and greenery and heavy open beams,
with substantial beef dishes and a super salad bar. *Chalet Swiss*
(525 Seventh Avenue, S.W.) is for fondue, veal as the Swiss
prepare it, that sublime potato preparation known as rosti, and
Swiss wines. *Moose Factory* (628 Ninth Avenue, S.W.) is for
reasonably priced pasta lunches and dinners in a colorful setting.
Oliver's (609 Seventh Avenue, S.W.) is at once very smartly decorated and very expertly operated, with delicious food—prime ribs,
steaks, lobster tails, Continental specialties—and a honey of a
lounge in connection. *Omi* (615 Second Street, S.W.) serves tep-
pan-style steaks prepared at table; other Japanese specialties. Fun.
Hudson's Bay's *Chinook Ranch Room* is a worth-knowing-about
cafeteria, in the downtown store. BANFF: *Banff Springs Hotel's* restaurants include the Alhambra, for table d'hôte meals in a luxurious setting, the Alberta Rooms for roast beef and steaks, and the
Riverview Lounge, where you'll want to have afternoon tea-with-
a-view. *Mount Royal Hotel Restaurant* is for steaks as well as fish
and seafood; *Ticino Restaurant*—Swiss ownership and cuisine;
Phil's Pancakes—steaks as well as flapjacks, and good; *Homestead
Hotel Restaurant*—tasty, moderate-priced lunches and dinners.
EDMONTON dining is at its best in the *Discovery Restaurant* (9929
108th Street, in Petroleum Plaza). The setting is discreetly handsome and contemporary. The menu ranges from Alberta trout and
crêpes Newburg through steak au poivre and roast lamb, Greek
style. Desserts rate a card of their own, and the wine list is com-

posed with care. Exceptional. *La Ronde,* atop the Château Lacombe Hotel, is a revolving restaurant with a difference: first-rate food. (Many of these places appear to substitute the view for the fare.) The menu is limited with steaks and prime ribs dominant, but everything is very good. The Lacombe's ground-floor *Chevalier Grill* is banner-hung, brick-walled, and also commendable. *Ingelnook* (Macdonald Hotel) is beautifully decorated in period-country style, with an equally attractive cocktail lounge adjoining. The menu is international, more interesting at dinner than at lunch. *Tower Suite* (CN Tower) is very tony, international in the scope of its menu and of its wines, and very good at either lunch or dinner. *Oliver's* (11730 Jasper Avenue) is quite as ritzy as are its counterparts in Calgary and Winnipeg. The menu emphasizes beef and seafood but extends into other delectable areas. Setting is opulent, wines good, and service that of pros. *Steak Loft* (9974 Jasper Avenue) is a convenient, heart-of-downtown beef house, reliable and moderate-priced. *Empress of China* (10404 124th Street) is among the city's better Chinese restaurants; the specialty is Cantonese dishes. *Italian Garden* (10169 104th Street) is recommended for a quality lunch or dinner, Italian style; good pastas, veal dishes, and salads. *Old Spaghetti Factory* (Boardwalk Shopping Centre, 10220 103rd Street) is a good way to see an old warehouse transformed into a maze of shops—and this restaurant, whose props include a retired trolley car, and lots of Tiffany lampshades. Pasta-accented meals are cheap, good, and fun. *Pyrogy House* (12510 118th Avenue) is for Ukrainian specialties. JASPER: The immense main dining room of *Jasper Park Lodge* is the region's best-known restaurant; it has a smaller, more intimate Steak House, as well. The *Marmot Motor Lodge Restaurant* is first-calibre, too—very attractive, with good steaks and ribs of beef, as well as seafood. Lobster tails and beef are the specialties of the *Iron Horse* in the Whistler Hotel. *Holiday Restaurant* (410 Connaught Drive) is still another source of good steaks and prime ribs. The *Athabasca Hotel Restaurant* is locally noted for its pizza.

British Columbia

LA COLOMBIE BRITANNIQUE

Best times for a visit: *This is an all-year-round vacationland. Winter, along the Pacific coast, is about the warmest in Canada, with temperatures in Vancouver and Victoria well above freezing, little frost, light snowfalls, but a good bit of rain to*

compensate. Eastern British Columbia is colder in winter and excellent for winter sports. Summer days are, in most parts of the province, pleasantly—but not overly—warm, and nights are cool; there can be cloudy and rainy days along the coast. The Okanagan Valley has exceptionally hot, dry summer days. Spring and fall are short seasons marking the extreme changes from cold winter to hot summer—in eastern British Columbia. But as one approaches the Pacific there is less seasonal contrast. Victoria in January (the coldest month) is only about twenty degrees colder than July, the hottest month. And Vancouver may be mild enough for a January golf game—and gloomily gray and wet in June. **Transportation:** *British Columbia can be reached by every available means of transport, except, possibly, pogo stick. It is, of course, the starting point (termination point, if you're coming from the east) of the Trans-Canada Highway. Mile 0 is in Victoria, the highway then cuts north across Vancouver Island to the port of Nanaimo, crosses the Strait of Georgia by ferry with you and your car, resumes in Vancouver and cuts across the province, via Kamloops, passes through the magnificent Rogers Pass (between Revelstoke and Golden), skirting Revelstoke National Park, goes across Albert Canyon to and through Glacier National Park in the dazzling Selkirk Range, then traverses still another national park— Yoho, before passing into Banff National Park, in Alberta. The Trans-Canada Highway is at no other point more exciting. U. S. Highway 99 is the most direct route from Seattle. It is in British Columbia that the largely unpaved Alaska Highway begins—at Dawson Creek, continuing north to Watson Lake over the Yukon frontier, thence through the Yukon and into Alaska (see the chapter on the Yukon Territory). Dawson Creek is reached by the Great North Road (Highway 97), a scenic, paved, 534-mile stretch beginning at Cache Creek and going north via Prince George. Another major highway—and the province has an extensive road network—is fully paved Highway 16, which runs through the Rockies on the Alberta border, through the heart of the province to Prince George and the terminal point, the port of Prince Rupert, on the Pacific. There are extensive bus routes* *serving the province (including Greyhound, Pacific Stage Lines, and Vancouver Island Coach Lines), and bus service to other provinces, as well as to U.S. points (Greyhound makes a number of runs each day between Vancouver and Seattle). A number of airlines serve British Columbia. Air Canada begins (and completes) its transcontinental routes in Vancouver and serves Victoria, as well. CP Air flies into Vancouver from Pacific points and from Edmonton and points east in Canada. It also flies north to the Yukon and to Prince Rupert. Pacific Western Airlines links Vancouver, Victoria, and Seattle, flies also to smaller B.C. points, Edmonton, and the Northwest Territories. United Airlines flies to Vancouver from U.S. cities. Quantas, the Australian line, flies from the Pacific to Vancouver. And there are others, both scheduled and chartered. Both major Canadian railroads —Canadian National and CP Rail—traverse British Columbia, with Vancouver the main terminus; CN has a terminal at Prince Rupert, as well. British Columbia Railway, provincially owned, operates a north-south route from Vancouver to Fort St. John and Dawson Creek. There is frequent steamer and ferry service between the state of Washington and British Columbia, between the state of Alaska and British Columbia, and between Vancouver Island (site of Victoria, the capital) and Vancouver (the city) on the mainland. The British Columbia Ferry System (B.C. Ferries, for short) runs its boats (with restaurants) between Vancouver and Nanaimo on Vancouver Island; and between Vancouver and Victoria (Swartz Bay). CP Ships connect downtown Vancouver and Nanaimo. Washington State Ferries operate between Anacortes, Washington, and Sidney. Black Ball Transport provides service between Port Angeles, Washington, and Victoria. Alaska State Ferry system plies between Prince Rupert, British Columbia, and Skagway, Alaska, a popular departure point (by train) for Whitehorse, Yukon. Cruise ships of Royal Viking and other lines plying between California and Alaska call regularly at Vancouver, Victoria, and sometimes Prince Rupert. Several sight-seeing boats make frequent tours every day of Vancouver Harbor and surrounding waters.* **Having a drink:** *Liquor and beer in dining lounges* *(combined restaurant-cocktail lounges), licensed dining rooms, lounges, and beverage rooms, which serve beer only, and at which beer may be bought to take out.* **Further information:** *Department of Travel Industry, Parliament Buildings, Victoria; 100 Bush Street, San Francisco, and 3303 Wilshire Boulevard, Los Angeles; Agent-General of British Columbia, 1 Regent Street, London; Canadian Government Office of Tourism, Ottawa and branches.*

INTRODUCING BRITISH COLUMBIA

British Columbia is not nearly as British as it sometimes likes to believe; was never, of course, seen by the explorer for whom it is named; provides enormous Canada with its only direct outlet to the Pacific; is the only Canadian province with American states flanking both its southern *and* northern frontiers. It is so big that it would encompass three Italies, seven New York states, or seventeen Nova Scotias; is almost wholly mountainous—no province is more scenically exciting, square mile by square mile; and has a population less than that of Greater Toronto, but which is at once industrious, hard-playing, culture-conscious, cosmopolitan, and, it would appear, eternally ambivalent in its attitudes toward those fellow Canadians—poor deprived souls—who live east of the Rockies barrier and are rarely as appreciative as they might be of the contributions British Columbia makes to the confederation.

There is, of course, no question but that British Columbia *does* contribute a great deal to Canada, or that its role is a very special one. Few contemporary visitors to the province leave without reluctance; indeed many stay on permanently, and I should not be surprised if the proportion of eastern Canadians in Vancouver was quite as high as is the proportion of eastern Americans in San Francisco. The lure of this lush, rich land is nothing new, and there seems little likelihood that its drawing power is about to diminish in the foreseeable future.

Drake and the Spaniards: The first known outsider to cruise about in the neighborhood of what we now call British Columbia was Sir Francis Drake, who came all the way north from Chile as long ago as 1579, on a search for a Northwest Passage. It's doubtful that he ever went ashore, but he did christen the land he viewed from shipboard as New Albion—and moved along. British Columbia remained Indian territory—up for grabs but with no comers—for almost two additional centuries. And it might so have remained for even longer had not Russian fur traders crossed the Bering Strait and set up posts in Alaska.

The globe-girdling Spaniards, always on the lookout for additions to their then vast realm, became concerned about the Russian activity. In 1774, they sent one Juan Perez on an expedition. The following year, the Heceta and Quadra Expedition laid claim to the area. But the Spaniards did not go unchallenged. In 1778 British Captain James Cook—searching for the Northwest Passage as was Drake almost two hundred years earlier—went ashore at Nootka, on the west coast of Vancouver Island. He was to die only a year later—in Hawaii—but fur-trading Captain John Meares set up a post at Nootka a decade later. For some time thereafter, the English and Spaniards were at odds over the area, for the Spaniards had settled in, too. (Place names there remain a souvenir of their presence—Strait of Juan de Fuca, Laredo Sound, Aristazabal Island, Bella Bella, Estevan Islands, Port Angeles, Anacortes, and San Mateo are examples.)

It took the Nootka Convention of 1790 to resolve the nasty situation. The Spaniards gave up their claims, the coast was declared British territory, and the following year Captain George Vancouver sailed from England with orders to take possession; that he did on August 28, 1792, and for two successive years he explored and surveyed the coastal area. In 1793, the remarkable Alexander Mackenzie crossed British Columbia at the termination of his epoch-making trans-Canada trek, in the name of the North West Company. He lost no time in establishing a profitable fur-trading business, and the early decades of the following century saw still more North West Company traders arrive in what they had come to call New Caledonia—no relation whatsoever to the French Pacific island bearing that name.

Riches and rivalries: Simon Fraser founded Fort McLeod in 1805, and later came David Stuart, an emissary of John Jacob Astor. The wilderness, before long, became a network of fur brigades. And like other parts of the west, this region was not spared the bitter rivalry which ensued between the North West and Hudson's Bay companies. That came to an end only in 1821 when the latter absorbed the former, and in the familiar Hudson's Bay pattern of that era, took over as both commercial and governmental leader of the region.

There were, however, other developments. The United States was interested in acquiring as much of this territory as it could, and Britain was not about to give up any of what it considered Union Jack domain. The squabble was temporarily terminated in 1846 when both the U.S. and the British agreed that the forty-ninth parallel would serve as the international frontier. Earlier, in 1843, Hudson's Bay had set up headquarters in Fort Victoria—predecessor of the current provincial capital, which it named for the then new sovereign. And in 1849 Hudson's Bay pulled out of the business of government in the area, and turned over Vancouver Island to the Crown. It became, at long last, a proper colony. The first governor, Richard Blanshard, resigned after less than two years. He was succeeded by Sir James Douglas, who had been in Canada as a fur trader—originally for the North West Company—since 1820. Later, for Hudson's Bay Company, he became chief factor and then commander of all the company's territory west of the Rockies. It was he who built Fort Victoria, in 1843. He remained affiliated with Hudson's Bay when he took over the Vancouver Island governorship in 1851, retaining that connection until 1858 when he was also made governor of the new colony of British Columbia on the mainland. By the time he retired in 1864, he had been knighted by Queen Victoria in recognition of his long service and the firm direction he had assumed of the new colony during a turbulent period.

Gold and progress: For it was in Douglas' time that gold was discovered in British Columbia. Discoveries in the Thompson and Fraser rivers in 1859 and a bit later in the Cariboo region brought new life to the colony, and led to settlement of the north. In 1866 the Vancouver Island and mainland colonies were united. New Westminster (just outside of Vancouver), which had been the capital of the mainland colony, took over as seat of government for the united colonies, but only briefly. In 1868 Victoria was made capital, and so it has remained ever since.

During this period, while the Pacific coast settlements were undergoing drastic political change, the British North American colonies to the east had not been quiescent. Indeed, the confederation of Canada had come about in 1867, and the Easterners were anxious for their distant neighbors on the Pacific to join them. In 1871 the British Columbians—on the condition that a transcontinental railroad would be constructed to link them with the east—went along and became a province of the new country.

The federal government's first attempt at building the railroad was unsuccessful, and it had British Columbia's secessionist movement to contend with as a result. But the secessionists failed, and the second attempt at the railroad—a private enterprise venture—was a rousing success. The Canadian Pacific reached Vancouver in 1885—half a decade ahead of schedule.

Growing pains: And none too soon. More gold was discovered in 1887 in the Kootenay country, and later there were still more gold strikes in the far north. Construction got under way in many parts of the province. Beginnings were made in industry. Vancouver's unique location served it well, and as Canada's only Pacific port of consequence it began to expand. There were, to be sure, difficult problems. It took nothing less than a German emperor—Kaiser Wilhelm I—to successfully arbitrate the boundary dispute between the U.S. and Great Britain over San Juan Island in the Strait of Juan de Fuca; that tempest in a teapot brewed from 1859 to 1872, and the U.S. was ultimately the winner. There were disputes over the Alaska boundary and over the rich Bering Sea fisheries. And there was friction between whites and the immigrants who came to British Columbia from China, Japan, and India, to the point where the federal government (not unlike that of the United States) disallowed their entry.

The good life: This is magnificently rich country. British Columbians live well, taking as much advantage of the splendid natural endowments of their land for recreation purposes as for trade and commerce. Almost three quarters of the province is tree-covered, and the forests bring British Columbia fifty cents out of every earned dollar. (A recent annual figure for timber was $1.9 billion.) If stretched out, the inlets along the province coastline would total some seven thousand miles. Here are thousands of miles of sheltered waters alive with superb salmon, cod, halibut, herring—nearly half of Canada's total fisheries wealth. (The average annual pack of canned salmon is nearly one and three quarter million cases!)

Mineral wealth? British Columbia extracts gold, silver, copper, zinc, and lead from its surface, to the tune of some $993 million annually. The soil is rich, too, and the province's famed apples, peaches, berries, and other fruits, as well as its vegetables, make their way all across Canada, and are exported to the United States, too. While using its natural resources wisely and well, the province does not neglect manufacturing. In a decade and a half, the gross value of manufacturing production has jumped from about $1.5 billion to $7.1 billion. And tourism is by no means a minor industry. More than four million Americans spent $267 million during 1974 in the province—a 15 per cent increase over 1973.

Lively politics: Still, with all this wealth, and their high standards of living, and the enviable beauty that surrounds them, British Columbians are anything but smug or apathetic. Politics in the province is as lively as in any, save Quebec. This has long been an essentially Social Credit province. Premier William Andrew Cecil Bennet was in office from 1952 until 1972. He was finally routed after two decades by the progressive New Democratic Party of former social worker David Barrett, who became Premier. But only until late 1975, when the elder Bennet's forty-three-year-old millionaire son, Bill, was swept into office, returning Social Credit to the fold.

YOUR VISIT TO BRITISH COLUMBIA

British Columbia has fewer dull stretches than any other province—which is saying a good deal. One is never far from mountains. The Rockies, bordering Alberta, stretch through northern British Columbia. Ranges and separate groupings of peaks, almost in parallel blocs, extend westward all the way to the Coast Mountains flanking the Pacific. There are five national parks, a wide-ranging network of provincial parks, a great city which is among the most beautiful in the Western Hemisphere, the lakes of the Okanagan Valley, the fjord-fringed seacoast, the maze of islands, not the least of which is Vancouver Island with its delightful rural vistas. There is the rugged, sparsely settled north where the

Alaska Highway has its origin. There is the lovely valley of the Fraser.

Vancouver: When Vancouver was incorporated as a city in 1886, it was home to some two thousand people. Today there are about half a million in the city proper (making it the third-largest city in the country), and Metropolitan Vancouver has a population of over a million. It includes, besides Vancouver itself, the even older city of New Westminster (which was British Columbia's first capital and is today the third-largest city of the province, with more than forty thousand people), North Vancouver, Burnaby, Richmond, West Vancouver, and a number of smaller north shore communities. Great port (its superb natural harbor has ninety-eight miles of water frontage), manufacturing hub, transport terminus, distribution point for the province, cultural center, tourist mecca—Canada's doorway to the Orient, Vancouver is all of these. "By Land and Sea We Prosper" is its official motto. And so it does. But what is there to attract us to this metropolis which occupies the peninsula lying between Burrard Inlet and the Fraser River, the whole magnificently fringed by a ring of majestic mountains? Well, to begin with, we have those mountains; we have water; we have a downtown of broad thoroughfares, tall skyscrapers, fine hotels and restaurants; we have some of the most splendidly situated residential areas of any North American city (picture windows must have been designed with Vancouver homeowners in mind). And we have an away-from-town area that lends itself to almost limitless excursions.

Vancouver, when the sun shines, is a sparkling sight. Its residents rush to their boats (there are well over thirty thousand registered pleasure craft in the area, not to mention countless thousands of smaller ones) for a lunch hour or weekend cruise. Or they rush to their beaches or to their golf courses. They support an art gallery, an opera association, theatre groups, and every summer the Pacific National Exhibition and Vancouver Sea Festival.

Bus tours take in all of the principal sights of Vancouver and environs, and I suggest one or two straight off because there is no Canadian city in which it is easier to get sidetracked while relaxing. One can easily spend far too much time lolling on the sands of English Bay or on the lawns of Stanley Park—and never really get elsewhere.

If a Vancouverite takes you sight-seeing, you can be sure he'll take you to Stanley Park first. Just north of the downtown area, and almost entirely water-bordered, it is a beautifully designed and maintained area of natural woods, formal gardens including paths for strolls, a zoo noted for its polar (and other) bears, an adjacent aquarium (as much a visitors' requisite as the zoo), rose gardens, picnic grounds, lookouts at Prospect and Brockton points, cricket grounds where matches may be watched on weekends, bathing beaches, a variety of restaurants and tea rooms, and Malkin Bowl, for summer theatre and other presentations.

On the crescent-shaped shore line of English Bay, which adjoins the western fringe of the park, the apartment houses give the area the look of Rio de Janeiro's Copacabana Beach. And there are other fine beaches, too.

It is this dazzling setting, and its attendant amenities, that can sidetrack the visitor curious about Vancouver's cultural fabric. It is perhaps even safe to conjecture that were Vancouver not so naturally smashing, given its coastal location and commercial and maritime eminence, it might expend more effort on matters of the intellect. The effect of mountains converging upon sea, with a verdant peninsula sandwiched in between, has obviously been something of a cultural deterrent to the populace. Instead of hieing himself off to an art gallery or concert or museum, the Vancouverite is more likely to head to the beaches or the ski slopes. A consequence is that, despite the build-up of the area's cultural establishment, considerable segments of the citizenry remain ignorant of it, or of much of it. The interested visitor must have an idea of what to look for. For example:

The Vancouver Art Gallery. It is smack in the heart of downtown in a substantial, elderly Georgia Street building which leads the newcomer or a visitor to expect more inside. There is, to be sure, a respectable permanent collection, including something like 200 paintings by the late Emily Carr, the province's most important painter; some of these are generally on display. There are paintings by Canadian Group of Seven artists (Lawren Harris, one of the seven, was a friend of Miss Carr's and played a part in the paintings selected for the museum). There are frequent traveling shows of the first rank, and the gallery has a many-faceted community program that embraces music as well as art. Still, the am-

bience of the place has a chill to it. One is not excited as one
enters, and walks about, as is the case in the Art Gallery of
Greater Victoria, or the art galleries in, for example, Edmonton
and Winnipeg—to name some others in the west.

The University of British Columbia's Museum of Anthropology
occupies a striking headquarters near Marine Drive, facing the
Strait of Georgia. Its architect was Arthur Erickson, the talented
Canadian who was responsible for the nearby Simon Fraser University complex. Erickson's Great Hall has 40-foot-high windows
and houses giant totem poles allowing them to be viewed in natural light against a natural background. But the collection is at least
as important as the setting. It embraces some 10,000 northwest
coast Indian artifacts (including a beautiful group of objects from
the Kwakiutl group). Additionally, there are some 10,000 objects
from other cultures—China, Japan, Korea, Tibet, other parts of
Asia, Africa, South America—which is the finest in the country
after that of Toronto's Royal Ontario Museum. Also worth visiting, while on the impressive 300-building UBC campus (ask for a
map at the entrance gates) is the Art Gallery (with frequently
changing shows) in the University Library's basement, and the No-
tobe Japanese garden, quite as elegant as the most elaborate in
Japan.

The museum's complex in Vanier Park near English Bay embraces the Centennial and Maritime museums and the aquarium.
The Centennial combines natural history with the history of the region; the latter exhibits are more interesting, but no match for the
Provincial Museum over in Victoria. The Maritime Museum also
has competition with a Victoria counterpart. This one is very big
on ship models, with amusing bits and pieces scattered about, including a Victorian-era poster no-nonsense in its aim: "Wanted:
Smart Active Boys for Royal Navy, 12-year Enlistment, £10 Pay
Per Year." To be seen in conjunction with the Maritime is nothing
less than a National Historic Site, a Royal Canadian Mounted
Police ship called the *St. Roch* which was the first to sail through
the Northwest Passage from west to east—Vancouver to Halifax
and return; the ship left Vancouver in June 1940 and reappeared
twenty-eight months later. The H. R. MacMillan Planetarium
houses a honey of a circular domed theatre in which are shown

multimedia presentations on matters astronomical. There's a cafeteria so that you may take between-museums refreshment breaks.

Simon Fraser University, in Burnaby, deserves inspection if only for its exterior architecture. It's an eye-opening series of connected poured-concrete quadrangles of varying heights, with a very mod geometric look, the lot dramatically plopped atop Burnaby Mountain; the architect was the same Arthur Erickson of the earlier-recommended UBC anthropology construction period. There are guided tours, but you may amble about on your own and take in the University Art Gallery—with changing shows not unlike those at UBC, and the Archeology-Ethnology Museum, strong on the beautiful arts and artifacts of the Northwest Indians. Peek at the theatre, too.

While you are in Burnaby, hop over to Heritage Village, an outdoor museum of B.C. life between 1890 and 1920, with structures ranging from Elworth House from the twenties, through a one-room schoolhouse, general store, village smithy, and, of course, an ice-cream parlor. All are skillfully re-created with commendable attention to detail. Still another Burnaby destination is the Burnaby Art Gallery; it occupies a turn-of-century mansion, and features changing exhibitions.

Would-be botanists will want to take in the Bloedel Conservatory—a handsome Plexiglas-domed structure in Queen Elizabeth Park sheltering several hundred species of tropical plants and the Van Dusen Botanical Gardens, more than half a hundred acres of both oriental- and occidental-style plantings.

Downtown Vancouver is among the more agreeable of urban Canadian locales. The main intersection—Georgia at Burrard—is distinguished by Christ Church, the smallish Anglican cathedral, a lovely neo-Gothic structure that goes back to 1895; its interior is a warm and inviting meld of Victorian stained glass and brass tablets framed by dark-wood arches. You may walk down Burrard Street to the harbor, take in the whole area from Granville Square at the foot of Granville Street, and wander through downtown's trio of browse-shop-eat areas. One, Chinatown (Pender Street, Abbott through to Gore streets) is locally adjudged to be second only in size after that of San Francisco. It is not without interest, but is nothing like that of the California city or, for that matter, New York's. Robsonstrasse, which is actually Robson Street as it meanders from Howe to Broughton streets, is even more locally over-rated than Chinatown; it contains some ethnic restaurants, food shops, and the like. A pleasant enough stroll. Gastown, named after a Vancouver early bird called Gassy Jack Deighton (because he gassed—talked—a lot) is an attractively restored area of elderly structures now seeing service as shops, art galleries, and places to eat and drink. Charming, this. Vancouver cultural life centers in the well-designed Queen Elizabeth Theatre and Playhouse. Both the Vancouver Opera Association (a partner in Opera West, sharing resources with the companies of Edmonton, Calgary, and Winnipeg) and the Vancouver Symphony give winter seasons.

I have saved a couple of requisite excursions. Make the lovely drive out to Capilano Canyon and cross the rather eerie suspension bridge that spans the Capilano River. Take the cable car ride up Grouse Mountain; so long as the weather is clear—night or day —the view can be counted upon to be unforgettable and one can lunch or dine at the summit. Head out to Queen Elizabeth Park's arboretum. Ascend to the observation post whose lawns are highlighted in summer by beds of brilliant flowers. From where you stand, you overlook the exquisite gardens built on a hill that slopes into a densely wooded area, and beyond will be the skyline of Vancouver, Howe Sound, and the North Shore Mountains. No other prospect, in this city of splendid prospects, is more beautiful.

Victoria: If it is true that Victoria remains quite the blandest-appearing of North American Pacific coast port cities, it is also true that it has begun to appreciate that as capital of Canada's westernmost province, and with a personality all its own, it need no longer kid either itself or its visitors with Outpost-of-England blather. For make no mistake: Victoria has a great deal more going for it than waxworks, bits and pieces of mock-Shakespeariana, and a sprinkling of genuine imported British expatriates. It can now stand on its own as a Canadian destination of consequence, with a collection of historic, architectural, and cultural attractions way out of proportion to its size.

You start with the Parliament Buildings, overlooking the pretty Inner Harbour area downtown. This complex, completed in 1897, is very grand Victorian (as well it might be in a city named for that monarch), set behind meticulously tended gardens, and illuminated at night. Pop inside and have a look around. East of

Parliament is Thunderbird Park, with one of the best collections of totem poles in the west. Another neighbor is the Empress Hotel, quite as imposing as Parliament and, until it got its first sign a decade or two back, often mistaken for it. The Empress owes its existence to two local men who, at the turn of the century, convinced Canadian Pacific, after its ferry operations began, that they could turn Victoria into a tourist magnet if it had a luxury hotel. Godfrey Holloway, in his book *The Empress of Victoria* (Pacific Productions, 1968) explains how Captain J. W. Troupe and George Henry Barnard were successful in their venture, how Barnard got himself elected to the city council as a means of helping insure municipal support for the project, and was later elected mayor, after which the voters agreed to grant Canadian Pacific the tax exemptions it wanted. A transplanted Englishman—Francis M. Rattenbury, who also designed the Parliament Buildings and the original Hotel Vancouver across the water—was the Empress' architect. (The pity is that he did not stay in Victoria; instead he returned to England, Mr. Holloway recounts, only to be murdered by his young chauffeur, reputedly the lover of the second Mrs. Rattenbury.) The Empress opened in 1908, with additions following in 1910 and 1929, and has kept a guest roster over the years that is one of the planet's more impressive.

From the Inner Harbour Area, lead Victoria's two main streets —Government and Douglas. Each is the site of an important—and ingenious—restored area. Bastion Square, on Government Street, is a cluster of handsome nineteenth-century buildings now housing restaurants, shops, offices, and—in the case of the one-time courthouse—the Maritime Museum of British Columbia. It was established after interest in its aims was shown by Prince Philip, the Duke of Edinburgh, on a post-World War II visit. Philip himself made contributions to the collection, the nucleus of which were Royal Canadian Navy objects relating to Victoria's role in provincial history. Today, in its capacious home, the exhibits go beyond those of the Navy, and run a wide gamut. Not the least amusing part of a visit is the antique elevator; don't miss a ride in it.

Centennial Square, off Douglas Street, has as its focus the 1878 City Hall, which the community was prepared to raze to make way for a new one, when some local architects and their supporters fought for the restoration of the original—and happily won. This square also contains McPherson Theatre—a cleverly converted early twentieth-century building—and a row of shops, the lot facing onto a fountain-dominated green.

Return, now, to the Inner Harbour. Just opposite Parliament is a contemporary complex, Heritage Square. Its carillon tower is a gift from Dutch-origin citizens. The tallish building adjacent is the Provincial Archives. The remaining structure is the one to head for: the Provincial Museum, one of the best such in Canada. The entrance hall features dramatic waterfalls and jumbo totems. The second floor's subject matter is natural history, and the exhibits focus about first-rate dioramas, handsome enough to look at, but with the added attraction of sound effects. Go up to the third floor —my favorite—for what the museum calls Human History. Allow time here. There's a street of structures even including two floors of a turn-of-the-century hotel, with furnished rooms and lobby, a theatre showing silent films (sit down and watch), a railroad station, sawmill, mineshaft, fur-trading post, fish factory, and a beautifully reproduced replica of Captain George Vancouver's eighteenth-century ship—interiors and all.

Helmcken House, nearby, is mid nineteenth century, with four furnished rooms as they were when a local physician inhabited them; the house is believed to be the oldest in B.C. still intact.

The Art Gallery of Greater Victoria is a car ride away from downtown. Its main building is a historic 1890 structure that had been an early Government House, official residence of the Lieutenant Governors, one of whom entertained King George V and Queen Mary there, when they were the Duke and Duchess of York, in 1901; there's a plaque telling that story in the entrance hall. Art works are displayed in the old house and in a modern addition. The permanent collection is a mixed bag—Canadian works by Victoria-born Emily Carr, by David Milne, and Group of Seven members, an unexpected cherub, or *putto,* by Sir Joshua Reynolds, Eskimo prints, English ceramics, and most important, a fabulous collection of oriental art, Japanese and Chinese for the most part—scrolls, jades, porcelains—but from India, Nepal, Tibet, and Persia as well. There are changing shows, too. And the ambience is among the more charming of any museum in the west.

Other houses, of one sort or other, constitute additional Victoria attractions. Point Ellice House is more than a century old, long inhabited by the O'Reilly family, which built it, and with a hodgepodge collection, from clothes to china. The look of the place is unprofessional, lived in, and fun. Craigflower Manor, built in 1855, in simple colonial style, is considered the best example of early house building in western Canada. It is unique in that it is operated as a Historic Site by both the federal and provincial governments (most such sites are the bailiwick of either one or the other government). And it's a gem of restoration and furnishing, with five handsome bedrooms upstairs, and a range of main-floor chambers. Craigflower School, not far distant, is of the same era as the house, a one-room schoolhouse full of mementos, including a photo of its last graduating class—that of 1911. Then there is another "Craig" structure, Craigdarroch Castle, a Victorian-era mock-Gothic gray-stone mansion, all turrets and towers and dark-wood interiors that now sees service as a music conservatory whose administration happily allows visitors. The entrance hall-cum-grand stairway is super, so are the fireplaces, and so are the paintings of Edward VII and his beautiful consort, Alexandra, along with photographs of the late Duke of Windsor when he was Prince of Wales.

Still another mock-Tudor castle is now the main building of Royal Roads Military College, set in a bucolic campus-estate that has traditionally been open to the public on weekday afternoons, thanks to the generosity of the Department of National Defense. The current Government House, also mock-Tudor, with a porte-cochère that is older than the house, opens its attractive gardens to the public, not to mention its vestibule, where in true British tradition, visitors may "sign the book" presumably to let the Lieutenant Governor and his lady know who's been to call, if only outdoors. Fort Rodd Hill and Fisgard Lighthouse, a good drive from town, is a national historic park. The setting is pretty, and one sees deer roaming over the great lawns bordering the water. But this is primarily for military buffs who enjoy coastal fortifications.

Victoria has a pair of commercial marine-life attractions—Undersea Gardens downtown in the Inner Harbour, and Sealand, at Oak Bay. Neither is requisite, in one visitor's opinion, unless the children insist. Neither, for that matter, is this city's Christ Church Cathedral, seat of the Anglican bishop, and a whale of a lot bigger —it is neo-Gothic on a grand scale—than the similarly named Anglican cathedral in Vancouver, if much less lovely. I need not advise you about Butchart Gardens; one misses seeing them at the risk of being labeled subversive. Victoria people consider them one of the seven wonders of the world. They are not, of course, any such thing, but they do constitute thirty-five acres of elaborate horticulture. There are Japanese, Italian, English rose, and sunken varieties and assorted other features, including a restaurant.

Vancouver Island: The largest island on the Pacific coast of either North or South America, Vancouver Island—beyond Victoria —is a sparsely settled land of dramatic fjords, forested mountain ranges, and occasional snow-capped peaks, with the highest, Mount Golden Hind, soaring 7,219 feet. The island is 280 miles long and as much as seventy-five miles in width, so that one needs some time to do it justice. A popular sight-seeing route takes one along the Island Highway, north from Victoria, at the southern tip, along the east coast to *Kelsey Bay,* 215 miles distant. With less time, and no car, an alternative might be a rail excursion, via Canadian Pacific, as far north as *Courtenay* (137 miles). The journey takes about six and a half hours, and the railroad follows, more or less, the Island Highway route. En route one finds a high proportion—about a fifth—of British Columbia's 321 provincial parks (the fact that the provincial capital is located on the island may or may not have anything to do with this). Going north, one has only to look to the left for vistas of the island's strikingly beautiful mountains, forests, and lakes. And to the right—with the splendid coastal mountains of mainland British Columbia as a backdrop almost too striking to be bona fide—are the islands and straits that separate Vancouver Island from the continent. The provincial parks—Elk Falls, named for the cascades that drop 120 feet into rocky canyon, is the most noted—are delightful recreation centers. And there are a number of pleasant villages, towns, and beauty spots en route. Elevated Malahat Drive offers superb views of Saanich Inlet. *Ladysmith,* smack on the forty-ninth parallel, is fine for swimming and is the site of the Crown Zellerbach Canada Museum and Arboretum, this being logging territory. *Nanaimo,* the island's No. 2 town, is, after Victoria, the leading ferry terminus on the island; there is direct service to Vancouver. Nanaimo is a former Hudson's Bay Company post, and its chief attraction is the Bastion, a part of the original fort, built in 1852 and now housing a museum worth perusing, along with the Centennial Museum, with Indian and local-history exhibits. At *Duncan,* midway between Victoria and Nanaimo—and a spectacular drive—is the British Columbia Forest Museum, a 40-acre, mostly outdoor complex that interprets the logging industry in a number of novel ways. From Nanaimo, excursions can be made inland to such spots as *Englishman River Falls, Little Qualicum Falls, Cameron Lake,* and *Port Alberni,* on its shore. Continuing north, one comes to *Courtenay,* the terminal point of the railroad; *Oyster River* with *Miracle Beach Provincial Park; Campbell River* and the aforementioned *Elk Falls Provincial Park,* and—after passing through small coastal settlements, *Kelsey Bay*—not nearly as remote as it would seem, for the mainland is but two miles distant, across Johnston Strait. The west coast of Vancouver Island is far less settled than the east and the site of *Pacific Rim National Park,* with beaches of extraordinary beauty, Barkley Sound—notorious for shipwrecks, inner hiking trails, and campgrounds. *Strathcona Provincial Park* is a major attraction of the interior, containing as it does the aforementioned Mount Golden Hind and other soaring peaks as well.

The mainland national parks: British Columbia's quartet of mainland national parks are all close neighbors of Banff and Jasper. They are smaller than the Big Two, and with considerably less international renown. But the Canadian Government takes its national parks seriously. No area is so designated unless it is of exceptional interest. Each of the parks in British Columbia has something distinctive to offer, and I suggest you take in as many of this group as your itinerary will allow, bearing in mind that the Rockies and neighboring ranges lose none of their beauty because of an arbitrary frontier separating British Columbia from Alberta. Yoho National Park is a near-neighbor of Lake Louise in Banff National Park (see the chapter on Alberta) and is conveniently visited from that point. Kootenay National Park, directly to the south of Yoho, can be taken in coming west on the Trans-Canada Highway through the Vermillion Pass from Banff. Farther west are the adjoining Mount Revelstoke and Glacier parks, both traversed by the magnificent Rogers Pass section of the Trans-Canada Highway.

Yoho National Park takes its name from an Indian word

roughly translated as "it's wonderful"—and Yoho is just that: five hundred square miles of pristine peaks, shimmering lakes, tumbling waterfalls, and thick green forest. The 133-mile Kicking Horse Trail is for cars—not horses—and takes one through the loveliest parts of the park. *Field* is the name of the hamlet that is park headquarters, and a center for accommodation, shopping, and the like. It is at the foot of 10,500-foot Mt. Stephen and not far from the park's most noted lake—Emerald. By means of Kicking Horse Trail, one can drive around lovely Wapta Lake, along the slopes of Cathedral Mountain, through the indescribably exciting Yoho Valley, past the 1,800-foot Takakkaw Falls, which drop from Daly Glacier into the Yoho River. On the way out of the park, after leaving Field, the chief attraction is the lofty summit of Mount Goodsir—nearly 12,000 feet high.

Kootenay National Park is, in effect, a seven-mile thriller-diller of a drive, between the Vermillion Pass—at which Alberta disappears and British Columbia begins—and *Radium Hot Springs,* to the south. The park embraces several miles of territory on either side of the highway, and one simply looks from one's car window both to left and to right at a succession of glistening lakes, fantastic canyons, effervescent mineral springs, icy peaks, and assorted wildlife (moose, bighorn sheep, and the like). There are campsites along the way, and before reaching Radium Hot Springs one has traveled along the Kootenay River for a period, driven through Sinclair Pass, and the steep sandstone "Iron Gates." At the springs one finds park headquarters and a variety of amenities, not excluding hot-springs swimming pools where the temperatures can be too hot for comfort.

Mount Revelstoke National Park is not big in area (one hundred square miles) but it's a dazzler. One enters it through the little town of *Revelstoke,* which is park headquarters. From town, one partially ascends the 8,000-foot mountain for which the park and town are named, by means of a hairpin-curve road that leads to an ingeniously placed lookout point at an elevation of 6,350 feet. From there the view is one of the most ethereal in Canada. One can walk about from the lookout to the summit or to other points of interest closer by. Revelstoke is one of western Canada's outstanding winter sports areas, with good accommodation and excellent facilities for skiing.

Glacier National Park is not to be confused with the similarly named area in Montana which adjoins Alberta's Waterton Lakes National Park. It embraces 521 choice square miles of the Selkirk Mountains—even bolder, snowier, and more glacier-covered than the adjoining Rockies. And until the *Rogers Pass* section of the Trans-Canada Highway was completed in 1962, it was the only Canadian national park that could be traversed only by train. The Rogers Pass section of the Trans-Canada Highway—one of the most incredible engineering feats of modern times—takes one through nearly thirty miles of Glacier Park territory. The highway is at its loftiest point when it climbs to 4,400 feet, at the foot of 9,482-foot Mount MacDonald. But that is not the highest of the peaks the highway skirts. Others, to give you an idea, include Tupper (9,229), Hermit (10,194), Sulzer (10,216), Swiss (10,515), Fleming (10,371) and Grant (10,216). Should you go by train, you'll pass through North America's longest tunnel—the Connaught, which is five miles in length, and has as its western terminal point the settlement of *Glacier,* where there are camp grounds. The nearest town to Glacier park is *Golden.* A small Columbia River settlement, it is the eastern terminal point of the Rogers Pass section of the highway; the road's western terminus is the aforementioned Revelstoke.

Kamloops and the Cariboo Country: *Kamloops* is the major town of what is known as the Cariboo Country, a historic British Columbia region which has known visitors from the days of the early fur traders and the later Gold Rush prospectors. A fairly substantial community where the routes of both major railroads converge—not to mention its location on the Trans-Canada Highway—it is the center of an area abounding in big fish and big game. There's an annual stampede (big cattle ranches, too), and a number of interesting points in the general neighborhood. *Wells Gray Provincial Park* (near *Clearwater*) is one of these—it abounds in glaciers, peaks, ice fields, lakes, and waterfalls, and is still largely undeveloped. And there are the Cariboo Country towns like *Williams Lake* (a cattle town that claims *its* stampede is the biggest after Calgary's), *Quesnel,* a modern town of some six thousand near the old Gold Rush center of *Barkerville*—elaborately restored to look as it did during its heyday some ninety years ago;

and a number of others, including a pair of memorably named places: *Horsefly* and *Likely*.

The Okanagan Valley is where much of that delicious B.C. fruit comes from. It is also the sunniest and (in summer) the hottest part of the province, and it's ideal in the spring (fruit blossoms), the winter (skating and skiing), and the autumn (hunting), as well as during the warm-weather months when its chief lakes (Okanagan, Kalamalka, and Skaha) are put to good use. The valley's principal centers are a trio of towns: *Kelowna, Vernon,* and, the largest of the three, *Penticton,* the biggest resort community in the interior of the province.

The Kootenays is a region of glacier-fed lakes and mountains that ranges around the *Kokanee Glacier Provincial Park,* to the south of the national parks and to the east of the Okanagan Valley. *Nelson,* a town of about ten thousand on Kootenay Lake, and *Trail*—a bit larger and the home of Consolidated Mining and Smelting Co., of Canada Ltd.—are the principal urban centers. If the making of fertilizers and metallurgical matters interest you, you're welcome to make a tour of Consolidated's plant in Trail. But you're more apt to be interested in the little resorts throughout the Kootenays area.

Prince George, Dawson Creek, and the north: *Prince George* is the principal town of the province's north-central region. To see is Fort George Park, with a historical museum within a reconstruction of the 1807 fort built in the area by Simon Fraser for the North West Company—early competitor in the west of the Hudson's Bay Company. There are farms, lumber operations, and mining in the surrounding area, and the fishing and hunting attract sportsmen. Two hundred fifty miles north, on the modern John Hart Highway, is *Dawson Creek,* at once the terminus of two railroads (Northern Alberta and Pacific Great Eastern) and starting point of the Alaska Highway—a remarkable 1,526-mile route that goes through the Yukon and terminates in Fairbanks, Alaska (see the chapter on Yukon Territory). The highway starts at the much-photographed "Mile 0" marker, and there are modern facilities in the town—which has the newness, briskness, and heartiness of the kind found even farther north, in the Yukon. Grain elevators attest to the fertility of the adjoining Peace River farmlands. There is a local historical museum. *Fort St. John* is a mecca for hunters.

A monument attests to the 1793 visit of Sir Alexander Mackenzie. Mackenzie stopped there long enough, on his historic trans-Canada trek, to set up a fort and trading post. The ruins of a mission, which went up shortly after his visit, still stand, outside of town. *Fort Nelson,* even farther north (some three hundred miles) on the Alaska Highway is a small but modern community with an ancient Hudson's Bay post background. It is the last stop of consequence before reaching the Yukon frontier. *Lower Post* is just this side of the border, and not far from Watson Lake, the first major Yukon settlement encountered on the highway.

Prince Rupert is northern British Columbia's Pacific port, the terminus of the Canadian Pacific Railway's northern line, and just below the southern tip of the Alaskan panhandle. The town's early boosters thought that, with the coming of the railway, it would develop as a serious rival to Vancouver. Well, it hasn't, quite. But it's a pretty perky town, with a lovely setting, an excellent ice-free harbor, a thriving fishing industry, some industrial plants, and the worth-visiting Museum of Northern British Columbia, with first-rate Indian exhibits. There are good hotels and restaurants. Prince Rupert can be reached by sea from Vancouver and is a take-off point for Alaska and a frequent port-of-call for cruise ships on the Alaska run. A paved 454-mile highway links it to Prince George in the interior.

The Fraser River Valley and Harrison Hot Springs: The valley of the Fraser is one of the province's loveliest regions and a boon to visitors in the province anxious to have a look at the interior, but with relatively little time in which to do so. In as little as a day, one can make a delightful excursion into the area from Vancouver. And if the prospect of green farms in the shadows of snow-capped peaks is one that appeals—and it most certainly should—this is for you. Stop off, en route, at *Fort Langley National Historic Park.* The fort was set up in 1827 by the Hudson's Bay Company, and became the first permanent British settlement in the lower mainland area of the province. It was at Fort Langley, in 1858, that the Crown Colony of British Columbia was officially transformed into a Canadian province at a ceremony presided over by Sir James Douglas, the governor. Not all of the fort has been restored, but a brief visit to the exhibits in the main building gives one a clear picture of what life in the province was like a century ago and more. Worth a visit too is *Harrison Hot Springs,* on the shores of mountain-backed, 46-mile-long Harrison Lake, and near the little town of *Agassiz.* This is a popular vacation area offering the full range of summer activity. It is the site, too, of a distinguished resort hotel, the Harrison. You may, in your Fraser Valley tour, conclude your drive at Harrison Hot Springs. But continue even farther east, if you like, to *Hope.* From there, continue west a bit to well-equipped *Ernest Manning Provincial Park* and return to Vancouver the same way you came—along the Trans-Canada Highway, or by means of Routes 9 and 7, on the opposite side of the river.

SHOPPING

The carved and decorated woodwork of British Columbia Indians—totems and masks especially—are the most interesting local crafts purchases. But there are others—ceramics, jewelry, weaving —from within the province. And some shops sell handicrafts from all over Canada. Department stores are excellent in Vancouver, good in Victoria. Here are some selected places. **Vancouver:** *Canadian Art Products* (976 Granville Street) is mostly for arts and crafts of the western Indians. *Maple Leaf House,* operated by Woodward's department store, at 142 Water Street in Gastown, vends all kinds of British Columbia wares, Indian and otherwise— including silver, ceramics, and paintings. *Gallery of B.C. Arts* (1974 West Georgia Street) is a traditional source of varied handicrafts as well as paintings. *Bowring,* in the Royal Centre Shopping Mall adjoining the Hyatt Regency Hotel, has a range of Eskimo soapstone carvings and prints, handmade quilts, Indian totems and masks, jewelry, pewter. *The Map and Print Centre* (438 Richards Street) specializes in old prints, etchings, and maps, many of them regional. *Khot-la-Cha Coast Salish Handicrafts* is at 270 Whanoak Drive in North Vancouver, and worth the trip if your interest is authentic Indian work; the range is extensive, and the owners are Indian. *Mrs. Willard Sparrow* has her own shop—Indian wares are the specialty—at 6508 Salish Drive, near the University of British Columbia campus. The *Vancouver Art Gallery Shop* sells a variety of handmade things, including Eskimo sculpture and prints; stocks change from time to time but are invariably of interest. The *Vancouver Aquarium Shop* has lovely British Columbia-made ceramics, a big selection of shells and coral, Indian crafts, and a seafood cookbook, with recipes contributed by Aquarium members and the Aquarium the publisher. *Eaton's* department store occupies five ultra-modern floors at the Pacific Centre Mall, Granville, between Robson and Georgia streets. Delicatessen, groceries, Canadiana and souvenirs, the licensed Rotisserie Restaurant and snack bar are all on the mall—or lower—level. There's a pharmacy on three, and the attractive licensed Marine Room Restaurant is on four. *Hudson's Bay Company,* nearby on Georgia Street, has a good Canadiana department, with Eskimo soapstone carvings and other handcrafts, on the second floor. Baron's Inn, a licensed restaurant, is on four, and there's a basement cafeteria. *Woodward's* downtown department store is at Hastings and Abbott streets, and runs the usual wide range, with a rather super food department. **Victoria:** There are a number of good handicraft shops, including long-on-the-scene *The Quest* (1023 Government Street)—with exceptionally fine handmade objects of varying kinds from throughout Canada, B.C. included; *Victoria Handloom* (Trounce Alley Shopping Centre and Empress Hotel lobby)—local as well as Canada-wide crafts, with Haida Indian argillite carvings among the local specialties; *Maple Leaf House* (operated by Woodward's department store at 620 Humboldt Street in Nootka Court Shopping Centre opposite the Empress) has British Columbia crafts of varying types the specialty; *Indian Craft Shoppe* (905 Government Street); *Bastion Handicrafts* (Village Fair Shopping Centre, Bastion Square)—with prints, textiles, pottery, paintings, among other things; *Gallery of the Arctic* (adjacent to The Quest)—for Eskimo soapstone, prints, and other Eskimo objects. There are shops in both the *Art Gallery of Greater Victoria* and the *Provincial Museum.* Let me recommend three special Government Street shops: *Rogers Chocolates,* in its own original building going back to before the turn of the century, makes plain creams, nut creams, varied types of "chews," and—most sublime of the lot—almond and chocolate brittle; unique in North America. *Robertson Ltd.* (1007 Government Street) keeps open stock in 90 patterns of Spode china—more than any other shop anywhere, even, they claim, Gered's in London—and I believe them. *E. A. Morris Ltd.* has been in its architecturally distinguished quarters since 1893, and smoker or not (I'm not), this is a tobacco shop you want to see with between twenty and thirty varieties of cigars in stock at all times. Victoria prides itself on its antiques shops. Better ones include *Connaisseur* (1156 Fort Street)—eighteenth-century furniture, silver, china; *Vauxhall Antiques Ltd.* (1023 Fort Street)—antique Chinese export porcelain; *Rosemary Wells* (839 Fort Street)—antique jewelry; and *Dorothy Wismer* (Empress Hotel lobby)—jewelry, silver, and china. *Eaton's* and *Hudson's Bay Company* are both downtown. Eaton's has two buildings, extending from Douglas through Government streets; groceries are in the main building basement; the Bay's big store has a good Canadiana shop on main, and the Nonsuch Buffet in the basement.

CREATURE COMFORTS

The visitor is taken good care of, by and large, in British Columbia. Vancouver, as the nation's No. 3 city, ranks right up there with Nos. 1 and 2 (Montreal and Toronto, respectively) as regards hotels and restaurants. Victoria, for so long overshadowed —and with good reason—by its long-time leader, has in recent years begun to offer a good, albeit largely unexciting choice of alternate accommodation and eating places. Major visitor destinations elsewhere in the province can usually be counted upon to provide modern places to stay. Here is my selection. **Vancouver:** The *Hyatt Regency,* smack in the heart of town at Georgia and Burrard, is a 656-room beauty, whose architects—unlike so many today—concerned themselves with the esthetics of its exterior, as well as what lies within. The lobby—four dramatic stories high—is among the more dazzling in western North America, and is only the beginning. Guest rooms are oversized with excellent baths. There are a number of places to drink and dine, including Truffles, one of the province's best restaurants, a coffee shop called the Regency Grill that has to be the most elegant in town, a roof-top restaurant-boîte with a superlative view, and the off-lobby Gallery for informal lunches and drinks. In connection: the spiffy Royal Shopping Centre. Hyatt fans, you won't be disappointed. *Hotel Vancouver,* long-time traditional hotel leader has undergone several million dollars worth of exceptionally stylish and tasteful refurbishing under the aegis of Hilton International who operate it —and skillfully—for its Canadian National owners. The exterior, with its châteaulike tower that is a landmark of the Vancouver skyline, remains, happily, as always. But the lobby, all 562 guest rooms and suites, and public rooms have all been given a bright new look, although the trio of suites on the fourteenth floor—the late King George VI and Queen Elizabeth were 1939 residents— retain the dignity of their original décor. The Panorama Roof remains popular for cocktails and dinner-dancing-cum-view, the capacious Spanish Grill—with lots of counter space for single diners in a hurry—is one of the best coffee shops in the west, and the Timber Club one of the handsomest—and most delicious—of quality restaurants. *The Hotel Georgia,* on the street whose name it takes in the core of downtown, is still another luxury-category traditional-style house that stays at the top of its form as a result of major refurbishing and alert management. With 315 rooms, it is smaller than its main competitors and manages to retain a smallish-scale warmth, the while offering excellent accommodation —the rooms and suites are charming—and restaurants, including the long-esteemed Cavalier-cum-lounge, a cozy back-of-house bar liked by locals, an atmospheric downstairs pub, the George V— that's fun for informal meals as well as drinks—and a coffee shop. *Holiday Inn Harbour Side* is precisely that: directly on the harbor, with its main entrance on Hastings Street, near Burrard, a pleasant walk from Georgia Street. This is a 455-room stunner, at once attractive as regards architecture and interior design, and functional. There's a big, inviting lobby, wide and handsome corridors off of which lead the super-looking guest rooms. Most are twins, but there are more than 80 singles, a dozen lovely suites, even rooms especially designed for handicapped guests, as well as an indoor pool with adjacent game room—Ping-pong, pinball machines for the kids—and sauna. There's a revolving restaurant-lounge and an off-lobby restaurant-lounge-coffee shop. *Bayshore Inn* is away from the center of town on Burrard Inlet, making it especially suitable for visitors with cars. The setting is resortlike, and the ambience is very good 1950s Modern, with skilled Western International management, comfortable rooms with views that can be sublime, public spaces that include a worth-knowing-about round-the-clock coffee shop, and a water-front room for dinner dancing, with entertainment. The *Four Seasons,* a branch of the international chain that has Canadian links in Calgary, Montreal, and Toronto, is typical of its counterparts, in that it is at once contemporary and luxurious, with a variety of stylish public spaces for dining, drinking, and lounging, and attractive bedrooms. The *Devonshire Hotel* is a traditional first-class favorite, heart-of-town on Georgia Street. There are 150 comfortable rooms—a number of them quite special—and places to eat and drink, including the locally liked Dev Seafood House and Carriage Room, this last-mentioned with entertainment. The *Sheraton-Landmark Hotel* is a pinnaclelike tower at 1400 Robson Street, ten or fifteen minutes' walk from the core of downtown. Rooms are balconied, spacious, and well equipped, and have mini-refrigerators. There's an excellent revolving restaurant on the roof and a coffee shop. *Blue Horizon Motor Hotel* (1225 Robson Street) is another modern tower—31 stories, with 200-plus well-equipped rooms, an elevated restaurant, coffee shop, and indoor pool. The *Rembrandt Hotel* (1160 Davie Street) has a convenient downtown location and is as contemporary as its name is otherwise. Close to 200 agreeable rooms-cum-balcony, in a 24-story tower, with restaurant, cocktail lounge, coffee shop, pool. *Georgian Towers Hotel* (1450 West Georgia Street) has 200 nice rooms, full facilities—including the Top of the Towers and Colonial House restaurants, and a situation convenient to Stanley Park. *The Ritz Hotel* (1040 West Georgia Street) is a smallish (124 rooms) older house worth knowing about because it is central and more moderately priced than its bigger competitors in the neighborhood. Two restaurants, a cocktail lounge. The *Grosvenor Hotel* (1840 Howe Street) is like the Ritz, another of the smaller (137 rooms) downtown hotels that is at once convenient (near Eaton's department store) and inexpensive. Restaurants, cocktail lounge. There are many hotels, motor hotels and motels away from downtown. Let me recommend just a few, to give you an idea. *Sheraton Plaza 500 Hotel* (500 West Twelfth Avenue), in the City Hall section, has 112 attractive rooms, all with balconies and many with sumptuous views of the downtown skyline and the mountains framing it. On premises: the handsome Town Planner Restaurant and lounge. *Denman Place Inn* (1733 Comox Street) is a 22-story complex near English Bay. There are

200 units, some with living rooms and kitchens, all with balconies, a top-floor restaurant-lounge with entertainment, coffee shop, indoor pool, sauna, and on-premises shops. *Vancouver Airport Hyatt House* (350 Cessna Drive, Richmond) is the definitive airport hotel, striking-looking façade, more than 400 super rooms and suites, a trio of restaurants—including a very posh one—and a coffee shop, atmospheric drinking parlors, and a honey of a pool.

Victoria: It was the *Empress Hotel* (as I pointed out earlier in this chapter) that created Victoria's tourist industry at the turn of the century, and it is the Empress that has continued all of these subsequent years as the city's dominant hotel. That is as it should be. This 416-room house is a national institution, beautifully operated by CP Hotels, whose management realizes all that that implies. Which means that in summer the queue for the hotel's famed service of afternoon tea in the lobby-lounge begins at 2 P.M., a good two hours in advance. And that during the high-season months the main restaurant—whose neo-Renaissance ceiling is in itself worthy of an Empress' visit—is eternally busy, along with the more casual Bengal bar-lounge, the coffee shop, and the zingy Paint Cellar disco. Not to mention guest rooms and suites. Which is by way of saying that advance booking is a necessity for late spring through early autumn. And which is also to say that the Empress is at its most enjoyable the rest of the year, especially during the mild Victoria winter. These are the queueless months when service throughout is at its unharried best. (There are special festivities at Christmas and through New Year's.) As for the accommodations, CP Hotels keeps refurbishing and refurbishing. The standard twins are a joy, and the suites—especially those overlooking the Inner Harbour—are very special. So, for that matter, are the corridors, which just have to be the widest and most elegant of any hotel anywhere. Seasonal differentiations notwithstanding, whenever your schedule takes you to Victoria, go. After the Empress, my next Victoria choice—assuming I was with car—would be *Oak Bay Beach Hotel.* This is an out-of-town charmer, directly on the water, and with the feel of a lovely country house, mock-Tudor without, cozy flowered chintz within. The rooms are very comfortable indeed, but mind, there are only three dozen of them, so you must book. There's a handsome restaurant-cocktail lounge, beautiful gardens out back, and an almost-next-door golf course. *Red Lion*

Motor Inn (3366 Douglas Street) is a brief drive away from down-town, with more than 80 attractive rooms, and a brick-walled warmth in its public spaces, which include a restaurant with enter-tainment, a coffee shop, and a lovely outdoor pool. Very pleasant. *Executive House* (777 Douglas Street) is modern, central, with nearly a hundred comfortable rooms and suites (some with kitch-ens), swimming pool, and best of all, a Hy's Restaurant-lounge. *Château Victoria* (740 Burdett Avenue) is a modern tower, châ-teaulike in name only. There are 77 rooms and suites (some with kitchens), and a roof-top restaurant-lounge. *Harbour Towers* (345 Quebec Street) is central, contemporary, with 75 rooms and suites (some with kitchens), indoor pool, sauna, restaurant-lounge. *Swiftsure Inn* (427 Belleville Street) is an 80-room house (some with kitchens); restaurant, lounge, coffee shop. And a central loca-tion. *Imperial Inn* (1961 Douglas Street) has nearly 80 modern rooms, restaurant-lounge, pool. *Colony Motor Inn* (2852 Douglas Street) is bright and modern, with 100 well-equipped rooms, indoor pool, sauna, and the Coach Light Restaurant, where there's week-end entertainment; coffee shop, too. **Vancouver Island** (going northward from Victoria)—**Duncan:** *Village Green Inn* is a hand-some, modern, low-slung complex with 80 lovely rooms, sports fa-cilities—including indoor pool, tennis court, putting green, and lawn bowling—a coffee shop, and an outpost of the Hy's Restaurant chain, for steaks and other beef specialties; nearby golf and fishing. **Nanaimo:** *Tally-Ho Travelodge,* in town, with 80 fully equipped rooms, pool, restaurant, cocktail lounge. **Parksville:** *Is-land Hall Hotel,* a long-popular resort, with more than a hundred rooms in a complex facing the beach. There's an indoor pool, as well, along with tennis and other outdoor diversions, including nearby golf and fishing. The dining room features weekend smor-gasbord. **Campbell River:** *Discovery Inn* has a hundred modern, fully equipped rooms, a heated pool, restaurant, and cocktail lounge, with superlative Campbell River salmon fishing the special local treat. **National Parks—Yoho:** *Emerald Lake Chalet,* the long-time leader, with 52 units, some in cottages, restaurant-cocktail lounge. *Wapta Lodge,* with nearly half a hundred units, restaurant, cocktail lounge, and coffee shop. **Kootenay National Park—** *Radium Hot Springs Lodge,* 80 balconied rooms with bath, res-taurant-cocktail lounge, sauna. **Mount Revelstoke and Glacier Na-**

tional Parks—*Northlander Park Lodge* (Rogers Pass), 50 rooms with bath, restaurant, cocktail lounge, cafeteria, and a heated pool; *Golden Arms Motor Hotel* (Golden, B.C.), 50 rooms, restaurant, and cocktail lounge. **Kamloops:** *Canadian Inn* (339 St. Paul Street) is a modern 100-room house with nicely furnished rooms with bath, a restaurant, cocktail lounge, and coffee shop, as well as a heated pool. **Williams Lake:** *Williams Lake Slumber Lodge* has nearly 60 rooms with bath, restaurant lounge, coffee shop. **Penticton:** *Pilgrim House Motor Hotel*—50 pleasant rooms with bath, a heated pool, restaurant, and cocktail lounge; *Penticton Inn*—100 modern rooms, some with kitchens, and facilities including a heated pool, sauna, restaurant-lounge, and coffee shop. **Kelowna:** *Caravel Motor Inn* (1585 Abbott Street), 40 pleasant rooms with bath, restaurant, cocktail lounge, and pool. *Stetson Village Motel* (1455 Harvey Avenue)—87 units of varying size, some kitchen-equipped, restaurant, cocktail lounge, coffee shop, and an indoor pool. **Vernon:** *Village Green Inn* (4801 27th Street, Highway 97) —nearly 90 agreeable rooms with bath, and facilities including pool, sauna, and tennis courts, with a coffee shop, cocktail lounge, and a branch of Hy's Restaurant—with their famed steaks. *Vernon Lodge* (3914 32nd Street)—140 modern rooms with bath, pool in a pretty garden, restaurant, and cocktail lounge. **Prince George:** *Inn of the North* (770 Brunswick Street)—160 attractive rooms with bath, restaurant, cocktail lounge-cum-entertainment, coffee shop, central location. *Yellowhead Inn* (Central and Fifteenth streets)—100 modern rooms with bath, restaurant, cocktail lounge, sauna. *Simon Fraser Inn* (600 Quebec Street)—90 rooms with bath, restaurant, cocktail lounge, coffee shop. **Dawson Creek:** *Peace Villa Motel* (1641 Alaska Avenue)—30 rooms with bath. *Park Inn* (10100 Tenth Street)—70 rooms, restaurant, cocktail lounge, coffee shop. **Fort St. John:** *Alexander Mackenzie Inn* (9223 100th Street)—70 rooms with bath, restaurant, cocktail lounge with entertainment, indoor pool, and sauna. **Fort Nelson:** *Provincial Motel* (Mile 300)—45 rooms with bath, restaurant, cocktail lounge. **Prince Rupert:** *Crest Motor Hotel* (2222 First Avenue West)—85 attractive rooms with bath, a handsome restaurant, cocktail lounge, coffee shop, and the nicest views in town of the Prince Rupert harbor. *Rupert Motor Inn* (First Avenue and Sixth Street)—51 lovely rooms-cum-view, and with the advantage of La

Gondola Restaurant—one of the best in town—on the premises. **Harrison Hot Springs:** *Harrison Hotel*—a 284-room-and-suite resort complex that is one of the most distinguished in western Canada, in a gorgeous mountain setting on the shores of Harrison Lake, with varied types of accommodations (some in cottages), an 18-hole golf course, tennis courts, health spa, cycling, indoor and outdoor pools, curling rink, and two restaurants including the first-rank Copper Room with dancing and entertainment.

Dining in Vancouver and Victoria: What I present here, for **Vancouver** dining, is a selection of the most interesting of many, many restaurants, in a variety of categories. First, my favorites in the HOTELS. *Truffles* (Hyatt Regency) is at once unusually beautiful to look upon, and top calibre, haute cuisine as regards its fare. There is an expensive à-la-carte menu at both lunch and dinner—from smoked B.C. salmon and lobster bisque for starters, through entrées like steak au poivre, veal Zurich style or roast pheasant, on to a magnificent dessert trolley. *Timber Club* (Hotel Vancouver) is inventively designed—and very smartly so—in the rustic style of the old Canadian west. The specialties are steaks in a variety of styles and roast beef, as well as B.C. seafoods, with hot apple fritters and baked Alaska among the desserts. Very smart. *Cavalier Grill* (Hotel Georgia) is elegant, for leisurely dinners with Caesar salad, Dungeness crab legs, and beef Wellington among the specialties. *Cloud 9* (Sheraton Landmark) is a handsome room atop this towering hotel, revolving and rewarding with the food—especially the steaks—as much a lure as the views.

DINING AND DANCING—*Sir Walter Raleigh* (409 Granville Street) is top-calibre for food, with an international menu, and perfect for dancing. *Panorama Roof* (Vancouver Hotel) is a traditional leader when a good meal, good music for dancing—and a breathtaking view—are to be combined; go for pre-dinner cocktails, too. *Odyssey* (Hyatt Regency) is mod-look, fun, and stylish. *Bayside Room* (Bayshore Inn) is a favorite with locals; the view is out over the water. FRENCH: *L'Escargot* (819 Pacific Street), with a French owner-chef who is one of the best cooks in the province, is smallish in an elderly house, with an intimate ambience, and perfectly delicious food—soups (try the bisque de homard), fish (try the broiled skate), beef (try the tournedos

Mirabeau) and desserts (try the poached pears). *Chez Joël* (217 Carrall Street, Gastown) is as good an excuse as any for a Gastown evening—the gigot d'agneau is roast lamb French-style, and the bouillabaise is good, too. You'll like the brick-walled look of the place. *Napoléon* (869 Hamilton Street) is rich reds and golds, a classic French menu, sumptuous service; the tournedos is special. *Côte d'Azur* (1216 Robson Street) relates its name to the pair of joined blue-hued houses it occupies. SEAFOOD: *Ship of the Seven Seas* is indeed just that—a one-time ferryboat now tied up at the foot of Lonsdale Avenue, North Vancouver, and seeing service as a seafood restaurant extraordinaire. The drill is this: You serve yourself buffet-style, with more than half a hundred hot and cold seafood dishes to choose from, including king crab, fresh shrimp, B.C. oysters on the half-shell, smoked salmon—among the cold dishes—and curried shrimp, fried oysters, sautéed frogs legs, and steamed clams among the hot specialties. There's a cocktail lounge in which you might well plan to spend some time waiting your turn, even if you've booked in advance. *Dev's Seafood House* (Devonshire Hotel) is more conventional, albeit good. ITALIAN: *Umberto's* (1380 Hornby Street) occupies a nicely restored house a half-century or so in years, and its fare is first-rate, with a range of soups (including Stracciatella), pastas (including linguine with clam sauce), fish and meat entrées (the veal specialties are toothsome) and luscious desserts. Lovely ambience and service. *Old Spaghetti Factory* (53 Water Street in Gastown) is essentially no different from its counterparts elsewhere—a trolley car for drinks, fun décor. But it serves no-nonsense food at excellent prices and is ideal for families. EAST INDIAN: B.C. has one of the highest proportions of East Indians in North America, so why not good Indian restaurants? Like *Punjab* (796 Main Street) where you may have your curries really hot. JAPANESE: *Kaede* (Royal Shopping Centre) is elegant and with a classic Japanese menu—sukiyaki, teriyaki, tempura, other favorites. *Kobe* (1012 Alberni Street) is for teppan cooking—steaks and the like at your table. CHINESE: *Chi Lin Palace* (Lotus Gardens Hotel, 455 Abbott Street) and *Noodle Makers* (122 Powell Street, Gastown) are among the better spots. UKRAINIAN: There is a considerable Ukrainian community in Vancouver as elsewhere in western Canada; specialties, including variations on the pirogy—stuffed pancake—theme and more familiar beef Stroganoff, at *Pirogy House* (3219 Oak Street and 4040 Cambie Street). SWISS: *William Tell* (772 Richards Street) has authentic fondue; other Swiss dishes and international as well —everything is delicious. RATHER SPECIAL: *Three Greenhorns* (1030 Denman Street) is at once smart and inventive—soups like Greenhorn Pot, starters like salmon bellies New Westminster, desserts like fireball and strawberries, interestingly prepared vegetables, more prosaic steaks. GREEK: *Greek Village* (1294 East Hastings) to understate, informal in the best Greek sense of that term. The decibel count can at times rise, and the Zorba-type music can become repetitious. But you can't help but enjoy yourself, with all manner of Greek fare—from the appetizers through the variety of lamb dishes and the eggplant-base moussaka, on into the desserts like baklava. STEAK AND ROAST BEEF: There are a trio of *Hy's;* one, the Prime Rib, on the fourth floor of 1177 Hastings, offers super views of the North Shore. The others, mainly steaks, are at 637 Hornby and 1755 Davie. For the best steak buys in town, consider *Keg & Cleaver,* a moderate-tab chain with numerous locations. And don't forget the original British Columbians, at *Muck-a-Muck* (1724 Davie Street), an authentic Indian restaurant, Indian-staffed and with such Indian dishes as salmon and duck chowders, roasted hazelnuts and steamed fernshoot among the vegetables, and roast rabbit a popular entrée, with such desserts as cold raspberry soup or sugared soapberries. The décor is appropriately Indian. As for the DEPARTMENT STORES: *Eaton's* licensed Marine Room is on four; the Rotisserie (also licensed) is on the mall level. *Hudson's Bay*'s Baron's Inn (licensed) is on four, and its Seymour Buffet—a cafeteria—is on six. OTHERS: *Rubin's* (974 Granville Avenue) is an ever-reliable deli—pastrami sandwiches on rye, and the like. *Smitty's Pancake Houses*—good for breakfast, snacks, quick lunches—are convenient; one is in the Royal Shopping Centre. Oh—and for Vancouver at its most charming and scenic: afternoon tea at *Ferguson Point Tea House,* overlooking the outer harbor in Stanley Park.

Victoria: Dinner in the beautiful *Edwardian Dining Room* of the Empress Hotel is, for many visitors, a Victoria requisite. The roast beef is celebrated, but the visitor must not otherwise fear mundane hotel food; the chefs take their work seriously. One may begin with excellent snails, Burgundy style, baked oysters, or onion soup. The salads, especially the Caesar, are very good. And so is the roast lamb and the grilled B.C. salmon. Traditionally, there are buffet dinners Thursday and Sunday. The Empress serves lunch in its *Bengal Bar;* menus are limited, with excellent curries—a different one each day—the specialty. *Hy's Steak House* (Executive House Hotel) is, like its counterparts, warm and clubby-attractive, with keen service, and an extensive menu with beef emphasized; a good place to sample the dry red wine from Kelowna, B.C. *Chauncey's* (614 Humboldt Street) is atmospheric in a way not often come upon in Victoria; the specialty is seafood—the local salmon poached with Hollandaise sauce, oysters Rockefeller, cracked crab. But there is New York sirloin for landlubbers. And try the crêpes for dessert. *Shah Jahan* (1010 Fort Street) is for curries and other Indian specialties, like chicken prepared both Tandoori and Biriyani styles; I am a nut for the former. *Dingle House* (137 George Road East) is a refurbished Victorian dwelling, with roast beef the big draw at dinner, along with a variety of fish dishes. Lunches are lighter, but nice; kids are discouraged after 6 P.M. *Parrot House* (the roof-top eatery in the Château Victoria Hotel) is attractive; steaks, roast beef, broiled salmon—and a view. *Coach and Four* (Bastion Square) is atmospheric English-pubby—for prime ribs, steaks, and chops. *Raven's* (Harbour Tower Hotel) sports an arresting B.C. Indian motif in its décor; nice for jumbo prawns, or roast rack of lamb, with perhaps a flambéed dessert at dinner. The *Marine Room* (Oak Bay Beach Hotel) is cozy and country-innish, with a sea view and tasty dinners. There is a convenient cafeteria—for lunch or snacks—in the *Hudson's Bay* department store. And hardly to be overlooked: the corned beef and other sandwiches at *Sam's Deli* (805 Government Street).

Manitoba

LE MANITOBA

Best times for a visit: *For most visitors, summer (June–September) is the choice season—hot (seventies and eighties), sunny days and cool nights. Winter is c-c-c-cold, but the low temperatures (Winnipeg has gone as low as thirty-five below)*

are not as bad as you might think, for the atmosphere is crisp, dry, and bright, and winter sports—ice fishing, skating, snowshoeing, skiing—are an attraction. Cultural life in Winnipeg—the ballet, symphony, theatre, opera—is at its peak in this season, too. Spring and autumn are brief seasons; the latter is a happy time for hunters and anglers. **Transportation:** *There are more than ten thousand miles of provincially maintained trunk highways, the majority of these paved; and there are considerable other roads. The lightly settled north has many fewer, as would be expected, than the south. The Trans-Canada Highway cuts across southern Manitoba—from Ontario and the town of McMunn in the east, through major communities like Winnipeg and Brandon (which it skirts) to Kirkella and Saskatchewan in the west. Major north-south routes lead into it. Bus service is well developed, both within the province, to adjoining provinces, and to such United States points as Minneapolis, Minnesota, and Fargo, North Dakota. Air Canada, CP Air, Northwest Orient Airlines, Frontier Airlines, and North Central Airlines connect Manitoba with the U.S. and other parts of Canada. Trans Air serves points in northern Manitoba, flies also to such other Canadian points as Toronto and the Northwest Territories. Additionally, there are more than a score of non-scheduled carriers flying small craft, mostly to northern Manitoba communities and "fly-in" fishing lodges. Both major railways— Canadian National and CP Rail—operate in Manitoba; the former maintain more than thirty-one hundred miles of track, the latter some seventeen hundred. A part of CN's route is the unique five-hundred-mile track between The Pas and the northern part of Churchill, on Hudson Bay.* **Having a drink:** *Liquor, wine, and beer in licensed restaurants, licensed hotel dining rooms, cabarets, cocktail lounges, and the simpler beverage rooms, which often serve food as well. Beer to take out may be bought in the retail stores of breweries in Winnipeg and from beer vendors, located in many of the province's hotels.* **Further information:** *Manitoba Government Travel, 200 Vaughan Street, Winnipeg; Agent-General of Manitoba, 83 Cannon Street, London; Canadian Government Office of Tourism, Ottawa and branches.*

INTRODUCING MANITOBA

Manitoba, for those not well acquainted with it—and that means a lot of us, I fear—is perhaps Canada's most underrated province. The eastern Canadian, if he thinks about it at all, considers it a largish blob on the map of his country—somewhere the other side of Toronto. The Canadian of the far west—from Alberta or British Columbia—feels a bit patronizing about it, lacking as it is in dramatic, snowy peaks. The American from the United States' Midwest too often regards it as an extension—not appreciably different—of his part of the world. And other Americans give it little, if any, thought whatsoever.

The heart of Canada: This most central of Canadian provinces —it is, indeed, the geographic heartland of the North American continent—is a great agricultural area, but is not without an Atlantic-outlet harbor of its own, and manufacturing industries so developed that they play the No. 1 economic role. It has known the white man since the early years of the seventeenth century, but still it is home to one of the largest proportions of red men in any part of Canada. It is plop in the center of a wide, wide continent, but its populace is more ethnically diverse than many east coast or west coast areas. It has one of the most highly developed transport systems in Canada, which is saying a good deal, but there are points in its northern area still accessible only by canoe or "fly-in" plane. It is a province of farms, with agriculture its leading source of income—but it has one of the largest and most valuable freshwater fisheries in the world, with nearly forty thousand square miles of inland lakes and streams yielding more than 30 million pounds of *commercially* caught fish each year. It is geographically isolated from the mainstreams and cross currents of the arts, but its capital is the seat of the only (and one of but two in the entire Commonwealth) ballet company in all of Canada honored by the Crown with the designation, "royal."

Manitoba is dynamic and full of verve, modern-minded and rich in history, physically massive and personally congenial, proud as a peacock over its accomplishments—but never smug, sophisticated but not snobbish, expert at blowing its own horn, but not to the point of boredom nor to the extent of forgetting that it is but one province of a great, united country.

Early visitors: Well, he didn't set foot on what is now Manitoba soil, but Henry Hudson, the intrepid Englishman who sailed up the New York State river now bearing his name, to Albany, in 1609, explored the great Canadian bay—also bearing his name—the following year. In 1612 the Nelson River was gained by Sir Thomas Button, the first white man to visit the province, whose land he took in the name of the King of England. Two decades later, explorer Luke Fox touched upon the region. The land they found had for long been the country of the Cree, Saulteaux, and Assiniboine Indians. (The last named worshiped a spirit, the Great Manito, and the province's name is believed to have been derived from it and from *waba,* the narrows portion of Lake Manitoba.)

By 1670 the intelligence had long since been spread abroad that this was rich fur country, and in that year Manitoba officially became a part of the enormous area—then known as Rupert's Land—under charter to the English Hudson's Bay Company, which set up a trading post at Port Nelson and later spread south to the Red River Valley, all the while in conflict with French interests. They had been on the scene ever since 1731 when La Vérendrye, a French-Canadian explorer, had reached what is now Winnipeg. The French-English competition abated, to an extent, in 1763 after the Peace of Paris, by which England gained control of Canada. Fur trading continued as the chief occupation mostly under the auspices of the Hudson's Bay and North West companies. And no important attempt had been made to take advantage of the rich prairie soil.

Lord Selkirk's settlements: But in 1812 things were to change, thanks to the resoluteness of a determined Scottish philanthropist-colonizer, the Earl of Selkirk. Earlier, he had established an agricultural settlement on Prince Edward Island as a new home for dispossessed, poverty-stricken farmers of northern Ireland and Scotland. Having heard of Manitoba's wide open spaces, he began, in 1808, to buy into the powerful Hudson's Bay Company; by 1811 he had obtained a substantial interest in it despite opposition from its fur-trading shareholders. He obtained, from the company, a grant of land in the Red River area, which included territory essential to the successful fur-trading operations of the North West Company—Hudson's Bay's big competitors. The first settlement, led by Miles MacDonnell, Lord Selkirk's agent, broke up not too long after it had begun in 1812. The North West interests had succeeded in turning the métis (French-Indian) trappers against the settlers, who went east to Ontario.

But Lord Selkirk was not easily defeated. In 1816 he sent another band of farmers west, under Robert Semple. This time, the North West gang and their métis followers resorted to bloodshed, slaying twenty-two of Semple's men at what has come to be known as the Battle of Seven Oaks. Meanwhile—in the best tradition of the West—Selkirk himself was en route to the territory. Learning of the Seven Oaks massacre, he and his men seized the North West Company's post, and re-established the colony, in 1817. This third attempt was successful, and even though Selkirk was later forced to pay damages to the North West Company, as a result of a lawsuit, his actions helped bring about a Hudson's Bay-North West merger in 1821. Agriculture had come to the plains for the first time, and it was to flourish.

Private landlord—and the métis: Settlement continued for some decades, under the aegis of the private landlord, the Hudson's Bay Company. In 1869 the Canadian Government bought the Northwest Territories from Hudson's Bay, but the transition was not as smooth as it might have been. Métis insurgent Louis Riel (the same who was hanged as a traitor after leading Riel's Rebellion in Saskatchewan in 1884) led the trappers of the region—mostly fellow métis—in a rebellion that resulted in the establishment of a short-lived provisional government. The métis believed that with the central government taking over from Hudson's Bay, their land rights and other interests would be threatened. The following year, Canadian and imperial troops were dispatched from the east to quash the rebellion, which they did—bloodlessly—at Fort Garry. The result was that Manitoba became a full province of the Canadian Confederation, with many of the rights Riel had sought.

If the province fought hard for its political birth, it struggled with equal difficulty for economic progress. The early provincial decades were rough going. Pioneer life was rugged and there were not a great many lures to induce settlement on a grand scale. And transportation was a severe handicap, although steamboat connections had long since been made with American communities on the Red River, and there had been trade with U.S. towns like St. Paul for some years. Manitoba shipped out its first wheat to Toronto in 1878, and in 1881, with the arrival of the Canadian Pacific at Winnipeg, both settlement and trade expanded.

The railroad arrives: German Mennonites and—of all people— Icelanders, had joined Anglo-Saxon newcomers even before the arrival of the CP; but by 1914, thanks to the railroad, Winnipeg's population exceeded the two-hundred-thousand mark; it had had but two hundred inhabitants in 1870. By the time of the First World War, Manitoba had become one of the great agricultural provinces, and Winnipeg had established itself as one of the great rail junctions of the world, serving Canada as a link between east and west, much as Chicago does the United States. It grew, too, as a banking and distributing center, and as this happened, the entire province began to make a break from dependence upon wheat and railroading alone. Manitoba looked beyond the wheat field (nineteen million acres are now farmed in the province) to the corral (more than one third of agricultural income now comes from live-stock), and the packing house (more than a quarter of the slaughtering in the prairie provinces is done in Manitoba).

And it looked below the ground, from which is now extracted copper, gold, zinc, silver, nickel—to the tune of more than $400 million a year. It looked to the forest—almost half the province is wooded, and now more than fifty-six thousand square miles are productive in this respect. It turned to the lakes and streams and the waters of Hudson Bay for fish and maritime products, and it revived fur trading as an industry; nearly eight thousand trappers and two hundred dealers provide pelts which, worth processing, are valued at more than $3 million annually. There is oil, too, with about five million barrels produced annually. Manufacturing employs close to 90,000 Manitobans and pays them more than $583 million in salaries each year. Tourism is rapidly climbing as a significant income earner, as well it might. For Manitoba has a great deal to offer—the provincial tourist office is one of the finest such operations in the country.

Modern Manitoba: The Manitoba government—the liberal New Democratic Party of Premier Ed Schreyer gained power in 1969 from the Conservatives who had controlled the province the previous eleven years—operates its own excellent telephone company. Along with municipalities and private interests, it wisely exploits water and power resources. In the field of social welfare, it maintains services ranging from child adoption to physical fitness. Its Health Department—from a section dealing with public health in the sparsely settled north to its Psychiatric Services, which operate hospitals and an imaginative Community Mental Health Service—is modern-minded, and embraces a medicare program. Its handsome university, just outside of Winnipeg, is one of Canada's best rated, and has been supplemented in recent years by the University of Winnipeg (in the downtown area of the capital) and Brandon University in the western part of the province. There are technical schools as well.

Manitoba adjoins Ontario, but it is far enough west so as not to be an eastern province. It borders Saskatchewan, but it is blessed with Hudson Bay, an outlet to the sea that has given it the kind of cosmopolitan outlook that Saskatchewan will be a long time achieving. Through it have passed so many bits and pieces of the east and the west, and to it have come so many peoples of diverse origins—Ukrainians and French, Mennonites and Scots—that it has achieved a degree of maturity, a style of its own, and a sense of humor a good deal sooner than many regions do. *Winnipeg Tribune* columnist Charles Lynch puts it this way: "[Manitoba] is neither a have province, nor a have-not. If you were looking for a Canadian norm . . . this is where you would . . . find it. It is not a hotbed of Canadian nationalism, nor do you hear much here about continentalism . . . Manitobans are less self-centered than most other Canadians, less inclined to boast about their blessings . . . [They] have broad horizons. . . ." Let me add that no Canadian province appears more intrinsically Canadian than Manitoba. And none is more able to make the traveler in Canada more optimistic about that country's future, nor more exhilarated by what it has already accomplished.

YOUR VISIT TO MANITOBA

We're dealing with a lot of land—and water—when we consider Manitoba. Provincial statisticians have added and juggled and come to the conclusion, supported by the facts, that the land and water areas of their province (in excess of 250,000 square miles) makes Manitoba larger than the combined U.S. states of Maine, New Hampshire, Vermont, New York, Massachusetts, Rhode Island, Connecticut, New Jersey, Maryland, Virginia, Delaware, Pennsylvania, and West Virginia. Or, to put it another way, Manitoba is just about five times the size of England.

This most central of the Canadian provinces, in the heart of the prairies of the midwest, is by an odd fluke of geography also a maritime region, for its northeast frontier is washed by the waters of Hudson Bay, which lead to the wide North Atlantic. The portion of the province flanking the bay—in the far north—is an area of rolling tundra rich in minerals, game, and fish. South of it are a trio of gigantic lakes—Lake Winnipeg (larger than Lake Ontario), Lake Winnipegosis (that's its real name, honest), and Lake Manitoba. Below and to the west is a land of rolling farms, green pine-and-fir forests, and quantities of smaller lakes. The south is the Manitoba you've heard most about—vast prairies with massive farms, and the cities, towns, and villages whose inhabitants constitute the great bulk of Manitoba's population. Manitoba reaches 761 miles from south to north, from the forty-ninth degree of latitude to the sixtieth. At its widest, it extends some five hundred miles.

Winnipeg, as I have earlier indicated, did not come to prosper without a long series of struggles during which it has been known by a number of names. In 1738 the Frenchman La Vérendrye built the first white settlement at the junction of the Red and Assiniboine rivers and called it Fort Rouge (red), after the name of one of the rivers. Later, under the North West Company, it became Fort Gibraltar, and after the merger of the North West and Hudson's Bay companies, the name became Fort Garry. The current appellation was first suggested in an 1864 newspaper editorial. Meaning "dirty water" in the Cree language, it had long been used to designate the large lake into which the Red River empties, and it had had a variety of spellings: Winnepeck, Winnipic, Winnipeek, Ouinipeg. When the city was incorporated in 1873—after both Garry (for the forts of that name) and Selkirk (for the British peer who established the Red River settlements) had also been proposed—Winnipeg came out as the winner.

In 1820 a visitor described it as comprising "a number of huts widely scattered along the margin of the river." Three decades later it was viewed as "a village of farm houses . . . [whole fields were] filled with . . . whites, half breeds and Indians . . . all reaping, binding, stacking in the golden grain."

Today, it is a metropolitan community of more than half a million, by far the liveliest between Toronto and Vancouver, and the most culturally rich and exciting of any Canadian city after Montreal and Toronto. Winnipeg's prowess in this regard is due not only to its lack of an especially gorgeous natural setting—it is without Vancouver's blend of mountains and sea—and its geographical isolation as an urban center—there is no major city for hundreds of miles in any direction—but also to its provincial pre-eminence. It is unlike Saskatchewan's competitive Regina and Saskatoon, Alberta's competitive Calgary and Edmonton. Discounting infinitely smaller and considerably less important Brandon, it is Manitoba's sole metropolis, and the province's government and citizenry—not only Winnipegers themselves—have concentrated considerable effort into making of their capital a city stimulating enough to make long cold winters pass quickly, and the other months so equally congenial that increasing quantities of visitors come to experience the place for themselves.

The Legislative Building is a great H-shaped structure dominated by a 225-foot dome atop which is the glistening Gold Boy statue—a five-ton sculpture of a gilt youth carrying a sheaf of wheat, the work of French sculptor Charles Garde. Within (there are free guided tours) are the Great Hall whose grand stairway is flanked by a pair of massive bronze buffaloes; the Legislative Chamber, with a mural by Frank Braynwyn commemorating the First World War; elaborate decorative details; and a worth-noting Legislative Library. The grounds are statue-dotted—Queen Victoria, as might be expected, but also Scottish poet Robert Burns, Icelandic patriot Jon Sigurdson, Ukrainian poet Taras Schevchenko, and Georges Étienne, a French-Canadian who was one of the Fathers of Confederation—all representatives of the province's ethnic groupings.

The Victorian-era mansion on the grounds is Government House, home of the Lieutenant Governor, the Queen's official representative in Manitoba. (Mention of the ethnic composition makes this as good a time as any to point out that for one week

every August, Winnipeg stages "Folklorama," a festival cele-
brating the score and a half of divers groups of which it is composed; each has its own pavilion and program.)

There are other Winnipeg destinations of some importance. The
Commodity Exchange offers guided tours. The parks are lovely—
Assiniboine especially so, with its zoo, and Kildonan with its open-
air theatre and sculptures. Historic Winnipeg is of note. The
Countess of Dufferin—the first railway locomotive to reach Manitoba back in 1877—is a downtown landmark. Even if—very sadly—
the marvelously gingerbread old City Hall (only somewhat
younger) has been razed, its modern successor is open to visitors;
and so is the splendidly equipped Convention Centre, built at a
cost of $25 million and opened with much fanfare in 1975. There
are some old houses doubling as museums. Ross House (1855)
was western Canada's first post office. Seven Oaks House (1851)
was a prosperous merchant home, with all the appropriate trim-
mings. MacDonald House (1895) was the home of Sir John A.
MacDonald, Canada's first prime minister, and is furnished in
elaborate late Victorian style.

There are visit-worthy churches. These would include St. James
(the oldest log church in the west), Kildonan (mid-nineteenth-
century Presbyterian), St. John's Anglican Cathedral (Mountie
hero Sir Samuel Steele is buried in its graveyard), and two Orthodox cathedrals—one Ukrainian, the other Greek. (If you are wondering, the Catholic cathedral is across the river in St. Boniface,
later described.)

And there are the smaller museums—relatively little-visited like
their counterparts in other cities, but an important part of the
city's cultural fabric. They include the University of Manitoba's
Art Gallery (mostly contemporary Canadian work, changing
shows as well) and its zoological and geological museums; the
Ukrainian Cultural Center—rich with artifacts, furniture, paintings,
silver, costumes, religious articles, books and manuscripts; and the
Transcona Museum, with its theme Manitoba history—both Indian
and settler. The shopping is good; so, for that matter, is the walking. Use the famed Portage and Main intersection as a focal point.
There is racing at Assiniboia Downs, and the Pan-American
Swimming Pool, created for the 1967 Pan-American Games, is

among the larger extant and has a museum pertaining to matters aquatic, in connection.

But what really distinguishes contemporary Winnipeg is the cultural and artistic prowess it has attained in recent years. Take the Winnipeg Art Gallery. Founded near the turn of the century it coasted along for years without achieving any special distinction. Then, in the early 1960s a plan evolved for a new building as a Centennial project. The board selected a Memorial Boulevard site and announced an architectural competition for the design. Winner was Gustavo da Roza, a Portuguese from Hong Kong. His elegant white triangle is at once irregular, striking, and functional. It houses one of Canada's best permanent collections, especially strong on Canadian work—David Milne, Emily Carr, members of the Group of Seven, and the largest collection anywhere of Eskimo sculpture. There are European Old Masters as well—and later Impressionists and moderns, even including Henry Moore sculpture. You never can tell what the show of the moment will be; there are more than half a hundred per annum, and a shop and licensed restaurant, too. All told, Canada's most important art museum west of Toronto.

Now consider the Centennial Centre and what it represents. The province's major hundredth-birthday project, it is a result of a collaboration among federal, provincial, and municipal governments as well as private citizens and corporations, whose gifts totaled more than $7 million. Focal point of the complex is the art-embellished 2,260-seat concert hall, with a restaurant, coffee shop, and cocktail lounge in the basement. The poured-concrete Manitoba Theatre Centre has a 785-seat auditorium (in which no seat is more than 75 feet from the stage) and backstage facilities that include capacious carpenter and wardrobe workshops with wall-size windows that allow visitors to watch artisans and designers at their work; the theatre's second stage is the adjacent, and older Warehouse Theatre.

Also a part of the Centennial Centre is the Manitoba Museum of Man and Nature, and the planetarium it operates. The museum proper attempts nothing less than Manitoba's story—historically and environmentally. There are fine dioramas, the multimedia Grasslands Gallery, a replica of the seventeenth-century fur-trading ship *Nonsuch,* used by the Hudson's Bay Company to open up the west; even an Urban Gallery, with Winnipeg as the subject. From the time it was opened by Queen Elizabeth II in 1970, the museum has been a major Winnipeg attraction, with good reason.

Back now to the Concert Hall and Theatre Centre. The hall is home to a trio of performing arts groups, notably the Royal Winnipeg Ballet. It was the first ballet group in the Commonwealth officially designated "royal." (London's Royal Ballet—ex-Sadler's Wells—followed it by three years.) Queen Elizabeth had first seen the Winnipeg group perform during a 1951 Manitoba visit while she was still a princess. Two years later, after ascending the throne, she granted the company the distinction of including "Royal" as a part of its name, and in so doing awarded the first Royal Charter of her reign. The name of the company is incidental to its excellence. It has remained small, with but twenty-five dancers, and it has emphasized Canadian themes and Canadian choreography in its repertoire, which embraces more than fourscore original ballets, including *Rose La Tulippe,* the first full-length ballet on a Canadian theme, and *The Ecstasy of Rita Joe,* widely acclaimed for its native-minority (Canadian Indian) subject. The repertoire of Saskatchewan-born director Arnold Spohr (whose assistant is ex-American Ballet Theatre soloist Vernon Lusby) runs a wide gamut, from the Canadian rock-theme *A Ballet High* to a specially created variation of Tchaikovsky's *The Nutcracker,* with works by Agnes de Mille, George Balanchine, Elliot Feld, John Butler, Todd Bolender and Montreal's Brian Macdonald (of Les Grands Ballets Canadiens) also danced. The Royal Winnipeg Ballet has a regular Winnipeg winter season and has danced for many summers outdoors at Assiniboine Park. In between, it tours Manitoba, the rest of Canada, and much of the planet. I hope you are lucky enough to catch it during your Manitoba visit, for it is not unlike the Bolshoi in Moscow or the Kirov in Leningrad, both of which are invariably dancing in distant corners of the globe with foreign visitors in their home territory anxious to see them.

The Winnipeg Symphony has been on the scene since 1948; Walter Kaufmann was conductor for its first formative decade. It gives a winter season, but tours the province each year as well, not to mention other Canadian points.

The Manitoba Theatre Centre dates back to 1958 and has performed more than a hundred plays in its relatively brief history. Like its sister companies, it tours the province and much else of Canada as well. It runs a wide gamut in the presentations of its remarkable resident repertory company, including original Canadian works. No matter what it's doing, in the course of your Winnipeg visit, be assured that it will be well done—and go see it.

The Manitoba Opera Association has been presenting fully staged operas only since 1972, wisely sharing resources—designers, technicians, singers—with Opera West, a co-operative whose other members are the western Canadian opera companies in Edmonton, Calgary, and Vancouver. Its usual season embraces three presentations—old favorites like *La Traviata, Il Trovatore,* and *Madama Butterfly.* The accompanying orchestra is the Winnipeg Symphony.

The Royal Winnipeg Ballet is not the only dance company in town. Contemporary Dancers had its beginnings when Rachel Browne, a Royal Winnipeg Ballet soloist, formed a small modern-dance group. Ere long it had financing, professional organization, and a repertoire, now totaling more than thirty-five original ballets in the modern style. The group tours Canada regularly. Small, talented, spirited, it has become the leading modern-dance group in Canada; another first for Winnipeg.

St. Boniface, a bridge ride over the Red River from Winnipeg, has taken on increased importance in recent years, with the Canada-wide emphasis—to a greater extent than ever before—on the country's French heritage. For St. Boniface is the seat of the largest French-speaking community in western Canada. (In 1975 it became the site of the first French-language book publishing house in the west, Les Éditions du Blé.)

Although it was the Frenchman La Vérendrye who in 1738 was the first man to settle at the junction of the Red and Assiniboine rivers, St. Boniface modestly dates its founding to 1818 when two Catholic priests were sent to the area by Lord Selkirk to serve as missionaries in his Red River Settlements. One, Father Provencher, later to become a bishop and one of the most beloved of local historical figures, established a church shortly after his arrival, and it attracted to St. Boniface many métis, a number of whom are buried in the grounds of the cathedral. The most noted of these graves is that of métis leader Louis Riel, which the visitor will probably want to see.

But the cathedral is noteworthy, too, as much architecturally as historically. What happened was that it burned in 1968. Instead of razing what was left of it, a new structure of stark, albeit lovely contemporary design was built within the old walls, and the effect is at once imposing, attractive, and of a piece. Have a look. There's a lovely *fin-de-siècle* Town Hall, identified in French, of course: Hôtel de Ville. And pay a call, if French Canadian culture at all interests you, on the Saint-Boniface Museum. It is located in the old Grey Nuns (Soeurs Grises) Convent, in itself a historic monument dating to 1846, and the oldest such structure in the west. The ambience within, as well as the exhibits, are in the same careful, precise, ever-so-agreeable vein of similar convent-museums in Quebec. Note, too, the Université de Saint-Boniface; it's the French-language affiliate of the University of Manitoba. Although not normally open to visitors, I make mention of the Centre Cultural Franco-Manitobain, at 340 Boulevard Provencher. Its aim is to promote French-Canadian culture throughout Manitoba by means of a multifaceted program, ranging from a little-theatre group called Le Cercle Molière, through art, music, and discussion groups, and special efforts in connection with the Festival du Voyageur, the week-long St. Boniface carnival that draws crowds every February.

Though without any especially Gallic cultural significance, there is still another St. Boniface Museum. It is called Aunt Margaret's Childhood Museum (*La Maison de la Poupée de Tante Margaret*), and the name of the game is nostalgia, by means of a miniature village inhabited by hundreds of dolls, with an immense assortment of elderly toys, as well. Not terribly unlike the doll-filled Museum of Yesterday's Childhood, across the river in Winnipeg.

Lower Fort Garry, some twenty miles northeast of Winnipeg, on the west bank of the Red River, was constructed in 1831 to replace the earlier Fort Garry—built of wood—which had been destroyed by floods in 1826. Lower Fort Garry was erected under the supervision of the Hudson's Bay Company's top Canadian officer, George Simpson, who planned it as "the most respectable looking establishment in the Indian Country." He built it sturdily—of heavy stone. And it is today much as it was well over a century

ago, thanks to affectionate maintenance through the years by the
Hudson's Bay Company. In 1951 the company presented it to the
Canadian Government, which has since maintained it as a National
Historic Site. And historic it is: from early Red River settlement
days . . . Riel's Rebellion . . . the signing of the first treaty between western Indian tribes and the Canadian government . . . the
training of the original troops of the North West Mounted Police.
You'll want to see the Governor's Residence, the penitentiary, the
retail store and fur loft, as well as its spacious grounds and walls
that enclose a precious heritage of Canadian history.

Riding Mountain National Park, a morning's ride (165 miles)
northwest of Winnipeg, is Manitoba's only national park—and a
unique one at that, situated as it is on the edge of the Great Plains,
atop a massive plateau with a twenty-two-hundred-foot elevation.
From eastern and northeastern portions, the park affords striking
views of the plains beneath and beyond it. And within its nearly
1,150 square miles—mostly thick green woods—are a series of
lovely lakes, a wide range of wildlife (from moose to buffalo),
splendid fishing (lake trout, northern pike, whitefish, perch), and
recreational facilities ranging from lawn bowling and tennis courts
to a movie theatre and a dance pavilion. The community of
Wasagaming is park headquarters, and a variety of accommodations—including camping grounds, trailer parks, hotels, and motels
are in its vicinity, along with shops and restaurants, administrative
buildings, a honey of a golf course, and an interesting little log-
cabin interpretive centre of Indian and animal lore. Clear Lake is
the park's major natural attraction, but there are a myriad of
others. (My favorite—Moon—is ideal for a quiet swim.) In a two-
thousand-acre enclosure near Lake Audy is to be found one of the
very few remaining herds of buffalo in North America. And in this
area, too, is one of Canada's largest herds of elk.

Brandon, a broad, low-slung city on the banks of the Assiniboine, first settled in 1878, is western Manitoba's chief town, in
the heart of prairie land. It is well equipped with facilities for visitors and is the site of Brandon University, with agriculture, home
economics, and music its specialties, and the B. J. Hales Museum,
with exhibits of Indian crafts, early settlers, and natural history.
Worth seeing, too, is the Log Fort—a reproduction of earlier ones
—and its museum, in Churchill Park. Every August Brandon is

crowded with visitors attending the Manitoba Provincial Exhibition, a mostly agricultural-type fair, but with other features, not the least of which are harness racing and a dazzling parade-and-show put on by the Royal Canadian Mounted Police. Outside of town is the nationally known seventeen-hundred-acre Experimental Farm, which welcomes interested visitors. Riding Mountain National Park is to the north, and there are a number of close-by lakes (Killarney and Rock among them) for excursions. Due south is the *International Peace Garden,* in the Turtle Mountains region on the international frontier, between Boissevain, Manitoba, and Dunseith, North Dakota. The garden—the only one in the world dedicated to global peace—comprises some 1,450 acres donated by the Province of Manitoba and nearly nine hundred acres that were the gift of the state of North Dakota; a score of clubs and organizations have contributed in various ways to the garden's development and maintenance as have the U. S. Congress, Canadian Parliament, and the legislatures of both Manitoba and North Dakota. I suggest you drive through both the Canadian and American sectors (both countries maintain customs stations at the frontier). To be seen are a variety of landscapes—from formal, sunken gardens to unspoiled lakes and forested groves. A plaque mounted on a simple stone mountain—surmounted by a granite globe—and flanked by the flags of the two countries bears this inscription: "To God in His glory, we two nations, dedicate this garden and pledge ourselves that as long as men shall live, we will not take up arms against one another." There are picnic grounds and a variety of facilities for overnight accommodations. Each June and July the garden is the site of the International Music Camp (with affiliated Schools of Art and Dance). Whom do we thank for conceiving the idea of the Garden to mark a century and a half of peace between two nations whose long frontier is without a single fortification? It was first thought of by a Canadian horticulturist, Henry J. Moore, who proposed it to the National Association of Gardeners of America at their 1929 convention in Toronto. The association appointed a binational committee to investigate possibilities, and the work got under way. The Turtle Mountains site was selected not only because of its beauty, but because it is midway between the Atlantic and Pacific and is but thirty-five miles from the point considered to be the geographic center of North America.

Whiteshell-Lac du Bonnet region: This fantastic maze of lovely lakes—some two hundred of them—in the southeastern corner of Manitoba, about two hours' drive from Winnipeg and even closer to the U.S. border—has developed into one of the province's most popular vacationlands. The canoeing and boating on the lakes and on such rivers as the Winnipeg, Lee, and Bird is first-rate. There's fine swimming, of course, but there's also water-skiing, skin-diving, fishing for bass and northern pike, and excellent camping in a region of pine and spruce forests through which roam deer and bear, beaver, and muskrat. And accommodation runs a wide gamut—much of it modern, modestly priced, and of great appeal to family groups. The town of *Lac du Bonnet* (seventy-two miles from Winnipeg) is at the gateway of the area. Translated as "Lake of the Cap," it is named after a delightful legend dating back to the eighteenth century, when a son of French explorer La Vérendrye fell in love with an Indian maiden named Minnewawa who lived in a village at the site of the present town. Forced to leave the place, he tacked his cap to a tree to symbolize his desire to return. The story of his romance and his headgear became legendary. The modern town, founded in the late nineteenth century, is named after the old legend. And Minnewawa is the name of its principal street. Lac du Bonnet is also the name of the largest lake of the region. Others include Brereton, dotted with islands and fringed by sandy beaches; West Hawk, noted for fishing; Falcon, location of the park town site, shopping area, and golf course; Big Whiteshell, Jessica, Betula, and White. There are scores and scores of others, many lying within the confines of the northern sector of Whiteshell Provincial Park, whose northern part is a preserve for wild game and for masses of birds, many of whom live along the wild-rice beds of the lakes.

Lake Winnipeg, seventh largest on the continent, has become one of North America's most popular cruise waterways. The modern *MS Lord Selkirk II* makes two-, five-, and seven-night cruises in the summer, departing from Selkirk, just north of Winnipeg. Accommodations run a wide gamut (from simple rooms without private facilities to de luxe, fully equipped ones); there are a full-service restaurant, and cocktail and other lounges, with dancing and entertainment. Ports of call include *Gimli,* the largest Icelandic community extant outside of Iceland, with a historical museum, Viking warrior statue on the lake front, and an annual midsummer Icelandic festival; *Berens River,* with its historic Indian and Hudson's Bay Company background; and *Grand Rapids,* a fishing port near the lake's north extremity.

Northern Manitoba: The vast but sparsely populated northern portions of Manitoba constitute its most unusual vacation destinations. For long relatively inaccessible to the ordinary visitor with a minimum of time at his disposal, they are now reached in a matter of hours by air from Winnipeg, although the railroad—if slower— remains a scenic means of transport. And there are roads, too. Aside from air service and the railroad to Churchill, the transport alternatives are canoe or pack trip in summer, and snowmobile or tractor in winter. Northern Manitoba is only just beginning to develop, and I hope your intinerary allows you time to explore a bit of it, for this is a bit of the Canada of the trapper and of the miner—the adventurers' Canada which few of us get to know.

The Pas is an up-to-date town situated at the junction of the Saskatchewan and Pasquia rivers, some 475 miles north of Winnipeg. The gateway to the north, it has known the white man since 1691 when fur trader-explorer Henry Kelsey camped on its site. Later, in the mid-eighteenth century, a small fort was built. Trappers and Indians were the principal occupants until 1907 when the Canadian National came north, and The Pas (whose name, incidentally, is believed to be a corruption of *opas,* the Greek for narrows) began to prosper as a distributing center and transport hub for the region. Today, it offers the visitor comfortable accommodations, a variety of amenities, the Little Northern Museum of Indian artifacts and historic objects, a rebuilt Christ Church (Anglican) still furnished with pews from the original, built in 1847; the original log building housing the first Roman Catholic Mission dating from 1887; and a colorful populace of lumbermen, prospectors, miners, fishermen, trappers, and Indians. The Pas's big moment each year comes in mid-February with the annual Trappers' Festival, a kind of northern Mardi Gras, when for three ebullient days the locals and a multitude of visitors celebrate with such events as the World Championship Dog Race, ice fishing, square dancing, snowmobile racing, goose calling, canoe packing, snowshoe racing, and the crowning of a Fur Queen. Uniform of the day? *Mukluk* boots, fur-trimmed parkas, buckskin jackets, and fur caps.

Just twenty miles from town is *Clearwater Provincial Park,* which is named for a unique lake—one of the few *truly* clear bodies of water in the world. The trout fishing is great and accommodations are modern and include camping grounds. Some fifty miles north of The Pas is *Cranberry Portage,* a small town that is still another center for anglers who fish the trio of nearby Cranberry Lakes and their neighbors, one of which—Athapapuskow—is among the loveliest in the north, and with good facilities.

Flin Flon is Manitoba's oddest town for two reasons: it is one of the few towns in the world built on a bed of solid rock, and it is unique, too, in that its strangely euphonious name derives from a character named Flintabbatey Flonatin, hero of a dime novel called *The Sunless City.* The book was popular with early miners in the area. They shortened the principal character's name and eventually it came to be the name of the settlement. For years no one much thought about Flin Flon's name, let alone the name of the book from which it came. And it was not for many decades that the town fathers, after instituting an international search for the novel—whose title no one remembered—came upon it in London. In 1962 a statue of Flin Flon—twenty feet high and of fiber glass—was created, based on a design by cartoonist Al Capp.

Flin Flon remains a mining town and is the site of one of the world's largest copper-zinc mines. Its major annual celebration is its Trout Festival, the first week of each July, during which there's a trout derby, a Gold Rush Canoe Derby, fish-fries, pulp-cutters' and flour-packing contests, the coronation of the Mermaid Queen, and, yes, dancing in the streets. A dozen lakes—full of fish—surround Flin Flon.

Thompson is a modern town that is the site of the second-largest nickel-producing enterprise in the world, operated by the International Nickel Company of Canada. Commercial production began in 1961. The town, on the banks of the Burntwood River, is four hundred air miles north of Winnipeg and is growing by leaps and bounds as a planned city. There are modern schools and houses, shopping areas, a hospital, and good accommodations, not to mention fishing, swimming, boating, and hunting in the surrounding districts.

Churchill is the remarkable sub-Arctic port through which Manitoba's earliest settlers arrived and because of which Manitoba is, despite its prairie position, able to call itself a maritime province. Built on a bleak peninsula that juts into Hudson Bay at the mouth of the Churchill River, and with a still-small population, it is without conventional beauty, to be sure, but it is one of Canada's most unusual towns thanks to its remote, far-northern location and a history that stretches back four centuries. Where else, after all, can one watch schools of white whales in the shadow of a five-million-bushel grain elevator? A thousand miles by rail from Winnipeg, Churchill—during the brief navigation season extending only from late July to early October—sees automobiles, tractors, and other products unloaded from ships in its harbor and transported by rail to the south. Not far from town is modern Fort Churchill. Across the river from town are the ruins of North America's most northerly fortress, Fort Prince of Wales—old cannon mounted in turrets of sixteen-foot-thick walls overlooking the harbor. You reach it by tour-boat in summer, and in winter—more fun this—by organized dog team. Now maintained by the federal government as a National Historic Site, the fort—built in 1731—is a replacement for an earlier wooden fort erected in 1717 by Captain James Knight for the Hudson's Bay Company. The present fort was all but destroyed by the French in 1782, but Churchill— named for a very distant ancestor of Sir Winston Churchill— managed to stay in business as a fur-trading post. Its history as a modern port dates only to 1927, when the Hudson Bay railway was constructed. It extends five hundred miles to The Pas over barren, lake-dotted Canadian Shield countryside; from The Pas there are earlier established rail links to Winnipeg. There are conducted train excursions every summer from Winnipeg and Saskatoon, but Churchill is now accessible by air, as well, and the short-time visitor does well to have at least a quick look—at the ruins of the old fort, the excellent exhibits of artifacts and handicrafts in the Eskimo Museum, the Anglican and Catholic missions, the immense grain elevator, the activity in the harbor, the white whales in the bay, and, of course, the motley populace of the town— Eskimos, Mounties, Hudson's Bay people, trappers, fishermen.

North of Churchill you might want to consider an expedition to *Brochet,* a mostly Indian community (Cree and Chipewayan) where fishing and trapping are the principal occupations. There's a Hudson's Bay Company post and a Catholic mission, and not far off is the Cochrane River, with arctic grayling the lure for anglers.

Far to the south of Churchill is *Norway House,* at the northern tip of Lake Winnipeg. It was founded as a Hudson's Bay post in 1825; sections of the old fort remain, there is a comfortable lodge for overnight guests, and good fishing.

SHOPPING

In **Winnipeg,** there are a number of sources of handicrafts— Eskimo, Indian, and otherwise. They include *Crafts Guild of Manitoba* (183 Kennedy Street); *Bowring's* (in the underground shopping concourse of the Lombard Place office building-hotel complex at Portage and Main); *Odjig Print Gallery & Gift Shop* (331 Donald Street)—Indian work exclusively; *Mamaj Art Gallery & Gift Shop* (409 Main Street)—Ukrainian folk art is the specialty; *Hand Made Gift Shop* (1328 Portage Avenue). Worth knowing about, for its books of Canadiana—the collection is probably the best in all Canada—is the eminently browsable *Mary Storer Book Shop,* 214 Kennedy Street. The *Winnipeg Art Gallery Shop* has a tempting stock of art books and crafts. *Eaton's* department store has souvenirs, including some Canadiana on the second floor; a good book department with a fairly extensive Canadiana section on three, along with groceries and bakery. *Hudson's Bay Company* has one of its best outlets in Winnipeg. Departments of interest to the out-of-towner might include souvenirs and Canadiana, as well as candy on main, books on five, and a big supermarket in the basement. (Department-store dining is dealt with under Creature Comforts, following.)

CREATURE COMFORTS

Winnipeg: *The Winnipeg Inn* gets my vote as Western International's best all-around Canadian operation, which is saying a lot. There are 350 exceptionally good-looking rooms, with electric blankets on all the beds—a Western International specialty—and well-equipped, spacious baths. I like the restaurants, too. The Velvet Glove is one of the town's poshest and with first-rank cuisine and wines. A floor below the lobby, actually in the Lombard Place shopping concourse, is Café Lombard for coffee and light meals. The zingy Stage Door is the nightclub, and there's a roof-top piano-bar-cum-view, not to mention an indoor pool and sauna on the same high floor. *The Fort Garry,* bless it, carries on in fine traditional style. It is among the more commendable in the commendable Canadian National chain. The 265 rooms have all been handsomely refurbished in recent seasons. The lobby is lovely, and so is Factor's Table, the handsome, period-style main restaurant. There's an inventively decorated coffee shop and cocktail lounge, too. And the exterior puts one in mind of the Plaza, in New York. The 411-room, 17-story *Holiday Inn,* connected with the Convention Centre, is one of the most tastefully decorated of any of the ever-multiplying links of that global chain that I have seen. And I've seen many. The guest rooms sport striped paper and Picasso prints. The cocktail lounge is atmospheric, the coffee shop a dilly, and the main restaurant handsome. There's a 2-story-high swimming pool, around which cluster a special group of guest rooms. The *Marlborough* is an elderly downtown house that has been attractively refurbished, with a smart main restaurant, an oddly neo-Gothic coffee shop, and a German rathskeller among its public rooms. All 300 guest rooms have been spruced up. The *Charter House Hotel* has just under 100 rooms, but it is full-facility, even including an outdoor heated pool that's a delight in summer. Good restaurant, agreeable cocktail lounge, coffee shop. Out near the airport is the 210-room *International Inn,* very mod, with its focal point a great dome-covered swimming pool in an inside garden just off the lobby. There are a variety of wine-dine rooms, including the Hollow Mug Theatre Restaurant, with shows and dancing. **Riding Mountain National Park (Wasagaming):** Leaders here are *Elk Horn Ranch,* with 21 varied units and all manner of facilities including restaurant, cocktail lounge, and swimming pool; *Mooswa Hotel,* with nearly 50 units, licensed restaurant, pool, and other amenities; and *Thunderbird Bungalows,* with 17 kitchen-equipped cabins. **Brandon:** My choice is CP Hotels' modern *Red Oak Inn,* with the chief lure a huge, high-ceilinged solarium embracing a capacious swimming pool, with an auxiliary pool for kids, a whirlpool bath, a sauna, even sunlamps for a winter tan. There are 100 attractive bedrooms, an inviting main restaurant, an informal coffee shop, and a cocktail lounge-cum-entertainment. The 63-room *Canadian Inn* is attractive and full-facility, with an indoor pool among its amenities and a downtown location. The Suburban Restaurant is a good bet for dinner. **Whiteshell Provincial Park area:** *Lakeview Motor Hotel*—(a dozen units and a licensed restaurant and beverage room)—on Lac du Bonnet; *Falcon Motor Hotel,* on Falcon Lake, full-facility, with 21 units, restaurant, and cocktail lounge, among other amenities. **Dauphin:** *Dauphin Community Inn*—restaurant, beverage room, and 17 rooms. **Clearwater Lake:** *Vickery's Lodge,* a fishing and hunting resort with a variety of facilities; 10 housekeeping units. **The Pas:** *Wescana Inn* has 41 rooms, a restaurant and cocktail lounge. *La Vérendrye Motel,* with 24 units, is similarly well equipped. **Flin Flon:** *Kelsey Trail Motor Inn* has a restaurant and cocktail lounge, 43 rooms, and a heated pool and sauna. *Flin Flon Hotel,* with an in-town location, has 26 rooms, restaurant, and cocktail lounge. **Thompson:** *Mystery Lake Motor Hotel* is a 40-unit house with restaurant and cocktail lounge. *Burntwood Motor Hotel* has 40 rooms, too, restaurant and cocktail lounge. The *Headframe* and *Rumaki Dinner Garden* are good restaurants. **Churchill:** *The Churchill Hotel* has a total of 36 units, only 20 of which have private baths. There are a restaurant, cocktail lounge, and beverage room. *Polar Hotel* has about a dozen units, no eating or drinking facilities. **Swan River:** *Nelson Motor Hotel,* 26 rooms with restaurant and beverage room.

Dining in Winnipeg: Canada's fourth largest city takes gastronomy seriously. One can eat very well indeed in Winnipeg. *Oliver's* (Main and Lombard) is at once elegant—there are a series of extremely tasteful rooms and lounges—and delicious, with such specialties as Australian lobster tails, Danish shrimp, and first-rank beef—steaks or ribs—for a festive lunch or dinner. *The Velvet Glove* (Winnipeg Inn) is a beauty of a paneled, chandelier-lit, eighteenth-century Georgian chamber, with perfectly delicious food —house pâté or oysters Rockefeller to start, the local goldeye fish, smoked or grilled, or rack of lamb for an entrée, black forest cake or crêpes Suzette for dessert. There is an adjacent lounge for pre- and post-meal drinks, and the service is skilled and cheerful. *Fac-*

tor's Table (Fort Garry Hotel) puts one in mind of early Manitoba when the Chief Factor—head man—at Upper Fort Garry hosted all manner of special guests. This is one of the most attractive restaurants in town, and especially interesting at dinner, with such specialties as steak au poivre, beef Wellington, bouillabaisse— or at least a Manitoba variation thereof—and rack of lamb boulangère. Start with the steak tartare or Caesar salad, made at tableside, and finish with one of the chef's pies, or the cheeseboard. (A good place for French-speaking visitors whose restaurant English is minimal, for the menus here—as in all Canadian National hotels—are in both languages.) *Old Swiss Inn* (207 Edmonton Street) is smallish, intimate, Swiss-cozy, and Swiss-owned. Everything is delicious—including the soups (lobster bisque, onion, real turtle), the veal dishes (escalope de veau cordon bleu) and the after-dinner (or lunch) drinks, most especially one dubbed The Burning Matterhorn. Don't neglect the choice Swiss wines. The *William Tell*, in the basement of the Concert Hall, is under the same management as Old Swiss Inn; you might enjoy it at lunchtime when it serves steak, Reuben and other sandwiches, and a super chef's salad. *La Vielle Gare* is just what the name indicates—an old railroad station cleverly converted into a restaurant. The locale is St. Boniface, across the Red River, and although the fare is not actually French, it is agreeable enough, with the ambience friendly and the setting attractive. *Koko's Steak House* (1133 Portage Avenue, and for long known as Pierre's) is a reliable spot for hearty meals—steak, lobster, ribs. And it has an oyster bar—not common in the interior of North America—and evening entertainment. *La Grande Canal of Venice* (175 Carlton Street) is, hardly surprisingly, Italian. The décor runs to an honest-to-goodness gondola, and the waiters—you guessed it—are gondoliers who double as singers. *Monty's Warehouse* (167 Bannatyne Street) is atmospheric, with Tiffany lamps dominating a turn-of-century ambience. Order steak or roast beef. *The Round Table* (800 Pembina Street) lacks King Arthur but is designed to put you in mind of him, as you look about. For beef. Bless *Hy's Steak Loft* (216 Kennedy Street). In its Winnipeg locale, as elsewhere throughout Canada, it is at once pleasurable, good-looking, and delicious. *Ichi Ban* (189 Carlton Street) is for beef, too, but as you can tell from its name, Japanese-style—prepared at the table with flair. The *Old Spaghetti Factory* (291 Bannatyne Street) shelters an ancient trolley car, and an astonishing variety of other amusing props; reasonably priced and ideal fare for all the family. The *Winnipeg Art Gallery Restaurant* is a wise choice for a lunch break in the course of inspecting the gallery. It is fully licensed, with daily special plates and hot dishes, salads, and sandwiches. DEPARTMENT-STORE eating is enjoyable: The *Hudson's Bay Company's Georgian Room* (fifth floor) is fully licensed and features a buffet at lunch and on evenings when the store is open; roast beef is among its choices. On the Bay's sixth floor is the *Paddlewheel*—yes, with a real paddlewheel—that just has to be the most amusing cafeteria you've come across; try the chicken pie. And there's a coffee shop in the Bay's basement. *Eaton's* concentrates two restaurants on five. Smarter of the pair is the good-looking *Grill*, serving lunch and tea, as well as dinner on open nights. There is the *Valley Room* cafeteria, as well. Las Vegas-style entertainment is the forte of *Town & Country* (317 Kennedy Street), with steak the fare at the dinner show.

New Brunswick

LE NOUVEAU-BRUNSWICK

Best times for a visit: *New Brunswick's high season extends from June through September; the summer months—through August—are typified by sunny days, often in the seventies, and cool evenings, while in September the daytime average is*

in the sixties. Autumn is cooler, of course, but pleasant, while winter is bracing and snowy. **Transportation:** *New Brunswick is reached by road from the provinces of Quebec and Nova Scotia and the state of Maine, which it borders; by ship from Nova Scotia (Canadian Pacific's* Princess of Acadia *is a commodious modern craft with lounges and restaurants, which plies the Bay of Fundy between Digby, Nova Scotia, and Saint John, New Brunswick, daily between mid-May and late October, in two hours and forty-five minutes—a beautiful voyage) and from Prince Edward Island (Canadian National's ferries connect—in less than an hour—Cape Tormentine, New Brunswick, and Borden, Prince Edward Island; almost hourly sailings from late June to early September), and by plane (Air Canada from eastern Canadian and U.S. points to Saint John, Fredericton, and Moncton, and Eastern Provincial Airways, from points within the Atlantic provinces and Quebec to Moncton). Both Canadian National and Canadian Pacific railways link the province with its neighbors. There is an extensive network of highways, with some sixteen hundred paved miles and good supplementary roads along delightfully scenic routes. There are free ferry crossings on the major rivers. The Trans-Canada Highway runs from the Quebec border south along the Saint John River to Fredericton, then southeasterly across the province to the Nova Scotia border. From a junction at Aulac, a branch (the only one on the entire highway) runs to Cape Tormentine. There is extensive bus service within the province; taxi drivers in the towns generally are not tipped.* **Having a drink:** *Top hotels have licensed dining rooms and cocktail lounges, and some of the better restaurants are licensed, as are some private clubs; taverns—for beer—are open only to men.* **Further information:** *New Brunswick Department of Tourism, Fredericton, New Brunswick; Canadian Government Office of Tourism, Ottawa and branches.*

INTRODUCING NEW BRUNSWICK

The special qualities of New Brunswick are not easy to define. I suspect that the province's lack of superlatives add to the difficulties of the observer. There are, to be sure, a river that flows backwards twice a day and a point at which cars may coast uphill. And there are few tides in the world higher than those of the Bay of Fundy. But little New Brunswick—only Nova Scotia and Prince Edward Island are smaller in area—is not distinguished by its natural phenomena. It has no great cities, and there is no single spectacular attraction to lure one.

But there is about the province an easy charm, a quiet beauty, a reserved friendliness. One has the feeling that New Brunswick is rarely accused of moving with anything even resembling deliberate speed, and at a time when in so many places to hurry is to move at the normal pace, this is comforting. The province's tempo today reflects its yesterdays. For it was a long time getting into even middle gear.

New Brunswick's native peoples were two tribes of the Algonquin family of Indians—the Micmacs (who also inhabited nearby Prince Edward Island) and the Malecites—mostly nomadic types who have left relatively little, other than a preponderance of multisyllabic place names retained by their successors.

Basque fishermen may well have sailed New Brunswick's shore very early in the sixteenth century. And it is sometimes said that a Portuguese navigator named Estevão Gomes cruised its waters in 1525, if indeed he was a real and not a mythical figure. At any rate, there is no doubt about Jacques Cartier. In 1534 he landed at Point Escuminac and explored Miramichi Bay in the north.

Champlain arrives: A quiescent period ensued until as late as 1604, when Samuel de Champlain discovered the Saint John River and named it for the date of his arrival—June 24—St. John's Day. Later, with his colleague, de Monts, he set up a settlement on an island in the Saint Croix River (which now constitutes part of the Maine-New Brunswick border). And the region called Acadia by the French—which comprised the present provinces of New Brunswick and Nova Scotia—was at last opened up to fairly active exploration. Englishmen came from what is now New England, Dutchmen went north from New Amsterdam, but the French arrived in the greatest numbers and with the help of international treaties signed in Europe, came to dominate the area through the seventeenth century.

They did not, however, always get along well—even with each other, as Saint John's founding indicates. One of their number,

Charles de la Tour, built a trading post in the vicinity of Saint John in 1635, which displeased a competitor, named d'Aulnay de Charnisay, who was trading out of Port Royal in Nova Scotia. Charnisay, in 1643, attacked La Tour's fort at Saint John and managed to hold on to it for two years, by which time La Tour—who had escaped—returned. Charnisay's men—in the presence of La Tour's wife, who was in charge during her husband's absence—killed La Tour's troops, destroyed the fort, and built one of his own across the river. Later, La Tour—after five years of exile—returned to find both his wife *and* his rival dead. Still undaunted, he married the widow of Charnisay and carried on, true to the spirit of that never-a-dull-moment era, until the British finally took the place in 1758—after many earlier attempts—and rechristened it Fort Frederick.

The British take over: It was during this period that the British gained complete control of Acadia and brutally expelled from the area the French-speaking Acadians, whose loyalty they doubted. Although it is the Acadians of the present Nova Scotia whose exodus has been most chronicled, those of New Brunswick—let it be noted—suffered also.

In 1784 New Brunswick was detached by the British from Nova Scotia, retaining the name by which it was called as a Nova Scotian county. Separate colony status resulted after a wave of settlers had come from England. They were later joined by another, more unusual group: the so-called United Empire Loyalists—British colonists from New England whose sentiments were with the Crown and against the American Revolutionaries.

The Loyalists found their new home harsh and not nearly so comfortable or developed as the American colonies. Some left after a short stay, but many remained, and with the colonists already on the spot—including those Acadians who had returned to their homeland—they slowly developed New Brunswick. Land was cleared for farming, and timber cut down in the process was put to good use in a newly founded shipbuilding industry.

More and more, the interior was opened up and settled. Fredericton, originally French, was renamed after a son of George III and designated by the governor of the time—to the chagrin of the colonists resident at coastal Saint John—as the colony's capital. By the mid-nineteenth century, Saint John had become a port and business center of consequence.

The province develops: Dissatisfied with the tactics of an arbitrary governor, the colonists petitioned the Crown for self-government, which was granted in 1849. And in 1867, with a good degree of the reluctance which has so often been reflected in its history, New Brunswick was a part of the first group of colonies to become provinces of the new Confederation of Canada. Since that time, growth has hardly been lightninglike, but it has been meaningful. The French-speaking New Brunswickers—most of them of Acadian stock, but some of Quebec origin, and almost all of them Roman Catholic—have multiplied their numbers to the point where they constitute more than 40 per cent of the total population of the province, much to the surprise of visitors who consider New Brunswick a largely Anglo-Saxon part of the world.

The forests account for the province's main industry—pulp and paper. But fishing and lobstering are of consequence, the northern mines are being exploited by Canadian and American interests, the province is the site of Camp Gagetown, the largest army training post in Canada, and communications and power facilities have improved to the point where secondary industries are being officially encouraged. Tourism is being wisely promoted both by the provincial government and private enterprise. Industrial development is especially noteworthy in the Saint John area, along with major improvements in shipping facilities (there is a new Harbour Bridge) and the province's first nuclear energy plant.

Acadian awareness: New Brunswick's French-speaking citizens began to assert themselves politically during the 1960s term of the first premier of Acadian descent in New Brunswick's long history, Louis J. Robichaud. The Robichaud era saw the increased use of the French language in official provincial communications, and concomitant cultural developments of the French-speaking sector of the populace. In 1970 the Liberal Party gained control after a full decade of Conservative rule.

YOUR VISIT TO NEW BRUNSWICK

New Brunswick is among the most thoroughly delightful of the Canadian provinces in which to travel, particularly by car. The towns are pleasant and hospitable, and a number have preserved enough of the past to make them more than stopover points. In the interior, the countryside is one of attractive, gently rolling farms whose meadows often flank the banks of quietly meandering rivers. And along the coast, one sees and savors maritime New Brunswick—great stretches of beach, tiny fishing villages in whose harbors bob masses of lobster boxes, populous resorts, verdant islands. There are picnic grounds, campsites, and trailer parks—nearly fifty of them that meet the government's inspection standards—scattered throughout the province, at scenic points. All about are historic sites, designated by monuments or plaques delineating New Brunswick's past. And covered bridges! New Brunswick has, sadly, allowed about 100 to disappear in recent years. Still, there are about 100 remaining, including the longest one in the world, at Hartland. (A group is now fairly active in the province, endeavoring to preserve the more scenic bridges and develop small parks around them.) With 80 per cent of its area still forested, and with a seacoast stretching well over six hundred miles, it is not surprising that New Brunswick has strong appeal to the rod-and-gun crowd, as well as the ordinary vacationer. The angler goes for Atlantic silver salmon, brook trout, and black bass, while the hunter's prey includes black bear and deer, as well as such game birds as ruffed grouse, spruce partridge, pheasant, woodcock, and ducks.

There may well be those who would dispute me, but there seems little question that New Brunswick is the most New England-like of the Atlantic provinces—far more so, in my view, than Prince Edward Island, Nova Scotia, or Newfoundland. Many of its people are, of course, the descendants of New Englanders. Their ties to Maine—just across the border—and Massachusetts are still strong. And the distinctive accent of the Maine Down Easter frequently influences New Brunswick speech. At the same time, it would be as fallacious to discount New Brunswick as little more than an extension of the American region it flanks as it would equate Manitoba with North Dakota or Quebec with New York.

Saint John requires a prefatory word as regards spelling. In order to distinguish it from the capital of Newfoundland, the first word of its name is always spelled out, never abbreviated. And the second word of its name is without a final apostrophe "s." We have, therefore, Saint John, New Brunswick, in contrast to St. John's, Newfoundland.

Saint John, through whose harbor Samuel de Champlain sailed in 1604, took a long while to forgive inland Fredericton for being selected the capital, but takes consolation in being the oldest incorporated city in Canada (1785), and in having achieved a number of other "firsts"—first paid police force in Canada (1826), first penny newspaper in the British Empire (a tri-weekly found in 1838), first public museum in Canada (1842)—and these are but a few.

Saint John is, of course, the province's largest city with a metropolitan population of about one hundred thousand. It is not, at first glance, a pretty town (it is the center of concerted industrial activity), but as one gets about, it becomes evident that it is not without attractions. Indeed, the centers of few Canadian towns are as appealing as old King Square, in the heart of Saint John. Laid out like the crosses of a Union Jack, and with a burial ground with stones going back to the eighteenth century across from it, it has been wisely preserved as an authentic period piece. Facing it is the handsome early-nineteenth-century Court House with a superb circular stairway within. The old City Market (1876)—I suggest you have a look—is nearby and so is the high-spired Trinity Church (Anglican), whose chief treasure is a royal coat of arms brought from Boston after the Revolution.

The harbor, at the foot of King Street—the main thoroughfare leading from King Square—is of great value in Canadian commerce, for it is ice-free the year round and invariably bustling with activity. (One of the world's largest dry docks is in Saint John—but on Courtenay Bay, on the other side of the city.)

Old Saint John is not confined to King Square, the adjacent burial ground, and the Court House. There are nearly a score of historical sites that the city fathers have cleverly combined in what they call the Loyalist Trail—a not overlong walking tour that includes stops at—among other places—the Loyalist House (1810) on Union Street, St. John's Stone Church (Anglican), a graceful structure (the city's first made of stone, imported from England as ship ballast in 1825); Mallard House on Germain Street, originally an inn and the meeting place of the colony's first legislature in 1786—when Fredericton was not quite ready to receive delegates; the Thatcher Sears House (1783) on King Street; the old stocks and pillory—modern traffic passes by them today—at the foot of King Street; and last (and perhaps least) a plaque marking the house which was home to Benedict Arnold, whom not even the Loyalists respected and who finally left North America to spend his final years in England.

The aforementioned New Brunswick Museum—Canada's oldest such public institution—occupies a fine building, and those exhibits dealing with New Brunswick marine and historical material— including some brilliant ship models—are of especial interest. The circular Martello Tower, an early-nineteenth-century fortification, in Saint John West (formerly known as Lancaster) across the Saint John River, is a National Historic Site with interesting exhibits. The biggest attraction in Greater Saint John is the Reversing Falls Rapids of the Saint John River, viewed from an observation point (at which have been constructed a restaurant, shop, and information bureau). The whole thing leaves me cold (cold, that is, not wet), but I seem to constitute a minority of one in this respect. At any rate, what happens is that when the tide of the river is ebbing, the current flows down a gorge into the harbor. However, when the tide is in flood, the water reverses itself and flows *up* from the Bay of Fundy and over the falls. There are two "performances" of this phenomenon of nature daily; for free printed timetables—indicating when to watch—you have only to ask any loyal resident, who will direct you posthaste to the tourist information centre on King Square and at the rapids. Guided tours of the city, incidentally, begin at the latter point.

There are two roads linking Saint John with Fredericton, the capital, which is up the Saint John River, in the interior. The shorter—called the Broad Road—is a modern sixty-seven-mile highway (Route No. 7), bypassing points of interest. The longer, scenic route (the River Road, Route 102) is ninety-four miles, and takes one through the delightful Saint John River Valley, following the route of the river, through small towns like *Evandale, Hampstead, Queenstown, Gagetown* (site of the Loomcrafters textile studios, which you'll want to visit); and past Camp Gagetown —Canada's largest military base built at a cost of a hundred million dollars and humming with training activity in summer—and *Oromocto,* a brand-new model town adjacent to the camp headquarters. If you've time, I certainly suggest the slower scenic route and, perhaps, a picnic lunch en route on the banks of the river.

Fredericton is a gem—quiet, smallish, and unexciting to be sure, but with great charm and considerable beauty.

The part of this Loyalist town of twenty thousand that will interest you most is its oldest section, along the green landscaped banks of the Saint John River. At the extreme end is a fine Georgian building that was built in 1828 as the colony's Government House. Beautifully preserved, it is still doing duty as an official headquarters currently for the Royal Canadian Mounted Police of the district. In central Fredericton, on Queen Street overlooking the river, is Officers' Square. Beside its reflecting pool is a bronze statue of modern New Brunswick's principal private benefactor, the locally reared English newspaper tycoon and wartime British Cabinet Minister, Lord Beaverbrook. And flanking the square is the Colonial-era Old Officers' Barracks, now occupied by the exhibits of the York-Sunbury Museum, a historical collection that I suggest you inspect.

Nearby is the Victorian-era Legislature Building, one of the most elegant in Canada. You'll want to see the Legislative Chamber and the Legislative Library, in an annex adjoining the main building. Situated on spacious grounds, to give it the perspective it needs, is Christ Church Cathedral (Anglican), one of the loveliest Gothic edifices in the country; it's a mid-nineteenth century master work considered one of all Canada's finest Victorian buildings. It has a nave copied from one in Norfolk, England, and a fine stained glass window (the one on the eastern side) given to it by New York City's noted Trinity Church.

On the next block is the eighteenth-century house of one of Fredericton's leading United Empire Loyalist fathers, Jonathan Odell of New Jersey; it now serves as the residence of the dean of the cathedral. Fredericton's modern showpiece—aside from the splendid new Beaverbrook Theatre—is the Beaverbrook Art Gallery, given to the people of the province by Lord Beaverbrook. The exhibits, reflecting the tastes—understandably enough—of the donor, are heavier on English art than they might be, and other schools suffer as a result. But one cannot complain, what with Gainsboroughs, Reynolds, some excellent pieces by Graham Sutherland (including portraits of Churchill, Beaverbrook, Somerset Maugham, and Helena Rubenstein), an outstanding group of Canadian work, from Cornelius Krieghoff (an exceptionally rich group of this nineteenth-century master) through the province's own Fred Ross and other contemporaries, and an exquisite miniature of Queen Elizabeth I by Nicholas Hilliard (in great contrast to the embarrassingly bad study of Queen Elizabeth II by Edward Halliday, which does justice neither to Her Majesty nor the gallery).

The University of New Brunswick, whose buildings occupy a spacious campus that you'll want to tour, is a granddaddy among higher-education institutions in North America. The well-educated United Empire Loyalists founded it in 1785, patterning it after the King's College (now Columbia University) of which they were so fond, in New York. It is the oldest provincial university and was established the same year as was the University of Georgia, which is the United States' oldest state university. The Old Arts Building (1825) is its choicest building and houses the first university chapel on whose original benches are still to be seen the carved names of early students. Lord Beaverbrook—until his death, in England, in June 1964—was honorary chancellor of the university, and buildings donated by him or his first wife are much in evidence on the campus as they are throughout the city of Fredericton, and in other parts of the province. No native son in modern times seems to have been more generous to his boyhood home than "The Beaver," as he was known to New Brunswickers. The other principal benefactor of contemporary New Brunswick, Lady Dunn, became the second Lady Beaverbrook. And one cannot travel any distance in the province without coming across a hockey rink or public building of some sort that is not a Beaverbrook or Dunn gift. (The exception to the rule appears to be Saint John, where the local millionaire is K. C. Irving, who developed a single gas station into a chain extending through the Atlantic provinces and Quebec; and from there went on to other major industrial and business enterprises, most of them in the Saint John area.)

Fredericton is justifiably proud, not only of the late Lord Beaverbrook and his benefactions, but of its repute as the "Poets' Corner of Canada," an official designation from the National Historic Sites and Monuments Board, in recognition of the work of Bliss Carman, Francis Joseph Sherman, and Sir Charles G. D. Roberts, as well as many other writers and artists. The area continues to attract practitioners of the arts, not the least of which are a group of outstanding craftsmen whose studios are of interest to visitors.

Other amenities? Well, there are municipal swimming pools, fishing in nearby streams, camping along the river, and harness racing all summer and into October. And a special treat is nearby (15 miles west): *Mactaquac Provincial Park*—with an 18-hole golf course, handicrafts center, a pair of swimming beaches, licensed restaurants and lounges, nature trails, a sailboat marina, and campgrounds. A near-neighbor is *Kings Landing Historical Settlement*—a restored New Brunswick village-museum, illustrating how the province lived between 1790 and 1870.

The Saint John River Valley: I have already alluded to the attractions of this valley in lower New Brunswick, from Fredericton south to Saint John. But I commend its upper reaches to you as well. You may want to settle for a half-day's drive through *Woodstock* (a frequent point of entry to the province from Houlton, Maine, where a visit is indicated to the beautifully restored old Court House, built in 1833, at Upper Woodstock) and to *Hartland,* site of the remarkable covered bridge whose 1,282-foot span makes it the world's longest such structure. Continuing north you find yourself in *Grand Falls,* named for the sadly underrated, eminently photogenic, 225-foot falls just outside of town. And at the northwestern tip of the province, near the U.S. and Quebec borders, is *Edmundston,* the metropolis of northern New Brunswick, a small city that has come to thrive as a result of the pulp and paper industry, and—after Moncton, in the south—the leading French-speaking community of the province. Edmundston is the first town gained by visitors entering New Brunswick from Quebec, on the Trans-Canada Highway, and it is linked with Madawaska, Maine, by a bridge and a pipeline that shoots pulp from Canada to the United States. About 85 per cent of the population of some twelve thousand is French-speaking and largely Roman Catholic. I suggest you acquaint yourself with St. Louis University (particularly its Laporte Art Museum), the Immaculate Conception Cathedral, and the Fourteen Stations of the Cross in the modern Our Lady of the Seven Sorrows Church, carved in wood by the New Brunswick artist Claude Roussel.

St. Stephen and St. Andrews are a pair of small southwestern New Brunswick towns that play a large role in the province's tourist picture. The former, just across the Saint Croix River from its sister city of Calais (pronounced, in this part of the world, Callas, as in Maria), Maine, is linked with the United States by an international bridge over which come many of the province's visitors. St. Stephen and Calais, the border notwithstanding, have been buddy-buddy communities through thick and thin during a long history, which dates back to St. Stephen's founding in 1783 as a haven for United Empire Loyalists fleeing from the anti-Crown colonies. They alone ignored the state of war that existed between Canada and the U.S. in 1812, and to this day they co-operate on a number of mutual matters, including firefighting; the brigades of both towns fight fires in their opposite number. (The water supply they share is interesting, too. It comes from the New Brunswick side, is piped across the river to Maine, from where it is sold back to St. Stephen.)

At one point they considered renaming St. Stephen Dover so that North America would have a Dover-Calais combination not unlike the British and French towns that are separated by the English Channel. But that seems to have had more support in Calais than in St. Stephen. There has always been a bit of industry—shipbuilding in the old days, chocolates, and wood products today. The Duncan McColl United Church—named for the clergyman who was instrumental in keeping the two towns friendly during the War of 1812—is St. Stephen's chief landmark. Twenty miles down the road a piece—and a pretty coastal road it is—lies *St. Andrews,* which is New Brunswick's Poshville—at least in summer, when the tourists come in quantity. Many have handsome homes of their own, others have been coming for years and with clockwork regularity to Canadian Pacific's rambling Algonquin Hotel (where newcomers sit on the oldtimers' porch rockers at the risk of imminent expulsion). St. Andrews also is lobster territory. And it is still an attractive old town—just a year younger than St. Stephen—with a number of monuments indicative of its maturity. The most noted is the classic white frame Greenock Church. The carved green oak tree on its tower was placed there as a reminder of home—Greenock (a contraction of green oak), Scotland—by the man who paid for the construction of the Presbyterian place of worship. The Court House is another architectural gem, and the Old Block House is a memento of early Loyalist days. Ministers Island, just off the coast, is accessible by car—over the floor of the ocean, at low tide, should you want to emulate Moses crossing the Red Sea.

The Isles of Fundy—at least the principal ones—are *Campobello, Deer,* and *Grand Manan.* Most noted of the trio is Campobello. For many years, the Roosevelt family summered there in their 34-room Dutch Colonial house. It was at Campobello that Franklin D. Roosevelt spent his boyhood holidays, and where he contracted infantile paralysis in 1921. *Sunrise at Campobello,* both movie and play, brought this beautiful island a degree of fame way out of proportion to its size in the 1960s, and it continues popular. It is now linked by bridge to Lubec, Maine, and in 1964 the Canadian and American governments began—after a Washington meeting of Prime Minister Pearson and President Johnson—to develop an international park there and to restore the Roosevelt house. But much earlier, in 1946, it was at Campobello that the first memorial was erected to the memory of the late, much beloved President by his island neighbors. Now the house and grounds are known as Roosevelt International Park and operated by an international commission. Campobello Island is gained by the Roosevelt International Bridge from Lubec, Maine.

Deer Island, only a half hour by ferry from the mainland, is the site of what is said to be the world's largest lobster pound, and is not unlike even larger *Grand Manan,* whose northwestern shore is a great mass of dramatic cliffs, rising as much as four hundred feet above the surf. The museum in the Grand Harbour High School is noted for its remarkable bird collection.

Fundy National Park (near *Alma*) is one of two national parks in New Brunswick. (The other, being developed, is a tongue twister: *Kouchibouguac,* on the east coast.) Fundy is relatively small, as national parks go, but it's a honey of a place for families on vacation. Within its eighty square miles are an eight-mile coastal area on the Bay of Fundy, with beaches protected by the steep cliffs of the coves in which they are situated; a beautiful 9-hole golf course, tennis courts, a salt-water swimming pool, trails for trekking, bowling greens, an amphitheatre where shows are often presented, picnic and camping grounds, and places to stay.

Moncton is New Brunswick's second largest city and by far the leading French-speaking community of the province. (Non-French speakers should know that virtually everyone is bilingual.) Its location on the Petitcodiac River in the southeast has helped it become a major transport terminus on the Canadian National Railways route, and for airlines as well.

To see: The campus of the Université de Moncton (ex-St. Joseph's), with its museum of regional Acadian lore; the Moncton Civic Museum, in the colonnaded former city hall, and the early-nineteenth-century Free Meetinghouse, for long an interdenominational church. Just outside town is Magnetic Hill, which appears to defy the laws of gravity. Motorists, to test it, drive to its base, put their cars in neutral, turn off the motor, and presto, the car "coasts" uphill. The secret? The terrain of the area makes the hill seem to head in the opposite direction from what is the case. And to add to the illusion, there's a stream alongside the road which appears to be flowing uphill. But Moncton has still another freak of nature, known familiarly as The Bore. The Petitcodiac, a tidal river, flows into the head of Shepody Bay, and at low tide it is little more than a weak stream. But it is converted into a navigable river by the advent of a tidal wave, and in minutes the muddy river flats are buried by some thirty feet of rushing water. The secret? The Bay of Fundy's tides are among the world's highest, and the converging shores pressure the tidal waters into the mouth of the river. "The Bore" arrives twice daily.

Dorchester, also near Moncton, is the site of Keilor House, a superb early-nineteenth-century stone mansion, furnished in period and operated as a museum by the Westmoreland Historical Society.

Newcastle, north of Moncton, was the boyhood home of Lord Beaverbrook, whose father was a local Presbyterian minister. Beaverbrook embellished the main square, years later, with a charming gazebo and special lighting. The Presbyterian Manse, or parsonage, is now the town's library. Neighboring **Chatham** was the birthplace of Joseph Cunard, who was to found the Cunard Line; his family house still stands on Water Street. And there are Beaverbrook benefactions (he once practiced law here): The Town Hall and Civic Centre.

Caracquet, north of Moncton, is the home of the Centennial Museum of Acadian culture, and a new Acadian village restoration similar to the Kings Landing Museum-Village near Fredericton.

Shediac, about fifteen miles from Moncton, is the site of the best public beaches on the New Brunswick side of the Northumberland Strait. The terrain is dully flat and infinitely less appealing than in other regions of the province, but the bathing is good and facilities are convenient.

Fort Beauséjour National Historic Park, not far from Moncton, occupies the ruins of a French-built fort constructed in 1751. A museum on the site is its chief attraction. Nearby is the pleasant town of *Sackville,* best known for Mount Allison University and Canada's major overseas broadcasting station.

SHOPPING

New Brunswick does interesting things with handicrafts. It teaches weaving, ceramics, and other crafts at its Craft Centre in Fredericton. Along the coast, wood carvers create delicately turned white gulls and perch them on bits of driftwood. Some of the weaving—tartans and otherwise—is distinctive; there are ships in bottles, model ships, hooked rugs, ceramics, jewelry, local cheeses, and maple syrups. I have found the *Sea Captain's Loft* in **St. Andrews** to have excellent and tasteful selections. In **Saint John,** visit the *Handcraft and Tourist Information Centre* in the Admiral Beatty Hotel and *Clara J. Woodland* (28 Sydney Street). In **Fredericton** visit the *Craft House* (610 Queen Street), and outside of town, *Mn'gwon Indian Crafts* on the Trans-Canada Highway. Note also: *Artisanat Henri Nadeau* (Trans-Canada Highway, **Edmundston**); *Campobello Island Gift House* (Herring Cove Road, **Campobello Island**); *Chalet Shop* (Fundy National Park, **Alma**); *Villa Providence Craft Shop* (215 Main Street, **Shediac**);

and at **Gagetown,** the long-established *Loomcrafters Shop,* for locally handwoven textiles. For general shopping: nearly fifty stores at Fredericton Shopping Mall are customarily open until 10 P.M. daily; and also for general shopping: an *Eaton's* branch.

CREATURE COMFORTS

Saint John: The traditional style *Admiral Beatty,* on King Square (downtown) remains the old-reliable—230 rooms with bath, dining room, cocktail lounge, garage, and tourist information-craft center. Competing with the Admiral Beatty is the modern 129-room full-facility *Holiday Inn,* on Haymarket Square. The 98-room, fully licensed *Wandlyn Motor Inn,* one of an ever-expanding chain, is good, too. The *Colonial Inn,* 175 City Road, is well equipped and with a licensed restaurant. And the *White House Lodge Motor-Hotel* (with a popular licensed restaurant) remains a leader in Saint John West. Favored *restaurants* include the *Riviera* (seafood) and the same management's summer-only restaurant at Reversing Falls; and the dining rooms of the *Admiral Beatty Hotel* and *White House Lodge.* **Fredericton's** long-time leader is the *Lord Beaverbrook*—heart-of-town, with 150 rooms, all with either bath or shower as well as color and cable TV, dining room, lounge with nightly entertainment, and coffee shop, as well as free on-premise parking. The 74-room *Wandlyn Motor Inn,* 58 Prospect Street, is fairly comfortable and with a licensed restaurant. The low-slung *Diplomat Motor Hotel* (225 Woodstock Road) has 80 units, a restaurant and cocktail lounge. *Colonial Inn,* 72 Regent Street, has 49 rooms and a licensed restaurant. Eighty-room *Keddy's Motor Inn* (Forest Hill), has a licensed restaurant and lounge. Two top restaurant bets are the *Wandlyn Motor Inn Dining Room* and the *Coffee Mill Restaurant,* at Fredericton Shopping Mall. **Oromocto:** The *Oromocto Hotel* features bath with all 50 rooms, some housekeeping units, licensed restaurant, and swimming pool. In **Grand Falls** the *Près du Lac Motel* has 70 units, and a licensed dining room and lounge. **Edmundston's** leaders include the *Wandlyn Motor Inn* (Trans-Canada Highway at Canada Road), with 86 rooms, licensed restaurant, and lounge; and the 47-unit *Lynn Motel* (unlicensed and without proper restaurant, but good withal), at 30 Church Street. **St. Stephen:** *Loon Bay Lodge* is a long-popular onetime private summer home on the St. Croix River twenty miles north of town, with 8 rooms; it's unlicensed. The *Wandlyn Motor Inn* (90 King Street) has 38 units and a licensed dining room. **St. Andrew's:** The drawing card here remains the *Algonquin Hotel,* in recent years owned by the provincial government although still operated by CP Hotels, and a product of extensive, expensive—and tasteful —refurbishing, to the point where all 200 rooms now have private baths. This is a lovely, long, rambling half-timbered summer resort of the old school. There used to be many like it in the northeastern U.S. and the Maritimes; more's the pity, very few remain. The Algonquin has a capacious licensed dining room, an amusing pub-lounge called Dick Turpin's, entertainment, dancing, a pair of golf courses, tennis courts, a heated pool. Summer only, of course. And a great place to unwind. In town is smaller, less elaborate but still inviting *Shiretown Inn;* all of its nearly 30 rooms now have private baths. There's a licensed dining room as well as the Smuggler's Wharf Restaurant, on the harbor. **Isles of Fundy: Campobello Island's** best bets are both smallish but with licensed restaurants: *Friar's Bay Motor Lodge* and the *Ponderosa Motel.* On **Deer Island,** there's the *45th Parallel Motel,* small and with an unlicensed restaurant. On **Grand Manan Island,** there are the newer 22-unit *Surfside Motel,* and the older 38-room *Marathon Hotel;* both have unlicensed restaurants. **Fundy National Park's** traditional trio carries on. All are unlicensed and without restaurants. Take your choice of the *Alpine Chalets,* 24 units, some with housekeeping facilities; *Fundy View Motel* (21 housekeeping units), or *Fundy Park Chalets* (29 units, all but seven housekeeping-equipped). At park-straddling **Alma,** there is additional accommodation, including the 16-room *Parkland Hotel,* with a licensed restaurant and lounge, and the 34-unit *Alpine Motor Inn,* unlicensed and without restaurant. **Moncton** is the site of the province's exceptional *Hotel Beauséjour,* one of the newer links of the nationwide Canadian National chain, with a contemporary façade and good-looking, traditional interiors. The 212 rooms reflect the side-by-side New Brunswick cultures: Acadian (French) and Loyalist (English), with décor in each chamber of one or the other motifs. Public rooms are all handsome—a mod-look coffee shop, the Acadian-style L'Auberge; a roof-top dine-dance room called Cloud 9 (on the office building connected with the hotel), and the most elegant of the lot, the Windjammer, with rich mahogany paneling and nautical brass fittings; interesting places for drinks, as well, and a high-up outdoor pool-cum-view, as well as meeting and convention facilities that are the best in the Maritimes, along with those of CN's Nova Scotian Hotel in Halifax. Also relatively recent in Moncton is *Howard Johnson's Motor Lodge,* at Magnetic Hill; it has 96 comfortable rooms, licensed Lamplighter Restaurant, Wayside Cocktail Lounge, coffee shop, heated indoor pool, and sauna. The 77-room *Wandlyn Motor Inn,* also at Magnetic Hill, has a restaurant and cocktail lounge. *Keddy's Motor Inn* (Shediac Road), has 83 rooms, a restaurant, and lounge. *Sackville's Marshlands Inn* is a smallish, traditional favorite, with a licensed restaurant. *Cy's Restaurant* remains a top Moncton choice for seafood.

Newfoundland

LA TERRE-NEUVE

Best times for a visit: *The temperatures—even in winter—are not extreme. Summer is, of course, delightful; June and July average sixty degrees, but days often are considerably warmer. August brings higher average readings, and sunshine*

hours can easily zoom to the eighties and even nineties, but nights are always cool. During the cold-weather months the temperature rarely goes below zero, and is usually well above that. The southeastern coast is famous for its fog. Spring arrives late—in May, and autumn is brief, generally confining itself to October. **Transportation:** *The fully paved Newfoundland sector of the Trans-Canada Highway extends 587 miles, from Port-aux-Basques, on the southwestern coast, to St. John's, on the east coast. Major roads are to be found in the Avalon Peninsula, on which St. John's is situated, others in the central and western portions, a number leading off of the Trans-Canada Highway. The Labrador region's main road links Goose Bay and Churchill Falls. Travelers wanting to motor through Newfoundland enter by way of Nova Scotia. From Sydney, in that province, they board—with their cars—Canadian National ferries for a nine-hour journey to Port-aux-Basques, where the Trans-Canada Highway begins. Port-aux-Basques is also the terminus for CN's bus route across the Trans-Canada Highway to St. John's. The bus takes some thirteen hours; there are six en route stops, Corner Brook, Grand Falls and Gander among them. Air Canada serves St. John's, Stephenville, and Gander on domestic routes, and also links Newfoundland directly with Europe by means of flights from Gander to Prestwick (Scotland) and London. Québecair links Montreal with Labrador. Eastern Provincial Airways connects a number of Newfoundland communities on intraprovincial routes and joins that province with New Brunswick; it flies also to Labrador, Nova Scotia, and Prince Edward Island and Montreal. An interesting way to see coastal Newfoundland and Labrador, after arrival, is by Canadian National steamers. The catch here is that the better accommodations are so limited that they're booked a year—or even two years—in advance. CN ships and those of Lake & Lake Ltd. link Fortune, Newfoundland, with St. Pierre, the major island of the little French Overseas Territory of St. Pierre and Miquelon (to which one may fly via Air St. Pierre from Sydney, Nova Scotia, which is described at the end of the Nova Scotia chapter).* **Having a drink:** *Leading hotels and motels*

have cocktail lounges and licensed dining rooms; better restaurants are licensed, too. Liquor is sold in government
stores. **Further information:** Newfoundland Department of
Tourism, Confederation Building, St. John's; Agent-General
of Newfoundland, 60 Trafalgar Square, London; Canadian
Government Office of Tourism, Ottawa and branches.

INTRODUCING NEWFOUNDLAND

Newfoundland is, to sum up even before beginning, extraordinary. It is Canada's newest province, but it had been, before
confederation, Britain's oldest colony. It is closer to Europe, geographically, than any other part of North America, but it was in
many ways, until fairly recently in its long history, one of the most
isolated of the continent's regions. Its rich fishing grounds, instead
of promoting colonization, were the cause of a policy—perhaps
unique in history—that discouraged settlement. It was without a
road linking its east and west coasts until the middle of the twentieth century, but received the first transatlantic cable in 1866 and
the first transatlantic wireless message in 1901, and it was from
Newfoundland's capital that the first successful transatlantic flight
was undertaken in 1919. Sparsely populated itself (there are about
six hundred thousand Newfoundlanders), it is landlord of a region
—Labrador—more than twice its size, and still sparsely inhabited,
even though it was probably the first bit of North America to have
been visited by Europeans—the Vikings—almost a thousand years
ago.

Oldest colony, youngest province: Newfoundland is still so new
to Canada that many of its residents still refer to fellow Canadian
provinces as "abroad." And many of the residents of those other
provinces—not to mention most Americans and other foreigners—
have not yet even learned how to pronounce Newfoundland. It
rhymes, if you are one of the uninitiated, with "under*stand*."

It was given its name by John Cabot, who landed there in 1497.
(Nova Scotians—and some historians—will tell you he first came
ashore on Cape Breton Island, in that province, but let's go along
with the Newfoundlanders, at least in this chapter.) Cabot was followed, in 1500, by Corte Real, a Portuguese who surveyed a por-

tion of the Newfoundland east coast and who, like Cabot, took back to Europe tales of the fishing riches in Newfoundland waters. Lack of modern communications notwithstanding, the word got around in seafood circles, and before long Spanish, French, Portuguese, and English fishing craft were using Newfoundland's natural harbors as bases for their operations. Nobody, though, much bothered with the flattish interior, and even though Cabot had made a second visit a decade after his first, it was not until 1583 that Sir Humphrey Gilbert formally claimed Newfoundland as a domain of Elizabeth I. And so began the settlement of Newfoundland, which has had its coat of arms—still in use—well over three centuries; they were granted by Royal Letters Patent in 1637, by Charles I (just a dozen years before he was beheaded). As with other colonies throughout the New World, it was not an easy matter, physically or politically. The English settlers had to contend not only with the French—who contested British claims to Newfoundland—but with powerful London-based fishing merchants who sent their fleets from English ports and—because they feared a substantial community on the spot might break their monopoly—conned the English government into forbidding permanent settlement.

The French are ousted: As a result, St. John's and numerous other communities on the magnificent east coast of Newfoundland came into being illegally—and therefore more slowly than might otherwise have been the case. Moreover, the French, whose stronghold was at Placentia, made nuisances of themselves with their proclivity for burning English settlements. (St. John's had it twice—in 1696 and again in 1705.)

Indeed, from 1708 until 1713 the French were virtual rulers of the Newfoundland coast, and it took the terms of the Treaty of Utrecht to oust them—if only temporarily—in 1713. They tried again, for the last time, in 1762 when the famed Lord Jeffrey Amherst (the "soldier of the king" for whom Amherst College in Massachusetts is named) repelled them at Signal Hill, now a National Historic Park, in St. John's. (But until as recently as 1904 the French had special fishing rights in Newfoundland waters, and the little islands of St. Pierre and Miquelon in that region still fly the *tricolore,* as a proud overseas territory of the French Republic.)

Newfoundland, despite its seniority at the Colonial Office, didn't rate a permanent governor until 1817. It was allowed to elect a legislative council of its own a few decades later, and in 1854 gained responsible government. In 1869 the colony turned down for the first time (it accepted only after the fourth) a proposal for confederation with Canada. The colony did, however, gain self-government, but it continued to have difficult times. Fishing had increased, lumbering and mining were developed, and there had long since been gains in the population through continued immigration from England and (as a result of the potato famine) from Ireland. The colony contributed heavily, particularly in terms of manpower, to World War I. Labrador—110,000 square miles—was officially placed under Newfoundland's jurisdiction in 1927 (although it had been given rights to that region's coast in 1763).

Government by a committee: The Depression of the 1930s was almost more than Newfoundland's marginal economy could weather, and in 1934 it had to appeal to Britain for aid. Britain responded by placing Newfoundland under a commission form of government. It was ruled by a committee of six, three from the United Kingdom, the remainder, Newfoundlanders. The period was not entirely a happy one—there was much dissension—but advances were made in education, health, and welfare services, and the economy improved.

With the advent of World War II, Allied eyes turned to Newfoundland. Its strategic importance made it a key locale. It was on the convoy route to Europe. It became the site of U.S. bases. It was in Newfoundland waters—off the coast of the venerable town of Placentia—that Roosevelt and Churchill drafted the Atlantic Charter in 1941.

The war not only brought prosperity to Newfoundland for the first time in its long history, it also oriented Newfoundland away from Europe and toward its North American neighbors—Canada and the United States.

With the coming of peace, Newfoundland found itself on better economic footing than ever before, and the question of its future governmental status presented itself. In 1946 a convention was called to delineate the choices: return to self-government, retain commission government, or become a Canadian province. But it took almost two years for the convention to complete its work, and it was not until 1948 that the voters had a chance to express their opinion, in a referendum that proved to be inconclusive; none of the three alternatives gained a clear majority. At a second referendum, later that year, confederation was the winner by a narrow margin, and the Terms of Union were signed in Ottawa on December 2, 1948, by the then Prime Minister, Louis St. Laurent, and the dynamic personality who was the province's first premier, Joseph Smallwood.

Smallwood and confederation: Premier "Joey" Smallwood's government took office on March 31, 1949. Using the no-nonsense slogan, "Grow up or Die," and with considerable help from the federal government, it tremendously improved the lot of the New-foundlander by accelerating and diversifying the economy, raising the standard of living, bettering transport facilities, building new schools, hospitals, and clinics, and giving the Newfoundlander sub-stantial reason to hope for a future that will entail less of the strug-gle and hardship that for so long has been his lot.

Labrador's great mineral riches are being exploited. Attractive new residential sections have sprouted in St. John's and other towns. The fully paved Trans-Canada Highway makes it possible to drive from one end of the province to the other. New public buildings have gone up. Tourism is being developed as an industry. The Newfoundlander—hard-working, self-sufficient—has emerged from a semi-isolation of centuries to the point where, in 1972, the province's voters felt secure enough to turn out Mr. Smallwood's Liberal Party—that had been in power nearly a quarter-century—and vote in the Conservatives. Frank Moores be-came the second Premier. Economic problems remain; more than half of provincial government funds come from Ottawa. Withal, today's visitor is charmed by the sincerity of the Newfoundland welcome, warmed by the Irish lilt or the Devon dialect distinctive to Newfoundland English, charmed by the whimsicality of the place names, excited by the exhilarating beauty of a seacoast surpassed by no other on any other continent.

YOUR VISIT TO NEWFOUNDLAND

Modern Newfoundland had its first taste of playing host on a substantial scale during World War II, when it came to know thousands of visitors from Canada (then still a foreign country) and the United States. But not even the experience of almost doubling as one vast military-naval base jaded the appetite of Newfoundlanders for company. They're as gracious and hospitable as ever they were. They want you to take them as you find them, for they're not yet in a position—with relatively few exceptions—to offer you the de luxe kind of accommodation afforded in most other provinces. But there are compensations, and before you go you would do well to study a Newfoundland map, if only for the place names. Let me cite just a few. There's Come-by-Chance, Run-by-Guess, and Blow-me-Down. Reflecting the Newfoundlander's difficult way of life, one finds Gripe Point, Famish Gut, and Empty Basket. Happier times? Well, choose among Heart's Desire, Sweet Bay, Little Paradise, Angel's Cove. Foreign origins? In Newfoundland, there's an English Harbour, a Portugal Cove, a Frenchmen's Cove, and, of course, an Ireland's Eye. There's Tea Cove and Sugar Loaf, Green Island and White Bay, Cow Head and Cat Gut, Goose Bay, of course, and Gander Bay, too; Petticoat Island and Stocking Harbour. But there have been, sad to relate, unimaginative Newfoundlanders; it's them we thank for Harbour Harbour and Nameless Cove.

There are a wealth of expressions that Newfoundlanders have brought into the English language: A fisherman is one rogue, a merchant is many . . . Empty vessels loom biggest . . . Far-off cows wear long horns . . . Pigs may fly, but they are very unlikely birds . . . In a leaky punt, 'tis always best to hug the shore . . . Wait a fair wind and you'll get one . . .

And there are individual words that are Newfoundland's own: ballyrag—to abuse; binicky—ill-tempered; glutch—to swallow with difficulty. An omadhaun is a foolish person . . . a gilderoy is a proud person . . . a jackeen is a rascally boy . . . an angishore is a weak, miserable person. And a bostoon is an ignorant person. But I don't think you need count on being called any of the last-mentioned during a Newfoundland visit, the core of which should be the capital, St. John's, and the surrounding Avalon Peninsula.

St. John's: I've already given a pronunciation lesson for Newfoundland (I repeat if you weren't paying attention: it rhymes with under*stand*). Now I offer a combination spelling-geography lesson. St. John's is the capital of Newfoundland; note that "St." is *always* abbreviated and "John's" is possessive. However, the major city of New Brunswick is Saint John. To avoid confusion, "saint" is *always* spelled out with the New Brunswick city and John, you'll note, has no apostrophe or final "s." Pronunciation? The Newfoundlander, with his Anglo-Irish origins, often pronounces it *sintjohn's,* and so do many other Canadians.

But what's it like? Well, it calls itself the oldest settlement in North America for, according to tradition, John Cabot, after having landed at Cape Bonavista in 1547, sailed into its harbor and named it for St. John's Day—on which he arrived. Sir Humphrey Gilbert, who came in 1583, no doubt traversed the waterfront path at the harbor's edge, which the locals term the continent's oldest thoroughfare. But alas and alack, there is very little else left of old St. John's, for it has probably endured more major fires than any other city of consequence in North America. The French burned it twice, in 1696 and in 1705; and there were other non-military—but nonetheless disastrous—fires, in 1816, 1817, 1846, and 1892. As a result, St. John's is largely Victorian, Edwardian, and thereafter—in its architecture. But its setting is nothing short of magnificent. It is built on steepish hills leading down to a perfectly splendid enclosed harbor. From the harbor to the open Atlantic, ships pass through the channel known as the Narrows, which is flanked on one side by the towering summit of Signal Hill, the site over the centuries of a succession of forts that guard the approach to the city and where, in 1901, Marconi received the first wireless message. Now a National Historic Park, Signal Hill affords one a splendid view of the city. The dramatic cliffs of the coastline and the blue-green sea appear to stretch endlessly. There are remains of the old forts and gun emplacements. A fine view is afforded from Cabot Tower, erected at the turn of the century as a memorial to the island's discoverer, but one does well to stroll about the hilltop for other perspectives, tarry a bit to watch ships wending their way in and out of port, and take in the exhibits at the Ranger-attended Visitor Center, for historic perspective. And note the signs indicating that London is 2,016 miles east distant, and New York, 1,005 miles southwest.

The older sections of the town—which cluster about Water Street, the main thoroughfare that hugs the harbor—put one in mind of Europe more than Canada. Aside from the steeples of churches, the effect is mostly of a mosaic of gaily painted frame houses and neat, hilly streets, one of which—Duckworth—is the site of some well-restored houses. Life is still not as fast-paced as in other Canadian urban centers. No one is in a great hurry—hurrying wouldn't pay, anyway, on such steep terrain—and it is not difficult to feel, here, that one is in a far more foreign place than Canada.

The oldest principal building is Government House, an early-nineteenth-century Georgian-style stone mansion on a hill of its own with a view of the newer sections of town. Now the official residence of the Lieutenant Governor (the provincial counterpart of the Governor-General), it had, before confederation, been home to a long line of colonial governors. The Colonial Building, dating from 1850, has a fine Greek-design portico. It is now the headquarters of the Provincial Archives and open to the public, and it served from the time of its construction until 1960 as the principal government building. Have a look at both the ex-Assembly and Legislative Council Chambers. The stairway, leading from the foyer to the upper floor, is very grand.

The huge, twin-towered St. John the Baptist Cathedral (Roman Catholic) was finished in 1855, at which time it no doubt could accommodate half the population of the city. Its interior is one of the finest of any church in Canada—with a superb Renaissance-style ceiling, a striking canopy-covered altar, and a magnificent situation affording the best-in-town vistas of the Narrows.

The Anglican Cathedral went up in 1897 to replace an earlier structure destroyed by fire. It is a tasteful Gothic specimen with an adjacent Chapter House whose contents include a gold communion service presented by King William IV. St. Thomas Church (Anglican) somehow or other managed to escape the fires despite its having been built in 1836. The Hanoverian Coat of Arms of the then-British Royal Family still is displayed within its sanctuary. St. Patrick's Roman Catholic Church (1864) is another interesting oldie. Almost every town has its war memorial. I mention St. John's only because it honors the Royal Newfoundland Regiment which, in a solitary day in 1916, lost almost every one of its members in battle.

New St. John's? There is the harbor-front Atlantic Place complex on Water Street. The Confederation Building is named for the union with Canada, and houses the unicameral Newfoundland

Legislature, the executive offices of the Provincial Government, and the interesting Newfoundland Naval and Military Museum, in the observation tower. (It is not to be confused with the inviting, old-fashioned hodgepodge that is the Newfoundland Museum, downtown; its catch-all exhibits depict bits and pieces of life in the province from the time of the now-extinct Beothuck Indians.)

The Memorial University embraces a modern 120-acre campus near the Confederation Building and honors Newfoundland's World War I and II dead. Of especial visitor interest are the Canadian paintings in its Art Gallery. Most spectacular of the newer St. John's buildings is the Arts and Culture Centre, the principal centennial project of the provincial government. Handsome, of brown brick, it includes a 1,000-seat theatre, an art gallery with changing exhibitions, the town's main public library, and a top-rank restaurant. Contemporary, too, is the spiffy City Hall (1970); it houses, among much else, a tower with a digital clock, and the helpful St. John's Tourist Commission.

The Avalon Peninsula, on which St. John's is situated, is about as beautiful an area as one can find in eastern North America, and I suggest that you earmark enough time in the capital to allow for some excursions. It is possible that by the time you arrive in Newfoundland you will have had a look at the Nova Scotia coast, or at least heard its praises told. Well and good. But Newfoundland's coast—considerably less publicized—is by no means a carbon copy. Where the fishing villages of Nova Scotia are charming, Newfoundland's are striking. Nova Scotian villages and fisherfolk are a pleasure to meet, but Newfoundland's have a ruddy, rugged, weatherbeaten quality that comes of this province's peculiarly isolated quality. There remains the terrain of the Avalon Peninsula— the magnificent vistas afforded from the rocky headlands which shelter, way below, the natural coves upon whose shores are the fisherfolks' little settlements. The contrast of neat frame houses— painted stark white and bright blue and vivid yellow and deep red —with that of soaring gray cliffs and the broad expanse of the Atlantic, is not to be duplicated anywhere else in Canada.

A pair of suggested *half-day tours:* One takes you directly north of St. John's, along the striking *Marine Drive* to *Outer Cove,* into the interior at *Torbay,* through green valleys interspersed with farms, to Pouch Cove, and beyond to *Cape St. Francis.* Alternatively, go due south from the capital to *Petty Harbour, Bay Bulls, Witless Bay, Mobile, Tors Cove,* and *La Manche*—each a dramatically situated fishing village, one more spectacularly placed than the other.

A *longer trip*—plan on a full day—will take you on the *Conception Bay* route—west across the peninsula from St. John's to *Topsail* (around which are beaches where you might want to bathe or picnic), then south along Conception Bay to its base at *Holyrood* and north, along its coast, through *Avondale, Brigus, Cupids* (a National Historic Site, where John Guy of Bristol established the first officially chartered Newfoundland settlement in 1610), *Port de Grave* (a breathtakingly lovely hamlet at the tip of a fingerlike peninsula), and *Harbour Grace,* early take-off point for transatlantic planes.

You might want to go farther afield, along the coast of Trinity Bay, through that delightfully named trio of villages—*Heart's Content, Heart's Desire,* and *Heart's Delight,* with *Whitbourne* your destination. Even more distant from the capital is the ancient French fortress town of *Placentia* on Placentia Bay, still with remains of the old forts and a seventeenth-century church.

Terra Nova is one of a pair of Newfoundland's national parks—a 153-square-mile preserve traversed by the Trans-Canada Highway on the eastern part of the island. The terrain offers one a blend of Newfoundland scenery—from the shores of Newman Sound through the forests, barren land, sparkling streams, and quiet lakes. There are fishing and modern accommodations. **Gros Morne**—the other national park—is newer (1970) and on the Gulf of St. Lawrence, on the west coast. It's named for 2,649-foot Mt. Gros Morne, of the Long Range Mountains. There's a Ranger-staffed visitor center, as well as dune-fringed beaches, interior lakes, salmon streams, and nature trails. And there's wildlife to be seen, if you're lucky.

Gander is perhaps Newfoundland's most visited point. At least it was in pre-jet days when transatlantic airlines of many nations touched down at its international airport, a then major fueling station. The airport became so popular that the government built a handsome new air terminal, dedicated by Queen Elizabeth in 1959. No sooner was it finished than jets replaced piston planes, and Gander's airport is now bypassed more often than not, although it remains in operation both for local regional services and as take-off point for transatlantic Air Canada flights to Prestwick (Scotland) and London.

Grand Falls is one of the province's major towns, thanks to the Anglo-Newfoundland Development Company's huge pulp and paper mills. Indeed, the town was created to serve the mills. The founders were Lord Rothermere and Lord Northcliffe, that remarkable brother team who founded the London *Daily Mail* at the turn of this century, introducing mass journalism to the United Kingdom. Grand Falls and its paper mills were established to supply their periodicals with newsprint. Grand Falls was one of the first modern company towns, well planned and attractive. Mill employees—all through the long, economically difficult period encountered by Newfoundland—were well paid and prospered. There is good fishing in the nearby Exploits River, and moose and caribou hunting nearby.

Corner Brook, Newfoundland's second city, is the metropolis of its western coast and owes its prosperity, like Grand Falls, to industry. In this case it is the Bowater mills, the largest pulp and paper mills in the world and open to the public for tours. There are, as well, cement and gypsum plants. Corner Brook, with good accommodations and facilities, is a pleasant stopover point and has become known for skiing and its Marble Mountain. From it, one can make excursions to *Bonne Bay,* reminiscent of the Scottish highlands and perhaps the prettiest point on the western coast, the nearby *Gros Morne National Park, Sir Richard Squires Provincial Park,* and *Pistolet Bay,* at the northern tip of the island. To the south is *Stephenville,* a small but handsomely situated coastal town whose unique seaside airport serves Corner Brook.

Port-aux-Basques: The western coast's southernmost town is of note principally because it is the terminus of the ferry from Sydney, Nova Scotia, and the starting point of both the Trans-Canada Highway's Newfoundland portion and the Canadian National Railway route that spans the province. Its name derives from the sixteenth century, when Basque fishermen from France settled it. Its principal occupation, aside from transport activities, is fish processing; there are fish factories within its confines as well as in the amalgamated community of *Channel.* Perhaps the principal point of interest is a monument to the 133 passengers who were killed aboard the SS *Caribou,* a ferry on the Sydney-Port-aux-Basques run, when it was torpedoed in 1942 by a German submarine.

Labrador, Newfoundland's New Frontier, has a coastline of more than forty-five hundred miles. Mostly low-lying and rocky, it is dotted with lakes, ponds, and forests. It is just beginning to be exploited by anglers and hunters, and its tremendous mineral resources—mostly iron ore—are now being mined in the area of the region's two modern boom towns—*Labrador City* and *Wabush,* in the southwest near the Quebec frontier. From this area comes something like 40 per cent of the all-Canada iron-ore total. *Churchill Falls,* to the northeast, is the site of a gigantic hydro-power project. The airport at *Goose Bay,* developed during World War II by the Royal Canadian Air Force as a military base, remains very much in operation for civilian purposes. Elsewhere, the sparse population lives mostly in coastal fishing villages, although there are minorities of Indian trappers in the interior and of Eskimo fishermen-sealers-hunters in the north. The major roads are around Goose Bay and in the mining areas of the west. The one railway runs from the mining town of *Sept-Îles, Quebec,* north across the western tip of Labrador to *Schefferville,* of interest to anglers because of the fine fishing in its neighborhood, out of lodges and tent camps. As for hunting: The bagging of caribou becomes increasingly popular in this area.

Seeing Newfoundland and Labrador by coastal steamer: What with much of its populace clustered in tiny fishing settlements along some six thousand miles of coast, and with relatively little settlement in the interior, Newfoundlanders travel extensively by ship, and considerable freight is transported in this way. Canadian National serves the area with a fleet of steamers, all of them containing minimal de luxe accommodation. Most of the ships begin their cruises in St. John's, but others depart from Argentia, Lewisporte, and Placentia. None of the numerous routes takes more than eighteen days round trip. On some, though, one may conveniently go one way by boat and return by either air or surface transport. All well and good. But. And there is a but: the good cabins on these ships are booked a year or more in advance. So if you want to see Newfoundland in this fashion, start planning way, way ahead.

Hunting and fishing: I have alluded to these major New-foundland-Labrador pastimes earlier in the chapter, and I mention them again at this point only to emphasize their importance in the province's tourism picture. The angler goes quite wild here—with species ranging from tuna to lake trout, and the hunter is in terri-tory through which roam moose, caribou, rabbit, and a variety of game birds. If you're interested, you do well to write, in advance of your trip, for free hunting and fishing booklets from the New-foundland Department of Tourism.

SHOPPING

Cut off for so long and in so many ways from the rest of Can-ada, Newfoundland's craft tradition remains alive, and continues to receive official encouragement. The result is a variety of in-teresting souvenirs. You'll find tiny objects—paperweights and the like—covered in sealskin, a variety of hand-knitted, hand-woven, and hand-embroidered goods, jewelry of the mineral known as Labradorite—as well as other local minerals—hooked rugs and mats, handsome fishing-boat replicas, fine hand-wrought carved mini-miniatures of the unique Newfoundland wood-and-stone anchors called killicks, and among much else, notepaper decorated with hand-blocked Newfoundland scenes. In **St. John's,** I am par-tial to *The Cod Jigger* (144 Duckworth Street). It's a co-operative supplied by some 300 artisans, with pottery, jewelry of the local Labradorite stone, hand-woven caps, and the unique New-foundland one-finger—or Baymen's—mittens, locally compiled cookbooks, among much else. Prices are right, too. Also good is *St. Mary's Bay Crafts* (28 Cochrane Street) with an interesting mix of hand-made things, and a commendable sense of style. A specialty is work in deerskin created by Indians in Labrador. Up-stairs in the same house is the gallery of the *Art Association of Newfoundland and Labrador,* with paintings, drawings, and sculp-ture of the province's artists—much of it worthy. *The New-foundland Weavery* (170 Duckworth Street) specializes in pottery but vends other crafts, as well. *The Gallery* (124 Water Street) is an interesting source of oil paintings and water colors, sculptures, and sketches. South of St. John's, at **Ferryland,** is the *Lighthouse*

Pottery; everything is locally made of local clay. West of St. John's, there are the *Corner Stone,* at **South Dildo** on Trinity Bay, and *Asdel Art Studio and Gallery,* at **Brigus** on Conception Bay. North of St. John's, at **Arnolds Cove,** the *Killick* is an important source of hand-fashioned knitwear—macramé, sweaters, afghans, shawls, place mats, and the like. In **Corner Brook,** *Island Pottery* is worth a stop for ceramics. All of the major towns have modern stores for more prosaic shopping needs. St. John's *Avalon Mall,* the province's largest shopping center, has half a hundred stores and services.

CREATURE COMFORTS

St. John's: If the elderly, albeit reasonably well-refurbished, *Hotel Newfoundland* is the least luxurious of the nationwide Canadian National chain, it is by no means to be despised, and it remains, for me at least, the premier choice in the capital. It's central (a harbor view from many rooms), with a capacious lobby, 130 comfortable rooms (including some suites) all with bath, an agreeable restaurant, and a pair of bar-lounges. The ambience is friendly, solid, and unpretentious, reflecting the better qualities of the city in which it is located. *The Battery Motel* is splendidly situated on Signal Hill, with smashing views of town and harbor. The pity is its cinder-block construction. Still, the 100-plus bedrooms are not at all bad (all have bath), there's an indoor pool, a sauna, an inviting cocktail lounge, and the Harbour Room—one of the best restaurants in town, with an exceptional wine cellar. The older *Kenmount Motel,* under the same management as the Battery, remains a reliable choice, well-maintained, with nearly 40 comfortable rooms, restaurant, and lounge. You would not call the *Hotel St. John's* beautiful, but it is clean and contemporary, with 80 kitchen-and-bath-equipped units, restaurant, and lounge. Outside of town, on Portugal Cove Road, is the esthetically unlovely *Holiday Inn.* Still, there is no arguing its facilities—190 spick-and-span rooms with bath, restaurant, lounge, even a little coffee shop. Eating in the capital can be pleasurable. Of the hotels, the top two as regards dining rooms, are the *Battery* and the *Newfoundland.* Of the independent restaurants, *Woodstock Colonial Inn* is consid-

ered the leader, hands down, with prix-fixe dinners that embrace
five courses, not one but two wines, the lot preceded by a cham-
pagne cocktail and topped off by a liqueur. The Colonial is seven
miles out of town on Route 3; dinner only, and if you are
culinarily daring, ask for seal flippers—a house specialty. *Act 3,*
in the handsome Newfoundland Arts and Culture Centre complex,
is smallish and mod in look, and a happy choice for lunch (legisla-
tors and top-rank civil servants from the nearby Confederation
Building frequent this place) or dinner, perhaps in connection with
a performance. First class, as regards ambience, fare, and wines.
And a good place to try the widely esteemed Newfoundland cod
tongues and/or fillets. Downtown's *Starboard Quarter,* overlooking the harbor in the Royal Trust Building, is adequate for lunch,
possibly more interesting for dinner. After-dark spots include the
Belmont pub—lots of local color and fun here, and the *Strand
Lounge,* at Avalon Mall Shopping Center, where the emphasis is
on singing with a Newfie-Irish lilt, and who can resist that combination? **Gander:** The *Albatross Hotel* leads. It has 111 rooms and
9 motel units (all with private bath), a restaurant, and cocktail
lounge. There is also the 64-room *Holiday Inn,* with restaurant,
coffee shop, lounge, and pool. In **Grand Falls,** consider the *Mount
Peyton Hotel*—75 rooms with bath, restaurant, cocktail lounge,
pool, and congenial management. **Corner Brook's** half-timbered
Glynmill Inn remains the traditional leader—66 attractive rooms
with bath, the best restaurant in the region (specialty: seafood),
and an inviting cocktail lounge that is a major congregating spot.
The 104-room *Holiday Inn* is well equipped, with dining room,
coffee shop, lounge, and pool. **Port-aux-Basques:** The *Grand Bay
Motel* has nearly 30 rooms, each with bath, and a dining room and
cocktail lounge. **Stephenville:** *Hotel Stephenville's* 25 rooms all
have private shower. There is a restaurant and cocktail lounge.
Other worth-noting places to stay include: **Black Duck's** *Dhoon
Lodge* (on Route 460), small (6 motel units and 5 cabins, all with
private shower) but well regarded, with restaurant and cocktail
lounge; **Deer Lake's** *Deer Lake Motel* (27 rooms all with bath,
restaurant, cocktail lounge); **Traytown's** *Traytown Tourist Cabins*
(10 units with private shower, no restaurant or lounge); **Clarenville's** *Holiday Inn* (Trans-Canada Highway, Route 230), with 64
rooms with bath, restaurant, coffee shop, cocktail lounge, pool;

Marystown's *Motel Mortier* (Routes 210 and 220), 78 rooms with bath, restaurant, cocktail lounge; and **Fortune's** *Clawbonnie Lodge* (14 units, licensed dining room). In **Labrador,** leaders include **Wabush's** *Sir Wilfred Grenfell Hotel* (52 of whose 69 rooms have private bath, restaurant, cocktail lounge), and **Happy Valley's** *Hotel Goose,* with private baths in 21 of the 29 rooms, restaurant, and cocktail lounge. Worth a try for the name alone.

Northwest Territories

LES TERRITOIRES DU NORD-OUEST

Best times for a visit: *For the southern part of the Territories, summer consists of June, July, and August, during which time days are warm and sunny (in the sixties and seventies) and nights cooler. Winters are long and severely*

cold; sixty below is not uncommon even in the south. In much of the region, there is virtually no spring or autumn. Rainfall is generally light, humidity is low, and during the height of the summer—this is Midnight Sun country—there is daylight round the clock. Mosquitoes and black flies can be bothersome, to put it mildly, and one is wise to have along insect repellent and a headnet. **Transportation:** *The Territories' only highway—the Mackenzie route—extends from Grimshaw, 320 miles north of Edmonton in Alberta, to Yellowknife, on the northern shore on Great Slave Lake. The gravel-surfaced road embraces 302 miles within the Northwest Territories, and passes through Enterprise, Hay River, Fort Providence, and Rae, en route to Yellowknife. Canadian Coachways operate buses between Edmonton and Hay River; N.W.T. Coachlines buses connect Hay River with Yellowknife. The bigger communities have car-rental firms. Otherwise, unless one travels by dogsled or boat, the only other means of transport is airplane. Pacific Western Airlines flies from Edmonton to major communities in the western portion of the Territories—including Fort Smith, Hay River, Yellowknife, and Inuvik. Transair flies from Winnipeg via Churchill, Manitoba, to Yellowknife, and smaller places like Coral Harbour, Baker Lake, and Rankin Inlet. Nordair flies from Montreal to Frobisher Bay and other Baffin Island points. Northward Airlines connects Inuvik with many Territories settlements. Northwest Territorial Airways links Yellowknife with certain Territories points, as does Ptarmigan Airways with still others. Private charter lines serve many points.* **Having a drink:** *Licensed dining rooms, cocktail lounges, and beer parlors (men only) are to be found in the major towns, along with retail liquor stores.* **Further information:** *Travelarctic (the Division of Tourism of the Government of the Northwest Territories), Yellowknife, Northwest Territories; Canadian Government Office of Tourism, Ottawa and branches. (Away from the larger settlements within the Territories, the local station of the Royal Canadian Mounted Police is a good source of information. Indeed, travelers embarking on trips into the wilderness by private* *plane or boat do well to leave their itineraries with the nearest R.C.M.P. post.*)

INTRODUCING
THE NORTHWEST TERRITORIES

We tend to think of Alaska—largest of the United States—as a vast, sparsely populated region. And with nearly 587,000 square miles and a population of some 300,000, it is just that. But in contrast to the Northwest Territories it's almost crowded. This incredibly tremendous area takes up almost a third of all Canada. Its 1,304,903 square miles makes it over twice the size of Alaska, or to put it another way, more than a third the size of the forty-eight "southern" U.S. states. It extends two thousand miles from Baffin Island in the east to the Yukon frontier in the west. Its northernmost reaches are within five hundred miles of the North Pole, and it extends some sixteen hundred miles south to the borders of the prairie provinces. To say it is underpopulated is to somewhat understate: about forty thousand Canadians are residents of the Northwest Territories.

A great mass of snow and ice? Only in part, and even then, not all year round. The Territories—as they are commonly called—constitute a region of fantastic variety.

Almost a third of Canada: The great Mackenzie River—one of the world's longest, stretching twelve hundred miles—is the dominant geographical feature of the western region. It flows from the inland sea that is Great Slave Lake all the way to the Arctic, at Mackenzie Bay. Its great, flat, forested valley is flanked on the west by the Mackenzie Mountains, which reach heights of nine thousand feet. And on its east is the rocky granite terrain of the Canadian, or Pre-Cambrian, Shield which extends east and covers much of the Territories' area—a mosaic of scrubby rock, rivers, and lakes, and occasional green patches. As one goes north, the trees become stubbier until gradually one has passed the tree line and is in true Arctic territory—devoid of trees, of course, but brilliant in summer with masses of blossoming shrubs and flowers. The extreme north is even more dramatic. Ellesmere, the northernmost island of the Territories, is a never-never land of snowy ten-thousand-foot peaks and never-melting icecaps, while Baffin Island, the most eastern extremity of the Territories, is distinguished by steep cliffs which drop two thousand feet into the sea.

It is strange, but a fact, that the part of Canada still not fully explored and still so sparsely settled was among the first portions of North America seen by foreigners. Sir Martin Frobisher, an intrepid English explorer, first reached the area in 1576 and within two years had made three trips to Baffin Island. In 1610 Henry Hudson, who had sailed up the New York State river bearing his name a year earlier, discovered and sailed through the vast bay that also is named after him to the very edge of what was the greatest fir forest in the world. Later, the Hudson's Bay Company —or, to give it the romantic full name which it still retains, The Governor and Company of Adventurers of England Trading Into Hudson's Bay—dispatched combination explorer-traders over a period of decades through the northern sea lanes. They, and others who followed them, were intent not only on the rich fur trade, but on finding a northwest passage to the Orient. In 1771 Samuel Hearne descended the Coppermine River. Less than two decades later Alexander Mackenzie, under the aegis of the North West Company—competitor to Hudson's Bay Company—went as far west as the mouth of the Mackenzie River. The Far North was not to be explored, to any substantial extent, until the first half of the nineteenth century, when Sir John Franklin made a number of remarkably fruitful scientific expeditions to the Arctic.

Progress toward self-government: The Northwest Territories was, for a long time, even larger than it is now. Northern sections of Quebec and Ontario were the first to be detached from it. Later, Manitoba was formed from it in 1870, and Saskatchewan and Alberta, in 1905. In 1918, the remaining area was divided into three administrative districts. Later that trio of districts became a quartet of regions so that now the Territories comprise Baffin—farthest north and east; Keewatin—central, fronting Hudson Bay; Fort Smith—almost but not all of the western area (with Yellowknife the capital); and Inuvik, the northwest corner.

Because of the tiny, widely dispersed populace, and a terrain that almost entirely precludes surface transportation, the federal government has, through the years, treated the Territories in a manner not unlike the way in which other nations govern distant colonies. Even with the growth of the town of Yellowknife into a basically modern community, the Territories' seat of government remained in distant Ottawa, and the chief executive officer, known as the Commissioner, ruled his domain—under the aegis of the Department of Northern Affairs and Natural Resources—from the federal capital, making only occasional "state visits" to the north. At least until 1967. That year, the seat of government of the Territories was moved from Ottawa to Yellowknife, and the people were given some voice in their affairs by means of a fifteen-member council, part elected, part appointed, until, in 1975, the entire Council became elective. Yellowknife gained in self-government, too. In 1970 it was officially designated as a city; it is governed by a mayor and a council of eight aldermen.

Until fairly recently there was little concern over the government of the Territories in the "south"—as provincial Canada is known in the northland. And even within the Territories, while there were no more than a relative handful of Euro-Canadians—the polite term for whites, in contrast to Eskimos and Indians, who constitute the vast majority—there was little reason to consider changes in the governmental setup. But as more whites—businessmen, teachers, miners, administrators, storekeepers, missionaries, and their families—went north, and with increased self-government granted the neighboring Yukon Territory, Northwest Territories residents began to assert themselves. And even in the provinces—where many residents could tell you more about the U.S. than the North—interest developed in the situation.

Big distances, small populace: Administering the Northwest Territories is anything but easy. Solutions to problems prove never to be as simple as they are in other parts of Canada. Climate, terrain, and the indigenous cultures of the majority of the little populace remain major stumbling blocks to development. Education is a prime example of the difficulties encountered. The Federal Government encounters relatively little difficulty in recruiting teachers to go north. Modern school buildings have been constructed, but because of the great distances that separate tiny settlements the government has, in many instances, established centralized residential schools. Students—mostly Eskimo and Indian—from outlying communities spend the school terms living a dormitory life away from home. For most months of each year they're deprived of the experience of home life during formative periods. Moreover, when they return home each summer, they must revert from the white Canadians' way of life to the traditional culture of their parents—a culture their education (at least indirectly) encourages them to reject. The result, too often, is a school graduate who is betwixt and between the Indian/Eskimo world and that of the modern Canadian. Educationally, he is little more than semi-literate and equipped neither for the traditional livelihoods of his parents nor for anything more than marginal work in the white world. The clash of cultures manifests itself in other ways, too. Alcoholism is a serious problem with newly urban Indians and Eskimos, and especially among the latter group, there have been alarming recent increases in the incidence of suicide, mental illness, and murders. At the same time, the development of this immense area, with a wealth of untapped natural resources, poses still additional weighty problems.

Development, communications, transport, education, culture, political structure, human relationships: in every area, the Northwest Territories present a major challenge to Canada.

YOUR VISIT TO THE NORTHWEST TERRITORIES

There is a very good chance that the Northwest Territories will not offer the slightest appeal to you as a pleasure traveler. Only an infinitesimal fraction of tourists in Canada even consider including it on their itineraries—and for perfectly understandable reasons. It is not equipped to handle quantities of tourists, and those it can receive must be prepared for minimal amenities beyond the major towns where the "informal" way of life can sometimes appear so casual as to border on the crude.

Despite the Territories' tremendous size, the number of vacation destinations are limited. The most popular area is the most developed one—that which is served by the Mackenzie Highway north of the Alberta border. But in my view, the great lure of the Territories is the Eskimo, his culture, and the stark, raw, and sweeping beauty of his homeland. They are often best observed in and about still other Territories' communities.

Yellowknife: The "metropolis" of the Northwest Territories with a population in the neighborhood of ten thousand and a location less than three hundred miles from the Arctic Circle, Yellowknife must be forgiven its inadequacies and credited with its accomplishments. It has sprouted in recent years to the point where it can boast many of the comforts of the "south." Its designation in 1967 as territorial capital gave it a special cachet and increased growth. There is an undeniably imposing Residential Boarding and Day School which serves the local youngsters through high school, as well as students—mostly Eskimos and Indians—who fly in from outlying settlements and board at the school during the fall and winter semesters. I would certainly recommend that you ask to be guided through.

There is the Con Mine of the Consolidated Mining and Smelting Company of Canada, where visitors are welcome to watch the operations. There is a considerable Indian population—the tribe is the Yellowknife, after which the town is named. But there is not an Eskimo in sight during the summer season. They appear only when the boarding school opens up in the fall.

The older part of the town—which was first settled in 1935—hugs the shores of enormous Great Slave Lake and has a certain degree of charm. There is a public bathing beach on an outlet of the lake whose waters are warmer than those of the parent body. And one finds movie theatres, modern shops, a good hospital, sports facilities including a golf course, and—during late July and most of August—daylight round the clock. Many local people have boats of their own which they use for almost nightly excursions on Great Slave Lake—excellent for fishing.

A worthy museum—the Museum of the North—is not without interest. High school students erected it in the early 1960s, and its exhibits include a memorable photo collection—explaining the region's history and its varied cultures. Aside from the lake, there is nothing to excite one in the way of aesthetics. The terrain is flat and scrubby, and the town is hardly of prepossessing appearance, although the accommodations scene has brightened considerably in recent years.

Rae, an hour's drive out of Yellowknife, just off the Mackenzie

Highway, is worthwhile as an excursion destination or as a stopover for motorists driving to or from Yellowknife. It is a largely Indian community with all of the features traditionally associated with such a place in the northland—a Royal Canadian Mounted Police post, a white-frame Catholic mission-church and school, an attractive Protestant church, the ubiquitous trading post of the Hudson's Bay Company—to be found in the settlements throughout the Territories (in interesting contrast to the giant department stores operated by "The Bay" in the great cities to the south)—and perhaps most interesting, the husky-dog teams of the Indians and the Mounties.

Fishing lodges: Rustic fly-in anglers' lodges are a special Territories attraction, with lake trout, Arctic grayling, walleye, whitefish, northern pike among the species. *Colville Lake,* an Indian settlement north of the Arctic Circle with an unusual Catholic church built of logs, is a favored fly-in spot. So are *Great Slave* and *Great Bear lakes* and *Snowbird Lake*—among others.

Hay River and Fort Smith are important communities in the southern part of the Mackenzie River District. The former, on the southern shore of Great Slave Lake, which is a busy commercial fishing center, has a variety of amenities, including boats for excursions and an architecturally striking high school. The nearby waterfalls—Louisa, Alexandra, and Lady Evelyn—are visit-worthy. Fort Smith is a regional administrative center, just north of the Alberta border and at the fringe of *Wood Buffalo National Park,* within whose confines is the largest herd of buffalo on the continent. The town's chief visitor lure is the first-rate Northern Life Museum, with exhibits relating to the Indian and Eskimo cultures, as well as to regional history. Noteworthy, too, is modern St. Joseph's Cathedral. Wood Buffalo National Park is headquarters for the new, still-developing *Nahanni National Park,* 1,840 square miles of wilderness in the Territories' southwest corner.

Inuvik is a key destination—one of the most interesting in the Territories. It is situated at almost the extreme northwestern tip of the region, near the northern point of the Yukon, and on a channel leading directly into the close-by Beaufort Sea (which adjoins the Arctic Ocean). Inuvik is government headquarters for the western Arctic and is a model Eskimo community, established in 1955, with modern public buildings—school, hospital, hotels, and the like. Its architecture, unlike those of makeshift design in other Territories towns, was especially designed for the north, and it is at once attractive and functional, with its most unusual structure Our Lady of Victory church—igloo-shaped with a bronze dome. This is whaling territory and a center for trappers and seal and walrus hunters—whose big season is summer and who sometimes can be induced to take visitors along. It is a center, too, for the brilliant handicrafts of the Eskimo, and a departure point for other Eskimo communities including *Aklavik,* whose All Saints Cathedral is the seat of the bishop of the Anglican Diocese of the Arctic, and whose décor blends local Eskimo with imported English motifs.

Frobisher Bay might be described as an eastern counterpart of Inuvik. It is the major community of the Territories' eastern area. Located on Baffin Island, it is dominantly Eskimo, with minimal amenities, and a retail outlet for Eskimo handicrafts. *Baffin Island National Park's* Pangnirtung Fjord—one of many in this spectacular park—is a relatively short flight away.

SHOPPING

The larger towns and "settlements" shops offer ordinary consumer requisites at prices understandably higher than those of the "south." In **Yellowknife,** *Northern Images* and *Studio Arctica* are good handicraft shops. In largely Eskimo communities such as **Frobisher Bay** (*Ikaluit Eskimo Co-op*) and **Inuvik** (*Inuvik Arts and Crafts Outlet*) the most interesting purchases are the superb Eskimo handicrafts, principally the soapstone carvings—mainly of animals. Also available are *mukluks* (the Eskimo decorated footwear), parkas, ivory carvings (from walrus tusks), carved whalebones, and striking prints. There are Indian crafts, as well, but they pale in contrast to the Eskimo work.

CREATURE COMFORTS

Yellowknife's leader is an 8-story, 120-room skyscraper—the first of its kind in the North—called the *Explorer.* Every room has color TV, telephone, and full bath, and facilities include a restaurant, cocktail lounge with nightly entertainment, coffee shop, games room, meeting and convention facilities. All thanks to the landlord, Pacific Western Airlines, for giving the capital the kind of hotel it needed. Other possibilities include the *Frontier Inn,* consisting of 9 housekeeping units with kitchen facilities and baths; the also-small *Northland Motel,* less than a dozen units, all with bath; and the *Yellowknife Inn,* the best available before the Explorer, with old and new sections, the latter preferable if somewhat more costly; all 162 rooms, both old and new, have private baths or showers, and there are places to eat and drink. Top eating spots include the Explorer Hotel and Hoist Room restaurant. **Hay River:** I opt for *Ptarmigan Inn* which has 44 rooms, all with bath, TV, radio, phone, as well as a restaurant, cocktail lounge, and coffee shop. Consider, also, the *Caribou Motor Inn,* with nearly 30 rooms, all with full baths, phones, radio, and TV, plus a restaurant and cocktail lounge. Motels include the *Migrator,* all of whose 18 rooms have bath and shower and TV. **Fort Smith's** *Pelican Rapids Inn* features 30 rooms, all with bath and TV. There's no restaurant or bar, but you may eat across the street, or at the older, licensed *Pinecrest Hotel,* 18 of whose 30 rooms have private bath. **Inuvik's** *Eskimo Inn* has nearly 80 rooms, all with private baths and phones. There are, as well, a restaurant, a pair of cocktail lounges, and a coffee shop. The *Arctic Inn* is smaller, featuring 14 rooms all with full bath and kitchen facilities; dining room and cocktail lounge. At the *Mackenzie Hotel* I suggest you ask for one of the 28 rooms (out of a total of 48) with private bath and color TV. This is a licensed house with restaurant, coffee shop, and cocktail lounge. **Frobisher Bay's** *Frobisher Inn* contains half a hundred twins, all with private bath; restaurant, cocktail lounge, coffee shop. Fishing and naturalists' lodges include *Colville Lake Lodge,* at the Hareskin Indian settlement at **Colville Lake,** and an outpost camp, as well, with Eskimo life, fish, and such animals as muskox and caribou the lures . . . *Indian Mountain Lodge, Jerry Bricker's, Frontier Fishing Lodge,* and *Trophy Lodge* on **Great Slave Lake** . . . *Arctic Circle Lodge* and *Branson's Lodge* on **Great Bear Lake** . . . *Arctic Outpost Camps, Ltd.,* on **Victoria Island,** 225 miles north of the Arctic Circle, with a modern main

lodge as well as heated tents . . . and *Bathurst Inlet Naturalists'*
Lodge—this last not only for fishing, but to observe a multitude of
birds, animals, plants and flowers, with an Eskimo staff, and a setting directly on the Arctic Ocean.

Nova Scotia

LA NOUVELLE ÉCOSSE

Best times for a visit: *Summer—with pleasantly warm but rarely overhot days, and with cool evenings—is the most favored season for visitors to Nova Scotia, but spring—late April and May, with the fruit trees in blossom, can be de-*

lightful, and autumn, particularly September and October when the leaves change and the hunting season is on, is attractive too. Winters are, of course, cold, snowy, and on the damp side, although coastal points can be warmer than you might expect. Halifax and Sydney, for example, have higher winter average temperatures than leading cities of the interior provinces. There is no point in hiding the fact that it rains a good bit in Nova Scotia. Indeed, Halifax has the dubious distinction of vying with Vancouver in this respect. But don't be discouraged: When it's clear and sunny, it's glorious.

Transportation: *Highways are excellent; there are several-thousand-plus paved miles, but the minor roads, more so in this province than some others, can make for especially atmospheric detours. The Trans-Canada Highway runs through northern Nova Scotia, from Amherst, just east of the New Brunswick border, through Truro across the causeway connecting mainland Nova Scotia with Cape Breton Island, and the port of North Sydney, which is the take-off point for ferries to Port-aux-Basques, Newfoundland, where the highway resumes. Paved highways from the United States connect with Route 2 leading into Nova Scotia. There is good bus service. Greyhound comes from U.S. points and connects with SMT Bus Lines at the Maine-New Brunswick frontier and Acadian Bus Lines in Nova Scotia. Voyageur Colonial buses, coming from Montreal, join with SMT in New Brunswick and Acadian in Nova Scotia. Three airlines serve the province, whose major airports are at Halifax, Yarmouth, and Sydney. Air Canada links the province with such Canadian cities as Montreal, Ottawa, and Toronto, and such American ones as Boston and New York. Eastern Provincial Airways connects Nova Scotia points with other Maritimes cities and Montreal. Air St. Pierre joins Sydney, Nova Scotia, with St. Pierre, major island of the tiny French Overseas Territory of St. Pierre et Miquelon, briefly described at the end of this chapter. Canadian National Railways runs daily trains through Nova Scotia as part of its coast-to-coast service. The approach by water—perhaps the most fun way of all—may be made from six Canadian and U.S. ports. From within Canada, there is ferry service between Saint*

*John, New Brunswick, and Digby, Nova Scotia, via CP
Ships' Princess of Acadia; between both Port-aux-Basques
and Argentia in Newfoundland and North Sydney, Nova
Scotia, via East Coast Ferry Service; and between the port
of Wood Islands, Prince Edward Island, and Caribou, Nova
Scotia, via Northumberland Ferries. From the U.S., ferries connect Portland, Maine, with Yarmouth, Nova Scotia
(Prince of Fundy Line), and Bar Harbor, Maine, with Yarmouth (Canadian National). Not all of the foregoing ferry
services are year-round; the emphasis is on heavy summer
traffic.* **Having a drink:** *Liquor, wine, and beer are obtainable in licensed hotel dining rooms and cocktail lounges,
licensed restaurants and cocktail lounges; by no means all hotels are fully licensed. Taverns and beverage rooms serve beer
only to men and women nineteen and over. (Taverns used to
be male enclaves.) Nova Scotia has local option, but Halifax,
the main towns, and some other areas are wet. Liquor and
beer may be bought in provincial liquor stores.* **Further information:** *Nova Scotia Department of Tourism, Hollis Building, Halifax; Nova Scotia Tourist Information Offices at
630 Fifth Avenue, New York City, 616 Forest Avenue, Portland (Maine), 45 Richmond Street West, Toronto, and Gare
Centrale, Montreal; Agent General of Nova Scotia, 14 Pall
Mall, London; Canadian Government Office of Tourism, Ottawa and branches.*

INTRODUCING NOVA SCOTIA

If one has any doubts about big things coming in small packages, Nova Scotia dispels them. It is the smallest of the provinces
save one (Prince Edward Island). It is richer historically than so
relatively tiny an area of the map has any business being, it is
scenically quite splendid, it is far more of an ethnic hodgepodge
than the uninitiated newcomer might believe, and though essentially conservative, it is very much a part of the fourth quarter of the
twentieth century, working aggressively to make itself at once a
haven for industry as well as for holidaymakers.

There is little question that it is the most exciting of the Atlantic provinces. Newfoundland is more dramatically rugged, but Nova Scotia is more developed. New Brunswick, though delightful, is more a part of the mainland, a bit more self-satisfied, a mite less in a hurry. And Prince Edward Island, though completely surrounded by water—a geographical feature which usually creates an atmosphere dear to the hearts of visiting mainlanders—is blander than one anticipates, particularly if one contrasts it with Nova Scotia.

Province of "firsts": Nova Scotia is the only North American province or state with a Latin name (I am not forgetting Regina, which is a city). But it has so many other distinctions that I shall numerate only a few. It was first in Canada with a post office, a Protestant church, a public school, a newspaper, representative government, a university charter, and—of all things—a distillery (the presence of which might well have been a cause of an excessively Puritanical attitude toward spirituous beverages which is only now beginning to be dispelled).

But most important, it is the site of the first permanent settlement in Canada—indeed, in all of North America north of the Gulf of Mexico. For in 1605 Port Royal (now Annapolis Royal) was established by Frenchmen Pierre du Guast—who had the impressive title of Sieur de Monts—and Samuel de Champlain. (Champlain, in order to maintain the morale of the lonely settlement's tiny populace, inaugurated the Order of the Good Time—*l'Ordre de Bon Temps*—in the winter of 1606. Members vied with each other in preparing sumptuous feasts and entertainments for themselves, and in so doing, established the continent's first social club. It remains in existence to this date, with Canada's Governor-General traditionally serving as its Grand Master. Visitors who spend at least three days in Nova Scotia may become members, at no charge, by registering with any of the province's information bureaus (at entry-exit points); each receives a handsome membership certificate with a reproduction of the painting depicting the Order's first dinner, held in the Habitation building which has been reproduced at Port Royal National Historic Park.)

Port Royal and Acadia: Europeans had, of course, seen Nova Scotia before they settled Port Royal. It is quite possible—though not proven as a fact of history—that Leif Ericson and his fellow Vikings landed there some nine centuries ago and named the area

Markland. It is also still debated as to whether John Cabot landed on Cape Breton Island in 1497 or on the coast of Newfoundland. (The Newfoundlanders, of course, contend that he came ashore on their territory; the Nova Scotians, understandably enough, hold to the Cape Breton theory; I have gone along with the former in the chapter on that province, and will not argue with the latter on this page.) At any rate, there is no doubt but that in 1518 Baron de Lery of France made the unsuccessful settlement on the Nova Scotia coast. It was abandoned, and there were no comers between that time and the landing of du Guast and Champlain, at Port Royal. The Port Royal adventure took hold. In 1632 some forty French peasant families settled in Nova Scotia, calling it Acadia. (The name is believed to have evolved either because Verrazano had used it, in his descriptions of the North American coast, or because it was the Micmac Indian word for "fertile land.")

Acadia was, in effect, the beginning of New France, and its birth set off a bitter Anglo-French struggle for the territory which was to last a century and to end only with the French and Indian Wars. As early as 1614 the British attacked and destroyed Annapolis Royal. In 1621 the Scottish Earl of Stirling gained title to the whole peninsula by means of a patent issued by King James (the First of England, the Sixth of Scotland). The area was named—not surprisingly—New Scotland, but in its Latin translation. And concurrently, a Scottish knighthood order, the Baronets of Nova Scotia, was founded; it was conferred upon 140 persons, each of whom was awarded a four- by six-mile plot of Nova Scotian territory. It was King James who designated Nova Scotia the "Royal Province"; the Royal coat of arms granted, as a result of this honor, is the basis for the beautiful blue and white flag still flown with great pride to this day throughout Nova Scotia. It was, indeed, the first flag granted to any British colony, and later became the first Canadian provincial flag.

New Scotland's early decades: But there were to be difficulties as regards flying it for some decades after it was designed, thanks to the almost unceasing French-English squabbling over the area. In 1667 the Treaty of Breda awarded Nova Scotia—or Acadia, if you will—to France. But by the terms of the Peace of Utrecht (1713) it reverted to England, although Cape Breton Island remained under French control. (Cape Breton Island was annexed to Nova Scotia Colony in 1763, but broke away to become a separately administered colony in 1784, remaining so until 1820, when it rejoined Nova Scotia with a reluctance never fully dispensed with.)

But gaining sovereignty over Nova Scotia—through the Peace of Utrecht—was not quite enough for the British. They could not rid themselves of the conviction—however erratic—that their Roman Catholic, French-speaking subjects in the colony—the Acadians— were disloyal, because they continued friendly with the Indians and, wanting to remain neutral, refused to swear allegiance to Britain. The British reaction? Get rid of them.

The Acadians expelled: And so began the cruel, harsh exodus of the Acadians, which Longfellow immortalized in *Evangeline,* even though he never visited Nova Scotia. In 1755 the British descended upon the peaceful Acadian farms, separated families, burned farmhouses, seized some seven thousand of the ten thousand Acadians, and shipped them southward, to colonies ranging from Maine to the West Indies (a substantial proportion went to southern Louisiana where, to this day, as Cajuns, they maintain their own distinctive culture). By the time the French and Indian Wars ended in 1763, the anti-Acadian hysteria subsided (although there had been an attempt at a second exodus the previous year, which was thwarted). The war over, a number of exiles returned; they, with those Acadians who had remained, took oaths of loyalty to the Crown and rapidly became Nova Scotians.

By that time, a couple of thousand Protestant Germans had settled in at Lunenburg and the surrounding region, and thrived as shipbuilders and farmers. Their German-accented English still is to be heard in the area. Later in the eighteenth century the first waves of Irish immigrants arrived. Many of their descendants are now Halifax community leaders, and the lovely Irish lilt—surely no people speaks English more beautifully than the Irish—is still a part of the speech of the capital. There had been Negroes, too— who came north as slaves from the British West Indian colonies, and whose descendants today give Nova Scotia the highest black population of any province, in proportion to the total population.

But there was other immigration. Thousands of New Englanders moved north to Nova Scotia, beginning with those who took over lands vacated by the expelled Acadians, mainly in the

Annapolis Valley. Still others came from Scotland and England, mostly to become farmers. And after the American Revolution some twenty-five thousand Loyalists—colonists who had sided with the Crown—settled in Nova Scotia, constituting what was quite possibly the largest single emigration of educated people in British history. (Half of the graduates of Harvard were among them, and their concern for education was manifested in the early beginnings of schools and universities in Nova Scotia and the present province of New Brunswick, which had then been a part of Nova Scotia.)

Later immigrants: Still later was the mass movement of Scottish Highlanders from their homelands to New Scotland. The early nineteenth century saw some fifty thousand Scots settle in the mainland counties of Antigonish and Pictou, as well as on Cape Breton Island, whose hills reminded them so much of home. Most Americans of Scottish descent have retained little more of their heritage than their names. But the Nova Scotian Scots are, it would seem, at least as Scottish as their relatives in today's United Kingdom. The clans still gather, some Gaelic still is spoken (the only Gaelic college on the continent is in Nova Scotia), and the tartan still is worn (there's one tartan for mainland Nova Scotia, another for Cape Breton Island, and the Lord help you if you confuse them, as I was once foolish enough to do—in Cape Breton Island, of all places).

This mélange of industrious immigrants was good for Nova Scotia. The colony did well by itself, and its people worked hard. They took their rights seriously, too. In 1848, under the leadership of Joseph Howe and James B. Uniacke, Nova Scotia became the first colony to win responsible government, after making the governor give up some of his power in favor of the elected legislative assembly; Uniacke became the first premier. In 1867 Nova Scotia became one of the first of the confederated provinces of the new Canada, with the hope that its changed status would help make a more prosperous economy possible for its people. For Nova Scotia, like its Atlantic neighbors, has never known the wealth of provinces like Ontario or Alberta, despite age and maturity, its rich coal mines, the marine wealth of its coastal waters (oh, those lobsters!), its fertile valleys, and its verdant forests.

Modern diversification: Its soil produces Canada's highest yield per acre of many crops, and it is second only to British Columbia in fisheries production. Its steel and iron mills are important factors in its economy. But it has needed even more industry, more diversification. In recent years its government has had a good deal of success in attracting new industries to the province, and in creating a new industry—tourism—which is bringing in a considerable number of dollars. World War II saw Halifax as a major naval and merchant marine base, and since that time Nova Scotia has been growing impressively—and is building as it grows. Manufacturing is now the largest single industry. Schools sprout up everywhere. New houses fill land until recently vacant on the outskirts of cities and towns. Universities have added to their technical faculties and facilities. During the peak summer season, some 1.3 million out-of-province visitors spend more than $76 million dollars in Nova Scotia.

Nova Scotia has not, bless its heart, swept away the best of the old in its leap toward the new. Nor has it neglected matters aesthetic in favor of matters economic. Through the Nova Scotia Arts Council, music, drama, dance, painting, and handicrafts remain and are encouraged and exploited. Halifax's Neptune Theatre is as first-rate and professional a repertory group as can be found in any North American city—including those far larger. The performing arts are otherwise thriving. The shopper in Nova Scotia finds more well designed and locally made craft objects than in almost any other province.

Nova Scotia is the most populous and richest of the Maritimes. Its Conservative Party under Premier Gerald A. Regan took over in 1970 after fourteen years of Liberal rule, and won again in 1974. Regional dominance notwithstanding, Nova Scotia still trails behind the other six provinces economically, and continues to promote diversity in its income-producing areas.

The Nova Scotian lives in a part of the world that just misses being an island. That tiny bit of land which geographically links his province to the mainland reflects, in a way, his attitude toward his neighbors. He is not as isolated as the Newfoundlander, and he is not as provincial as the Prince Edward Islander. But he is not, on the other hand, as urbane as the Montrealer or the Torontonian. No, the Nova Scotian is in between—pleasantly, comfortably, hospitably in between. One hopes, oncoming modernity or no, that he'll long stay that way.

YOUR VISIT TO NOVA SCOTIA

Nova Scotia is not massive in area (the "mainland" peninsula is but 374 miles long), but the traveler wanting to do it justice does well to give it some time. There are two national parks and a national historic park (one of a number)—Fortress of Louisbourg—the restoration of which is among the greater such accomplishments of modern times. Attractions are well distributed geographically, and even though one resolutely starts out of a morning with a definite destination in mind, points along the way present themselves so appealingly that one makes a stop here . . . and a stop there . . . with the result that a journey or an excursion inevitably takes longer than anticipated. It is not, therefore, easy to advise one on Nova Scotian requisites. But as a rough guide, I would certainly recommend Halifax, the capital, and its environs; nearby Atlantic Ocean points like Peggy's Cove and Lunenburg; Bay of Fundy points such as Grand Pré, Annapolis Royal, Digby, and Yarmouth; on Cape Breton Island, the aforementioned Louisbourg, Cape Breton Highlands National Park; Sydney; and such mainland towns as Amherst, Truro, and Antigonish, depending upon the course of your itinerary. Always remember that you are never more than thirty-five miles from water and usually much closer than that. Take your choice of the Bay of Fundy (with the world's highest tides) to the northwest; the Atlantic to the south; and the Northumberland Strait, on the northeast—forty-six hundred miles of seacoast in all.

Halifax: From a grim port that earned the dislike of countless thousands of Canadian troops who passed through it during World War II, Halifax has become the metropolis of the Maritimes, with a renewed core, a not insubstantial skyline, and a cultural fabric with but one major lack: a first-rank art museum.

Ever since it was founded by Lord Cornwallis in 1749—as a base to defend Britain's North American territory and to counteract the importance of the then-French base at Louisbourg on Cape Breton Island—Halifax has been of military and naval importance. Its great natural harbor has not only made it attractive to the Navy, but to merchant marine activity as well, for it is ice-free and operates the year-round, picking up in activity during winter when St. Lawrence ports are forced to close. Halifax has played a major martial role for more than three centuries. The British attacked the French from Halifax during the French and Indian Wars. They used it as a base against the Americans during the Revolution and during the War of 1812. Halifax saw service during World War I and, of course, World War II. And its greatest attraction to this day is one of military significance: the brilliantly designed, star-shaped Citadel, straddling the 270-foot-high Citadel Hill, which dominates the peninsula on which the oldest parts of the city are built. The Citadel one sees today—known also as Fort George—is the fourth to have been constructed on the site; it went up in 1828 and was in operation to and through World War II. British troops were garrisoned in it until 1906, when Canada—which that year assumed responsibility for its own defenses—took over with its own soldiers, thus terminating over a century-and-a-half occupation by Imperial forces.

In 1914, with the coming of World War I, the Citadel served as a detention camp for aliens suspected of disloyalty and for prisoners of war brought into port by the Navy—Leon Trotsky among them. During the Second World War the fort was at once a signal post, antiaircraft gunsite, and communications center. The federal government, in 1951, took control of it from the military, and in 1956 it was opened as a national historic park—surely one of the most significant in Canada. Within are a pair of excellent historical museums whose exhibits depict the history of the fort and, concurrently, the life of Halifax through the centuries. There is a gallery of contemporary painting, as well. And just below the fort is that beloved Halifax landmark, the Old Town Clock, a restored frame tower that has been in use since 1803 when it was erected by Queen Victoria's father, the Duke of Kent—at that time the military Commander in Chief of the colony.

But there is, I am happy to say, more of Old Halifax to be seen. Province House, the legislative building, is the only such Georgian building in any of the provinces still serving its original function. It is a gracious, exquisitely designed structure which dates back to 1818. Even older are the Martello Tower, in Point Pleasant Park (1796); the Little Dutch Church (1756) and its graveyard with the graves of early German settlers; and the elegant white-frame

St. Paul's Anglican Church—another great Georgian specimen—
built in 1750 and, like Province House, eminently worthy of interior inspection.

The Public Gardens—sixteen acres of flower-accented, path-
strewn lawns—opened in 1873 and are based upon an earlier park
dating back a century. I challenge you to produce a prettier city
park elsewhere in Canada. The former Admiralty House, for long
the headquarters of the British commander of the naval base, is
now the seat of Canadian Forces Base Halifax and a naval training
station. Away from the center, near Bedford, is the rotunda of
Prince's Lodge, all that remains of the suburban home—from 1794
to 1803—of the aforementioned Duke of Kent; it has been restored
as a historic site by the provincial government. Government House
is still another old building—early nineteenth century. The former
home of governors of the colony, it is now the official residence of
the province's lieutenant governors.

Quite as important to the spiritual life of the city as the Anglican cathedral—for Halifax, with its heavy Irish-descended population, is about half Roman Catholic—is St. Mary's Basilica, with
what is said to be the highest granite spire extant, and an impressive, visit-worthy interior. St. Mary's University, a Jesuit institution whose chapel serves as a parish church for the neighborhood,
has a functional, mostly modern campus. It is not nearly as attractive as that of Dalhousie University, which was founded in 1818,
has produced many a Canadian leader, and houses on its campus
King's College, originally situated, in 1788, at Windsor, and the
oldest such institution in the Commonwealth outside of the United
Kingdom. The Dalhousie campus, mostly Georgian in design, is
eminently worth a visit. On the grounds are the Public Archives of
Nova Scotia, in effect a historical museum—and a good one—and
the Dalhousie Arts Centre, a handsome contemporary complex
with a fine auditorium-theatre-concert hall (watch the papers for
current attractions), and a gallery for changing art exhibits, and
with a permanent collection, as well.

Barrington Street, long Halifax's principal business thoroughfare, has been supplemented by newer shopping areas, including that of the Scotia Square complex, a downtown harbor-front
cluster—ultramodern, and an interesting contrast to the well-restored two-century-old buildings—shops, restaurants, and the Nova

Scotia College of Art and Design at the Privateers Wharf area.
The modern Nova Scotia Museum has a mostly historical theme,
and seems geared more to children than adult visitors. (Much
more interesting is the network of lovely historic houses throughout the province, operated by the Nova Scotia Museum.*) You'll
want to see the activity of the harbor and get the perspective of the
city while crossing the Murray McKay or Angus L. MacDonald
bridges—to *Dartmouth,* the town across the harbor which is largely
a residential area.

Outside of Halifax, excursions might well be made to *North
West Arm,* a two-and-a-half-mile inlet of the sea with facilities for
swimming, sailing, and boating. *Point Pleasant* is a two-hundred-
acre wooded park containing, among other things, the aforementioned Martello Tower. The countryside all around the city is
inviting. Indeed, the ride into town from modern Halifax International Airport is an unusually scenic airport-city route. And you
might consider brief outings to such nearby spots as *Shad Bay,* a
fishing village pleasant for fishing and picnicking; *Hubbards,* with
cabins, a sand beach, Saturday dances in summer, and *Lawrence-
town* for swims and picnics, are spots on the Dartmouth side of
the harbor.

Coastal excursions out of Halifax: With as little as a day at
your disposal you can take in a choice bit of maritime Nova Scotia
—the fishing communities along the Atlantic, east of the capital.
Peggy's Cove, though tiny, is perhaps the most photographed—and
painted—coastal village in the Western Hemisphere. It is built atop
solid rock, and there is no doubt that its tiny harbor, the gaily
painted frame houses that surround it, and the craft anchored in
the water are photogenic as all get-out. It's just that upon occasion, you have almost (not quite) got to wait your turn to get your
camera at a good spot. I hope I do not exaggerate the over-
popularity of Peggy's Cove, but in contrast to the much less
frequented fishing villages of the much more rugged New-

* Be on the lookout for them in your Nova Scotia travels; historic houses
operated by the Nova Scotia Museum include: Uniacke House in Mount
Uniacke; Prescott House, Starrs Point; Perkins House, Liverpool; Lawrence
House, Maitland; Ross Thomson House, Shelburne; also the Old Woolen
Museum, Barrington; and Sherbrooke Village, a restoration project, at Sher-
brooke.

foundland coast, it is rather a weak cup of tea. Still, for the traveler who has not been—and is not going—to Newfoundland, it's
worth taking in; there are little souvenir and food shops, and an
artist's studio or two, where the paintings—how did you guess?—
are for sale. The villages of *Prospect* and *Terence Bay* are less-
frequented alternatives. *Chester,* on Mahone Bay, first attracted
visitors from New England in 1759 (they founded the place), and
it's been popular ever since with all manner of transients from pi-
rates (some time back) to tourists and summer residents, many of
whom have houses. The population is about a thousand, the yachting is excellent, and the swimming is great. Restored *Ross Farm*
(late nineteenth century) is nearby. *Mahone Bay* is the name of a
town as well as of a body of water. The town is about the size of
Chester, is beautifully situated at the head of the bay and, like
Chester, dates back to the mid-eighteenth century. There's quite a
ship-building industry—fishing schooners, yachts, and the like.
Lunenburg, largest of this group (nearly three thousand population), is the town founded by the Teutonic Hanoverians (and
some Swiss, too) to which I referred earlier in this chapter. It is, as
well, the seat of the continent's most important deep-sea fishing
fleet (there are two harbors, for the town juts out on a peninsula),
and it was—and you hear about this wherever you travel in Nova
Scotia, so you might as well learn now what it is they're talking
about—the home of the schooner *Bluenose,* undefeated champion
of the North Atlantic fishing fleet and the winner of a quartet of
international schooner races. (*Bluenose II* is a contemporary replica, owned and operated by the provincial government; it sails on
charters out of Halifax.) The town is a charmer—harbor views, or-
ange and yellow boats on the blue water, lobster traps and fish
nets on the piers, frame houses of brown, blue, and red all with
neat white trims, in the background—is one of the loveliest in the
east. St. John's Church, built in 1754, was chartered by the Crown
and still has the communion vessels given it by King George III,
and other ancient objects. See, too, Zion Evangelical Lutheran
Church, built in 1776—an easy year for Americans to remember.
Check to see if a Yacht Club race is going on during your visit
(there are two a week in the summer). Take in the unusual
Fisheries Museum; old ships are its home. Visit the Fishermen's
Memorial Room in the Community Center to see the records of

local sailors who were lost at sea; visit the studio of Earl Bailly, a
paralyzed artist of unusual gifts who paints with the brush held in
his teeth. And motor over to Blue Rocks (five miles), a fishing village less celebrated than Peggy's Cove but no less photogenic. I
don't need to tell you to listen for the unique Lunenburg accent;
you can't miss it. But I might suggest a stop in nearby *Bridgewater*
for the Des Brisay Museum—full of local regional lore.

Annapolis Valley and Bay of Fundy highlights: An understandably favored segment of Nova Scotia is that embracing the
heart of the lovely rolling farms and orchards of the Annapolis
Valley—extending from north of Halifax to the Bay of Fundy, and
ranging eastward on the bay from Kentville to Digby and Yarmouth. Working out of Halifax and going in the direction of Yarmouth, here are the major points: *Mount Uniacke* is a little hamlet
that would not be of consequence were it not for Uniacke House,
the fine mansion built in 1815 by the Irishman with the odd name
for whom the town is named. A white-frame, Greek Revival structure, with a graciously columned portico, it is operated as a historic site by the provincial government, complete with the original
furnishings—which are every bit as elegant as one would expect in
the home of a dashing adventurer who was Nova Scotia's attorney
general for the not inconsiderable period 1797–1830. *Windsor,*
happily placed at the juncture of the Avon and St. Croix rivers, is
a port and rail terminus of some consequence, is rich in historic
associations (having been founded by the French as Piziquid in
1703, and renamed by the British in 1764—as who could blame
them), and is the site of Clifton, the long-time home of Nova Scotian author Thomas Chandler Haliburton, who wrote the "Sam
Slick" stories (more familiar to Canadians than Americans). Clifton now is operated by the provincial government as the Haliburton Memorial Museum, and is largely decorated with original furnishings. While not Mount Uniacke by a long shot, it is not
without interest. Windsor was, as mentioned earlier, the original
site of King's College, the oldest Canadian college, long since
moved to the campus of Dalhousie University in Halifax. A plaque
outlining the college's history is in the chapel of King's Collegiate
School for Boys, itself a properly venerable institution. Windsor is
the site, too, of the only golf course with which I am familiar that

is laid out on the grounds of an ancient fortress, with the exception of that at El Morro, in San Juan, Puerto Rico. The old moat of Fort Edward is still there, as is the blockhouse, and there's a plaque explaining that it was from Fort Edward that the British shipped out the expelled Acadians from the surrounding region, in 1755. *Grand Pré*—great meadow, in English—is the site of the most romantic of the National Historic Parks. It is here that *Evangeline* comes to life, for this is the site of the Acadian village of which Longfellow wrote. There is a replica of a narrow, high-steepled church of the period, which is actually a museum with a number of early Acadian farm implements and other objects. The grounds—rose gardens with the plants imported from Orleans, France, great lawns, a statue of Evangeline—are quiet and restful. To be seen, too, are the Protestant Church of the Covenanters, a 1790 edifice built by New England migrants, and historic Prescott House, at nearby *Starrs Point*. *Wolfville* and *Kentville* are two towns of the Grand Pré region. The former is in particularly scenic country (take in the views from the Gaspereau Valley and the Blomidon Lookout), with the campus of Baptist-founded Acadia University (1838). Kentville—a larger town—is in apple country, and has a federal government agricultural experimental station, and 100 species of roses at Antcroft Gardens. *Fort Anne National Historic Park,* just outside of the town of Annapolis Royal, is a tiny reserve that is actually a museum of seventeenth- and eighteenth-century Nova Scotian history. It is housed in the former Officers' Quarters of the old fort, which was dedicated in 1797 by the Duke of Kent, and restored in 1935. The oldest exhibits (1604–1710) are in the Port Royal Room; in the Queen Anne Room are objects dating from the period of that sovereign. The Acadian Room relates to the French-speaking colonists and their heyday prior to the expulsion of 1755. The Loyalist Room concentrates on exhibits dealing with the settlers from New England (middle and late eighteenth century). And the Garrison Room contains military memorabilia. To be seen, too: an ancient well, and a statue of the Sieur de Monts, who established nearby Port Royal with Champlain in 1605, which is just minutes away and now is *Port Royal National Historic Park*. The park is a masterful re-creation of the first permanent settlement in Canada—Port Royal "habitation," as it is still called in both English and French.

Based on a drawing of Champlain's and on historical accounts, the reconstruction is a series of buildings circling a central courtyard and is worth the better part of a morning or an afternoon from even the most blasé of travelers. To be seen: the Governor's Residence, the Priest's House, the Community Room (where were served the famous dinners of the Champlain-founded Order of the Good Time—as described earlier in this chapter), the Guard Room; a chapel, kitchen, bakery, blacksmith shop, artisans' studio, and traders' room—where Indian trappers transacted their business with the resident Frenchmen. An excellent audio-visual presentation, produced by the federal government, depicting the life of the fort is shown a number of times each day during the summer in the community room, and I suggest you—and your children—give it a few moments of your time. Another tip: let the well-trained guides show you about; they're full of fascinating tidbits of the Port Royal period. *Digby,* a pleasant town of about two thousand, dates back to the mid-eighteenth century, is imposingly situated on a height overlooking the Annapolis Basin and Digby Gut, is the site of the noted resort, the Pines Hotel, and is just across the Bay of Fundy from Saint John, New Brunswick, with which it is connected by ferry. If you like scallops, Digby is for you: it's the headquarters of our planet's biggest fleet of scallop boats. *Yarmouth,* considerably larger than Digby, is hardly without interest. The great lighthouse known as Yarmouth Light is quite possibly the most dramatic—and most dramatically situated— of such edifices on the continent. Yarmouth dates from 1761, when it was settled by New Englanders from Massachusetts. Returned Acadians later added to the population, and afterward still other Americans came from New York and other U.S. cities. The county Historical Museum's exhibits give one a clear picture of the area's history, and the Firefighters' Museum is a requisite for buffs, with more than thirty engines of various eras. There is a lively lobstering industry, other fishing, and a good bit of manufacturing— wood products, mostly. The surrounding countryside—stone-fenced farms with sea beyond—is very easy on the eye.

Amherst, just over the border from New Brunswick, is a humming community. Like Amherst, Massachusetts, and the college in that town, it is named for the eighteenth-century Lord Jeffrey Amherst. Amherst has a variety of amenities, varied sports facilities, a good bit of industry, but it need not be considered a requisite stopover, except perhaps to see its Confederation Building, named in memory of no less than four hundred men who were Fathers of Canadian Confederation. The surrounding countryside is nothing if not diverse—coal mines, diked farms that have been cultivated since Acadian days, and some rather eye-filling vistas.

Truro, even bigger than Amherst, is about as central as a Nova Scotian city can be, is most noted for its thousand-acre Victoria Park, and is the site also of Nova Scotia Agricultural College and Demonstration Farm (both of which welcome visitors), Nova Scotia Teachers College, and an out-of-town mosque—unique in this part of the world. There's a good bit of manufacturing.

Pictou has a pretty harbor setting, a thriving lobster industry, Norway House—a stone mansion of the early nineteenth century that's now a lodge hall—a wonderfully situated golf course, and a pair of museums—the Micmac (Indian and other historic lore), and Hector National Exhibit Centre (recognizing locals of Scottish descent who have distinguished themselves). You're in luck if you hit Pictou during its Lobster Festival in July. Nearby (five miles) is little *Caribou*—terminus for ferries from the village of Wood Islands, Prince Edward Island, and *New Glasgow,* a mainly industrial town whose satellites include *Little Harbour* (for excellent swimming) and the photogenic little settlement of *Abercrombie,* on Pictou harbor.

Pugwash, an oddly named community with a population of little more than five hundred, has become internationally renowned in recent years as the site of the newsmaking East-West conferences of political leaders, scientists, and other intellectuals from both non-Communist and Communist countries, hosted by Cleveland industrialist Cyrus Eaton, a son of Nova Scotia. There is good swimming on Northumberland Strait beaches (the waters are among the warmest in this part of the continent), good boating, and excellent deep-sea fishing.

Antigonish is the largest town near the Canso Causeway which connects mainland Nova Scotia with Cape Breton Island. Handsomely set amidst hills covered with neat farms, fronted by a deep harbor leading into George Bay and the Northumberland Strait, it is the most Gaelic-speaking of Nova Scotian communities outside of Cape Breton Island. Have a look at St. Ninian's Cathedral

(Roman Catholic) and the campus of St. Francis Xavier University. It is noted for its pioneering work in adult education—mainly dealing with the organization of fish and farm co-operatives. Originally intended for local people and residents of nearby provinces, the university's adult education department now attracts students from many of the developing countries.

Cape Breton Island: One does not, I should explain, go through customs when passing from mainland Nova Scotia to Cape Breton Island. But one might just as well. Cape Breton Islanders consider themselves residents of almost a province apart. The island has its own tartan; the words "Nova Scotia" are, whenever possible in printed matter, abbreviated to "N.S."—or not used at all. It is, of course, over a century since this hundred-mile-long, eighty-mile-wide island ceased being a separate province. But the feelings of isolation which islands can promote sometimes die hard—even in the case of Cape Breton which, for several years now, has been connected with the rest of Nova Scotia by a modern causeway. One could do with a bit less of this excessive separatism, and at times, one has the feeling that the island tries to be more Scottish than the Scots of Scotland. But Cape Breton is, indisputably, Nova Scotia at its most beautiful—particularly the highlands region—and it is eminently hospitable. To visit this province without taking in the Cape is to commit a touristic blunder of major proportions.

Sydney is the island's principal city and, I suppose you might say, its "capital." Though dominantly industrial—it is home to the largest self-contained steel plant in North America, and other factories as well—it is far from being grim or grimy. Built for the most part on a peninsula flanked by a spacious harbor on the one side and the green hills on the other, it is of interest to the traveler more because of its location and its amenities than for specific attractions. St. George's Church (1786) is the fourth-oldest Anglican church in Canada and contains a chair from the wardroom of Lord Nelson's ship, the *Victory*—a souvenir of the vessel's visit to the town's harbor. Old St. Patrick's Church is now open as a museum. Wentworth Park is attractive, there is harness racing in summer at Cape Breton Sports Center, and boating at the Royal Cape Breton Yacht Club. *North Sydney,* the port for ships plying the run to Port-aux-Basques and Argentia, Newfoundland, is nearby. Sydney, should you be wondering, is not—like Peggy's

Cove—called after the Christian name of a beloved local figure. It was, rather, named for Lord Sydney, an eighteenth-century British Colonial Secretary. Its founders were New York State people who came north in 1785, under the leadership of Abraham Cuyler, a mayor of Albany.

Fortress of Louisbourg National Historic Park: Nothing of this magnitude has been, or is being, attempted anywhere else in North America. The Louisbourg restoration is a multiyear, multimillion-dollar project being undertaken by the federal government. The idea, put simply, is to re-create eighteenth-century French Colonial life—from governor to cod fisherman—as it was lived in what had been an incredibly elaborate fortress-community built by Louis XV as a major ploy in France's efforts to remain a dominant New World power. Designed to guard the mouth of the St. Lawrence River and built on a damp, frequently fogbound, windswept peninsula of Cape Breton Island, the fortress first fell to an invasion from New Englanders, was later returned to the French, and again fell, a second and final time, to the British. Decay and neglect were its subsequent enemies. But when, in the middle decades of this century, the government's restoration plan evolved, it was found that documentation on Louisbourg was nothing short of astonishing. Historians and archeologists have discovered—in Canada, as well as in England and France—some half a million documents, journals, maps, and plans, as well as some two million artifacts excavated on the site.

The project began when, in 1961, a force of out-of-work coal miners was formed and trained in eighteenth-century-style stone-cutting, carpentry, wrought-iron work, timber-hewing, and other crafts. They formed the nucleus of the Restoration staff. Since then, experts in all requisite fields have been retained. Once an aspect of a job has been determined, a design group composed of historians, archeologists, draftsmen, engineers and architects is formed to come up with specific details for construction. Only then is a go-ahead given.

About a fifth of the entire fortress complex and its defenses are to be reconstructed, with a target date of 1980 for completion. About half a dozen buildings a year are finished, each one taking more than half a decade to complete, so meticulous is the attention to detail and historical accuracy. Costumes are hand-sewn, stockings hand-knit; candles are reserved for the governor's chandeliers, with lamps elsewhere burning fish oil as was the case originally. When completed, Louisbourg is expected to be the largest historical reconstruction combining military and civil structures in the world.

The King's Bastion Barracks, a long, elegant-lined triple-story structure houses the sumptuous Governor's Wing which embraces ten magnificently furnished chambers, most especially His Excellency's bedroom, dining, and reception rooms. Other highlights include the officers' mess, enlisted men's quarters, prison, courtroom, and chapel, not to mention such detached buildings as guardhouse, stables, even an icehouse. Even the guides are special —in authentic garb, of course, but actually trained to work and behave as soldiers, fishermen, laundresses, cooks, maids, blacksmiths, or whatever occupation they are costumed to represent.

The Cabot Trail is an ingeniously plotted 184-mile circular drive that begins and terminates at Baddeck (on the Trans-Canada Highway, north of Sydney) and takes one through the splendid highlands of Cape Breton Island, including, of course, the Cape Breton Highlands National Park. It requires, *as a minimum,* about twenty-four hours on one's itinerary, but I would be even more leisurely if I were you, for this is extra-special tourist territory. *Baddeck* is approached either from mainland Nova Scotia, via the Trans-Canada Highway (which crosses to Cape Breton Island by means of the Canso Causeway) or from Sydney, to the south. Baddeck is a hamlet with a population of fewer than a thousand. But it is set in one of the prettiest regions of eastern Canada, where one still hears a good bit of Gaelic spoken, and where Alexander Graham Bell—among others—had a summer home. Bell, who was probably one of the most creative, original-thinking men of modern times, did a great deal more than invent the telephone (as if that would not have been sufficient for any one human being!). And he carried on a great many of his experiments in Baddeck. The range of his remarkable work is excellently portrayed in the modern, strikingly designed Alexander Graham Bell Memorial Museum, which is operated by the Federal Government, and where I suggest you plan on spending the better part of a morning or afternoon. *The Margaree River Valley* is another Cabot Trail highlight; it embraces the tiny settlements of Northeast Margaree, Margaree Forks, and Margaree Harbour; and has a sylvan beauty that, though quiet, is most appealing. *Chéticamp* is an almost entirely French-speaking village, and like almost all such communities in Nova Scotia it is dominated by an immense Roman Catholic church designed to hold the total populace—and then some. Chéticamp's is St. Peter's, with an elaborate décor and a tall spire. There are a number of sources (often private homes) of the hand-woven rugs indigenous to the area. Just beyond is the entrance to *Cape Breton Highlands National Park,* a four-hundred-square-mile natural wonderland sandwiched between the Atlantic and the Gulf of St. Lawrence. The scenic caliber is of a magnitude not to be met with in any national park between the east coast and Alberta, in the west. The park occupies an extensive, forested plateau some seventeen hundred feet high, and at its most dramatic, it drops down to the sea by means of fantastic cliffs, through which part of the Cabot Trail winds. The vistas, as one drives through, are, upon occasion, almost stupefyingly beautiful. One finds oneself simultaneously stunned and delighted by this succession of natural masterworks—from the fir forests and streams through to the seaside cliffs. There are designated ooh-and-aah points such as Mackenzie Mountain Lookout and Sunrise Lookout along the way, but almost all of the Cabot Trail is one vast lookout. Park Headquarters are at *Ingonish*. There, and in the surrounding area, one finds a variety of accommodations—from the provincially operated Keltic Lodge (with a magnificent situation) to camping grounds and trailer parks. Going south on the Trail from Ingonish, one may either return to Baddeck and proceed into mainland Nova Scotia—or drive south to Sydney. Accommodations are available at Baddeck, the Margarees, Chéticamp, Pleasant Bay, and the Ingonishes.

SHOPPING

Nova Scotia handicrafts run a wide and thoroughly delightful gamut. The provincial government wisely encourages the crafts movement and sponsors crafts exhibits as a part of the annual Nova Scotia Festival of the Arts, in Halifax every mid-August. To look for in the crafts shops are the unique hooked rugs, chair seats, and drinks coasters out of Chéticamp, ceramics, ships-in-bottles and ship models, carved seagulls mounted on fragments of driftwood, miniature chests filled with miniature shells, tiny carved boats, homespun textiles in varying shades and colors, cards and notepaper illustrated with local scenes, hand-wrought jewelry, Nova Scotia and Cape Breton Island tartans, as well, of course, as crafts from other parts of Canada—Eskimo and Indian especially. **Halifax** has several good shops. One particularly interesting one is *Sea Chest Boutique* (1593 Dresden Row) near the Dresden Arms Hotel. Also good are the *Spinning Wheel* (6300 Quinpool Road), *Waltoncraft Studio* (58 Dutch Village Road), and the *Maple Tree* in Scotia Square shopping center. *Nova Pine Shop,* in the Privateers Wharf area downtown, specializes not only in furniture, but in handmade quilts, pillows, throws and place mats. Smart shops are to be found on Spring Garden Road, from Barrington to South Park streets, and in the Halifax and Micmac shopping centers, the last-mentioned in Dartmouth; *Eaton's* and *Simpsons* department stores are at these locations. **Chester:** *The Warp and Woof* is an old favorite. **Mahone Bay:** *The Teazer.* **Lunenburg:** *Captain's Cache.* **Grand Pré:** *The Apple Barrel* is noteworthy in that it handles only Nova Scotian-made crafts. **Kentville:** *Fourspears Gifts.* **Yarmouth:** *Hoods.* **Amherst:** *Village Gift Shop.* **Truro:** *Round the Corner Gift Shop.* **Pictou:** *Grohmann Knives.* **Antigonish:** *The Curiosity Shop.* **Sydney:** *Normaway Handcrafts,* long on the scene at the corner of Charles and Townsend streets; *Cape Co-Op Books and Crafts* (358A George Street); and—both of these are on Main Street—the *Quilt Shop* (quilts, of course, handmade and machine-stitched, in traditional Nova Scotia designs), and the *House of Crafts and Art Gallery,* in a well-restored old church. **Louisbourg:** *Royal Battery.* **Baddeck:** *Lynwood.* **Chéticamp:** *Cooperative Artisanale de Chéticamp; Edna's Gift Shop; Foyer du Souvenir.*

CREATURE COMFORTS

Of the smaller provinces, it is probably safe to assert that Nova Scotia comes through as having the most consistently high-standard accommodations, province-wide. By that I mean the visitor can count on being quite comfortable away from the capital, as

well as within it. The same rule obtains as regards the inner man.
Provincial Nova Scotia leads the smaller provinces in the fre-
quency with which one comes across interesting restaurants. Now,
down to some specifics: **Halifax,** as befits its standing as the major
city of the Maritimes, leads in this quartet of provinces with its
hotel plant—and by a long shot. *The Nova Scotian Hotel,*
Canadian National's centrally located traditional-style property,
has been first-rate as long as I have known it. After a mid-1970s
refurbishing of major proportions, it emerged as an even finer
hotel, with commendable attention to detail—especially noticeable
in the various furnishing schemes of its 316 rooms and suites. This
is, needless to say, full-facility, with one of the best restaurants
in the province, a good-sized and handsome coffee shop, and a
cocktail lounge that is a major congregating spot. My candidate
for the Maritimes' best all-round hotel. The *Lord Nelson,* also
traditional-style, but larger as regards room-total than the Nova
Scotian (355 rooms), is a long-time leader, and remains agreeable
indeed, with attractive public spaces, inviting wine-dine facilities
(good restaurant, coffee shop, popular Victory Lounge, and comfortable rooms—I prefer those in the older section to those in the
new wing) and a lovely location overlooking the Public Gardens.
Citadel Inn: This modern, well-located downtown house is at its
most outstanding with the rooms of its tower section—about 80 of
the total of 189. Business travelers with paper work will like the
desk space and the otherwise inventive design of these chambers,
not to mention the views of town and harbor from their windows;
restaurant, cocktail lounge, and outdoor pool. *Dresden Arms
Motor Inn* is long popular, like the Nova Scotian and Lord Nelson. Although less grand than those competitors, it is well
equipped and managed, with one of the best restaurants in the
capital, pleasant rooms, and a nice perky ambience. *Holiday Inn* is
away from the center of town, and therefore more suitable for motorists than car-less visitors. It's a 237-room tower, with attractive
lobby, restaurant, cocktail lounge, and coffee shop. The rooms are
good-sized and good looking, and there's an indoor pool. *Keddy's
Motor Inn* (20 St. Margaret's Bay Road, **Armdale**) is a worth-
knowing-about house; it has 132 rooms with the usual amenities,
as well as a licensed restaurant and cocktail lounge. Another good
albeit un-central spot is *Wandlyn Motor Inn* (Bedford Road just

north of the Fairview Overpass), a link of the eastern Canada
chain that has 75 nice rooms and a licensed dining room. **Dartmouth,** Halifax's across-the-water neighbor, offers a number of
possibilities, including the 120-room *Holiday Inn,* with restaurant,
cocktail lounge-cum-entertainment, and pool; and the 92-unit
Wandlyn Motor Inn, with restaurant and cocktail lounge. **Chester:**
The smallish *Sword & Anchor Inn* is a long-time charmer; a
dozen of its 14 rooms have bath, the harbor-view setting is lovely,
and there's a licensed dining room that's a good lunch or dinner
bet, especially for the local fish or lobster. *Windjammer Motel* is
smallish (15 units) but nice, and with its licensed dining room—
noted for seafood and home-baked cakes and pies—a special lure.
Lunenburg: *Bluenose Lodge* has baths in 9 of its 10 rooms, and a
locally heralded licensed dining room, with home-baked goods and
seafood the specialties. **Windsor:** *Kingsway Inn* has 30 modern—
and very good-looking—rooms, a heated indoor pool, a licensed
restaurant, all part of a low-slung contemporary complex. *Old Orchard Inn,* anything but old, is a smart-looker of a motor-inn, with
a one-of-a-kind neo-medieval lobby, a Colonial-look licensed restaurant, cocktail lounge with entertainment, tennis courts, indoor
pool, and a choice of accommodations either in conventional-style
bedrooms (74 of these) or 30 frame chalets, some kitchen-
equipped. **Kentville:** *Wandlyn Motor Inn* has 75 fully equipped
rooms, as well as a licensed restaurant—among the better area eateries—cocktail lounge, and coffee bar. **Annapolis Royal:** *Royal
Anne Motel* remains a leader; 20 pleasant rooms, and croquet on
the lawn. Have a lobster dinner at the nearby *Sea Shell Restaurant.* **Digby:** *The Pines* is the relatively recent label for what several generations of holidaymakers fondly recall as the Digby Pines
—for long Canadian Pacific's pre-eminent eastern resort hotel.
Since the Nova Scotia Government took over its ownership and
operation, the first word of the title was unceremoniously dropped.
But, otherwise, the place remains a winner, with its baronial-style
main building overlooking the bay, 92 attractive rooms as well as
31 two-bedroom cottages, a handsome dining room, cocktail
lounge both in the main hotel and in the golf-course clubhouse
(the course is 18 holes), swimming in a heated glass-walled pool-
cum-bay view, and facilities including tennis, shuffleboard, croquet, movies—even afternoon tea. If the Pines is full-up, consider

another area favorite—*Mountain Gap Inn;* it embraces motel rooms (102 of these) and cottages (10 of these, some with three bedrooms). Swimming and other active diversions, restaurant, and cocktail lounge. *Hedley House,* at nearby Smith's Cove, is at once a hostelry (smallish but nice, with 14 rooms, some kitchen-equipped), and a restaurant—one of the better ones in the Digby area. Worth noting, too: Digby's *Fundy Restaurant,* for reasonably priced seafood. **Yarmouth:** *Manor Inn,* five miles from town, is a big white-frame house—the ex-Commodore Raymond estate. It's set amidst four acres of gardens, with a half-mile lake front. There are 6 bedrooms, each with bath, in the main house and each distinctively furnished. Additionally, there's a motel wing with 20 modern rooms with bath; dining room and bar-lounge, as well. Downtown Yarmouth offers the commendably contemporary *Grand Hotel,* a convenient Main Street house with 138 functional rooms with bath, restaurant, and handsome cocktail lounge, with entertainment. *Braemer Lodge,* for long the traditional Yarmouth "resort," is eleven miles from town and embraces a main house sheltering nearly 70 rooms with bath, as well as nearly a dozen cottages. Varied activities, from swimming in the lake to shuffleboard and tennis; licensed restaurant. *Harris' Restaurant* is a good Yarmouth choice for a reasonably priced lobster dinner. **Amherst:** *Wandlyn Motor Inn*—a good bet, with 60 well-equipped rooms, licensed restaurant, and the usual Wandlyn coffee bar. **Truro:** My choice is *Keddy's Motor Inn*—70 comfortable rooms, as well as a restaurant and cocktail lounge. **New Glasgow:** *Heather Motor Inn,* at nearby Stellerton, has 76 rooms, restaurant, and cocktail lounge. *Peter Pan Motel*—54 rooms, restaurant, lounge. **Antigonish:** *Claymore Motel* has more than half a hundred rooms, restaurant, cocktail lounge, and a heated outdoor pool. *Antigonisher Motel-Hotel* is agreeable, too, with 35 units and a convenient albeit unlicensed restaurant. **Sydney:** *Holiday Inn* is perky, bright, and good looking, with 122 generous-size rooms, a sea-view restaurant, cocktail lounge, and coffee shop. *Keddy's Motor Inn* has 73 modern units as well as a licensed restaurant. *Wandlyn Motor Inn* has 71 rooms, a licensed restaurant that's one of the best in town, and the usual Wandlyn coffee bar. *Isle Royal Hotel,* long on the scene, has 141 rooms, restaurant, cocktail lounge, coffee bar, and a central location. It has a motel—

at another location, on King's Road—containing 110 rooms, restaurant, and cocktail lounge. **Baddeck:** *Inverary Inn,* a traditional favorite in this area, continues popular although it's hardly fancy. There are 13 (out of 17) rooms with bath in a onetime farmhouse, as well as 7 cottages, a beach, and a commendable—albeit dry—dining room that serves dinner only. *Telegraph House* has 10 rooms and suites in its main building, and a dozen-odd motel units, as well as an unlicensed restaurant. **Chéticamp:** *Parkview Motel*—17 rooms, a pool, and a licensed dining room that is probably the best in the neighborhood with top-notch seafood and baked goods. *Acadian Motel:* 16 modern units, and a restaurant and cocktail lounge. **Ingonish Beach:** *Keltic Lodge,* owned and operated—like the Pines at Digby—by the provincial government, is superbly situated on a high cliff overlooking the sea, offers a variety of attractions—beaches, pool, deep-sea fishing, shuffleboard, tennis, golf in the national park, hiking, fishing, evening entertainment, and movies. There's a first-rate restaurant that serves afternoon tea as well as the usual meals, cocktail lounge, coffee shop, handsome and capacious public rooms, and a variety of accommodations: 32 main-lodge bedrooms, 40 motel rooms, and half a dozen cottages of varying sizes. Transients are welcome to dine but in limited numbers, with residents having priority. *Glenhorn Resort* embraces three dozen motel rooms, and 9 cottages of varying sizes. There are both restaurant and cocktail lounge, and a variety of diversions. *Ingonish Motel:* 32 modern units, a licensed restaurant, and both pool and beach. **Louisbourg:** *Fleur de Lis Motel*—18 rooms and an unlicensed dining room. Consider lunch or dinner at *Le Potager Restaurant,* unlicensed but nice.

Dining in Halifax: The Nova Scotian capital does as well with restaurants as with hotels, with a disproportionately large proportion of good places. To me the restaurant with the most ambitious, interesting—and successful—cuisine is Ohioan Frank Metzger's *Fat Frank's* (5411 Spring Garden Road), which has become a local gustatory landmark with good reason. There are longer menus at many top-rank restaurants, but Frank keeps his within reason. And you have a wide enough choice—his own pâté or oysters Rockefeller to start, onion or other soups, several seafood and fish choices, entrées like chicken Marengo and filet of beef, fresh-only vegetables, splendid desserts (most especially the black forest cake as it should be—but rarely is—made). Everything is cooked to order. The setting is two floors of a private house, with waitresses in long gowns, the silver and coffee services antique, the paintings on the wall choice. Dinner only. *Henry House* (1222 Barrington Street) occupies a dilly of an early-nineteenth-century merchant's home that has been handsomely restored. The two-foot thick walls remain, and so do many of the decorative details. Go for either lunch or dinner and ignore the clam chowder—to start—and the trifle—to finish—at your own risk. There are a variety of in-betweens from coq au vin to broiled steak to boiled lobster. Everything is delicious and the presentation is expert. *The Evangeline Room* (Nova Scotian Hotel) is a handsome, traditional-décor restaurant that serves à la carte dinner only, with specialties including a house pâté, Malpecque oysters in season, a variety of seafood dishes including lobster Newburg—and boiled—and delicious desserts. The wine list is the most elaborate in town. Have a pre- or post-dinner drink in the hotel's *Griffin Bar,* where there's a daily buffet lunch. *Dresden Arms Motor Hotel Restaurant* is a traditionally popular spot with the locals for seafood—lobster and fresh fish—along with good desserts and breads, all nicely served, and with tabs moderate. The setting is inviting, too. *The Gondola* (5175 South Street) is a wise choice for an Italian meal, always pleasant for a change in the Maritimes. Pasta in variety, and good veal dishes, too. *Mario's* (5680 Spring Garden Road) though newer, is still another good source of Italian food. *French Casino* (2150 Gottington Road) does not belie its name. It is indeed French, with the standbys like coq au vin and steak au poivre invariably reliable. Cleverly named *Duke of Granville* occupies an old house at the corner of Duke and Granville streets and is a good bet for lunch, with good clam chowder and hamburgers.

FROM NOVA SCOTIA TO FRANCE

SAINT-PIERRE ET MIQUELON

Less than 200 miles from the Nova Scotia coast is the ancient—and tiny—French Overseas Territory of Saint-Pierre et Miquelon. Now, make no mistake, this cluster of a dozen little islands—only

two of which have permanent populations—is to this very day a part
of the French Republic; it is *Old* France, not New, not Québecois;
not, in other words, a part of Canada. There is plane service via Air
St. Pierre from Sydney, and much slower and less convenient ship
service, too, to Saint-Pierre, the major island of the group. The lure
is the populace—descendants of settlers from four centuries back,
who are mostly fishermen, and whose language remains that of
Metropolitan France rather than the North American-accented
Québecois. There's a worth-visiting historical museum—small but
to the point. There are several comfortable hotels (Île de la
France—with a good dining room—and Champlain are the leaders);
good restaurants (Le Caveau and Chez Dutin, most especially);
and excursion destinations around the island, and to the even
quainter island of Saint-Miquelon, where Pension Chez Paulette is
a recommended stopping place. Meanwhile, back on Saint-Pierre,
the principal visitor-occupation is shopping—for French perfumes
and colognes, French scarves, gloves, and other clothing accessories, French porcelain (including Limoges) and kitchenware,
French wines, as well as whiskey and other spirits. Stores worth
checking out include: B. Leroux Deschamps, Les Galleries
Françaises, Albert Briand, and Marc Moraze. If you can, time
your visit to include Bastille Day, July 14, and you'll really appreciate that you're in La Belle France. Further information: French
Government Tourist Office, 610 Fifth Avenue, New York City;
Services Officiels Français du Tourisme, 1840 Avenue Sherbrooke ouest, Montreal.

Ontario

L'ONTARIO

Best times for a visit: *If one excepts its far northern reaches (which can be fifty below in winter) Ontario is pleasant the year-round and with attractions for vacationers during every season. Southern Ontario (including such places as Toronto,*

Niagara Falls, Windsor) juts down into the United States and constitutes the southernmost bit of all Canada, with the country's mildest winters. (Toronto, for example, rarely goes below seventeen degrees, and is usually warmer in winter.) As one goes north (Ottawa, Sault Ste. Marie, for example) winters are, of course, progressively colder. Winter sees Ontario cities at their liveliest, with activities ranging from hockey to legitimate theatre. And winter sports are well developed in many parts of the province. In summer, southern Ontario sets another all-Canadian record: it is the warmest region of the country, and days can be humid as well as hot. But once again, as one goes north to the lakes and forests, temperatures drop and nights are cool; they also can be buggy, so insect repellent is imperative. Spring—April and May—is pleasant in the central region and the south—particularly the latter. And brisk autumn—late September to mid-November—is popular with hunters and (in October) with motorists who enjoy the brilliant panorama of tree leaves changing color. **Transportation:** *No province is better equipped with roads. The Trans-Canada Highway extends almost fifteen hundred miles in Ontario. It begins in the west, just east of Kenora near the Manitoba border, passes through Thunder Bay on Lake Superior, follows the shore of that lake to Sault Ste. Marie, at which point it continues along the shore of Lake Huron, goes north to Sudbury, then southeast along Georgian Bay to Orillia and Lake Simcoe, from where it goes through the interior to the federal capital, Ottawa, and passes over the Ontario-Quebec frontier to Montreal. There is an extensive intercity bus system, and buses also link major Ontario towns with those of nearby Canadian provinces and U.S. states. Both major Canadian airlines—Air Canada and CP Air—serve Ontario, and so do a number of American and other foreign carriers. Some two dozen airlines fly in and out of Toronto International Airport, including American Airlines, Alitalia, British Airways, BWIA, KLM, Lufthansa, United, and Swissair. Ontario is served by both CP Rail and Canadian National, as well as by the Ontario Northland Railway, a 222-mile route linking the city of North Bay, 180 miles north of Toronto, with Moosonee, on James Bay, a satellite of Hud-*

*son Bay. CN runs extra-speed turbo trains, with two classes
of service between Toronto, Ottawa, and Montreal; running
time Toronto–Montreal is four hours, ten minutes. Public
transport is modern and efficient in all principal cities.
Toronto's subway system is one of the best in North
America; it is essentially T-shaped, with two routes—the
longer east-west Bloor-Danforth, and the north-south Yonge-
University; the two converge as the central Yonge and St.
George stations, which are inter-line transfer points.* **Having a
drink:** *Liquor by the glass is available at licensed cocktail
lounges and—with meals—at licensed hotel dining rooms and
licensed restaurants. There are beverage rooms serving beer
to men only, and women's beverage rooms serve beer to
women only; or to women who bring male escorts with them.
Liquor by the bottle is available at provincial government liquor stores.* **Further information:** *Ontario Ministry of Industry and Tourism, Hearst Block, Queen's Park, Toronto;
Agent-General of Ontario, 13 Charles II Street, London;
Canadian Government Office of Tourism, Ottawa and
branches.*

INTRODUCING ONTARIO

When one considers that one out of every three Canadians lives
in Ontario, the significance of that tremendous—and tremendously
rich—province is apparent. Ontario is home to more than 8 million
people—nearly 2 million more than Quebec, which has the second
largest population. But it is not by any means crowded. Its area—
and here, among the provinces, it *is* exceeded by that of Quebec
and only Quebec—is larger by a good bit than that of Nigeria,
which is the largest country in Africa—a continent of big countries.
It would accommodate over twenty-six lands the size of the
Netherlands, eight states the size of New York (and then some),
more than four United Kingdoms. From east to west it stretches a
thousand miles, touching the province of Manitoba on the west,
the province of Quebec on the east, Hudson and James Bays on
the north, and the states of Minnesota, Michigan, Wisconsin (with
which it shares Lake Superior), Ohio and Pennsylvania (with

which it shares Lake Erie), and New York. The only Great Lake it does *not* border is Lake Michigan. Its Niagara region, Canada's southernmost bit of territory, puts Windsor—one of its major cities —to the *south* of such U.S. points as Boston and Minneapolis. And from that fertile heavily populated region it extends north for a thousand miles to the sparsely inhabited mineral-rich shores of Hudson Bay.

The richest province: Though Ontario, to most North Americans, is generally ranked with the eastern part of the continent, it is the hub of Canada. Quebec and the four Atlantic provinces are to its east, and the quartet of enormous western provinces lie in the opposite direction. Except for the matter of area, in which it is topped among the provinces only by Quebec, Ontario leads Canada in every important respect. It is the richest province, with the highest per capita income. It has the biggest industrial capacity, producing about as much in value as all of the rest of Canada. It has great forests, immensely productive farms, and tremendous mineral wealth (copper, nickel, uranium, gold, iron ore). It abounds in hydroelectric power. It fronts a maze of major Great Lakes waterways, and from its territory the St. Lawrence Seaway wends its way to the Atlantic. It is the seat of Canada's second-largest city—and largest English-speaking city—a center of industrial, financial, and intellectual activity. And hardly to be underestimated is its political importance on the national scene. Ontario sends to the federal capital—this, too, lies within its borders—no less than eighty-five of the 265 members of the House of Commons.

The contrast between today's Ontario and today's Quebec could not be more startling. No two neighboring provinces in Canada appear more dissimilar. Quebec's personality is as Gallic as Ontario's is dominantly Anglo-Saxon. Even the automobile license plates of the two provinces reflect their personalities: Quebec's reads *"Québec—La Belle Province"* and carries the French fleur-de-lis. Ontario's, on the other hand, is distinguished by a crown—the insignia of the English-speaking Queen of Canada, to whom it is devotedly loyal. But this strongly Anglo-Saxon province is a region of French origins. Its original inhabitants were, of course, Indians—the Algonquin group (nomads who roamed the rocky, lake-dotted Canadian Shield area of what is now northern Ontario, and included such tribes as the Cree, Ottawa, and Missisauga) and the Iroquois (who included such tribes as the Hurons and Petuns, who lived sedentary lives in their great bark-roofed longhouses).

Early French days: Their way of life was first disturbed by the Frenchman Étienne Brule, who came upon the Ottawa River Valley in 1610, and who was followed a few years later by Samuel de Champlain, who reached the eastern shores of Lake Huron in 1615. Their countrymen—missionaries, traders, explorers—followed, setting up posts at strategic points. (The most famous of the missions, Fort Sainte Marie I, lasted but a decade—from 1639 to 1649. It was given up after eight priests were murdered by Indians; now partly reconstructed, it may be seen today, near the town of Midland.)

The French continued in the region—and the wealth they accumulated through fur trading with the Indians did not go unnoticed by the British in their colonies to the south. A difficult period—embracing hostilities as well as competition—ensued until 1763, when the Peace of Paris decreed that the French were to turn over their North American mainland territories to the British. In 1774 the area was made a part of Quebec, but shortly thereafter—beginning in 1783—substantial waves of colonists loyal to the Crown came north from the American colonies to escape the turmoil of the Revolution, and made known their demands for a government of their own. The British, in 1791, acceded to their request and decreed the land west of the Ottawa River a separate colony, to be known as Upper Canada—in contrast to Quebec, which then became known as Lower Canada.

The Yanks burn York: The War of 1812, among other things, impeded settlement, for the area was a series of battlefields, and the United States did not win friends north of the border when it burned York (the capital, now Toronto). Indeed, many of the forts where the British and their colonists fought the American invaders—who would have liked adding Canada to the U.S. but did not succeed—still dot the Ontario countryside. Neither side admitted being the loser in that war, but for Canada, a tangible result was a sense of unity and nationhood which was to serve it in good stead and lead ultimately to its becoming a sovereign state.

After the war, immigration picked up. Englishmen, Scots, and Irish were drawn to British North America in great numbers. By

1837 there were some 350,000 people living in Upper Canada. They liked their new homeland, but the more radical among them were not pleased with the autocratic, aristocratic clique of old-timers—known as the Family Compact group—who were running the colony highhandedly. After Robert Baldwin—an advocate of responsible government—had failed to dissuade the discontent group under William Lyon Mackenzie from drastic action, the Rebellion of 1837 ensued. It was quelled, but partially as a result of it, a change in government did come about in 1841. That year, the two Canadas—Upper (now Ontario) and Lower (now Quebec)— were united, and Upper Canada got still another name—Canada West. What followed was, perhaps, inevitable—the clash of two cultures, English and French. It was not resolved until almost three decades later when, in 1867, the Canadian Confederation was born. The area that had been known, successively, as Upper Canada and Canada West became Ontario—a province of the new country, while its neighbor took its old name and became the Province of Quebec.

Today's Ontario: The transcontinental railroad, in the 1880s, brought new groups of settlers to Ontario, industry and commerce developed, new towns were born, older ones grew rapidly. With the turn of the century came mineral discoveries in the barren northern regions of the province. In 1912 Ontario's territory was increased when it was given parts of the Northwest Territories. In the 1930s, new gold strikes were made.

Ontario's Conservative Party has set an enviable twentieth-century record. By 1975 it had been in office for more than two and a half decades, having won no less than eight provincial elections since 1943.

Economically, Ontario makes for a mass of superlatives. Its industrial output is about 40 per cent of Canada's; within Ontario are made more than 90 per cent of such commodities as cars, heavy and agricultural machinery. Ontario's steel production is 80 per cent of the nation's total, while its pulp and paper industries represent a third of the Canadian output. The natural resources are there, too. Forty per cent of Canada's mining activity originates in Ontario, Canada's Shield region.

Despite the continued importance of farming, commercial fishing, and lumbering, Ontario is the most urbanized of the provinces. It has been attracting immigrants from a variety of lands, in quantity, since World War II, and since French became the sole official language of neighboring Quebec in 1974, it is expected to be even more of a magnet to those new Canadians who want English to be their—and their children's—New World language.

No province has a consistently higher standard of living, which reflects itself—as far as the visitor is concerned—in a commendable province-wide standard, as regards hotels and restaurants. Ontario is not—Niagara Falls excepted—Canada at its most naturally scenic. And in contrast to neighboring Quebec, it is anything but exotic, at least for fellow North Americans. Still, it holds its own touristically. As how could it not, as the seat of one of the continent's most dynamic cities (Toronto), the remarkable federal capital (Ottawa), countless lakes and hunting grounds, a variety of parks—national, national-historical, and provincial—and an underappreciated network of culturally rewarding smaller cities that can pay surprisingly large visitor dividends.

YOUR VISIT TO ONTARIO

Ontario's highlights—the really outstanding places for the newcomer—are relatively few, and would, to my mind, include Ottawa, the national capital; Toronto, the provincial capital—and Canada's second largest city; Stratford, in summer the site of the noted Shakespeare Festival; Niagara Falls, indisputably one of the great natural phenomena of the universe. But there are, as well, a number of other interesting places—substantial cities, points of historic interest, and a variety of rural vacation areas. The most important of these are dealt with in the pages that follow, working in a generally east to west direction. Ontario, it might be noted, has four national parks; all are popular and eminently visitable, but none has the exciting quality of such parks as Banff to the west or Cape Breton to the east. There are, as well, more than half a dozen national historic parks and sites—interesting, but not of major historic significance; a number of well-equipped provincial parks, and a chain of parks operated by the St. Lawrence Parks Commission along a 170-mile area, from the Quebec border to Adolphustown on Lake Ontario. Some of these are for day-camping and picnicking, some for overnight visits, and two are of historic interest: Upper Canada Village, near Morrisburg, and Old Fort Henry, at Kingston. There are, as well, literally hundreds of campsites, roadside parks, picnic grounds, and recreation areas throughout the province.

OTTAWA AND THE EAST

Ottawa: There is probably no important world capital with as odd a background as Ottawa's. It surprised even its own most loyal boosters when it was designated the Canadian seat of government in 1857 by no less a personage than Queen Victoria.

Built on the south bank of the Ottawa River, at its junction with the Gatineau River, Ottawa was first inhabited as a farm by one Nicholas Sparks at the start of the nineteenth century. In 1826 the Royal Engineers—come from England to build the Rideau Canal—made the area their headquarters, and in 1832—when the canal was finished—there remained a community of some two thousand souls who named their village Bytown, in honor of the engineer in charge of the canal, Colonel John By. Before long, Bytown might well have been called Lumbertown. Gristmills and sawmills went up, and the populace was not without its share of rough, tough lumberjacks and laborers. English-speaking Bytowners were not always above brawling with French-speaking Bytowners, but there was enough unity among the lot for the town to be incorporated in 1847. Along about that time, the "two Canadas" of the period— Upper (Ontario) and Lower (Quebec) were being united, and a competition had ensued among the principal cities of the region for selection as the new capital. Bytown, by then a metropolis with a population of ten thousand, entered, and convinced that its name was not as glamorous as it might be, changed it to Ottawa—after a local Indian tribe. Still, no one took the entry of this unrefined lumber town seriously. The other contenders, after all, were such respected cities as Quebec, Toronto, Kingston, and Montreal. But in 1857 the following word came from across the Atlantic to the Governor of Canada, "I am commanded by the Queen to inform you that in the judgment of Her Majesty, the City of Ottawa combines more advantages than any other place in Canada for the permanent seat of the future government of the province and is selected by Her Majesty accordingly."

Lumberjack background or no, Ottawa took its new honors in its stride, not aware at the time that a decade later it would be the seat of government not only of the area now embracing Ontario and Quebec, but of a vast country that would span a continent.

But even before 1867—when the Confederation of Canada came into being—construction started on the Parliament Buildings. Queen Victoria's son Bertie, the Prince of Wales—later Edward VII—came all the way from London to lay the cornerstone in 1861. Government departments were established and attracted quantities of personnel to staff them, and at the same time, lumbering continued to thrive, and industry—thanks to the development of cheap power—had its beginnings. In 1880 Ottawa had some twenty-seven thousand inhabitants; by the turn of the century there were sixty thousand, and since then the city has never stopped growing; it now numbers some 300,000 (half a million-plus in the metro region) and recent years have seen it sprout not only a new skyline—to augment that of the towers of Parliament and the Château Laurier Hotel—but a perky, lively ambience that agreeably surprises visitors too long away.

The original Parliament Buildings were burned almost completely in 1916, but were rebuilt—almost duplicating what they replaced—and completed in 1921. Majestically situated on the spacious lawns of Parliament Hill, this beautiful complex—the greatest neo-Gothic complex in North America and of the same high calibre as the also neo-Gothic Parliament in London—is invariably the visitor's first Ottawa destination. The three-hundred-foot Peace Tower dominates Parliament Hill. Its fifty-three-bell carillon peals forth several times weekly, and from its observation deck one has a splendid view of the city and the town of Hull, Quebec, just across the Ottawa River. The doorway of the central building is framed with an arch in which are carved the coats of arms of all ten Canadian provinces. Within are the circular Confederation Hall, through which one passes to the two chambers—House of Commons and Senate—and the elegant, wood-paneled Parliamentary Library, which is housed in an adjoining polygonal building of its own and is the only part of the original Parliament bloc to have survived the 1916 fire. Both legislative chambers are superb. The House of Commons, larger of the two, has a Speaker's Chair of English oak, while the members' chairs are of Canadian oak, and the ceiling is of hand-painted Irish linen. Even more elaborate is the smaller Senate chamber, with striking murals depicting Canada's participation in World War I, rich red carpeting, stained-glass windows, and a marvelously gilded ceiling. On either side of the main building are satellite structures; in the East Block are the Governor-General's, Prime Minister's, and the Privy Council offices, and in the West Block other government departments have their headquarters. The Parliament Buildings are open to the public daily the year round; uniformed personnel take groups around on free guided tours, which leave from the Confederation Hall every half hour or so. And on the grounds of Parliament Hill—before the Parliament Buildings—the splendid Changing of the Guard ceremony takes place at ten o'clock every morning in summer. Parliament, it might be noted here, is one of the few places in all Canada where one sees the Royal Canadian Mounted Police in the red tunics that are a part of their full-ceremonial dress. However, though Mounties are on duty during the Changing of the Guard ceremonies, they do not constitute the members of the guard; this honor goes to the soldiers of the elite units known as the Canadian Grenadier Guards, and the Governor-General's Foot Guards. There are two guard units in the ceremony, the "new" and the "old"; each consists of an officer and forty noncoms and guardsmen. There is, too, a Colour Guard carrying the Queen's Colour or Regimental Colour, and there is musical accompaniment from the Regimental Band and the Corps of Drums or Pipes and Drums. The guard ceremony is by no means a time-honored daily practice on Parliament Hill. We may thank Queen Elizabeth II for having inspired its inauguration during her 1959 visit. The public was so attracted to it that it has been repeated each summer since then, and I shudder to think of the disappointment it could cause if it were stopped. Well over a thousand tourists—Canadian, American, and others, are on hand to watch every morning during July and August, for this—along with a similar ceremony at the Citadel (summer residence of the Governor-General) in Quebec City—represents ceremonial spit-and-polish at its finest, and cannot be duplicated elsewhere in the Western Hemisphere.

The grounds of Parliament are dotted with statues of former Prime Ministers, and of those statesmen—known as the Fathers of Confederation—who helped bring the united Canada into being nearly a century ago. Just across the way, on Wellington Street, is the United States Embassy, and nearby are the old Supreme Court Building, the new Supreme Court which Queen Elizabeth the Queen Mother dedicated in 1939 while on a visit with her husband, George VI. In the vicinity, too, are the Bank of Canada, St. Andrew's Presbyterian Church (the oldest in Ottawa), and Sparks Mall, Ottawa's leading commercial thoroughfare.

The Rideau Canal (which may be traversed by sight-seeing boats leaving frequently throughout the day, in summer) is a part of central Ottawa; beside the canal is the great castlelike Château Laurier, the leading hotel; during sessions of Parliament it is the temporary home of many lawmakers. It is the across-the-street neighbor of the onetime Union Station, cleverly converted to contemporary use as a conference hall. (The train terminal moved to a south-side location.) In this neighborhood, too, is the Canadian National War Memorial, a seventy-foot-high arched monument unveiled by King George VI in 1939. There is a fine view of Parliament Hill to be had from Major's Hill Park, but I urge that you time your visit so as not to arrive on weekdays at noon—when Ottawa is given the time by means of a crashing cannon boom.

I suggest you drive about town, taking in the modern City Hall, the contemporary Carleton University campus, and the older grounds of the University of Ottawa. By all means, photograph the sentries in their pillboxes at the entrance to Government House (known also as Rideau Hall), the official residence of the Queen's representative, the Governor-General. When the Governor-General is not in residence, the grounds of the estate are usually open, and upon occasion the house is open to the public, as well. It was built in 1835 as the private home of Thomas McKay, a wealthy citizen of what was then called Bytown. The government leased it for the Confederation's first Governor-General, Viscount Monck, in 1865 (while he was still Governor-General of British North America), and in that year bought the building, later making extensive alterations, not the least of which was the great stone façade of the main entrance, in which is carved the Royal coat of arms—believed to be the largest extant. It is at Government House where foreign ambassadors present their credentials to the Governor-General, after being brought there in His Excellency's horse-drawn State Carriage, with an escort of Mounties. Ambassadors present Letters of Credence to the Governor-General in the ballroom; he accepts them on behalf of the Queen. Government House is the Queen's home when she is in Ottawa, and it is where other heads of state stay when on official visits to Canada. Principal public rooms include the Drawing Room, the less formal but larger Long Drawing Room; the elegant, Chippendale-furnished Dining Room, and the Tent Room—scene of large state dinners, investitures, and major receptions; its walls are covered with portraits of the Royal Family and of former Governors-General, and there is a crystal chandelier that was given to Canada by the British Government. The grounds—some eighty acres—include natural woods, green lawns, and meticulously tended formal gardens.

The official residence of the Prime Minister—a stone mansion built in 1951—is near Government House; known by its address—24 Sussex Drive, and not open to the public. Other official residences of note are Stornoway, a 1914 mansion in Rockcliffe Park that is home to Her Majesty's Loyal Leader of the Opposition; and Earnscliffe, the mid-nineteenth-century home of the first Prime Minister, Sir John A. Macdonald, and now the official residence of the British High Commissioners. (High Commissioners are what Commonwealth countries call the ambassadors they exchange with each other.) A good example of modern Ottawa is the Garden of the Provinces, which is dedicated to the component parts of the confederation, and in which the coat of arms of each is reproduced. To be seen, too, are the many government buildings—including a number of new ones away from the center of the city, and part of a long-range plan of reconstruction, rehabilitation, and redesign being executed by the National Capital Commission.

Ottawa's two cathedrals are both underappreciated and under-visited. La Basilique Notre-Dame d'Ottawa, the Catholic cathedral, is a mid-nineteenth-century (1841) neo-Gothic gem, with an interior so beautiful—the ceiling of gold stars on a blue background alone makes a visit worthwhile—that it ranks with the similarly named but far more reputed Notre-Dame in Montreal. Christ Church Cathedral is the newer (1872) seat of the Anglican bishop of Ottawa, handsome English Gothic in style. It replaces an earlier structure that was adjudged inadequate, after Ottawa was designated the capital of Canada. Still, more than a century old, it is pleasantly mellow, and hung with military colors that make clear its long-time relationship with Establishment Ottawa—an interesting contrast with Francophone Notre-Dame.

Contemporary Ottawa is nowhere better typified than in the National Arts Centre, the federal-capital counterpart of the striking performing arts complexes found in the provincial capitals and, appropriately enough, the most impressive of the lot. Occupying six gardened acres on the west bank of the Rideau Canal, the hexagonal-shaped centre (designed by Montreal architect Fred Lebensold who won the esteemed Massey Award for it) embraces a splendid 2,300-seat Opera House, the 900-seat Theatre, the more intimate Salon for small-scale performances, and a luxury-category restaurant.

Then there are Ottawa's museums. No city this size in North America has a more remarkable museum plant, and the visitor does well to allow himself enough time to do this group full justice.

The National Gallery, one of the planet's superlative art museums, is No. 1 in Canada; only Toronto's Art Gallery of Ontario and Montreal's Musée des Beaux-Arts are in a class with it. The National Gallery has no weaknesses, as regards major schools of painting. By that I mean that it does not disappoint with European paintings—Old Masters, later English portraitists, French Impressionists and post-Impressionists. It is strong, too, on the Canadians, early on with well-known artists like Krieghoff through to relatively little known but nonetheless exciting contemporary practitioners. There are older Canadian works like a Christmas-card Krieghoff of a wilderness farm, or of Robert Todd's "Montmorency Falls," and of this century's Lawren Harris ("Toronto Houses"), Tom Thomson ("Red Leaves"), David Milne ("Billboards"), and Arthur Lismer ("A September Gale")—to name a few. Or Claude Tousignant's "Chromatic Accelerator" and Joyce Wieland's "Confedspread"—to name a couple of more recent beauties. Then cross the Atlantic—Bronzino's "Portrait of a Man," Chardin's "The Governess," Renoir and Picasso, Léger and Monet.

The little-visited National Archives (which shares a building with the National Library) is worth popping into, if only for the frequently changed exhibits in its impressive lobby. The National

Museum of Man is anthropology for the laymen—graphic and very easy to take. It shares a nicely restored mock-Tudor building with the also-worthy National Museum of Natural Sciences, with super dioramas relating to Canadian bird and animal life. The Canadian War Museum sounds off-putting but is absorbing with exhibits ranging from the World War II Mercedes Benz of Nazi Hermann Goering, through to the tunic of General Sir Isaac Brock, out of the War of 1812. The National Museum of Science and Technology is Ottawa's answer to Toronto's highly touted Ontario Science Centre—and much more easily visitable and less frenetic, with great appeal for the kids. The National Aeronautical Collection is a great hangar full of airplanes dating back to the time when they were spelled aeroplanes. Lots of fun. Laurier House is a cozy mid-nineteenth-century mansion that had been inhabited by two Prime Ministers—Sir Wilfred Laurier and W. L. Mackenzie King. Canadians who know their history enjoy it, and only less so do Americans and other foreigners. As an added treat, there is a relatively recent appendage—the study of more recent Prime Minister Lester B. Pearson, full of objects having to do with his distinguished career, which included the winning of the Nobel Peace Prize. Bytown occupies the old stone structure of the same Colonel By for whom Ottawa was first named; its chock-a-block full of early Ottawa lore. And then for more specialized interests there are the National Postal Museum, the Canadian Film Institute (exhibits for movie buffs), and the Museum of Canadian Scouting.

Hull, Quebec, just across the river from Ottawa, is a largely French-speaking community (Ottawa itself has become heavily Francophone), and is of note chiefly because it is the site of a number of good French-style restaurants.

Cornwall, the easternmost of major Ontario towns, is just across the St. Lawrence from New York State (near Massena). It is an old city, dating back to the late eighteenth century, thrives on pulp and paper and rayon industries, and is near the St. Lawrence Seaway Authority. Visitors are most attracted here to the Seaway, and its locks, canals, and the Robert H. Saunders generating station, which may be toured. A good way to see them is by means of sight-seeing-boat trips.

Upper Canada Village, near *Morrisburg,* is the *chef d'oeuvre* of the chain of parks operated by the St. Lawrence Parks Commission. It is a faithful, accurate—and charming—re-creation of a mid-nineteenth-century village, typical of the area's settlements of the 1850s. Set amidst a green and wooded area is a group of some forty buildings—from tavern to church, from home to school. All of the buildings are original, relocated from sites throughout the St. Lawrence Valley, beautifully restored and appropriately furnished. Most are from old villages that had to be inundated with the widening of the St. Lawrence for the great seaway project. The park itself was the site of the Battle of Chrysler's Farm in 1813. There is a Memorial Mound, dedicated to the soldiers who lost their lives, but it is Upper Canada Village that is of the most general interest. You'll want to take in a broad sampling of the two-score buildings—the schoolmaster's stone house, the elegant drawing room of Loucks' Farmhouse, green-shuttered Cook's Tavern, the general store, the doctor's house with its unique root fence, and possibly last—but not least—Willard's Hotel, once again serving lunches and dinners, as it did a century ago.

The Thousand Islands (St. Lawrence Islands National Park) and Brockville: You may count them if you like; the point is, there *are* a lot of them. The Thousand Islands—varying in size—lie along the St. Lawrence between Brockville and Kingston; those on the western side are mostly Canadian; those on the east, in New York State. This is a traditionally popular vacation area and understandably so: pleasant climate, all manner of water sports—boating, canoeing, sailing, swimming, sunbathing, a variety of resorts, and excellent fishing for such species as pike, bass, pickerel, and salmon trout. Nearly two hundred acres' worth of Canadian islands and a bit of mainland comprise the St. Lawrence Islands National Park. Principal islands—with various types of recreation facilities—include Aubrey, Beau Rivage, Gordon, Georgina, and Constance. On the mainland, there are additional park amenities at Mallorytown, a good bathing spot. Cruises through the islands are available, and one can also take river tours from the town of Brockville. Twelve miles east of Brockville is *Fort Wellington National Historic Park,* whose highlight is a military blockhouse from the War of 1812, with walls four feet thick. Brockville is close to the Thousand Islands International Bridge, which makes ingenious use of various islands in the river as stepping stones to connect its span with the United States and Canada, and was dedicated by Prime Minister Mackenzie King and President Roosevelt in 1938. The crossing is from Alexandria Bay, New York—the American center of the Thousand Islands—to Rockport, Ontario.

Kingston and Old Fort Henry: Kingston saw its first white man in 1615 when Champlain went exploring in the neighborhood. Later in the seventeenth century, the French built a fort where the city now stands. They were impressed with its location—at the mouth of the Cataraqui River, where Lake Ontario flows into the St. Lawrence River. And others after them have been, too. The British took it from the French in 1758. Later, United Empire Loyalists—American colonists on the side of the Crown—started emigrating to the area, and the name Kingston came to replace Fort Frontenac—which was what the French had called the place. It was in Kingston, in 1872, that the first Executive Council of Upper Canada was held. During the War of 1812 Kingston was a key military-naval base, and it was at that time that Fort Henry was constructed. From 1841 to 1843 Kingston was the capital of the united provinces of Upper and Lower Canada. By the turn of the century it had a population of under twenty thousand. It is now much larger, but the time has long since passed when it was among the handful of leading cities of the east. Still, today it is far from unimportant. It is, for one thing, the site of the Royal Military College of Canada, wherein are trained officers for all of the nation's armed forces—Army, Navy, and Air Force. Situated on a peninsula overlooking the harbor, it is a handsome spot and its museum in Fort Frederick is open to visitors. Just across Navy Bay from the college is Fort Henry, which saw service as a British garrison up to 1870, and as a Canadian post for the ensuing two decades, after which it was abandoned as obsolete. The great fort's restoration was begun in 1936 and finished in 1938. It is now operated as part of the chains of parks of the St. Lawrence Parks Commission. There are more than 120 rooms within, including a military museum, and the noted Fort Henry Guard—whose members are well-trained university students in the natty bellman-capped uniforms of the old Imperial garrisons—bring life to the old ramparts, with their daily summer drills for visitors and regular firings of the muzzle-loading cannons which date back a century and a half.

But Kingston has other monuments: St. George's Church (Anglican), where the first Upper Canada executive council met in the late eighteenth century; the lovely mid-nineteenth-century Court House; St. Mary's Cathedral (Roman Catholic, 1843); the boyhood home of Canada's first Prime Minister, Sir John A. Macdonald, and a National Historic Site; a number of fine early-nineteenth-century houses; the handsome campus of Queen's University (with its Etherington Art Gallery), the Royal Signals Museum—with military communications its theme; and the rather grim-themed Penitentiary Museum.

Oshawa is of interest because it rivals Windsor as a Canadian car-manufacturing center, with General Motors of Canada providing its major industrial activity. To see are the Canadian Automotive Museum, the gardens of the estate of auto-builder Robert McLaughlin, and two mid-nineteenth-century house-museums: Henry and Robinson.

TORONTO AND THE SOUTH

Toronto: If Canada has a wonder city—and no country should be without one—it is Toronto. This is Canada's largest English-speaking city. This is Canada's financial capital. This is Canada's industrial headquarters. This is one of North America's great inland ports. And this is Ontario's capital. Within its own city limits —a thirty-five-square-mile area—it is home to more than 700,000 persons. With the dozen surrounding communities embracing some 240 square miles, which, with it, form the incorporated municipality of Metropolitan Toronto, it has a population of more than 2.5 million.

There is no disputing Vancouver's superiority in the realm of natural esthetics; the British Columbia metropolis is Canada's most beautiful city, thanks in great part to its superb situation. One cannot deny, either, that venerable, Gallic-flavored Montreal is more socially sure of itself, more appealingly mellow. But Toronto remains among the more stimulating cities within the interior of North America. Indeed, it has become a city that—judged by the frequently accepted criteria for such distinction—can be called great, or at least on the verge of greatness. In matters of commerce, it can boast a stock exchange second only on the continent to New York's. Educationally, it is top-rank. Abroad, the university bearing its name is one of the least-appreciated North American institutions of higher learning, although it is the second-largest in the British Commonwealth (after the University of London) with one of the finest academic reputations. The Royal Ontario Museum is one of the great cultural repositories of the world. The O'Keefe and St. Lawrence centres have helped make Toronto a leading performing arts headquarters on the continent. Even in the area of self-government, Toronto is a leader; the Municipality of Metropolitan Toronto is one of the most creatively administered of any in the Western Hemisphere.

Toronto is the principal Canadian melting pot. (The locals prefer calling it a Canadian mosaic.) It is to Canada what New York and San Francisco are to the United States, drawing the gifted youth of the country from every province and attracting the greatest proportion of the new Canadians—Europeans (many with special skills and talents) who have immigrated in recent decades. If today's Toronto can be excessively aggressive in blowing its horn, there is no denying that it has bounce and drive, curiosity, and a willingness to take stock of itself. Its contemporary atmosphere is one that attracts thinkers as well as doers, planners as well as makers. Its people are quite possibly the most widely traveled of any in Canada. One has the distinct impression that Toronto has a higher proportion of citizens who know Canada well than does any other Canadian city—not to mention the United States and other parts of the universe.

The marvel of Toronto is that it had such a slow, discouraging start. It was a small city with a population well under fifty thousand as recently as a century ago. The first settlers of the area were, like those of neighboring communities, French. Fur traders set up Fort Rouille in 1720; the English took over a few decades later, and toward the end of the eighteenth century Toronto was named York—after the then Duke of York—and became the capital of Upper Canada. During the War of 1812, by which time it had attracted United Empire Loyalists from the United States, it was burned by American troops. Indeed, it was Toronto's destruction that inspired the British to burn Washington to the extent that the soot-scarred Executive Mansion was painted white—and given a new name. After that war Yonge Street—still a main thoroughfare—was constructed and named after a British Cabinet member. In 1834 York—then ten thousand strong—was incorporated and changed its name to something more indigenous, taking *toronto,* an Indian word for "meeting place." The new city's first mayor was William Lyon Mackenzie, a leader of the 1837 rebellion against the province's autocratic leadership (alluded to earlier in this chapter). Mackenzie was the grandfather of William Lyon Mackenzie King, Prime Minister of Canada for more than two decades.

It was not until well after the middle of the nineteenth century that Toronto began to pick up steam. The birth of this century saw it a proper city of well over two hundred thousand—four times what it had been four decades earlier. And in the last seven decades, all of Toronto's advantages—its location, its nearness to raw materials, power, and fuel, its transportation links—combined to further boost its growth. By the time of World War II the city was eminently substantial, but almost too respectable and prudishly Anglo-Saxon to have many boosters beyond its borders. Since the war half-a-million-plus Europeans have made the Toronto area their home. They brought to it what it had for so long lacked: a cosmopolitan quality, a conglomerate populace, new folkways and foods, new languages and habits, a new acceptance of the strange, a new pride in diversity.

But how does one discover Toronto? It is, thanks to its public transport system—including Canada's first subway, so neat and clean that a New Yorker like myself becomes most envious—one of the easiest of large Canadian cities in which to get about. And it is not geographically difficult. The earlier-mentioned Yonge (pronounced *young*) Street separates its eastern and western sectors, and lower Yonge Street is the heart of the business district, with the hotels, department stores and shops, and many of the important public buildings within walking distance of each other. Queen's Park is the green setting for the provincial Parliament Buildings—a massive Victorian-Romanesque pile within which one is welcome to see the immense Legislative Chamber and other elaborately decorated public rooms. (Of the provincial-legislative interiors, this ranks at the top along with Quebec and Nova Scotia.) Next door to the Parliament is the principal campus of the University of Toronto. Founded as King's College in 1827, the university embraces a number of professional schools and under-graduate colleges, three of which are church-related—as in a number of large Canadian universities. At Toronto, these are Victoria (the United Church), Trinity (Anglican), and St. Michael's (Roman Catholic). University College is provincially supported and non-denominational. There are a number of new buildings— the John Robarts Library is a dazzler—and among the older structures you might want to inspect are Hart House, University College, which for many years after its erection in 1859 housed the entire university, and the lovely Gothic chapel at Trinity College.

There are other public buildings nearby—the splendid Victorian-Romanesque Old City Hall, and, nearby, its successor, the new City Hall (1965), with its crescent-shaped twin towers enclosing a central block housing the open-to-visitors City Council Chamber, with capacious Nathan Phillips Square adjacent.

The Anglican and Roman Catholic cathedrals are both under-rated. St. Michael's is the seat of the largest English-speaking Catholic diocese in Canada, was completed in 1848 in English Gothic style; it's a beauty. Anglican St. James has an imposing interior with an elaborate—and very high—wood-beam ceiling; it's about the same age as St. Michael's. And there is St. Paul's—after Montreal's Notre-Dame, the largest church in the country. There are the Maple Leaf Gardens, the indoor arena noted for its hockey games; Exhibition Park, site each summer of the tremendous—and tremendously well-attended—Canadian National Exhibition, late in spring of the Canadian International Trade Fair, and in winter, of the Royal Agricultural Winter Fair. There are quite literally scores upon scores of public parks and recreation areas, including those of Toronto Island, in the harbor, and easily reached by ferry; Casa Loma is the elaborate but not overly tasteful 98-room "castle"— with towering battlements, secret stairways, underground tunnel, hidden panels, and the like—built just before World War I by Sir Henry M. Pelatt, a local man who—quite literally—made good and felt compelled to let the world know about it. This slightly absurd, essentially Tudor Gothic Monument to Money is open to the public, and like most visitors, I'm sure your curiosity will get the better of you and you'll want to have a look.

There are, however, monuments of Old Toronto more representative than Casa Loma. Old Fort York, beautifully restored and much as it was in the early nineteenth century, should be a requisite, with the officers' quarters the most impressive of the interiors, and guides in period uniforms. And so should Black Creek Village, an out-of-town reconstruction of a country settlement as it might have been in 1867, the year of Confederation; there are some 30 buildings. Colborne Lodge, an early-nineteenth-century house of a leading citizen in bucolic High Park, is also eminently visitable. And so is Mackenzie House, the dwelling given to the city's first mayor after his return from exile in the United States. He lived there until he died in 1861, and the place is furnished with articles typical of his period. Campbell House is a gem of a house in the Osgoode Hall complex. It was the home (1825–29) of the first Canadian judge to be knighted—Sir William Campbell—and is smartly furnished in period style.

There are a number of museums. One, the Marine Museum of Upper Canada, is housed in an Exhibition Park building that went up in 1841 as a British Officers Quarters and was mercifully spared from destruction when other old buildings surrounding it were torn down in 1953. The Toronto Historical Board (which also operates—and with consummate taste and skill—Fort York, Colborne Lodge, and Mackenzie House) took over and turned the place into a repository of artifacts typifying the marine life of the region—from Indian canoes on upward.

The Art Gallery of Ontario (if you've been away, you'll remember it as the Art Gallery of Toronto) occupies handsome quarters in a pair of connected buildings that join up with an 1817 structure that was the gallery's first home, and has been restored as a house-museum. The Art Gallery ranks with the National Gallery in Ottawa, and Montreal's Musée des Beaux-Arts as one of Canada's top trio of museums. To visit it is an exceptional esthetic treat because it is rich with fine works—Canadian and foreign, old and new. The permanent collection of some 5,000 objects (of which never more than a fraction are on display) ranges from the fourteenth to the twentieth centuries—Brueghel the Younger's "Peasants' Wedding," Canaletto's "Bacino di San Marco," Hogarth's "Boy in a Green Coat," Gainsborough's "The Harvest Waggon," into Impressionists like Monet, Sisley, Renoir, Pissaro, Degas. Picassos early, middle, and later; Canadians including favorites like Paul Kane, Cornelius Krieghoff, F. A. Verner, Homer

Watson, Paul Peel, James Wilson Morrice, David Milne, Tom
Thomson, A. Y. Jackson, Lawren Harris, Emily Carr. American
representation is commendable, too, from John Singer Sargent
through to Frank Stella. And then there are the Moores. Henry
Moore himself gave the gallery the bulk of the more than 300 of
his works in a separate pavilion built to house them. They include
18 bronzes of varying sizes, 40 original plasters, and about that
same number of plaster maquettes (the models on which large
sculptures are based). There are, as well, 200 lithographs and
etchings. A passage leads from the Gallery proper to the Grange,
the early nineteenth-century house that had been its first home,
and that is now restored as a residence typical of the period
1835–40. The curved stairway of the entrance hall is the
knock-em-dead curved stairway of all time. But the Regency
drawing room and dining room, and the bedrooms and kitchen are
super, too. Just as requisite for old-house buffs as earlier recommended Mackenzie, Colborne, Campbell houses. A good shop,
too. And both a licensed restaurant and cafeteria.

The Art Gallery of Ontario is not Toronto's only great museum.
The other is the Royal Ontario Museum, founded in 1852 and in
its present Avenue Road building since 1933. The ROM embraces
three acres of galleries (not counting the satellite Sigmond Samuel
Collection in its own building, and the McLaughlin Planetarium).
The best known of the ROM specialties are those relating to the
Orient. If one's time is limited, the thing to do is head for the third
floor. The order is chronological. Start at Gallery I and move
along counterclockwise and you'll encounter Chinese Art from
Neolithic times through to the last royal dynasty, as well as Japanese, Korean, and Indian art, with the Chinese most heavily
represented and most outstanding. There are sculptures, jades,
bronzes, china, textiles, lacquerware, paintings, screens, and monumental sculpture, and the quality is even more impressive than
the quantity.

But there is so much more to the ROM. Go down a floor to
two, and you'll find five galleries of Greek, Roman, and Egyptian
works. Move down to main—oddly neglected in favor of the upper
levels—and there are sumptuous decorative arts collections, especially of English furnishings, with Elizabethan, Queen Anne, and
eighteenth-century period rooms, and gallery after gallery of Euro-

pean furniture, porcelain, and glass; a room full of medieval and Renaissance treasures, another of clocks and watches, and for a surprise, Art Nouveau from the turn of this century, and the later Art Deco. Don't skip the basement—with Indian, Eskimo, African, and South Pacific collections. And don't neglect the shops. Not far away, just opposite Parliament, is the ROM's Sigmond Samuel Gallery. It was a gift of Dr. Samuel in 1951 and houses the museum's Canadiana collections. Only in the Province of Quebec can one see early Canadian furniture such as is exhibited at the Samuel Gallery. The main floor is a series of rooms, each devoted to furniture and related objects of a different province or region. There are rooms for Quebec (1750–1820), the Maritimes (mid-nineteenth century), an Ontario dining room, and an Ontario parlor. There are collections of silver, glass, and—in the upstairs galleries—ceramics, along with a Quebec area of folk sculpture and toys.

The McMichael Canadian Collection is some twenty miles north of town in the village of Kleinburg. It is worth the trip, at least if one likes Canadian painting. There are some 700 works in a handsomely designed complex of rustic galleries embracing some 30 rooms, with the setting properly green and bucolic. Emphasis is on the Group of Seven—A. Y. Jackson, J. E. H. MacDonald, Lawren Harris, Arthur Lismer, F. H. Varley, Franklin Carmichael, Frank H. "Franz" Johnston—and associates like A. J. Casson and Edwin Holgate, as well as other greats like Emily Carr, David Milne, Tom Thomson, not to mention a choice group of Eskimo sculpture and Indian wood carving. There's a restaurant as well as a shop.

The Hockey Hall of Fame is among Toronto's most popular museums, in this hockey-crazy land. To see are impedimenta of the game—sweaters, pucks, sticks, trophies, with the Canadian Sports Hall of Fame (devoted to other sports) on the same Canadian National Exhibition Park premises.

More contemporary Toronto is manifested in a pair of attractions whose popularity top the Toronto list. Both employ World's Fair-type display techniques. One, Ontario Place, is a warm-weather-months only proposition—96 water-born acres in Lake Ontario that meld restaurants and cafés with the performing arts (concerts, opera, dance, rock, kids' magic shows), and other attractions ranging from handicraft shops to movies in a spherical-shaped theatre with a screen six stories high. Then there is the out-of-town Ontario Science Centre (770 Don Mills Road), a futuristic-look complex that serves up popular science, mostly to the kids but also to those adults who tag along. The idea is to touch, push, pull, wind, and pedal wherever and whenever you want. There are no guides; you find your own way, or at least you are supposed to.

The Metro Toronto Zoo opened in 1974 and like so much else in Toronto, abounds in superlatives. There are some 5,000 animals in a 710-acre tract, with natural settings dominant, and a division by geography—South America, North America, Eurasia, Indomalaya, and Australia, plus the Rouge River Valley, with Canadian fauna, viewed from slow-moving trains, not unlike the buses of the San Diego zoo. There are places to eat, and otherwise spend one's money. It's fun.

Back to town, then, for another Toronto superlative—the CN Tower, focal point of Metro Centre, North America's largest single downtown redevelopment project, 190 acres all told, and embracing transportation, communications, offices, and residential facilities, under joint CN-CP aegis. Height is 1,458 feet, with the main observation level at 1,122 feet, and the restaurant at 1,150 feet.

For the rest, enjoy yourself. O'Keefe Centre, first of the post-World War II performing arts centres that were to sweep Canada, seats 3,200 and is the home of the Canadian Opera Company, and the widely traveled National Ballet of Canada—with the Royal Winnipeg Ballet and Les Grands Ballets Canadiens of Montreal, one of the country's top dance companies. In contrast to the Royal Winnipeg, which concentrates on innovative new choreography and Canadian themes, with a smaller-than-usual complement of dancers, the National Ballet is a large group, and dances the classics. It performs elaborate full-length versions of *Swan Lake, The Sleeping Beauty, Coppelia,* and *La Sylphide,* and although its own personnel appeared overshadowed, on performances both at home and abroad, by guest superstar Rudolf Nureyev, it has a skilled resident company, including ballerinas Karen Kain, Veronica Tennant, and Vanessa Harwood, and premier danseurs Frank Augustyn, Gary Norman, and Tomas Schramek, with David Haber the artistic director. Complementing O'Keefe Centre is the newer St. Lawrence Centre—a pair of halls, the larger with some 800 seats. There are a number of older theatres as well, most notably the atmospheric turn-of-the-century Royal Alexandra. Massey Hall is headquarters for the esteemed Toronto Symphony.

In warm weather, Toronto is dotted with pockets that make for happy strolling or sitting. Nathan Phillips Square, opposite the City Hall, is activity-packed all summer long. Allan Gardens is the city's beautiful botanical park—ideal walking territory. The Commerce Court skyscraper complex encircles a mall with a big shopping center below it. Kensington Market is in New Toronto—street stalls with vendors from all of the countries that have sent the city post-World War II citizens. Markham Village is a charming quarter of trendy shops, artsy boutiques, and engaging cafés in snappily restored elderly houses. Yorkville Village is more of same, a variation on the Markham theme and quite as agreeable. For elevated promenades: Toronto Dominion Center, a trio of pinnacles, in the tallest of which there is a 55th-floor observation tower from where, as any Torontonian worth his salt will assure you, on a clear day you can see Niagara Falls. Toronto is a major Canadian center for television and radio production. There's racing, too —at Greenwood (on Lake Ontario, within the city limits) and at the more distant Woodbine track.

Peterborough, 80 miles northeast of Toronto, in the Kawartha Lakes area, lies on the Trent-Severn Waterway, joining Georgian Bay with Lake Ontario. There's a history-filled Centennial Museum, the ultra-modern architectural Trent University, and an early-nineteenth-century mock-Gothic Catholic Cathedral.

Hamilton, one of Ontario's major cities, is a bustling steel town —the most important steel-producing center of the country, for that matter. To see are the eighteen-hundred-acre Royal Botanical Gardens, a contemporary City Hall, the campus of McMaster University, beautifully restored 35-room Dundern Castle—the Regency-style home of an early Prime Minister, the Art Gallery of Hamilton—for its excellent Canadian painting collection, neo-Gothic Christ the King Cathedral, the Canadian Football Hall of Fame, a really super farmers' market, and—thirty miles distant— the eight-lock, twenty-five-mile Welland Canal, which links Lake Erie and Lake Ontario and is a part of the St. Lawrence Seaway.

St. Catherines is a pretty, garden-dotted city in the heart of the fruit-growing region of the Niagara Peninsula and is the center of the area's wine-making industry. There's an interesting, thrice-

weekly farmers' market in the heart of town. St. Catherines is
proud of its annual grape and wine festival, and of the Royal Canadian Henley Regatta, held every July at nearby Port Dalhousie.
It's a good center in the spring, when the fruit trees are blossoming
brilliantly in the surrounding countryside.

Niagara Falls is at once a natural and man-made binational
phenomenon. There is hardly an American or a Canadian who
does not look forward to seeing Niagara at least once before he
dies, and I have yet to meet a foreign visitor to North America
who has not included the Falls in his itinerary if it was humanly
possible. Statistically, Victoria in Africa and Iguazú in South
America surpass Niagara. Both of them—while magnificent—are in
relatively sparsely traveled areas of the globe and attract relatively
few visitors. They are, as a result, still in unspoiled regions of scenic beauty. Niagara, on the other hand, is on the U.S.-Canadian
frontier, with an American city on one side and a Canadian one on
the other. It is located in one of the most populous parts of North
America and it attracts—get ready for this figure—some twelve million visitors each year, so that, presumably, one must be grateful
that the carnival atmosphere is no more dominant than is the case.
On my first visit to Niagara, made at the age of five, I do not recall
being at all appalled by the mob scene and the tawdry commercial
surroundings. But on more recent return visits—after having seen
both Victoria and Iguazú falls—I was far from completely cap-
tivated with what I encountered. Nonetheless, the Falls themselves
are spectacular. They are, to refresh your elementary-school geography, cascades of the short (thirty-mile) Niagara River that nature created to link higher Lake Erie (572 feet above sea level)
with lower (245 feet) Lake Ontario. The Falls are best seen—and
I say this at the risk of appearing an un-American American—from
the Canadian side, where the perspective is infinitely better. In all
fairness to the authorities, I must give credit to the Province of
Ontario for the success it has achieved in keeping the area imme-
diately adjacent to the falls as protected parkland. I wish only that
some of the territory it borders was not quite so tacky.

Something like 90 per cent of the river's water flows over
Horseshoe Falls—162 feet high and 2,600 feet wide. Across the
frontier are the narrower but somewhat higher American Falls—
167 feet high, 100 feet wide. There are, of course, a number of

ways of seeing the Falls, short of going over them in a barrel, which has been attempted on a number of occasions (not always successfully). Most visitors do not rest easy without a view from one of the commercial towers built for the purpose. They include the 525-foot Skylon and the 325-foot Royal. There are no other really significant points of interest, but the mock-Tudor ex-mansion of tycoon Sir Harry Oakes is rather impressive, and so is the landscaped amphitheatre that he presented to the community. Regional lore is the subject of the Willoughby Historical Museum, and there are a pair of nice old churches that are quite lost in the touristic shuffle—early-nineteenth-century St. John's and somewhat later Holy Trinity. A ride aboard the little steamer *Maid of the Mist* is highly recommended; it chugs right along the edge of the Falls and right into the mist and spray which they create. Every passenger is given a heavy-duty raincoat for the trip, and those at the forward end of the ship are advised to wear them with collars up and cameras protected!

Niagara-on-the-Lake has all of the charm that neighboring Niagara Falls lacks. It's a little town of early-nineteenth-century houses, an old-fashioned hotel, restored Fort George, the worthy Niagara Historical Museum, a pair of lovely old churches (St. Andrew's Presbyterian and St. Mark's Anglican) and—in startling contrast—the ultramodern, multimillion-dollar theatre used for the annual Shaw Festival every summer, and throughout the rest of the year, as well. This is a nice place to stay on your visit to the Falls.

Guelph, between Toronto and Kitchener, goes back to the early nineteenth century, revolves about central St. George's Square, and numbers among its monuments a Catholic cathedral—Our Lady of the Immaculate Conception—that mostly resembles that of Cologne, in Germany, a pair of square front towers (added in this century) being major exceptions to the Cologne-look. There's a museum, the Civic, that is local-historical in theme. And the old John McCrae House, named for a man born in it who wrote the World War I poem, *In Flanders Fields,* is a national historic site. A rather nice Guelph touch is Wyndham Street, all of whose buildings must by law be built of the same local limestone used when the town was established; a good specimen is the Victorian-style City Hall.

Kitchener's ace in the hole is its Pennsylvania Dutch flavor—a surprise of surprises in the Province of Ontario. Pennsylvania Dutch were dominant among its settlers, and on a Saturday morning its Farmers' Market is well sprinkled with bonneted, black-gowned Mennonite women come to sell their produce. Woodside was the childhood home of Prime Minister Mackenzie King; it and its grounds are now preserved as a National Historic Park by the federal government. *Waterloo,* adjacent to Kitchener, is the seat of the University of Waterloo. Worth a visit, too, are surrounding villages like *Doon*—an artists' magnet with its old mill and brick houses, and heavily Scottish *Fergus,* with its annual Highland Games.

Stratford is a charming town, settled in the nineteenth century by immigrants from the English town of the same name. The Canadian Stratfordites not only called their new home after Shakespeare's birthplace, but also named the stream on which it is situated—a branch of Ontario's Thames River—after the Avon, which flows through the Warwickshire Stratford. Indeed, the Canadian Stratford is full of names associated with its English antecedent—and has been for many years. The town's modern claim to fame is the Shakespeare Memorial Theatre, whose summer festivals attract visitors from all over North America and Europe, as well. The theatre was conceived by Tom Patterson, a local newspaperman, and with Sir Tyrone Guthrie as its first director, opened under canvas—in a vast tent—in 1953. The first season's stars were Sir Alec Guinness and Irene Worth, and the first production—*Richard III*—was a rousing success. So, indeed, has the festival been ever since. In 1957 the theatre moved into its own specially designed permanent building—an ingenious, contemporary adaptation of the Elizabethan-era theatre, with a permanent platform stage into which are built a balcony, trap doors, seven acting levels, and nine entrances. Seats are on three sides of the stage, there is an 858-seat balcony, and the total seating capacity exceeds twenty-two hundred. Since it opened, the theatre has presented more than a score of Shakespeare's plays, as well as a number of other classics, and even some contemporary Canadian drama, this last performed in the 1,000-seat Avon Theatre—a restored turn-of-century opera house. There are several museums. Rothman's Art Gallery displays contemporary work and, sometimes, Festival costumes. The Thompson Memorial Museum is a mixed bag of local lore. And the Brocksden School Museum is a charmer—a mid-nineteenth-century school with texts and other impedimenta of the period.

The theatre straddles a hill overlooking the Avon, and in the midst of the parkland running through the city; the town fathers have wisely preserved this parkland through the years. There are good places to eat and stay in the town, and in nearby towns like Kitchener. On matinee days one can leave points as distant as Toronto, lunch in Stratford, take in the play, and be back at the point of departure in time for a late dinner.

London, as one might perceive from its name, makes no secret of its British origins. An attractive city of about 170,000 population at a junction of two tributaries of the Thames River, it is primarily industrial, but it has a legitimate theatre of note and is the seat of the University of Western Ontario, with an art gallery and an Indian-Pioneer Life Museum—both recommended. Its pride is 325-acre Springbank Park—with a zoo, miniature railway, bird sanctuary, and lovely gardens. To visit also are the London Art Museum—a part of the Public Library, and with Group of Seven and other Canadian paintings; Eldon House—a nineteenth-century home furnished in period; the multistructure Fanshawe Pioneer Village; and a reproduction of a venerable brewery, courtesy of Labatt's. And so that there will be no question of Anglophile proclivities, one finds a St. Paul's Cathedral, a Covent Garden, a Piccadilly, a Hyde Park, a Regent Street, and a Pall Mall.

Chatham, a Thames River city, is in the heart of rich agricultural area, and has a good bit of industry as well as the Chatham-Kent Museum, which depicts the region's history. Nearby is the partially restored eighteenth-century village of *Moraviantown,* and the town of *Dresden,* where the Reverend Josiah Henson—the original of Harriet Beecher Stowe's Uncle Tom, escaped from the United States in 1830. Henson ran Dawn Settlement, a three-hundred-acre farm worked by other refugee ex-slaves, and lived there until he died in 1883. His grave is still at the site of the original farm, and the house in which he lived is still to be seen. *Rondeau Provincial Park* is just southeast of Chatham on Lake Erie; there are fine bathing beaches, picnic and camping grounds, boats for rent, and good fishing.

Point Pelee National Park, a forest-beach region of six square miles, flanks Lake Erie and constitutes the southernmost tip of the Canadian mainland. Its unusual flora and fauna attract plant, animal, and bird buffs. The park's natural attributes are the subject of its museum, and there's a nature trail. There are camping grounds, but the nearest accommodation, otherwise, is at little *Leamington,* six miles distant.

Windsor, just across the Detroit River from Detroit, is, like its neighbor, an automobile-manufacturing center, with Ford of Canada, General Motors of Canada and Chrysler of Canada all on the scene, and all with plants open to visitors. It is the site, too, of a number of other factories, many of them Canadian affiliates of U.S. firms. Windsor is the home of the Hiram Walker distilleries, which gave the community, on the company's hundredth birthday in 1958, the Hiram Walker Historical Museum, located in an 1811 brick house—the city's oldest—in downtown Windsor. The exhibits relate to the Windsor-Detroit area, and the house—beautifully restored—is chief among them. Also located in a onetime mansion is the Art Gallery of Windsor, with extensive Canadian collections, top-caliber Eskimo sculpture, and some European paintings, too. Dieppe Gardens are strikingly situated on the riverfront, just opposite Detroit's impressive skyline; a plaque in the gardens recalls Windsor's importance as an underground railway station to which American slaves escaped. There are sumptuous sunken gardens in Jackson Park. To be seen, too, is the Gothic-design campus of the University of Windsor, long known as Assumption College. Detroiters and Windsor residents cross the international frontier at their door almost as though it didn't exist. (The Detroit-Windsor tunnel, extending under the river and about a mile in length, was finished in 1930, a year after the Ambassador Bridge—longest international suspension bridge extant.) The visitor does well to acquaint himself with both cities while he's in the area.

GEORGIAN BAY AND THE NORTH

Lake Huron's immense Georgian Bay, north of Toronto, and the lakes to the east and north of it constitute an important Ontario playground, and are tremendously popular with hunters and anglers. But the newcomer to the region should be warned: there are no mountains in the area. It is mostly flat, uninspiring country, of no particular scenic beauty, and with no outstanding resorts.

Orillia, on the northern fringe of *Lake Simcoe,* is the principal town for the Simcoe area. It has a beachside park of its own and a monument to Champlain, who passed through the area in 1615. The home of humorist Stephen Leacock is open to summer visitors. There is excellent fishing in the surrounding lakes.

The Muskoka Lakes region, emanating from the town of *Gravenhurst,* has a number of resorts, but none that I could perceive of the de luxe character to be found in regions like the Laurentians of Quebec. The area is minimally pretty but almost completely devoid of charm and of benefit, it would seem to me, chiefly to city dwellers who live fairly close by.

Midland, on Georgian Bay, has several recommendable features: the Huronia Museum of Indian and early-settler artifacts (including a Huron log hut), a replica of a Huron Indian village, and the Martyr's Shrine, a modern stone church on the grounds of old Fort Sainte-Marie, the first permanent white community in the area. The shrine—Roman Catholic—commemorates the martyrdom of eight Jesuit missionaries killed by the Iroquois in the seventeenth century and canonized in the twentieth (1930) as the first North American saints. The fort's burial ground has also been restored; it was the first Christian cemetery in Ontario. Sainte-Marie, among the Hurons, is a mixed-media interpretation depicting the area's history.

Georgian Bay has any number of bathing points. That at *Wasaga,* on its southern fringe, is one of the most popular, extending for a number of miles along the flat terrain, and fringed by quantities of rentable cabins and other accommodations.

Georgian Bay Islands National Park, north of Wasaga, embraces six square miles and includes some of twenty-five of the bay's myriad islands. *Honey Harbour* is the focal point of the park's territory. Of the islands in the park, Flowerpot—with a pair of unique rock pillars on its beach—is the most unusual. There are a number of camping areas and clothes-changing pavilions. Honey Harbour has accommodations.

North Bay is the principal community on enormous *Lake Nipissing,* considerably to the north of Georgian Bay Islands National Park. It is the departure point for northern Ontario and James Bay, and it straddles, besides Lake Nipissing, the much smaller Trout Lake. The fishing and hunting is excellent—and draws considerable quantities of practitioners. But for the ordinary traveler, there is Champlain Park, for picnics, daily boat cruises on the lake during the summer excursions to nearby Cuehesnay Falls, and an Indian village in the neighborhood.

Timmins, *really* in the heart of the north country, has mine tours—gold, zinc, silver—as its chief visitor lure.

WESTERN ONTARIO

Sault (pronounced "soo") **Sainte Marie,** like Niagara Falls, is the just-across-the-border of an American city with the same name. Sault Sainte Marie is about midway between Toronto, to the east, and the Lakehead city of Thunder Bay, to the west. It and its Michigan counterpart (linked by an international bridge) lie on the St. Mary's River, which links Lake Huron and Lake Superior by means of the Soo Locks and Canal, through which pass the vast cargoes of the lake traffic. The Sault, as the city is called, has a rich French-trapper background dating to the days of the North West Company—that long-formidable rival of the Hudson's Bay Company. The Algoma Steel Corporation is a major employer, and there is considerable other industry. There are two scenic parks (Bellevue, on the river, and huge Hiawatha), and the Sault Historical Society Museum tells the region's story. So, in a different way, does Ermatinger House—oldest in the region, beautifully restored, and open as a museum. Nearby are the lakes and streams of the Algoma region, offering spring and autumn fishing and big-game hunting, with deer and moose the principal trophies. There are day-long summer train tours to and through this area, with Agawa Canyon the highlight. At nearby Wawa, on the Trans-Canada Highway, is a giant, much-photographed, but not particularly well-executed snow-goose statue.

The Lakehead is the terminology for Canada's western shore of Lake Superior, and it is the site of *Thunder Bay,* the amalgamated former twin cities of Port Arthur and Fort William. (Geographic note: Thunder Bay North is ex-Port Arthur, while Thunder Bay South was formerly Fort William.) Lures are the largest single-unit grain elevator in the world, a fine reconstruction of early-nine-teenth-century Fort William, the Thunder Bay Historical Museum, a logging camp replica in Centennial Park, the relatively recent Lakehead University, the gorge of Guimet Canyon, and a pano-ramic view of the region from atop 1,800-foot Mount McKay.

Kenora and Lake of the Woods: This is Ontario at its west-ernmost, with Manitoba just across the border. Kenora is a splen-didly situated town, largely devoted to catering to the needs of Trans-Canada Highway stoppers-off and tourists come to delight in the beauty of island-dotted Lake of the Woods and the sur-rounding country. One may take a short cruise around the lake from Kenora, or undertake longer forays of this enormous body of water, which extends sixty miles in length, is fifty miles wide, and has no less than fifteen thousand islands. The fishing is, as would be expected, excellent; there is deer and moose hunting in autumn; and the sightseer will want to see as much of the lake's area as possible—hopefully Whitefish Bay and the Western Peninsula, as well as Lake of the Woods Museum, in Kenora's Memorial Park, the better to obtain a graphic picture of the area's history.

SHOPPING

Toronto leads the province, if not—along with Montreal—all Canada. CANADIANA SHOPS include *Pinecraft Limited* (116 York-ville Avenue), with a wide range of handcrafted objects, smallish through to Ontario-made reproductions of early Canadian country furniture. *Canadian Guild of Crafts* (140 Cumberland Street) offers Eskimo soapstone carving and prints, Indian work, jewelry, and other wares. *Royal Ontario Museum Shop* (Avenue Road at Bloor) has the expected replicas of objects in the museum collec-tion—and some very striking ones. But there are Canadian crafts, too—especially pottery and jewelry, as well as Eskimo soapstone carving and prints. *Canadian Guild of Potters* (100 Avenue Road) is for this country's ceramics, in a variety of shapes and sizes and running a gamut of prices. *Art Gallery of Toronto Shop* (317 Dundas Street) has color postcards of paintings in the collec-tion that are among the town's best buys. Art books and related items. *Trade Wind Gifts* (138 Cumberland Street) has crafts of charm and interest among a varied stock. ANTIQUES: Toronto, along with Victoria and Montreal, is a major Canadian source. *Robert Dirstein and Partners Ltd.* (77 Yorkville Avenue) features fine quality objects, furniture, and accessories, mostly European. *Upper Canada House* (467 Eglinton Avenue West) specializes in early Canadian antiques, prints, and maps as well as furniture and accessories. *Simpson's* department store's Treasure House (sixth floor) is a bona fide antiques shop, both furniture and accessories. *Sotheby & Co. (Canada) Ltd.* (170 Bloor Street West) is affiliated with the noted antiques and art auction house of London and New York. ART GALLERIES are many and varied. They include: *Polack Gallery* (356 Dundas Street West), new works, both domestic and imported; *Marlborough Godard* (22 Hazelton Avenue), works of international caliber, mostly contemporary; *David Mirvish* (596 Markham Street)—trendy names regardless of nationality, Canadian painters, too. *Innuit* (30 Avenue Road), Eskimo work—soapstone sculpture, prints, ivory carving, other specialties. *Marcilipman Graphics* (223 Avenue Road), posters a specialty. *Nancy Pool* (16 Hazelton Avenue), Canadians only in a variety of media. DEPARTMENT STORES are super, invariably with a variety of restaurants and snack spots, post offices, pharmacies, supermarkets, bakeries, and Canadiana departments, whose wares range from quality handicrafts to the more prosaic junk-type souvenir-type souvenirs. *Eaton's* has downtown stores at College and Yonge, and Queen and Yonge. *Hudson's Bay Company* (The Bay), has capacious downtown quarters at Bloor and Yonge. *Simpson's* is on Yonge from Richmond through to Queen—just across from Eaton's. There are a number of BOOKSTORES (and the department stores all have book departments). *W. H. Smith,* familiar to travelers in Britain and, for that matter, Montreal, is at 100 Yonge Street. *Britnell's* (765 Yonge Street) is another good shop. SMART SHOPPING AREAS, away from the core of downtown, include *Yorkville* (Avenue Road to Bay Street), with the concentration on Cumberland Street and Yorkville Avenue, and the Hyatt Regency Hotel as a landmark; and *Markham Village,* which in effect is Markham Street to Bloor, with *Honest Ed's* cut-rate variety store the landmark. SMART CLOTHING SHOPS are to be found in abundance in this smart, rich city. Two basics are *Holt, Renfrew* (144 Bloor Street West), a link of the chain with both men's and women's clothes and accessories, some gifts and kid's things—all of it expensive and stylish; and *Creeds* (Manu Life Centre) purely local, purely distaff as regards wares, and beloved of affluent Toronto ladies. SUBTERRANEAN SHOPPING has become prevalent downtown, in several skyscraper clusters, including those of the *Sheraton Four Seasons Hotel* opposite City Hall, and the earlier-mentioned *Commerce Court* (Bay and King streets) and *Toronto-Dominion Centre* (between Wellington and King, with entrances also on York and Bay).

Ottawa: Good handicrafts sources are *Canada's Four Corners* (93 Sparks Street Mall)—a branch of the Pinecraft-Four Corners group country-wide, and with sheepskin rugs among its diverse wares; and the *Snow Goose* (40 Elgin Street)—whose Eskimo soapstone carvings are notable for quality as well as price. DEPARTMENT STORES include *Oglivy's* (126 Rideau Street) where old establishment Ottawa shops, *Simpson's* (Spark Street Mall), and *Hudson's Bay Company,* on Rideau Street. *Books Canada* (50 Elgin Street) specializes in Canadiana. *Byward Market* is nice, old-fashioned, and with meats, produce, deli, and flowers.

CREATURE COMFORTS

Ottawa: If it is true that the *Château Laurier* is almost as much an Ottawa institution as the neighboring Parliament cluster, it is equally true that it keeps abreast of the times. The 500-room queen bee of the Canadian National chain is regularly refurbished. Bedrooms, suites, and mini-suites (these last are convenient for travelers wanting a small sitting room) are bright and welcoming, the lobby buzzes, and the public rooms—Canadian Grill for a smart dinner, L'Auberge for breakfast or casual meals, Cock & Lion lounge for drinks—are all pleasurable. What is helping keep the Château Laurier on its toes is relatively recent competition, something it did not have for many years. For example, the *Carleton Towers Hotel* (150 Albert Street) is just what Ottawa needed —top-rank de luxe-category competition for the Château. This is an ultra-modern, understatedly elegant house in the heart of town, with 240 rooms and suites (the suites are stunners, but then the standard twins are smart, too)—just about half the size of the

Château, and that much more intimate. Personal-style service is the name of the game, along with amenities that include one of the best restaurants in town, a coffee shop-snackery called the Sidewalk Café—and just that—an inviting bar-lounge, indoor pool-spa, and Old Bytown, for late-hour drinks and entertainment. Without the cachet of the Carleton, but bigger (450 rooms), modern, and very attractive, the *Skyline Hotel* (101 Lyon Street) is major-league—tall and skyscraping, with nifty bedrooms and suites, and a range of places to eat, drink, and be amused, including the Top of the Hill boîte, Diamond Lil's-90s-style pub-lounge, and a handsome main, never-closed restaurant. Very nice indeed. *Holiday Inn Ottawa-Centre* (100 Kent Street) is accessible from the Skyline by the Galeries des Boutiques shopping center that separates the two. The Holiday Inn is a neat 500-room tower that is among the better looking of this chain in a country where Holiday Inns are generally a cut or two above the international average. The rooms are attractive and full-facility, and the suites luxurious. Amenities include a revolving roof-top restaurant with the best view in town, a softly lit main restaurant, a coffee shop, and places to drink and relax. *Park Lane Hotel* (111 Cooper Street) is a centrally located, subdued contemporary tower with 238 smart and spacious rooms, equally smart restaurant and cocktail lounge; coffee shop, too. The traditional style, long-popular *Lord Elgin Hotel* (100 Elgin Street) remains good. There are 400 cozy rooms, nice restaurant and lounge, central location. Other Ottawa suggestions: The 116-room full-facility *Sheraton El Mirador Motor Inn* (480 Metcalfe Street) and the ultra-mod *Hotel Quai d'Orsay* (210 Somerset Street West)—named, oddly enough, for the Paris palace that is the seat of the French Foreign Ministry—with 112 rooms, restaurant and lounge; and already recommended in the chapter on Quebec, but repeated here for convenience sake, the *Sheraton Le Marquis* at 131 Laurier Street, across the river in Hull. **Cornwall:** *Flamingo Motel* and *Parkway Inn*—both full-facility, and with pools—are good choices. **Brockville:** The handsome *Skyline Hotel* has 80 attractive rooms, restaurant, cocktail lounge, coffee shop, pool. **Thousand Islands—Gananoque:** *Glen House* has both cottages and motel units; licensed restaurant. *Colonial Motel* has more than half a hundred modern rooms, restaurant. *Provincial Motel* is smallish but with a good restaurant and pool. **Kingston:** *410-Inn* (Division Street) is a comfortable 164-room house, with a restaurant, cocktail lounge, and pool. *Holiday Inn* (Princess Street) is quite as well equipped as you'd expect: 126 nice rooms, restaurant, coffee shop, cocktail lounge, outdoor pool. **Belleville:** *Hotel Four Seasons* (11 Baybridge Road) is a looker: 125 zingy rooms, smart restaurant, cocktail lounge with entertainment, coffee shop, outdoor pool (a link of the Four Seasons chain). *Sun Valley Motor Inn* (407 North Front Street) has 110 rooms, restaurant, coffee shop, cocktail lounge. **Hamilton:** *Royal Connaught Hotel* (for long the Sheraton Connaught, at 112 King Street East) is traditional style, with 250 rooms and suites, restaurant, coffee shop, cocktail lounge, and heart-of-town location. *Holiday Inn* (150 King Street) is central, has 231 rooms, restaurant, coffee shop, cocktail lounge, and pool. Try the *Shakespeare Restaurant* (181 Main Street East) for a good steak lunch or dinner. **St. Catherines:** *Holiday Inn* (North Service Road) has 158 snappy rooms, and a range of facilities including restaurant, cocktail lounge, coffee shop, and outdoor pool. *Leonard Hotel* (259 St. Paul Street) has 90 modern rooms, restaurant, cocktail lounge, coffee shop, outdoor pool. *Howard Johnson's* (Lake Street) has about 100 rooms, restaurant, coffee shop, and cocktail lounge. **Kitchener:** *Valhalla Inn* (King Street) may not be quite Valhalla, but it's very nice, with 130 rooms, restaurant, coffee shop, cocktail lounge-cum-entertainment, pool. *Holiday Inn* (30 Fairway Road) is modern with 122 rooms and suites, restaurant, cocktail lounge with entertainment, coffee shop, outdoor pool. **Stratford:** *Festival Motor Inn* (Ontario Street East) has a hundred rooms, restaurant, coffee shop, cocktail lounge, and an outdoor pool. *Victorian Inn* (10 Romeo—yes Romeo—Street) is older, with 188 rooms, plus restaurant, cocktail lounge, coffee shop, and indoor pool. *Stratford Suburban Motel* (Highway 7) is another old-reliable, with 22 rooms and an outdoor pool, but no restaurant or lounge. *Majer's Motel* (Highway 7) has 32 rooms and pool, but no wine-dine facilities. **Toronto** has one of the finest hotel plants of any North American city. The choice is wide and the choice is good. Here is my selection: *Hyatt Regency Toronto* (21 Avenue Road) is a graceful tower that's become a landmark in the Yorkville section—one of the most agreeable parts of town. There are 540 beautiful rooms and suites, all with bay windows, super baths, electric blankets, and other nice touches. The public rooms are among the more estimable in the province. The Regency Grill, for example, is the ultimate in coffee shops. Up on high is the Odyssey for dinner dancing. The SRO Lounge is congenial; there's a honey of an outdoor pool-sundeck, and more later about Truffles Restaurant. The *Four Seasons Sheraton* (13 Queen Street West) is a splendid 1,466-room structure with an enviable location: overlooking Nathan Phillips Square, the ultramodern plaza of Toronto's landmark City Hall, smack in the heart of everything. This ever-so-contemporary hotel's major asset is the winning architecture of its many and varied public spaces—walkways that overlook waterfalls in a rock garden, an 80-foot outdoor pool, the Long Lounge, with its 70-foot bar overlooking City Hall, and a number of other places to eat and drink, including Traders, just off the spectacular, high-ceilinged lobby and locally popular for its sandwich lunches. The *Royal York* (100 Front Street West) is CP Hotels' beloved old-timer with a new look that cost not a sou under $12 million. And it shows, from the very grand lobby (with its double spiral staircase leading to the lower level), every one of the 1,600 rooms and suites bright and appealing, and more rooms in which to eat, drink, dance, and be entertained than any other hotel in North America—at least to my knowledge. They range from the Imperial Room, with really top-rank stars in its shows, and the also top-rank Acadian Room Restaurant (of which more later), through to Dick Turpin's for drinks and hearty fare, or light-look Gazebo for the buffet. The location is heart of downtown-convenient. Very pleasant indeed. The *Sutton Place Hotel* (955 Bay Street) is at once well-located, smartly high style, and not so big (350 rooms and suites) that it can't provide the kind of service that one expects in a luxe-category house. Rooms are comfortable, and among the suites are some of the poshest in Ontario, especially the so-called Prime Minister's, whose living-dining room combines Empire-period antiques with contemporary pieces, and whose pair of bedrooms are no less stylish. Go to the roof-top bar-lounge-boîte called Stop 33 for a drink. The *Park Plaza Hotel* (4 Avenue Road) is the Hyatt Regency Toronto's near-neighbor and complements it nicely. This is a long-time traditional-style favorite, as popular as ever, with quietly tasteful rooms and suites (550 all told), the very good Prince Arthur Dining Room, and an amusing

bar, the Emmett's Corner so called for the murals by *Punch* Magazine cartoonist Rowland Emmett. *Hotel Toronto* (145 Richmond
Street West) is Western International's 32-story, 600-room representation on the Toronto scene. The look throughout is contemporary, the ambience winning, and the public rooms include the
Polynesian-accented Trader Vic's Restaurant-Lounge, the Terrace
Grill—a coffee shop plus (afternoon tea is a feature)—off the
lobby, and a lounge for lunch (order the steak soup), drinks, and
entertainment known as the Barrister's. Outdoor-indoor pool, too.
Central situation, adjacent to the Guardian of Canada Tower, the
pair comprising the Toronto Place complex. The *Harbour Castle*
(Harbour Square) does not belie its hardly immodest name. You
might call this 983-room twin-tower a castle, late-twentieth-cen-
tury style. And there's no doubt about its harbor location. Lake
Ontario and the Toronto Islands are the view from one side,
downtown Toronto—a short walk away—from the other. Lots of
pluses here—ten passenger elevators, for example, an indoor-out-
door pool, an abnormally large number of suites (115 all told),
and a variety of restaurants and lounges, ranging from the roof-top
revolving Lighthouse, to a welcome Oyster Bar-seafood room. The
Four Seasons Hotel (415 Jarvis Street, and not to be confused
with the earlier recommended Sheraton Four Seasons) is among
the smaller hotels in the top rank. There are 164 lovely rooms and
suites, very nice places to eat and relax and a honey of a year-
round pool, surrounded by an engaging café. The atmosphere is
unhurried. A charmer. *Holiday Inn Downtown* (89 Chestnut
Street) is a 750-room-and-suite house that ranks in looks and facilities with its counterparts in the other major Canadian cities.
There are roof-top and more-intimate restaurants, coffee shop,
cocktail lounges, indoor and outdoor pools. One of half a dozen of
this chain in the Toronto area. *Chelsea Inn* (33 Gerrard Street
West) is brightly contemporary, capacious (there are just over
800 rooms, studios, and suites), central, with restaurant-coffee
shop, bar-lounge, health club, and underground parking. *Lord
Simcoe Hotel* (150 King Street West) has been on the scene for
some years, fills a need for functional, conveniently located accommodation. Public rooms include a handy cafeteria, the Captain's
Table Restaurant, a pair of lounges. *Prince Hotel* (900 York Mills
Road in Don Mills, Ontario) is a long way from central Toronto,

in its own 15-acre park. But if you've your own car and hanker for a bucolic setting with a Japanese flavor, this may be a wise choice. There are more than 400 perfectly lovely rooms and suites that nicely blend Occident and Orient in their design, nice places to eat including a smart French restaurant and a honey of a coffee shop, as well as a night club and cocktail lounge. Swimming pool, tennis. *Sherway Inn* (5487 Dundas Street West, Islington) is another away-from-the-center winner. An agreeably understated contemporary theme is common to the décor throughout, including the 88 rooms, La Casserole Restaurant, cocktail lounge, coffee shop, and outdoor pool-sundeck. *Toronto Airport Hilton* is a gracious 263-room hotel, with typically comfortable Hilton International rooms, an all-year-round-heated pool, coffee shop, a zingy basement disco called Attila's Cave that brings out the crowds from town, and a first-rate restaurant worth knowing about if you would like a good pre-flight lunch or dinner. The *Bristol Place Hotel* (950 Dixon Road) is under the same management as the earlier-recommended Sutton Place in town, and is among the more architecturally striking and innovative hotels, airport or otherwise, in Canada. There are 221 fine rooms, and handsome places to eat and drink, any one of which I suggest you sample—to get an idea of what an unusual place this hotel is. The *Skyline Toronto Hotel* (655 Dixon Road) is another airport leader and a part of the same chain that operates the commendable Skyline in Ottawa. This one is big—800 rooms and suites, round-the-clock coffee shop, roof-top Cloud Room for dinner dancing, variety of lounges, indoor pool. **Peterborough:** *Red Oak Inn* (100 Charlotte Street) is a contemporary, heart-of-town haven, in Peterborough Square with its shops a branch of Eaton's department store. The handsome rooms in the U-shaped hotel enclose a central pool area, complete with sunlamps, whirlpool, sauna. There's an elegant main dining room, English-style pub, coffee shop. One of CP Hotels' newer operations. *Holiday Inn* (150 George Street North) has 171 rooms, restaurant, cocktail lounge, coffee shop, and outdoor pool. **Niagara Falls:** The situation is this. There are only two proper hotels that directly overlook the Falls. *If,* by the time of your arrival, the Brock and the Foxhead (both Sheraton-franchise operations under joint local management) have treated themselves to thorough stem-to-stern refurbishings, *then* they're the favored places to stay, for the views from their front bedrooms and public rooms are spectacular. Otherwise, consider the one motel with a Falls view from some of its rooms: *Michael's Inn* (5599 River Road). There are 110 modern rooms, restaurant, swimming pool. Nothing fancy, but neat and well-operated. Other motel suggestions: *Cairn-Croft Motor Hotel* (6400 Lundy's Lane) with more than 80 full-facility rooms, attractive dining room, lounge, and outdoor pool; *Fallsway Motor Hotel* (4946 Clifton Hill) with 173 comfortable rooms, in a series of connected 2-story pavilions, good restaurant, cocktail lounge with entertainment, outdoor pool; and *Park Motor Hotel* (Clifton Hill Road), 180 rooms, restaurant, coffee shop, cocktail lounge with entertainment, enclosed glass-roofed pool. (Note: Although this is a book about Canada, let me mention that across the bridge, on the American side, there are a number of places to stay in Niagara Falls, New York, including the de luxe-category *Niagara Hilton,* with 401 rooms and suites, restaurant, coffee shop, trio of lounges, indoor pool, barber and beauty shops; a two-minute walk to the American Falls. Also on the American side are a *Treadway Inn, Holiday Inn, Quality Inn, Ramada Inn,* and a pair of *Howard Johnson's Motor Lodges.*) **Niagara-on-the-Lake:** This charmer of a little town has as its ace-in-the-hole the *Oban Inn* (Gage Street). There are not quite two dozen rooms, of which no two are alike, and every one is a delight, air-conditioned and with bath. This is an old-fashioned house with an old-fashioned dining room—the whole experience a happy antidote to so largely vulgarized Niagara Falls, and the place to stay if you're in town for the Shaw Festival. *Pillar & Post Inn* (King Street) is more motel than *auberge,* but with some style and a nice restaurant-lounge; 59 rooms. *Angel Inn* (224 Regent Street) is an eighteenth-century house, by no means large, with a handful of antique-furnished rooms, each with bath, and a dining room. *The Buttery* is the town's best-known restaurant, for lunch, dinner, or after a Festival Theatre performance. Virtually everything is good—from snacks like Welsh rarebit and Cornish pasties through stews and steaks right on into desserts including apple dumplings and trifle. **Guelph:** *College Motor Inn* (716 Gordon Street) has 63 nice rooms, dining room, cocktail lounge, outdoor pool. **London:** *Sheraton Oxbury Inn* (Oxford Street at Mornington Avenue) is a Sheraton franchise downtown, with 204 rooms, a restaurant, coffee shop, cocktail lounge, and night club. *Ramada Inn* (817 Exeter Road) has 130 rooms, and a range of places to dine and relax, including the Scorpio 1 night club. There's an indoor pool with sauna. *Howard Johnson's* (1150 Wellington Road) has 120 cheery rooms, restaurant, coffee shop, cocktail lounge, and heated pool. There are a pair of *Holiday Inns;* the downtown one is at 299 King Street, has nearly 300 rooms, restaurant, coffee shop, lounges with entertainment, indoor and outdoor pools. The other, called *London South,* is smaller, at 1210 Wellington Road, and is full-facility, too. Try *London Place* (340 Wellington Street) for a posh dinner. **Chatham:** The 160-room *Holiday Inn* (25 Keil Drive North) has restaurant, cocktail lounge, coffee shop, and both indoor and outdoor pools. **Windsor:** *Holiday Inn* (480 Riverside Drive) is river front, with 231 rooms and suites, a restaurant, coffee shop, lounge with entertainment, and outdoor pool. *Seaway Inn* (430 Ouellette Avenue) has a convenient downtown location, 150 nice rooms, a good restaurant, cocktail lounge, and indoor pool. *Wandlyn Viscount Motor Inn* (1150 Ouellette Avenue) has 210 modern rooms of various types, restaurant, never-closed coffee shop, cocktail lounge, and outdoor pool. *Ye Olde Steak House* (46 Chatham Street West) is old-reliable, and *Mario's* (755 Ouellette Avenue) is also good for beef, primarily prime ribs. **Orillia:** Long-on-the-scene *Fern Resort* (Lake Couchiching) has some 70 rooms of varying types, swimming in both the lake and a pool, tennis and other diversions, including evening entertainment and dancing; restaurant and cocktail lounge. *Sundial Motor Inn* (Sundial Drive) has 74 rooms, licensed restaurant, coffee shop, and outdoor pool. **Muskoka Lakes region:** *Milford Manor,* on Lake Muskoka, at Milford Bay, embraces 50 rooms and 36 cottages, with a dining room, pool and beach swimming, variety of sports, and other activities, including nightly dancing. *Cleveland House,* on Lake Rosseau, at Minett, is a good-sized all-the-family resort, accommodating some 300, in main-house rooms and bungalows; lake and pool swimming, wide range of diversions for adults and kids, restaurant and cocktail lounge. **Georgian Bay:** *Delawana Inn,* at Honey Harbour, is a long-time area favorite, with nearly 300 units, pool and lake swimming, all manner of additional activities, including nightly dancing; restaurant, cocktail lounge. **North Bay:**

Empire Motor Hotel (425 Fraser Street) has 142 rooms, restaurant, cocktail lounge. *Sands Motor Inn* (366 McIntyre Street) has three dozen modern rooms, restaurant, and cocktail lounge. **Timmins:** *Empire Motor Hotel* (11 Spruce Street) has more than a hundred modern rooms, restaurant, and cocktail lounge. *Sheraton Caswell Motor Inn* (Highway 17) has 76 rooms, restaurant, coffee shop, cocktail lounge, and outdoor pool. *Diplomat Motel* (844 Queen Street) has 31 rooms, restaurant, cocktail lounge, coffee shop. **Thunder Bay:** *Red Oak Inn* (555 West Arthur Street), CP Hotels' modern Thunder Bay outpost, is a $5 million complex whose special lure is an enclosed solarium complete with free-form pool, saunas, and whirlpool, the lot surrounded by trees and greenery year-round. Most of the 183 guest rooms have a solarium view, as do most diners in the coffee shop. There are a main restaurant and cocktail lounge, as well. *Landmark Inn* (Dawson Road in Thunder Bay North—ex-Port Arthur) has more than 100 mod-look rooms, and range of facilities include the Iron Gates Restaurant, Expressway Den (big) and lounges (intimate), pool, and sauna. *Holiday Inn* (130 South Brodie Street in Thunder Bay South—ex-Fort William) is a well-equipped 125-room house with dining room, cocktail lounge, coffee shop, and indoor pool. **Kenora:** *Holiday Inn* is directly on Lake of the Woods, with nearly a hundred well-equipped rooms, restaurant, coffee shop, cocktail lounge, and indoor pool.

Dining in Toronto: Toronto, in what appears to be a never-ending effort to prove that its pre-World War II reputation as North America's squarest metropolis is reversible, continues to expand and improve and innovate in the restaurant realm. It is an all-continent leader in this respect, following close on Montreal's heels within Canada's borders. What follows is but a selection, enough to give the temporary visitor a good choice, but not too much so as to overwhelm him. HOTELS in this extra-special hotel-city are by no means to be gastronomically slighted. *Truffles* (Hyatt Regency Toronto) is at once beautiful to behold, elegant of ambience, skilled as regards service—and perfectly delicious. The menu is an imaginative meld from a variety of countries, most of them European. Steaks and ribs of beef, delicate bisques, superbly sauced ragouts, masterwork-desserts, fine wines. *Acadian Room* (Royal York) attempts, and with considerable success, an evocation of an earlier Canada, in its décor, and of culinary Canada, with its fare. Watch bread being baked, note the open-to-view kitchen, enjoy typical dishes—Nova Scotia smoked salmon, Maritimes oysters, clam chowder Nova Scotia style, pea soup *habitant* style from next-door Quebec, B.C. salmon, Ontario duckling. And presented with flair. *Westbury Hotel Main Dining Room:* If the Westbury as a hotel is no longer what it was, its restaurant continues to be highly regarded. This is an old-school, haute-cuisine French-style place. Order the simpler grills—steaks or lamb chops if you like. But consider the seafood (shrimps especially) and the poultry (chicken dishes are a highlight). Everything is treated with respect—vegetables, fruits, cheeses, salads, and the desserts tend toward the classic French, praise be. *Victoria Room* (King Edward Sheraton): Not unlike the Westbury (which is much newer, to be sure), the King Edward has seen better days. But its principal restaurant remains beautifully kept, and a first-class spot for a good meal in a beautiful neo-baroque setting, all illuminated by Toronto's prettiest crystal chandeliers. No surprises here, but a range of hors d'oeuvres including imported Beluga caviar, top-notch salads, trout and imported English sole among the fish dishes, with favored entrées running to prime ribs from a silver trolley, chicken Kiev, and curried shrimp. The steaks-for-two are a special treat. And there are flamed desserts. *Royal Hunt Room* (Sutton Place Hotel): The treats here are twofold, a trencher-men's Royal Hunt Breakfast, buffet style and rather super, and—at lunch or better yet dinner—specialties of game and beef. Lovely ambience. FRENCH: *Napoléon* (79 Grenville Street) is the next best thing, this side of the Atlantic, to stepping into a French provincial town house for an intimate meal. The setting is a joy, the service likewise, and most important, so is the fare—whether (at dinner) you choose the duckling, a fish dish, the coq au vin, or whatever. Lunches are less elaborate. *L'Aiglon* (121 Yorkville Avenue) offers a nice choice: an oyster bar with seafood dishes downstairs, or an intimate French restaurant upstairs. *Le Provençal* (23 St. Thomas Street) does nice doughy things—quiche Lorraine, crêpes variously stuffed, savory hot pies. But meats and seafood invariably reliable, too. *L'Hardy's* (634 Church Street) is small, intimate, and pleasing; try the bouef bourguignonne. *Gaston's* (595 Markham) has among its attributes a commendable soupe à l'oignone, and a perky sidewalk café. *Le Tour de France* (197 College Street) has the bicycle race it is named for as its décor theme and serves dishes you remember from France but seldom see in North America—like pissaladière Niçoise, cassolette de poissons (a super fish casserole), and the genuine cassoulet Toulousain. Good wine list, too, and outside tables in summer. *L'Omelette* (48 Wellington Street East) is under the same management as Le Tour de France, and its name prepares one for what to expect: omelets a score of ways, but quite as many non-egg entrées of meat and fish. And a sidewalk café. ITALIAN: *Luigi's* (819a Yonge Street) has a nice bright look and hums with apparently happy customers at lunch and dinner. The pastas are first-rate and in considerable variety. Veal dishes are good entrée selections. Good bread, good wines, smiling service. *La Scala* (1121 Bay Street) rarely disappoints, from the antipasti and minestrone though the pasta and veal in variety, into salads and desserts. Attractive looking. *Mister Tony's* (100 Cumberland Street): You had better work up a respectable appetite, for this is a no-nonsense seven-course prix-fixe proposition; tasty, too. *Noodles* (60 Bloor Street West) has the kind of mod-Italian-look you find more in Milan than in the south—much steel and glass and style—with delicious food—antipasti, pastas, meat dishes—to match. You enter from Bay Street. *Old Spaghetti Factory* (54 The Esplanade) is one whose counterparts throughout North America are no doubt familiar—the crazy-mixed-up-antique-and-almost-antique décor, the friendly staff, the nice low prices, all of which make this a perfect family locale. STEAKS AND ROAST BEEF: *Hy's* (73 Richmond Street West and 133 Yorkville Avenue) is as reliable in Toronto as throughout Canada, for steaks and beef (seafood, too) professionally prepared and served in a stylish, posh-club ambience. *Gatsby's* (504 Church Street) name should prepare you for the décor. It's very amusing Twenties, with good steaks, and lobster, too. *Rib O' Beef* (220 Bay Street, at Wellington, and 140 Dupont Street) has a warm, pubby look and specializes in what it is named for—with no less than seven cuts at varying prices. *Hayloft Sirloin Pit* (37 Front Street East) is for steak and other beef dishes, in a casual setting, with a self-service salad stand a happy bonus. ESPECIALLY TORONTO: *Winston's* (104 Adelaid Street West) is at once smart and delicious, with pheasant

the specialty in its downstairs Game Room, and a wide variety in
the French-accented main restaurant. *Three Small Rooms* (Windsor Arms Hotel, 22 St. Thomas Street) is at its best in the areas of
ambience and wine. It embraces a trio of rooms—restaurant, grill,
and so-called wine room, with the latter having the most limited
menu. The wine selection is probably the most extensive in the
country; give the list some study. And concentrate on the more
hearty entrées when it comes to ordering. *Julie's Mansion* (515
Jarvis Street) is a town house restored and pressed—rather grandly
—into restaurant service. An eclectic menu and lots of local color.
The Fifty-Fourth (Toronto Dominion Centre) is a glossy restaurant with a glorious view, on the 54th floor of one of the downtown office towers. Steaks, chops, and the prosaic but hearty
dishes that affluent business and professional types thrive on. This
is the place to observe their midday rites. DEPARTMENT-STORE
EATING is first-rate in Toronto. *Eaton's* is at its fanciest in the
high-ceilinged, colonnaded Georgian Room, on nine. Go for lunch,
afternoon tea, and—on open evenings—dinner; licensed. Other Eaton's places for sustenance include the Viking Room and a convenient cafeteria. *Simpson's* impresses with the Arcadian Court, an
immense and eye-filling licensed restaurant on eight; its roast-beef
buffets are a specialty. The Panorama Room is a very nice cafeteria. DELI: *Shopsy's* (295 Spadina Avenue) and *Switzer's* (322
Spadina Avenue) are both sources of corned beef sandwiches and
the like, and both good. ASIAN: Consider *Moon Wan* (459 Dundas
Street West) for delicious Chinese food; *Michi* (459 Church Street
and 328 Queen Street West) for Japanese specialties; *Tanaka*
(1880 Bay Street) for Japanese teppan foods—grilled-at-table—
steaks, and other dishes; *Rajput I* and *Rajput II* (1303 Bloor
Street West and 376 Bloor Street West) for curries and other Indian specialties. SPANISH: *Don Quijote* (300 College Street) has
favorite Iberian foods like gazpacho and paella, guitars in the evening, and courteous service in that special Spanish way.
HUNGARIAN: Hungarian Village (990 Bay Street) for goulash,
stuffed peppers, and the Magyar version of mixed grill.
   Dining in Ottawa and Hull: *The Carleton Room* (Carleton
Towers Hotel) is all brown and black and chrome and intimate,
with an haute-cuisine menu and skilled service; for a posh leisurely
dinner. *L'Opéra* (National Arts Centre) is another locale for a

grand dinner, not necessarily one that has to be rushed in time for the curtain. Opulent setting, delicious fare with a wide range, beef being noteworthy. *Canadian Grill* (Château Laurier Hotel) is smart and with an interesting clientele that can include parliamentary and government faces. Dancing, too. Traditional favorites like roast beef, steak, grilled chops are popular. Nice desserts, too. *Top of the Hill* (Skyline Hotel) is as much for the view as for the fare. Both are agreeable. *La Ronde* (Holiday Inn Downtown) is another on-high restaurant, and it revolves. The view is the best in Ottawa with the fare secondary. *The Parliament Restaurant* (Parliament) is open only to members and their guests; try and get invited if only for the buzzy atmosphere and the mostly political clientele. *Chez Pierre* (753 Montreal Road) is a good French choice, and so is *La Guillotine* (513 Sussex Drive); don't let its name frighten you off. *Mamma Teresa* (281 Kent Street) is for substantial Italian lunches or dinners. *The Mill* (555 Ottawa River Parkway) is just that—an old restored one—handsome to look at, and wherein roast beef is the specialty. *Friday's* (150 Elgin Street) occupies a restored house, too, with roast beef and steaks its specialties. *Hayloft Sirloin Pit* (Rideau at Waller) is casual, moderate-tabbed, and with a help-yourself salad bar; as is its counterpart in Toronto. *Japanese Village* (170 Laurier Avenue West) is for Japanese food, teppan style—steaks and the like prepared at your table. *Nate's* (316 Rideau Street) is for delicatessen—corned beef on rye, most especially. In Hull, French, or at least Québecois-French (which is not necessarily the same thing) restaurants are the big draw. *La Ferme Columbia* (376 Boulevard Saint-Joseph) occupies a lovely old stone farmhouse, handsomely restored and furnished. The wine list is possibly the longest for miles around, the menu—also extensive—includes specialties mostly of veal and duck, with good grills. Dinner is more interesting than lunch. *Café Louis IX* (703 Boulevard Saint-Joseph) is another Hull leader in another lovely house. *Café Restaurant Sur l'Île* (94 Rue Principale) is still another popular Hull choice, atmosphere attractive, food tasty.

Prince Edward Island

L'ÎLE-DU-PRINCE-EDOUARD

Best times for a visit: *Summer—June through August—is the ideal season, with sunny days in the seventies (upon occasion, the eighties) and cooler evenings. Autumn—through October—is delightful, and spring, which comes in early May, is*

also pleasant. Winter is not overly cold but with no special inducements for a holiday visit. **Transportation:** *The most popular means of access to the island is via ferry, from two points. Canadian National operates car-carrying boats across the Northumberland Strait from Cape Tormentine, New Brunswick to Borden, Prince Edward Island. The crossing takes less than an hour; most of the ferries have restaurants, and all have comfortable lounges. The other crossing is made from Caribou, Nova Scotia, to the village of Wood Islands, Prince Edward Island. This is a somewhat longer journey (about an hour and a half). Flying to the island is quick and effortless, via Eastern Provincial Airways, whose Boeing 737s connect Charlottetown with Montreal and Halifax. The road network within the province is highly developed, and thanks to the low, even terrain, driving is a pleasure. The Trans-Canada Highway crosses the province, and U.S. visitors might note that Interstate 95, coming from Maine, connects with it at the Houlton, New Brunswick, frontier crossing. Abegweit Sightseeing runs tours of the island on imported double-deck buses out of London.* **Having a drink:** *For long the only Canadian province that completely prohibited the sale of any alcohol—even beer—by the drink, P.E.I. has now joined the twentieth century, with both licensed dining rooms (restaurants where you may drink in conjunction with a meal) and licensed lounges. Provincial liquor stores sell spirits by the bottle.* **Further information:** *Tourist Information Division, Department of the Environment and Tourism. Charlottetown, Prince Edward Island; Agent-General of Prince Edward Island, 40 Trafalgar Square, London; Canadian Government Office of Tourism, Ottawa and branches.*

INTRODUCING PRINCE EDWARD ISLAND

Canada *does* run to extremes. Its Northwest Territories are more than a third as large as the lower forty-eight U.S. states. But Prince Edward Island is just about the size of Delaware. It is the most densely populated of Canada's provinces, but has the

smallest population (about 110,000) by a good margin. It is by
far the smallest of the provinces or territories in area, and is the
only one completely surrounded by water. (Newfoundland, by virtue of its jurisdiction over mainland Labrador, does not pass the
"water test," while Nova Scotia—attached to the mainland at one
relatively narrow point—just misses, too.)

There is something about a purely liquid frontier that tends to
make islands conservative by nature, and "P.E.I."—as it is called—
is no exception to the rule, despite its status as a full-fledged province of one of the world's most progressive countries. It is proud
as a peacock because in 1864 it was the site of the first meeting of
the leaders of the various British North American colonies who
voted to confederate and become Canada. But it didn't see fit to
go along with them until some years later. With its tiny population,
its lack of industry and mineral resources, and its fine bathing
beaches, it continues to make most of its money from farming
(potatoes, mostly) and tourism, which it has never promoted aggressively. The one major hotel chain (Canadian National) that
had been represented on the island, got out. Only one airline—a regional carrier at that—links the island with the mainland, and even
with tourism's economic importance, it's been possible to order a
drink, or even buy a bottle of booze without a provincial permit
only in the last decade. P.E.I. probably pays the lowest wages of
any in Canada, and there is so relatively little opportunity for most
of its young people that one finds a higher proportion of transplanted P.E.I.-ers throughout Canada and the U.S. than from any
other province.

The bland island: The compelling personalities of so many islands is lacking in the case of P.E.I. It is pretty and pleasant
enough, but the visitor expecting anything remotely resembling the
tangy flavor and the strong character of even so near a place as
insular Newfoundland is in for disappointment. Still, it can boast a
history a bit more spirited than its present personality would indicate.

Jacques Cartier is recorded as the first white man to have gone
ashore on the island in 1534, at a time when its original inhabitants, the Micmac Indians, still called it Abegweit. Far from being
fierce, the first of their number to see Cartier and his party fled as
they stepped ashore. "We landed that day," Cartier wrote, "in

four places to see the trees which are wonderfully beautiful and very fragrant. . . . The soil where there are no trees is also very rich. . . . It is the best tempered region one can possibly see and the heat is considerable. There are many turtle-doves, wood pigeons and other birds. . . ."

Hardly, it would seem, a discovery of earth-shaking consequence. Indeed, no one seems to have visited the place again until Samuel de Champlain did so in 1608. He dubbed it Île St. Jean, but there were no settlers until more than a century later, when a French group, in 1720, arrived and established Fort la Joie (Fort of Joy)—so happy were they to have arrived safely in the New World. Shortly thereafter, they were joined by additional French-speaking people—from Acadia, the current Nova Scotia.

Name change: Things then began to move more rapidly. In 1758, the British took control of the island from the French and proceeded without delay to anglicize its name; it became St. John's Island. In 1763 it was annexed to the Colony of Nova Scotia, and six years later—as a result of its residents' unhappiness with that situation—it was detached to become a colony on its own. Three decades later it appears to have dawned on the English that the island's name, a direct translation from the French, had no particular English significance. They then renamed it Prince Edward Island in honor of Edward, Duke of Kent, fourth son of George III and—later—father of Queen Victoria.

There was during this longish period, with change of name and of landlord, no really heavy immigration. But in the first half of the nineteenth century many Scots came, a good portion of them impoverished peasants drawn to the island by Lord Selkirk, the same peer who was later to establish the Red River Settlements of Manitoba. The Scots found, upon arrival, that Lord Selkirk's agents had exaggerated the island's attractions. Decades before they arrived, the Crown had divided the entire island among Englishmen to whom it was financially obligated, and for generations, farmers on the island were no more than the tenants of absentee landlords.

Absentee landlords: Representative government came to P.E.I. in 1851, and in 1864 Charlottetown—the capital since 1765—was the site of the first confederation conference. But the absentee landlord system continued until 1875, two years after the island became a province of Canada. Under the terms of the Land Purchase Act, the proprietors had to sell their land to the government which, in turn, turned it over to the tenants who were working it.

Industry has never had continued success on the island. Shipbuilding, which took place concurrently with the clearing of the forests during the early waves of settlement, has long since subsided. There was, for a period, a thriving silver fox-farming industry, but it disappeared when the silver fox went out of fashion. Agriculture and tourism are the principal sources of income today, and many farmers double as fishermen. P.E.I.'s potatoes are of exceptional quality, and its dairy products are first-rate, too. Industry today has mainly to do with food processing—butter and cheese, fish, poultry, and the like.

YOUR VISIT TO PRINCE EDWARD ISLAND

Prince Edward Island is not a big place—140 miles long, from four to forty miles wide, and with its highest elevation some five hundred feet. Aside from the great stretches of sandy beach—often beneath red-clay cliffs—there are no spectacular physical attributes. The rolling dairy farms are neat and well cared for. There are but two towns of consequence. The villages have a sameness throughout the province—spick-and-span and only occasionally charming. The sole national park is, in actuality, a stretch of bathing beaches, convenient to the capital. Families with young children (most P.E.I. visitors are from Ontario, with the northeast U.S. following) find the island meets their needs for a budget vacation. For others, a brief visit usually suffices.

Charlottetown, with its population in the neighborhood of twenty thousand, is home to about a fifth of all islanders. It has the best harbor on the island (this is where the happy French colonists built their Fort la Joie), and it is the center of the island's political, cultural, educational, and commercial activity. Province House (1843), is a handsome Georgian-style stone structure which houses the legislature and contains the chamber—now a museum that is a requisite destination—where delegates from the British North American colonies met in 1864 to plan the confederation that would signify the birth of the Canadian nation. "In this historic chamber," reads a tablet, "around this table on September first, 1864, were gathered those statesmen whose deliberations led to the formation of the Dominion of Canada." The delegates had handsome Regency chairs for their historic work. Just down the hall is the Provincial Legislative Chamber, with its red-canopied Speaker's chair, and an unusual feature: the seating of the Opposition on the Speaker's right rather than left—a carryover from the building's opening when the Government's members opted for seats on the left—closer to the room's sole stove.

Government House, Charlottetown's second major antique building (1834) is a gracious colonnaded, white-frame mansion, on a capacious lawn overlooking the harbor and verdant Victoria Park, within whose forty acres are the venerable cannon of a much earlier Fort Edward.

Government House is not open to the public. (It is inhabited by the Lieutenant Governor, the Queen's representative in the province, from whom you'll need an invitation in order to go inside.) However, just across the street is Beaconsfield, a handsome Second Empire-style house (1870) originally the home of an affluent merchant, later a nurses' residence and a boarding house, and from 1970 onwards, headquarters for the commendable Prince Edward Island Heritage Foundation. The foundation, funded by the provincial legislature as well as private gifts, aims to conserve, preserve, and restore the island's historical resources. Besides its administrative offices, Beaconsfield contains several rooms of selected exhibits, and a library; you are most welcome.

Another don't-miss is St. Dunstan's Basilica, which along with the Roman Catholic cathedral in St. John's Newfoundland, is among the major architectural sleepers of the Maritimes. St. Dunstan's, a post-World War I Gothic structure, appears large enough to seat at least half the population of Charlottetown. It is 271 feet long and 90 feet wide, with a trio of slender spires, a splendid Bavarian-imported rose window behind the main altar, an elaborate choir, perfectly splendid proportions all round, the lot constituting one of the loveliest ecclesiastical interiors in all of Canada. Actually a cathedral, St. Dunstan's was honored with the designation of a basilica in 1929, when it was officially consecrated, as a

tribute to its serving as the seat of the oldest Roman Catholic diocese in the Maritime provinces (1829) and the second-oldest
English-speaking diocese in Canada.

The Anglican cathedral, St. Peter's, is distinguished by murals
in its All Souls' Chapel, by Robert Harris, a top-rank turn-of-the-
century painter of local origin. Mock-Gothic, turn-of-century St.
Paul's Anglican Church was first established by royal warrant in
1769. Have a look at the fine carvings on the interior arches and
pillars, and note the unglazed tile, made of island clay, in the
vaulting of the chancel.

If the foregoing—what remains of old Charlottetown—are not
without distinction, then the much newer Confederation Centre is
nothing less than socko. Indeed, no North American city anywhere
near as small as Charlottetown, be it seat of government or not,
has anything like this remarkable complex. No less a personage
than Elizabeth II came, as Queen of Canada, to Charlottetown to
dedicate it in 1964, to mark the centennial of the meeting of the
founding Confederation fathers in Province House—just down
Grafton Street—a century earlier. Confederation Centre, occupying
two full city blocks in the heart of town, was a joint federal and
provincial project, and still enjoys heavy federal operating sub-
sidies (the annual budget is about $2 million). Its board of honor-
ary presidents comprises the premiers of all ten provinces, and the
patrons of its satellite Confederation Centre of the Arts is an all-
star trio consisting of the Governor-General of Canada, the Prime
Minister, and the leader of Her Majesty's Official Opposition, in
the Government at Ottawa. Set off by plazas, terraces, and foun-
tains and of striking contemporary design—which makes it appear
as a group of joined structures rather than a single building—the
center revolves around a domed Memorial Hall, whose principal
decorations are a dozen abstract-design banners, each by a
different Canadian artist. The names of the Fathers of Confederation are inscribed over the main doors. From Memorial Hall,
one reaches the theatre (black walls, white cloudlike ceiling
fixtures, nearly 1,000 red seats, with its own professional resident
acting company, a trio of choirs, and a Charlottetown Summer
Festival production in July and August), library, and public
archives, a licensed coffee shop, meeting rooms, a gift shop, and
an art gallery. The gallery has a collection of more than 1,500

paintings by Robert Harris, the same local painter whose murals decorate earlier-described St. Peter's Cathedral, and which had been located in the Harris Memorial Gallery, razed to build the Confederation Centre. The gallery also owns a trio of specially commissioned murals; most striking is Jean-Paul Lemeux's "Charlottetown Revisited," and a wide variety of Canadian works ranging from a Cornelius Krieghoff mid-nineteenth-century painting of Indians, to a superb Eskimo soapstone carving, as well as frequent traveling exhibitions, many of them exceptional, thanks to the gallery's association with the National Museums of Canada. Officials claim that thanks to summer crowds—more people visit it than any other art museum in the country, including Ottawa's National Gallery.

The relatively recent *University of Prince Edward Island,* with its attractive red-brick campus, is an outgrowth of Prince of Wales and St. Dunstan's Colleges. There are about 1,500 students.

Charlottetown Racetrack is synonymous with the trotters— P.E.I. at its most wicked. Downtown Charlottetown is easily and pleasantly walkable (see "What to Buy" and "Creature Comforts"). Then one leaves town to explore the rest of the island.

Prince Edward Island National Park stretches for some twenty-five miles along the north coast of the island, is as close as ten miles to the capital and was established back in 1937. Within its excellently tended confines are seven major beaches—with lifeguards, bathhouses, and nature trails lying beneath cliffs of red sandstone, and with waters warmer than at many points hundreds of miles south along the Atlantic Coast. *Dalvay, Stanhope, Brackley* and *Cavendish* (the latter, my favorite) are the most popular beaches. In the general area are campgrounds, trailer parks, picnic areas, hotels and motels. Near Cavendish Beach is the farmhouse where Lucy Maud Montgomery—the island's most celebrated native—set *Anne of Green Gables;* it's open to visitors and provides a picture of Victorian-era rural life on P.E.I. An 18-hole golf course doubles as its back yard.

Summerside is the province's second metropolis, if one may be so bold as regards terminology. It is an agreeable enough little town, with a range of contemporary amenities, albeit nothing of historical or esthetic significance.

If P.E.I. is without the supercharged drama of parts of Nova Sco-

tia and Newfoundland, and if it lacks the architectural distinction
of New Englandlike New Brunswick, it can still reward the sightseer who looks more carefully than he might elsewhere in the Maritimes. For example: At *Belfast,* note the early-nineteenth-century
St. John's Presbyterian Church and its resemblance to Sir Christopher Wren's London churches. A monument outside honors the
village's first Scottish immigrants and within, in the archives, is
Lord Selkirk's deed for the land on which the church stands. At
Burlington, the Woodleigh Replicas—locally promoted far out of
proportion to their importance—comprise a group of replicas—the
size might be termed life-size doll house—of such British structures
as Anne Hathaway's cottage, the Tower of London, and York
Minster. *Cavendish,* as I have earlier mentioned, is within the National Park, and fronting its golf course is the house that Lucy
Maud Montgomery used as the setting for *Anne of Green Gables,*
around which P.E.I.'s literary sun rises and sets. (A musical version is a perennial hit at the summer Charlottetown Festivals.) If
you are not old enough to remember, or not Canadian enough to
care, there were *Anne* novels reborn twice as movies (the first
starring Anne Shirley in the 1930s) not to mention the locally—
and frequently—produced musical play. If you're an unrecon-
structed Montgomery buff, see the little house where the author
was born at *Clifton.* At *Georgetown,* one finds the smallish Linden
Lea Museum, with not a few exhibits of interest, including what
remains of a little-known early-eighteenth-century French settlement in the region. At *Malpeque*—which gave its name to the esteemed local oysters—the Cabot Park Museum proves that all need
not be lost when an old building is razed. The walls of this ten-
sided structure are made of handsome peaked window frames
saved when the Cabot Building in Charlottetown gave way for
Confederation Centre. Within, the exhibits are an inviting mix of
domestic implements and farm tools. At *Montague,* still more
P.E.I. history; the locale is the Garden of the Gulf Museum. *Rustico's* Farmers' Bank building, more than a century old and now
part-church-hall, part-museum, is where an early Catholic priest
founded a tiny bank and other local institutions, as well; insightful
memorabilia. At *York,* the lure is a no-nonsense collection of old
Canadian glass in the museum of Jewell's Country Gardens, which
is less corny than its name implies. See also the antique one-room

schoolhouse and country store. *Rocky Point's* attraction is Micmac Indian Village, or at least a latter-day interpretation of such a community—wigwams, souvenirs, and all. At *Milltown Cross* is the phenomenon of Harvey Moore's Bird Sanctuary. A quarter of a century ago the late Mr. Moore started luring wild ducks to his pond, which is now home to thousands of birds—a half dozen species of ducks as well as Canada Geese—every autumn, and many others that stay on for months at a time. Have a look at them—in the ponds, on the lawns, overhead—and if you like, rent a boat and fish the ponds for rainbow trout. At *Strathgartney,* the Strathgartney Homestead is a nineteenth-century farm, open to inspection. The interior is furnished in period, but there are outbuildings, as well. *Port Hill:* Though not especially relevant to the province, the Green Park Museum, in an old house, is interesting if only because its initial exhibits (it opened in 1969) came from England's world-reputed National Maritime Museum in Greenwich. The theme, not unsurprisingly, is transatlantic navigation. Old and elderly *churches* dot the island. Some to bear in mind are Montague's Church of Christ (made of local brick of about a century ago), Milton's St. John's Anglican (interior décor by William Harris, brother of earlier-described painter Robert Harris), St. Eleanor's St. John's—the oldest Anglican church on the island (1838) with fine stained glass—Springfield's St. Elizabeth's Anglican (1847), and the Disciples of Christ's white-frame Cross Roads Chapel (1836). Along the coast one finds *lobster pounds* and co-ops, where the seafood is for sale; worth considering, if you've a place to cook it, and worth inspecting, even if you haven't. At Victoria's Fisherman's Wharf, clam chowder and clam fritters are on sale, as well as lobster.

SHOPPING

There is not a province in Canada whose handicraft output has improved so remarkably in recent years. You'll find—all locally made—patchwork quilts, pottery, dolls, knitwear, woodcarving (including bird miniatures), ship models (including ships in bottles), jewelry of local materials, paintings, and other crafts. In **Charlottetown,** head first for the *Island Crafts Shop* (31 Queen Street); it's the capital's outlet for the P.E.I. Craftsmen's Council. Also good is *Cook's Cove* (75 Dorchester Street), and the nearby *Old Warehouse,* whose specialty is elderly things. The *Wool and Yarn Shop* (Grafton Street) carries a big stock of handknitted sweaters, both men's and women's. The nearby *Bookmark* is well-stocked with reading material, including volumes on local and regional subjects. The leading DEPARTMENT STORES are a branch of the cross-country *Eaton's*—quite small this—and the bigger locally owned *Moore and McLeod,* with clothing, housewares, furniture, and—of especial interest to visitors—a souvenir department. Away from the capital, consider, the old reliable *Of the Isle Shop* at **Brackley,** with as complete a selection of interesting wares as was the case when this book was first published; *Flat River Crafts Studio* (stoneware, hand-blocked batik cloth, sculpture) at **Flat River,** near the Wood Islands ferry terminal; the *Village Craft House* at **Central Bedeque** (quilts and dolls); the *Village Pottery,* at **New London,** for made-on-the-premises ceramics; *Stoneware Pottery and Crafts,* **South Milton;** *Laughing Lobster,* **Meadow Bank** (model boats and other woodwork), *Cupboard Gifts,* **Summerside East** (assorted island crafts), and *Wood Islands Handcrafts Co-op Association* (**Wood Islands** ferry terminal) for ceramics, woodwork, leatherwork, and weaving. To be noted, too, for a selection of Canadawide crafts is the *Gift Shop* in **Charlottetown's** Confederation Centre.

CREATURE COMFORTS

So long as it is understood that the very grand and/or opulent is not a part of the P.E.I. accommodations scene, one can be comfortable and content. What follows is a selective group of places to stay. Please note that all are fully licensed. In **Charlottetown,** the traditional leader, *Hotel Charlottetown*—once a part of the nationwide Canadian National chain—is now on its own, but considerably refurbished, with its bedrooms more attractive than ever, the town's handsomest restaurant, a coffee shop, and the capacious Tudor Lounge for drinks. The location could not be more central. *Inn on the Hill* (15 Euston Street) is an exceptionally attractive in-town house, very contemporary, with capacious bedrooms (each with two double beds), equally attractive suites, a honey of a cocktail lounge, a smart coffee shop with a Scandinavian Modern look, and professional management. *Kirkwood Motor Hotel,* a mile from the center of town, is a low-slung complex with the Florentine Restaurant and Sweet Charlotte coffee shop, modern and well-equipped bedrooms, and a heated pool. *McLauchlan's Motel* has the advantage of an in-town location, pleasant rooms, a licensed restaurant, sauna, and barber-beauty shop. *Motel Charlottetown,* on the Trans-Canada Highway just outside of town, is well kept, with comfortable rooms, a licensed restaurant and coffee shop, and a heated pool. In the **National Park area,** on the North Shore, *Shaw's Hotel and Cottages* remains an inviting, old-fashioned resort, on 75 rambling acres, with the same congenial Shaw family management that has run the place continuously since 1860. The dining room is among the island's better eating places, and the Lobster Pot lounge, in its own quarters near the main house, is a happy choice for relaxing drinks. Not all main-house rooms have bath, but those in the cottages—for from two to ten persons—are all so equipped. And Brackley Beach is adjacent. *Dalvay-by-the-Sea,* at **Dalvay Beach,** which is where National Park headquarters are located, is the resort that comes closest of any on the island to being elegant. The main house is a former private summer mansion with a quite marvelous grand stairway leading to a balconied second story; the management is French-from-France, the food has a delightful Gallic flavor, and facilities include tennis, golf driving range, bowling green, playground, and—for the lake on one side of the hotel—canoes and rowboats. All 26 main-house rooms have private bath; there are a pair of cottages, one originally built years ago for Governor-General Viscount Alexander and his family. Dalvay goes back to 1895, when it was built for Alexander MacDonald, a Standard Oil partner of John D. Rockefeller. *Links Inn,* at **Cavendish,** is pleasant, with rooms in a main house and cottages, a good restaurant, and a next-to-the-Green Gables Golf Course setting. *Cavendish Motel,* with both regular rooms and housekeeping units, has a restaurant and lounge. At **Stanhope Beach,** also on the North Shore, is the *Stanhope Beach Inn and Motel,* with 54 modern rooms, restaurant, and lounge. At **Roseneath,** four miles north of Montague, on the southeast corner of the island, is

Brudenell Resort, with 50 twin-bedded rooms and a smaller number of housekeeping units, restaurant, coffee shop, and cocktail
lounge—all very contemporary. In **Summerside,** is the *Linkletter
Motel,* with half a hundred pleasant rooms, restaurant, coffee shop,
and cocktail lounge. P.E.I. makes a specialty of farmhouse vacations; a number of working farms let rooms during the summer
months to couples and families.

Dining in P.E.I.: Civilized dining came late to Prince Edward Island. It was the last of the provinces to legally permit the con-
sumption of a pre-dinner cocktail, not to mention the even more
depraved practice of the between-meals libation, unaccompanied
by solid nourishment. Which is not to say that all hell has broken
loose in Charlottetown, or beyond. Only to be grateful that in
this most conservative of the provinces, the contemporary
holidaymaker can sip his beer or scotch and not be in violation of
the law.

In **Charlottetown,** the good-looking *Georgian Dining Room* of
the Hotel Charlottetown has remained consistently reliable over
the years. Its lobster dinners remain especially good, but there is
other local seafood (don't forget the island's Malpeque oysters)
and fish. And quality steaks, as well. As for desserts: whatever the
pie of the day, order it. *Le Petit Café,* the hotel's coffee shop,
serves lobster lunches and dinners, as well as hamburgers, sandwiches and short orders. The *Florentine Restaurant* of the Kirkwood Motor Hotel has achieved an enviable reputation with the
locals for dinners featuring lobster, steak, and roast beef, with the
first-mentioned—and other local fish and seafood—taking prece-
dence. The hotel's coffee shop—officially the *Sweet Charlotte Restaurant,* in honor of the consort of George III for whom the capital is named—is less formal, but with a surprisingly extensive lunch
and dinner menu and hearty breakfasts. *Davy Jones' Locker* has
perhaps the most extensive seafood menu in town—Malpaque oysters, cherrystone clams, seafood chowder, steamed clams and mussels, oyster stew, lobster bisque, fresh trout, halibut, and scallops,
and of course, lobster in a variety of presentations. Attractive setting, too. *The Schooner* has a nautical look to it; there's seafood,
but European-accented meat dishes, as well. Very pleasant. *The
Gondolier* is authentic Italian. *Gentleman Jim's,* just outside of
town, is for steaks. Out on the island, the specialty is the com-

munity-organized lobster supper, at bargain prices. Best of the lot is probably that served at the *New Glasgow Recreation Centre,* near Cavendish, with local ladies baking the bread, pies, and cakes, and smiley high school girls working as waitresses. Usual serving hours 4 to 8:30 P.M., and the menu comprises boiled lobster in the shell, hot or cold, with drawn butter, a variety of salads and relishes, those homemade desserts, and a beverage. Another recommended lobster-supper locale is *St. Anne's Church* on the North Shore. Other good out-of-the-capital eating spots are *Dalvay-by-the-Sea,* for both lunch and dinner; *Shaw's,* and the *Stanhope Beach Inn*—at all of which advance booking is recommended, for these are hotels where residents get seating preference. Also agreeable: *Lobster Shanty North,* at Montague; and the *Chowder Hall Restaurant* of the Bay Vista Motel, at Bayview, near Cavendish.

Quebec

LE QUÉBEC

Best times for a visit: *In a word—anytime, except, of course, for frigid winters in the north of the province, which is of relatively little visitor interest. Summers in the south—from Quebec City downward—are hot and—I speak from experi-*

ence—can, on occasion, be humid. Spring (late April through early June) and fall (late September and October) are delightful for touring, both urban and rural. And winter—crisp, cold, and with quantities of skiable snow—is a major tourist season in Quebec City, Montreal, the Laurentians, and other winter sports areas. **Transportation:** *The road network is enormous, and with a high proportion of paved highways. The Trans-Canada Highway passes through—or near— Quebec's most interesting attractions. Going from east to west, it begins on the northern New Brunswick border, near Edmundston, in that province; goes through Rivière du Loup, starting point for tours of the Gaspé Peninsula, and then heads south along the St. Lawrence River, passing by the Murray Bay region, to Lévis (the across-the-river neighbor of Quebec City), continuing to Montreal (gateway to the Laurentians), after which it crosses over into Ontario and Ottawa, the national capital. The province is approached from the American states of New York, Vermont, New Hampshire, and Maine by a number of modern highways. Bus service, within the province and to out-of-province points, is extensive. Quebec is served by more airlines than any other province. The major airports are Montreal's sprawling, older Dorval—principally for domestic Canadian services, and flights to and from the U.S.; and immense still-a-building Mirabel (35 miles northwest), whose first section, built at a cost of $440 million, is nearly five times the size of what had been the largest airport—Dallas-Fort Worth. A feature of Mirabel's terminal is that travelers need walk no farther than 280 feet between arrival and departure—a happy contrast to the interminable passageways of Dorval. Mirabel users include Air Canada, CP Air, British Airways, Air France, KLM, Alitalia, Iberia, Sabena, Swissair, Lufthansa, Aer Lingus, CSA (Czechoslovak), SAS, TAP (Portuguese), Aeroflot, and Olympic. Air Canada, through Dorval, links the province to its transcontinental, Canadian, and U.S. routes. It makes several flights daily between Montreal and Quebec City, and to other provincial destinations. Québecair flies to northeastern and eastern points within Quebec and Labrador. Also flying regionally are Eastern*

Provincial and Air Gaspé, among others. Eastern Air Lines has frequent service from New York and points south. Delta Airlines flies to and from Boston. Railroads: *Both Canadian National and CP Rail are on the scene; Montreal is national headquarters for both (and for Air Canada, as well). CN's noted* Super Continental *runs from Montreal all the way west to Vancouver, while its* Ocean Limited *goes east to Halifax. CP Rail's* Canadian—*the first of Canada's dome-topped trains —links Montreal and Toronto with Vancouver; that line also serves the Maritimes. There is frequent train service linking Montreal, Toronto, and Ottawa, via both CN and CP Rail; CN's extra-speedy turbo trains make the Montreal-Toronto run in four hours, ten minutes, and run also to Ottawa. America's Amtrak trains connect Montreal with New England, New York, Philadelphia, and Washington, with connections to other cities of the Amtrak network. Luxury cruise ships call at Montreal, Quebec City, Saguenay river ports, and Gaspé. Urban transport, particularly in Montreal and Quebec, is well organized. In both of these cities, buses are the principal public vehicles, as well—in the case of Montreal —as one of the planet's handsomest and best-designed subway —or Métro—systems. The Montreal Métro, though infinitely smaller, is patterned on that of Paris in that each line has two terminus stations; you check the station maps to find your station stop, and board a train going in that direction—at one end or the other—of the line. There are three lines—Nos. 1, 2, & 4—with 28 stations; two additional lines are being built. Stations are handsome with no two alike. And the whole system is spotless. In short: urban transport at its best.* **Having a drink:** *The most permissive and most sensible liquor laws of any province, one finds many licensed hotel dining rooms, restaurants, cocktail lounges, cafés, cabarets, and brasseries; these last serve beer and cider, as well as meals to both sexes and are often former male-only taverns. Liquor and wine by the bottle are sold in provincial liquor stores operated by La Régie des Alcools du Québec; beer to take out is sold in licensed grocery stores.* **Further information:** *Direction Generale du Tourisme, Cité Parlementaire, Quebec City; Province of Quebec Tourist Office, 17 West*

50th Street, New York City; Quebec Government Office, 31
St. James Avenue, Boston; Quebec Government Office, 111
West Jackson Boulevard, Chicago; Quebec Government Office, 1412 Main Street, Dallas; Agent-General of Quebec, 12
Upper Grosvenor Street, London; Agent-General of Quebec,
66 Rue Pergolèse, Paris; Canadian Government Office of
Tourism, Ottawa and branches.

INTRODUCING QUEBEC

There are, constituting the confederation of Canada, four provinces to the east of Quebec, five provinces to the west of Quebec, and two territories to the north and west of Quebec. And there is Quebec. It calls itself *la belle province*. Indeed, it is beautiful. But it might well be styled *la province extraordinaire*.

For Quebec has seen to it for centuries—and continues to see to it—that wherever possible, what obtains for the rest of Canada does not quite obtain in the case of Quebec. Every province has, of course, its individualities, its rights and prerogatives, its eccentricities, if you will. But such manifestations of each province's personality are almost unnoticeable in contrast to those of Quebec. And even if they were more strongly pronounced than they are, they would not be as important as Quebec's. For Quebec is Canada's largest province in area. (Texas, pardner? Quebec has room for two Texases.) And it is second only to Ontario in population, which means that within its borders live close to a third of the Canadian people.

Ici on parle Français: There are French-speaking Canadians in every province and territory. (New Brunswick is 40 per cent French-speaking, but its population is small.) Still, to all intents and purposes, Quebec *is* French-speaking Canada; only about 12 per cent of its people consider English their principal language.

And its distinctiveness lies not only in language, but in its way of life. Quebec has retained the system of civil law which it inherited from its French founders. It maintains a dual school system; one part is for the largely Roman Catholic, French-speaking populace, and its schools are largely staffed by clergy and religious. The other part is for the minority of English-speaking (mainly Protestant) residents.

Quebec, while recognizing that it is but a division of a larger land, tends to think of itself as a separate entity whenever it can. In every Canadian province the provincial government is strong and clings to the prerogatives allowed it under the laws of Confederation, to the point where the concept of States' Rights—even in the southern United States—appear pallid. But Quebec is special. Its legislature is called the National Assembly, even though it is but one province of a nation. It sends delegations to international meetings, much as a sovereign nation would, accredits consular personnel stationed within the province, and has even worked out cultural pacts on its own accord with a major power like France.

Sound as though there's sentiment for a Republic of Quebec? Well there is, currently, and there has been, recurrently, in the past—during both the First and Second World Wars. Still, the great majority of the people of the province vigorously supported World War II efforts and, of course, fought and died in the armed services alongside other Canadians. Today, despite the activities of the Separatist *Parti Québecois,* many citizens remain in favor of a united Canada, although fewer than before seem to support the monarchial form of Canada's government; although members of the Royal Family have visited the province without unhappy results (Queen Elizabeth the Queen Mother did so in 1974), visits of the Sovereign, Elizabeth II, as Queen of Canada, are increasingly rare.

Quebec has not yet fully accepted the British conquest of New France two centuries ago. The majority of its people—who have clung stubbornly to their language and to many of their traditional ways—continue to resent the English-speaking Canadians' indifference to and, at times, hostility toward the French language. They have not forgotten, either, the discrimination they have had to face, through the years, in social, occupational, and professional fields. They have only in recent years come to realize that they have been passed over when jobs were handed out not only because of the language barrier and indefensible snobbism, but because so relatively few of them were trained to be competent in the ways of contemporary commerce and technology. They are only now beginning to recognize that Quebec is a mélange of the eight-

eenth and twentieth centuries, with the nineteenth—by and large—
omitted. They do not consider that their fellow countrymen understand as well as they might that had it not been for their ancestors,
the Canada of today might not have come about.

Cartier and New France: For it was the French who initially
settled Canada. The first permanent settlement in North America,
north of Mexico, was the French Port Royal, in what is now Nova
Scotia. Champlain first visited there in 1604. The original settlement in Quebec followed; but a good bit earlier, in 1534, another
Frenchman, Jacques Cartier, had planted a fleur-de-lis-encrested
cross at the Gaspé Peninsula. Cartier had set sail in search of a
western passage to the Orient, but after landing at Gaspé, he
claimed it (and the country beyond) for the King of France.

A year later he sailed through the St. Lawrence as far as the site
of Montreal, but went back to where Quebec now stands to winter
at what was then an Indian village known as Stadacona.
Champlain was not to arrive in the area until 1608—after he had
established Port Royal. He built at Quebec a small, two-story,
moat-surrounded building, and it was he who gave Quebec its
name. Its origin, though, is not fully established, although many
authorities believe it to be derived from an Indian word meaning
"narrowing of the waters." At any rate, New France was in business. More fur traders, missionaries, and explorers came to the
new land from the old. They settled the St. Lawrence Valley, and
they went as far afield as the Rockies in the west, Hudson Bay to
the north, the Mississippi Valley and the Gulf of Mexico to the
south. (Montreal was founded as a religious settlement in 1642.)

Wolfe's victory on the Plains of Abraham: In 1663 Quebec
passed from the management of the fur-trading companies to the
Crown of France, and became a royal colony. Later, during the
French and Indian Wars, the French attempted to strengthen and
expand their military hold on the region, but were to lose to the
British at the tragic, albeit dramatic, battle on the Plains of
Abraham—above Quebec City—in 1759, when British General
Wolfe's troops were victorious over those of French General
Montcalm. (Wolfe, however, was killed in battle, and Montcalm
died of wounds, just after the battle.) The tide had turned. In
1763, New France's sixty thousand colonists went under British
rule. A little more than a decade later the British Parliament—in

order to assure the loyalty of its French-speaking subjects in the incipient American Revolution—passed a measure known as the Quebec Act. It allowed the people of Quebec to retain their semi-feudal land-tenure system, their language, their religion, and their legal and political institutions.

The Quebec Act was one of the most far-reaching of laws having to do with the history of North America, for it (a) aroused so much resentment among the American colonists—the concessions in favor of Roman Catholicism were decried by the Protestant colonists, who also lost land to Quebec which they coveted—that it helped bring on the American Revolution, (b) helped keep Canada loyal to the Crown during the Revolution, and (c) was the basis for Quebec's maintaining its French-language flavor through both the colonial and confederation periods, to this very day.

Unhappy Lower Canada: In 1791, representative government came to British North America when it was divided into two provinces: Upper Canada (today's Ontario), on one side of the Ottawa River, and Lower Canada (Quebec), on the other. But the French-speaking Lower Canadians were not happy with what they considered discriminatory, high-handed treatment from their British governors. In 1837 the *Patriotes*—a group of reform-minded followers of Louis Joseph Papineau—staged a rebellion against the government. Papineau, Montreal-born and the eloquent founder of the French-Canadian Reform Party, fled the country, and the rebellion was a failure. But it did have the effect of making the British aware of the intensity of their French-speaking subjects' feelings.

In 1840, under the Act of Union, Quebec was joined with Ontario. In 1846 it was styled Canada East, and in 1849—after a considerable struggle—it gained responsible government. The liaison with Ontario was never a particularly happy one, what with strains of various sorts between the French-speaking and English-speaking peoples. That difficulty was partially resolved with confederation. In 1867 Quebec regained its old name and became a province of the new Canada, along with the other original members.

Lopsided development: Aside from the foregoing political developments and the transformation of Montreal into a great city, the nineteenth century saw few other changes in the province. Descendants of the peasants who had immigrated to the region in the previous century—tilling land held by feudal *seigneurs* and dependent upon the counsel of the traditionally conservative parish priests —continued to carry on as their antecedents had. Life in the small communities was built around the family (and families were very large). Farms were self-sufficient; spinning, weaving, and other home handicrafts were retained. What education there was centered around the three R's and, in advanced-learning centers, the classics. The semi-feudal land system was modified in 1854; it was not to be completely eliminated for decades thereafter.

But much of the wealth that was accumulated was controlled by English-speaking bankers and industrialists in Montreal, and elsewhere. There were, to be sure, successful French-speaking Canadians, but they were exceptions to the rule, at least in the realm of commerce. The provincial government, while ever mindful of the powers decreed it when the province entered Confederation under the British North America Act, tended to be hyperconservative, and not without more than its share of corruption. (The government of Maurice Duplessis, Premier from 1936 to 1939, and again from 1944 until 1959, gave Quebec an international reputation which it could well have done without.)

The more recent Liberal Party government of Prime Minister Robert Bourassa (elected in 1970, again in 1973, and as nonseparatist as contemporary Quebec politics allow) made considerable progress. Industry—especially pulp and paper—has been aggressively encouraged and has multiplied along with hydroelectric output. Mining production has risen to the fore. Farmers—now a minority of the population—still play an important part in the economy.

The modern province: At the same time, education improved. (There has been substantial increase in high-school graduates and in university enrollments.) Health care is improving with the provincial government earmarking considerable budgets to public health and social security, and with a provincially sponsored health insurance program.

But with these improvements, many Quebec people—whose counterparts a generation or two ago might not have cared—have become aware of the Anglo-Saxon dominance of Canada—politically, culturally, occupationally. The mid-1960s terrorist tactics of the Quebec Liberation Front have led to non-violent but politically strong sentiment for nationalist political evolution to the point where many—if not all—observers of the scene that believe that secession of Quebec is a matter of when—not if. This conviction became more widespread than ever when in 1974 the province enacted legislation ironically signed into law by the Queen's representative, the Lieutenant Governor, declaring French the sole official language, rather than one of two such tongues, along with English. The English-speaking minority protested, as did much of the rest of Canada, the sentiment being that the so-called Bill 22 contravened nationwide official bilingualism, a policy strongly promoted by Prime Minister Pierre Trudeau and his predecessor, Lester Pearson.

The federal government continues efforts to recruit more French-speaking civil servants to work in the Ottawa ministries and throughout the country, and teaches intensive French to those English-speaking civil servants whose jobs are such that they should be able to conduct business in either language. Federal documents—from postage stamps to income tax forms, to signs in federally supported airports and in the national parks—have long been printed in both languages, and nationally distributed products —from toothpaste to canned vegetables—generally are prepared with bilingual labels. Still, the resistance of many English-speaking Canadians to French remains widespread. I have heard otherwise rational and intelligent Canadians turn color and nearly lose control, in exclaiming their distaste for the language. Indeed, French— long the language of international diplomacy, long the universally respected language of culture in every corner of the world (including the United States)—appears to be looked upon by many Canadians in much the same way as certain bigoted New Yorkers view the Spanish spoken by Puerto Ricans in their midst. Still, the language situation is not beyond lighter touches, if not always intended. The English-language magazine, *Montreal Calendar,* in a review of the classic film *Gone With the Wind,* pointed out that Vivien Leigh has the role of "the flirtatious Dixie belle, Scarlette O'Hara."

Prejudices and problems: Bill 22 has changed things, but up to relatively recently—particularly in the city of Montreal—it has been the French-speaking citizen who learned English (and learned it beautifully), rather than the English-speaking citizen who learned French. (The current fear, among thoughtful Québecois and Anglo-Canadians both, is that Bill 22 will discourage French-speakers from troubling to learn English, and eventually make of Quebec a linguistically isolated enclave in mainly English-speaking North America.) Even the most highly educated and sophisticated of French-speaking Québecois resent the patronizing attitude taken by their English-speaking fellow citizens toward their language, their culture, and often themselves. Canadians whose English grammar is not always first-rate incorrectly dismiss Canadian French as nothing more than a shadow of the French language, when in fact, scholars from many countries (including the United States, where there is much excellent instruction in French) travel to such universities as Montréal and Laval to take advanced degrees in French. The idiomatic French—it is called *joual,* and it can indeed be earthy—spoken by the man in the street is no more to be criticized than the English of the London Cockney, the Ozark American, or the Newfoundland Canadian. As a matter of fact, it is objected to—when it is used in current novels and plays—by Québecois parents who want their children to speak proper French as it is taught in the schools, and as it is spoken by educated people. Make no mistake: The visitor need not fear that his "French-style" French will not be understood, or for that matter, that it will not be appreciated. It is true that outsiders' grammar and accents are, on rare occasion, made fun of. But by and large—certainly in my experience—Québecois are glad when fellow-North Americans from the major-language group take the trouble to speak the language of their hosts.

The wonder of today's Quebec is that despite its French-speaking people's preoccupation with their relationship toward the rest of Canada, their nationalist sentiments, and the chips on their shoulders, they remain, by and large, gracious and hospitable to visitors, congenial, good company, and the inhabitants of a province that has a special interest for the newcomer unmatched by any other in Canada. The point is, this stubbornly Francophone province is like no other corner of North America. It is not, of course, France. But the language of the Gauls is there, the ambience has been strongly influenced by them, the countryside is lovely, the capital is a truly unique city, and Montreal is not only Canada's largest city; it is indisputably its greatest.

YOUR VISIT TO QUEBEC

Quebec, as has already been indicated, is enormous, but there is no need for the prospective visitor to feel he must travel from the lower fringe of this 594,860-square-mile province all the way to its northern reaches on the shores of Hudson Strait, just south of the Northwest Territories' Baffin Island. For the most visitable—and most visited—sectors of Quebec lie roughly within the southern third of its territory, from the Saguenay River to Montreal on the St. Lawrence, and the eastern townships fringing the United States. Requisite Quebec destinations are relatively easy to pinpoint: Montreal and the nearby Laurentians; the lovely farmland and towns which flank the St. Lawrence, north to—and including—the capital, Quebec City, along with its environs; Murray Bay and the Saguenay River; the Gaspé Peninsula. There are a national park, many provincial parks, and other visitable destinations as well. Travel in Quebec is pleasant. A tremendously high proportion of French-speaking city-dwellers are conversant in English, as are many of the country people who deal with travelers. And, of course, there is an English-speaking minority.

Montreal: To describe Greater Montreal as the home of one out of every ten Canadians is only to indicate its size. To state—as Montreal is fond of stating—that after Paris it is the largest French-speaking city in the world is but to quote a fairly impressive statistic. To amplify by emphasizing that this is the world's most important inland port is to shed some—but only some—additional light. The truth of the matter is that Montreal is not easy to categorize. It is a quite marvelous freak. It was founded by the French as a religious settlement and it is today a city where French is spoken as a mother tongue by more than two thirds of its inhabitants. It was started on the road to greatness by early French traders and trappers. But it was made great by English-speaking Canadians—largely in the nineteenth century—at a time when the province which it dominates largely stagnated economically, technologically, and socially. Its fast pace and its modern façade set it apart from the rest of Quebec and make of it almost a world apart. With its dominance in the commercial, transportation, and banking fields, it is the part of Quebec with the closest links to the rest of Canada. And were it not a dominantly French-speaking community, influenced by the traditionally conservative climate of the province to which it belongs, its cultural importance would be far more widespread throughout Canada.

But despite its peculiarities—perhaps, in part, because of them—Montreal is Canada's sole representative among the relative handful of truly important urban centers on our planet. Vancouver is infinitely more beautiful, thanks to its splendid setting. Toronto is perhaps more aggressive and more accurately reflects the English-speaking Canadian majority and the new Canadians from Europe who have helped transform it into a cosmopolitan metropolis.

But Montreal has the advantages of a longer history and a location which—though a thousand miles inland—give it more of an Atlantic Seaboard ambience than its neighbor cities to the east. Montreal had a head start commercially, time to develop aesthetically, the wealth to indulge itself culturally. And the result is maturity. This is the mellowest, the most socially sure of itself of all major Canadian cities. In no other large city in the country do ethnic groups speaking different mother tongues exist side by side the way English- and French-speaking Montrealers do. In no city anywhere, on any continent, is the visitor speaking a language foreign to the great majority—I refer to the English or the American or the English-speaking Canadian—at once more comfortable or more at home. In Paris, the waiter or *concierge* will speak a passable English to his customer. But in Montreal, the French-speaking Montrealer—and he is the waiter in the hotel, the bartender, the bus driver, the chambermaid, the room clerk, the shop clerk more often than not—has learned to speak excellent, almost unaccented English.

Jacques Cartier saw the site of Montreal in 1535, and it was he who named the island on which the city is largely built. He called the mountain overlooking the area *Mont Réal*—royal mountain. And it stuck. The Indian village at the foot of the mountain, extant during Cartier's visit, had disappeared by the time Champlain arrived in 1611, and there was no settlement to replace it until 1642 when Paul de Chomedey, Sieur de Maisonneuve, set up a mission—"for the glory of God"—which was developed as Ville-Marie de Montréal, named in honor of the Virgin Mary. Maison-neuve, a French army officer, had as his chief colleague Jeanne Mance, who was the founder of the Hôtel Dieu hospital in 1644. The original group of twenty-three colonists included, also, a Jesuit priest, Bartholémy Vimont. Ville-Marie de Montréal, de-spite attacks from the Iroquois and other vicissitudes, thrived both as a religious mission and as a fur-trading post.

In 1657 the St. Sulpice Seminary was founded. In the early eighteenth century the Château de Ramezay—happily, still to be visited—was built as the governor's residence. In 1760 Montreal—then a town of some eight thousand population—surrendered to the British, under whom it began to grow by leaps and bounds. It was in Montreal that the North West Company, long-time rival of the Hudson's Bay Company, was founded in 1783 by French in-terests. But at this time, substantial numbers of Englishmen ar-rived and established businesses, the while living separately from the French and setting a pattern which exists, by and large, to this day.

The latter half of the nineteenth century saw Montreal expand phenomenally, thanks to increased trade, the coming of respon-sible government, the advent of the railway. In 1840 the popula-tion was about fifty thousand; with the dawn of the twentieth cen-tury it had leaped to 360,000, and the city limits had spread from the confines of Montreal Island to the southern shores of the St. Lawrence. Half a century later, in 1950, Montreal had more than a million inhabitants. A decade later, the figure exceeds 1,190,000. Greater Montreal is now the home of something like three million persons.

This is a city to be reckoned with. The core of Montreal is Do-minion Square and the contiguous Place du Canada, focal point for the stranger destined for hotels, transport terminals, the great department stores, shops and restaurants of Rue Ste.-Catherine—the main commercial thoroughfare—and surrounding streets (espe-cially Sherbrooke, Bishop, Crescent, and Montague or Mountain). It is a hop and a skip to the enormous, crucifix-shaped Roman Catholic Cathedral of Marie-Reine-du-Monde—a rather as-tonishing small-scale replica of St. Peter's Basilica in Rome that deserves interior inspection, if only to see the brilliant copy of Bernini's baldachin, or altar canopy—and to still another cruciform building: the Royal Bank, principal edifice of the Place Ville-Marie, in whose elegant basement promenades one finds shops of limitless variety and underground passages to the Gare Centrale and the Queen Elizabeth Hotel—another of the city's modern landmarks. Place Ville-Marie is the core of Montreal's unique underground city—more than 40 acres of arcades, and especially popular in snowy winter. There are some 500 shops, 30-plus restaurants, as well as many places to snack and drink, plus below-street access to office buildings, including the Place Bonaventure hotel-shop-convention hall complex.

Place Victoria is Montreal's skyscraper-filled financial district, with the Bank of Canada and other leading financial institutions. But it is the Place d'Armes—and surrounding Vieux Montréal—to which the visitor should give next priority. Fronting the harbor—itself worth a tour, for it is here that the St. Lawrence Seaway has its start—is what remains of the oldest part of the city; it is an official Provincial Historic District. A good deal has, mercifully, been preserved and in recent years restored, including uncelebrated—but nonetheless valuable—old buildings converted into restaurants, boutiques, and museums. Dominating the square is Notre Dame Church, whose exterior of pleasingly neat but unspectacular Gothic belies the opulence of what lies within. Notre Dame was built between 1823 and 1829 as the third church by that name on that site. The carved wood detail of its nave, the statues of saints in Gothic niches surrounding its brilliant main altar, the stained glass windows depicting the history of Montreal, the elaborate décor of Our Lady of the Sacred Heart Chapel, the octagonal baptistery, the lovely *objets*—religious and otherwise—in the church's museum, the six-thousand-pipe organ—all of these combine to make a visit to Notre Dame one of the most memorable of Montreal moments.

St. Sulpice Seminary, headquarters of the order that sent members to North America in the seventeenth century to help found the city, is to the left of Notre Dame. Nearby, around Place Jacques Cartier, one comes upon the Château de Ramezay, built in 1705 as the French governors' residence, and now an exceptional—and charming—museum, full of memorabilia dating back to the French period, including some excellent early Quebec furniture. Here, too, is the mansard-roofed City Hall, a Franco-Victorian souvenir of nineteenth-century Montreal. There are cafés all about—al fresco in summer. The piers of the harbor are close by, as is colonnaded old Bonsecours Market, to which farmers used to bring their produce from the country, and the so-called Sailors' Church or Notre-Dame-de-Bonsecours, built in 1771—the city's oldest—with ship models throughout, and a subterranean museum whose subject is Marguerite Bourgeois, the beatified nun who founded the church in the seventeenth century.

The mountain for which Montreal is called retains the name given it by Cartier—Mont Réal or Mount Royal—and most of it is now a municipally operated park offering a super view of the city from its famed observation point, and with a fleet of horse-drawn *calèches* that may be engaged for rides. This is a ski (and ice-skating) mecca in winter and agreeable at any time of year for walks and picnics by the shores of Beaver Lake. It is perhaps most famous for its 100-foot luminous cross; it is visible at night from as far away as fifty miles, and was erected in 1924 on the site of the wooden cross placed there by Maisonneuve, the city's founder, more than three centuries ago.

La Fontaine Park is the site of a Children's Zoo, lagoons with boats for rowing, and an open-air theatre. Maisonneuve Park is home to Montreal's superior Botanical Gardens, and a range of sports facilities, including a gymnasium and pool, 36-hole golf course, tennis courts, and Maurice Richard Arena—for hockey and skating. More unusual is the park that occupies Île Sainte-Hélène, alongside the Jacques Cartier Bridge over the St. Lawrence. Named by Champlain in 1611 (for his twelve-year-old wife), Île Sainte-Hélène is the site of the Montreal Aquarium and of the excellent Maritime and Military Museum before which—in summer—soldiers parade each day, wearing the colonial-period uniforms of the *Compagnie Franche de la Marine*. They culminate their maneuvers by firing a genuine antique of a cannon. But, as if that were not enough, Île Sainte-Hélène has more to offer—swimming pools, picnic and playgrounds, a municipally operated French-cuisine restaurant and a theatre—La Poudrière—in a converted stone powderhouse.

St. Joseph's Oratory is on the western slope of Mount Royal. Along with Sainte-Anne-de-Beaupré, near Quebec City, it is perhaps the most noted such Roman Catholic shrine in North America. It was founded at the turn of the century by a monk known as Brother André who was devoted to St. Joseph, the first patron saint of Catholic Canada. He obtained permission to build a simple oratory, and it was not long before news spread of cures effected at the shrine as a result of Brother André's intercession. St. Joseph's, now a great stone church, attracts some three million pilgrims a year. In connection is a museum dealing with St. Joseph and three centuries of Canadian devotion to him.

Cité du Havre is a sector of the Expo 67 site whose buildings have been put to contemporary uses. They include the important Musée d'Art Contemporain—with modern Quebec works and changing shows; the architecturally socko Habitat apartment house, and the Théâtre Expo, used regularly for plays.

I am not ordinarily drawn to residential districts—they have a sameness in all cities—but I do consider Montreal's Westmount—a traditional stronghold of the city's rich Anglophiles—an exception and urge that you pass its palatial houses. Historically important Outremont—still with some of its early farmhouses, now on built-up streets—is visit-worthy, too. The Boulevard Saint-Laurent area is what might be called Ethnic Montreal—in and around Rue Roy, it's Italian and Greek; beyond, near Rue La Gauchetière, it's Chinese, with shops and restaurants, according to nationality.

Montreal's universities are invariably of interest to visitors. The best known in the English-speaking world is McGill, which received a royal charter in 1821 and now has an enrollment of some ten thousand students, a particularly famous school of medicine, and a charmer of a mostly-nineteenth-century downtown campus. The Université de Montreal is headquartered in a graceless albeit enormous, many-winged main building on the upper reaches of Mount Royal; it's the biggest French-language university outside of France. Among its many faculties, that of engineering is probably the most noted. Concordia University, created in 1973, embraces the former Loyola College (Jesuit) and Sir George Williams University and is the province's biggest, as regards enrollment. There is, as well, the relatively recent campus of the Université du Québec à Montréal.

Montreal's only peers as regards museums are Ottawa and Toronto. Aside from those already recommended on earlier pages of this chapter—such as Château de Ramezay in Vieux Montréal, Musée d'Art Contemporain in Cité du Havre, Maritime and Military Museum on Île Sainte-Hélène—there are others. Most important—indeed its only competitors in all of Canada are Ottawa's National Gallery and the Art Gallery of Ontario in Toronto—is the Musée des Beaux-Arts (Museum of Fine Arts). It had the genius —and indeed the courage—to close its doors for more than three years (April 1973 until mid-1976) in order to undertake a $10 million reorganization, refurbishing, and expansion, with one result a doubling of exhibition space. The museum occupies an early-twentieth-century neo-classic building and appended exposed-concrete five-level extension, housing—in 34 galleries—one of the continent's most diverse collections. (Many paintings were wisely loaned to museums throughout Canada during the refurbishing period; in the course of crossing the country to research this revised edition of this book, I came across Montreal loanshows in museums from Halifax to Vancouver. Every one was a pleasure, as is the museum itself.) Going back to 1860 (it is the country's oldest art museum), the Beaux-Arts has a permanent collection that includes old European masters—Italian, Flemish, German, Dutch, eighteenth-century English portraitists, and a superb French group including Boudin and Daumier, Cézanne and Corot, Courbet and Dérain, Monet and Renoir, Picasso and Pissarro. And there is more: first-rank Quebec and other Canadian art, including Indian and Eskimo; treasures from ancient Rome, China, and Egypt; and a relatively recent acquisition of more than 500 choice African and South Pacific works, collected by a priest-professor and a gift of his order, the Society of Jesus. This is the only major Canadian museum combining the fine and decorative arts—beginning with ancient glass and continuing through varied eras and cultures into our own. In addition, there are frequently changing exhibitions, a many-faceted community program including concerts and movies, and a restaurant that is a feature of the new wing.

After the Beaux-Arts, and along with the Musée des Arts Contemporain, the most important in town is McGill University's McCord Museum, occupying a handsomely refurbished building on the campus, designed by the same Fred Lebensold, architect of the new wing of the Beaux-Arts. Nucleus of the collection was a gift of collector David Ross McCord in the nineteen-twenties. It embraces Canadian history and ethnology. There are paintings— prints, photographs, and the decorative arts as well—furniture, silver, glass, china, carved wood, wrought iron. Exhibition space is limited so that each visit allows for no more than a sampling of the collection. But whatever one sees is an esthetic treat—thematically selected, handsomely mounted. Maison des Arts la Sauvegarde occupies a restored Vieux Montréal house at 160 Rue Notre Dame est. On view are frequently changed shows of the works of contemporary local artists; have a look. Not far away is Maison du Calvet, an early-eighteenth-century house owned by Ogilvy's department store and beautifully restored, in period style, and operating as a museum—and a charmer. Dominion Gallery (1438 Rue Sherbrooke ouest) is the largest commercial art gallery; invariably browseworthy. Sadye Bronfman Centre (5170 Rue Côte Sainte Catherine) presents mountworthy shows. And so does the Sir George Williams Gallery of Concordia University (1455 Boulevard de Maisonneuve—on the mezzanine). Away from the center of town, and eminently worth the drive, is Maison Saint-Gabriel at 2146 Rue Favard. It is a rambling fieldstone house built as a convent for the Sisters of Notre Dame in 1669—and still used as such. The nuns very kindly open their treasure-filled home for visitors seriously interested in old Quebec furniture and furnishings, not to mention architecture. There's a lot to see—a stone-walled basement, the community room-refectory, kitchen, and reception room on the main floor, and the second floor with nuns' dormitory, and —most interesting, this—a reproduction of a bedroom of a Fille du Roi. Les Filles du Roi—Daughters of the King—were eighteenth-century ladies who crossed from the old France to the new to find husbands, under a sensible plan whereby they were sheltered in convents, such as this one, during the courtship period. There's an antique-furnished chapel and an attic, all of whose beams and rafters are held in place by wooden pegs. Aside from the already-recommended churches (Cathedrale Marie-Reine-du-Monde, St. Joseph's Oratory, Notre Dame, Notre-Dame-de-Bonsecours), there are others worth noting. Christ Church Anglican Cathedral is a lovely, not overlarge neo-Gothic structure with a handsome ceiling and frequent noontime concerts in the heart of downtown, next to Eaton's on Rue Sainte-Catherine—symbolic perhaps of the historic mercantile dominance of the city's English-speaking minority. St. George's, also Gothic-style and Anglican, is a Dominion Square landmark, dating to 1870, with carved woodwork within from the mother country, and a pulpit dating to 1842. Little St. Stephen's, built in 1822, is the city's oldest Anglican church. St. Patrick's, as its name might imply, is at once Catholic and English-language; its style is severe early Gothic. Shaar Hashomayim Synagogue in the Westmount district is one of the major Jewish temples; another is Temple Emanuel, also in Westmount. Other churches of note include St. James United (Rue Sainte-Catherine ouest), St. Andrews and St. Paul, Presbyterian (Rue Sherbrooke at Redpath), St. John's Lutheran (Rue Jeanne-Mance), and St. George's Greek Orthodox Cathedral (Rue Sainte-Catherine).

Place des Arts—the first of the splendid performing arts centers now found in all major Canadian cities and one of the most esthetically rewarding—is where one sees the Montreal Symphony, Les Grands Ballets Canadiens—one of the country's three top dance companies—and L'Opéra du Québec—all with annual seasons. These three organizations perform in the Place des Arts' Salle Wilfred Pelletier. But the complex also includes the smaller Maisonneuve and Port Royal theatres. Legitimate theatre, mostly in French (Théâtre de la Poudrière and others) but in English too —especially at the Centaur, noted for its experimental work, and with a pair of halls in the Old Stock Exchange building—flourishes. Visiting attractions, musical and otherwise, often play the Forum, and the Paul Sauvé Arena. The Forum is home to Les Canadiens, Montreal's hockey team, and to other sports events, including lacrosse and wrestling. The Expos (baseball) play at Jarry Park, and the Alouettes (football) at the Autostade. There's racing at Blue Bonnets track. Night life is as lively as one is apt to encounter in Canada. Stores and boutiques are smart and stylish only in Toronto. And Man and His World is the every-summer successor to Expo 67—the great and still beloved Montreal World's Fair. It takes place on Île Sainte-Hélène, site of the original, utilizing some two dozen pavilions and a 135-acre amusement section, La Ronde. As if a mid-twentieth century global exposition was not accomplishment enough, Montreal played host to the world once again, at the 1976 Summer Olympics. Both of these monumental events, each skillfully planned and organized well in advance, were the handiwork of the city's long-time and indefatigable Mayor Jean Drapeau. The Olympics, which cost the City of Montreal and the Province of Quebec some $600 million to prepare for, attracted competitors from more than 130 nations, resulted in the sale of some four million tickets, with the various events transmitted from a hundred-odd radio and a score of television studios, in more than seventy languages, to sports fans on all five continents. The principal Games-site (in Olympic Park, ex-Maisonneuve Park, in the eastern part of town) was the Olympic Stadium, elegantly elliptical in design and embracing a 72,000-seat stadium proper, swimming center, and a structure called the Velodrome. This last was created for cycling and judo during the Olympics, and for conferences and conventions afterwards. The stadium proper remains a visitor attraction and a sports-venue. Olympics Village, a quartet of striking triangular-shaped structures built to house athletes, was also planned for post-Games use—as condominium apartments.

The Laurentians and Mont Tremblant Provincial Park: The four-season climate of the North Temperate zone has been no kinder to any resort area in North America than to the Laurentian Mountain region, some thirty-five miles north of Montreal. But, be it understood from the very beginning, they are by no means an eastern Rockies. Reputedly the oldest mountains on the continent —mellowed and leveled through many, many centuries—they constitute an area of relatively gentle if substantial hills, extending over a 110-mile area, in and about such charmingly French-named villages as *Sainte-Agathe des Monts* (site of an annual Laurentian winter carnival), *Sainte-Adèle, Saint-Jovite, Val-Morin, Val-David, Saint-Sauveur-des-Monts,* and *Mont Tremblant.* Go in the winter for skiing; go in the summer for swimming, sunning, yachting, and riding. Go in the early autumn to see the leaves turn, and in the spring to see that season evolve. A Laurentians treat is Village de Séraphin—a reconstructed mid-nineteenth-century village, typical of the region—in Sainte-Adèle. The range of accommodation is wide. And for roughing it, the provincial government offers the natural beauty of Mont Tremblant Park (ninety miles north of Montreal) for camping, fishing, and canoeing holidays.

The Eastern Townships (Cantons de l'Est) constitute the pleasantly rolling area of the province in its southeastern corner, bordering Vermont and New Hampshire. This is a land of farms and lakes, orchards and ski-runs, modern towns and still-quiet villages, asbestos mines and deer-inhabited hills. Originally settled by United Empire Loyalists—American colonists siding with the Crown during the Revolution—in the eighteenth century, and for long a traditionally English-speaking area, the Eastern Townships have in recent years become dominantly French speaking. *Sherbrooke* is the principal city of the Townships. Its Magog River location has provided it with hydroelectric power for industry, and its hills—within and without the city—are well equipped for skiing. On one, there is a 75-foot illuminated cross, on the order of that atop Mount Royal in Montreal. Amenities are modern, and you may want to take time to see the surprisingly high-calibre Art Museum at the relatively young (1954) Université de Sherbrooke (Picasso and Chagall are among the artists) and the stained glass windows of St. Michael's Basilica. *Granby* is the second town of the region. Its zoo is exceptional (and a lot of fun), there's an ancient Roman fountain in Pelletier Park, and a museum of antique cars. *North Hatley* is a year-round resort (skiing through swimming) on Lake Massawippi, and near such other resorts as Ayer's Cliff and Knowlton. *Magog* shares 33-mile-long Lake Memphremagog with the Vermont town of Newport; they're at opposite ends of the lake, which is excellent for fishing. The area around Magog is a winter sports center, as well.

The Outaouais is a quiet region of rivers, lakes, and forests, which serves the adjoining cities of Hull and Ottawa (in next-door Ontario) as a year-round holidayland. It takes its name from the Outaouais—or Ottawa—River separating the two cities. *Hull,* a pulp-and-paper town with a mainly French-speaking populace, attracts many Ottawa residents and visitors to its good restaurants. Its Ottawa River Museum—with exhibits depicting the importance of pulp-and-paper to the region—occupies a fine old house. Just outside of town is the Gatineau Park, a twenty-by-five-mile region of woods and lakes for skiing, fishing, and camping, developed by the Federal Government's National Capital Commission. Kingsmere, long-time home of Prime Minister Mackenzie King, is in the park and open to visitors.

Trois-Rivières lies on the north shore of the St. Lawrence, about midway between Montreal and Quebec City. The Trans-Canada

Highway, on the opposite side of the river, does not traverse it, but the traveler interested in a town loaded with seventeenth- and eighteenth-century buildings does well to have a look at this city— Canada's second oldest after Quebec. (Indeed, the route following the north side of the river, between Montreal and Quebec City— while less speedy than the Trans-Canada Highway—passes through delightful countryside, and is recommended to the motorist who would see the Old Quebec of the St. Lawrence Valley.) There are fine old houses (de Gannes, de Tonnacour), the Ursuline Convent (whose walls are late seventeenth century and enclose a fine museum), the former Recollet Monastery (eighteenth century), which is now St. James's Anglican Church, the mid-eighteenth-century Vallières de Saint Réal House opposite it, the Pierre Boucher Historical Museum in St. Joseph's Seminary, and the formidably titled, but still interesting Museum of Prehistoric Archaeology—most of whose exhibits are of the area. Near Trois-Rivières is *Cap de la Madeleine,* whose Shrine of the Holy Rosary—dating from the seventeenth century—attracts hundreds of thousands of visitors and pilgrims each year.

Quebec City: The brilliant—and brilliantly strategic—situation of this quite literally fantastic city is not something that the Europeans were the first to appreciate. When Jacques Cartier first saw Quebec more than four centuries ago, in 1535, it was the site of a thriving Indian village known as Stadacona. What Cartier found, the Indians called *Kebec*—"the place where the water narrows." For it is at Quebec that the 350-foot-high promontory known as Cape Diamond (*Cap Diamant*) juts forward, flanked by the St. Lawrence (*St. Laurent*) and its tiny tributary, the St. Charles, and facing the promontory of what is now the town of Lévis. Control of Quebec means—and long has meant—control of the traffic on the St. Lawrence, for here below Cape Diamond it is less than three-quarters of a mile wide, although it is several miles wide to the north, and even wider to the south. Word of Cartier's discovery prompted the luckless attempt by Roberval to establish a European settlement at Quebec in 1549, but the bitter cold of winter, the scurvy, and the not-always-hospitable Indians already resident made this difficult. Champlain first saw the great Cape Diamond in 1603 and was quick to realize the potential of a settlement there.

He went back in 1608 to found a trading post near what is now the Place d'Armes. It prospered to the point where the English felt it worth trying to take, in 1629; they kept it, though, for only three years, when it reverted to French hands.

In 1659 Quebec's first Roman Catholic Bishop, Laval, came on the scene. His arrival signified the beginning of a long history of Church participation in the affairs of the region and of difficulties between the Church and the fur-trading interests, who at first ran the area, and later, the government of New France. For in 1663 King Louis XIV took over control from the mercantile interests, and none too soon. After a few quiet decades it became apparent that the English colonies to the south had their eyes on this rich French area. In 1690 Sir William Phipps' forces tried to take Quebec; they failed, but the attempt led to the building of the city's great walls, portions of which still are to be seen. There was a second unsuccessful attempt to take the place in 1711. But New France's days were numbered. Half a century later General Wolfe, fighting General Montcalm on the Plains of Abraham, came out the victor (even though he—as well as Montcalm—died as a result of the tragic battle).

Quebec grew slowly during the nineteenth century, despite its location as a center of government, as headquarters of the Roman Catholic Church in Canada, as an important seat of education. (Here were established the first general hospital, first chronic-disease hospital, first boys' school, first girls' school, and first university-level institution in Canada.) But the nineteenth century saw Montreal leap to commercial and industrial eminence, to Quebec's detriment. Only after the twentieth century was well under way did the old city again pick up steam, thanks to shoe manufacturing, pulp and paper, and a variety of other industries.

Though it had known fairly substantial English-speaking populations in earlier years, Quebec today is almost entirely (92 per cent) French speaking—if one excludes the great quantities of tourists who visit it at every season of the year. The area population exceeds 400,000. This is a proud city, which takes seriously its great age and its rich past, and at the same time its singular importance as the seat of government of the unique Francophone state that is the largest and second most popular of Canada's provinces. Quebec has not the sense of humor of more cosmopolitan

Montreal. But one does not look for in Quebec what one seeks in the larger city; this is a town like no other in North America.

The city's great skyscraper—Château Frontenac—is a hotel out of a fairy tale, built in 1893, and one of the most remarkable of the world's hostelries. It is named for an early governor, with the Place d'Armes at its front door and the delightful Dufferin Terrace —with the river far below—at its rear. The Château Frontenac is as good a starting point as any for a tour of Vieux Québec, which includes both the Upper and Lower towns of this double-decker of a city. Starting with the top level, I suggest you acquaint yourself with places like these: the Champlain Monument, perhaps the most impressive and memorable piece of historic sculpture in a province that is loaded with such works; Kent House, built in the seventeenth century and so named because Queen Victoria's papa lived in it in the late eighteenth century when he was the Duke of Kent; the early-nineteenth-century Anglican Cathedral—one of the handsomest such edifices in a country full of handsome Anglican cathedrals; the chapel and museum of the remarkable seventeenth-century Ursuline Convent; much restored but very old (1650) Notre-Dame Basilica, seat of the Archbishop of Quebec—who heads Canada's oldest diocese—with an interior that is appropriately elaborate; the Musée du Fort, an unusual three-dimensional, diorama-style interpretation of the city's derring-do history; the Franciscan Convent (with nuns' needlework); the museums of both the Hôtel-Dieu and General hospitals; and Maillou House, with its collection of fine old Quebec furniture.

Place Royale, historic center of the Lower Town, is undergoing elaborate restoration—with some seventy houses included in the project. The square is dominated by Notre-Dame-des-Victoires Church—built in 1688, and lovely within. Museum-houses include Hôtel Chevalier—with local furniture going back four centuries and Place Royale relics—and Maison Fornel—orientation center for the square's restoration. Also interesting: the early buildings of Université Laval (most of which is now in newer quarters in a newer part of town).

The Plains of Abraham—from which is afforded a memorable view—is known as Battlefields Park. Within it is the requisite Musée du Québec, a provincial government repository with a distinguished collection of Quebec art, both contemporary and old, of splendid-quality early Quebec furniture and decorative objects, and of the

Provincial Archives. There are, as well, frequently changed exhibitions. The nearby Citadel is at once the official summer residence of Canada's Governor-General, and a long-functioning military post-cum-regimental museum; at 10 A.M., the Changing of the Guard takes place there daily in summer. The ceremony is in many ways as impressive as the similar one enacted on Parliament Hill, in Ottawa. Not far from this seasonal home of the Crown's No. 1 official for all Canada, is Bois de Coulange, official residence of Quebec's Lieutenant Governor, the Queen's representative to the province; it is on Boulevard Laurier.

The creamy façade of the Quebec Seminary complex, part of it going back to the late seventeenth century, houses an underappreciated museum—silver, ceramics, antique books, paintings. Quite literally, a treasure trove, this. To see as well: the seminary's chapel, with remains (1708) of Quebec's Bishop Laval: *"Premier Évêque de la Nouvelle France."*

Quebec's legislative building, officially termed its Parliament, ranks in style and interest with the architecturally lovely—if smaller—legislative buildings of Nova Scotia, New Brunswick, and Prince Edward Island, and their grander counterparts in British Columbia and Ontario. Indeed, the elaborate green chamber of its Assemblée Nationale is quite the most beautiful of any in Canada, and I suggest you have yourself a guided tour of this gem of a French Renaissance-style structure, completed in 1886. The initials "V.R." in the molding stand for Victoria Regina, who reigned at the time of construction; a crown and the royal coat of arms remain on view above the Speaker's chair. Separatist sentiment or no, Quebec respects tradition.

In between bouts of sight-seeing you'll want to allow time for aimless rambles—daytime strolls through the narrow streets of the Upper and Lower towns; evening promenades along Dufferin Terrace (in summer there are public entertainments of various sorts). There are interesting shops, pleasant restaurants, cafés, nightspots. Concerts, ballet, theatre, and opera are staged in the Grand Théâtre du Québec—a multimillion-dollar cultural complex completed in 1970: Salle Louis-Fréchette is the main hall (1,800 seats); there's an 800-seat theatre and a restaurant.

From January to the beginning of Lent, Quebec is one long, event-packed Winter Carnival. "Bonhomme Carnival," a giant papier-mâché snowman, reigns (with the aid of a human emcee). There's a boat race across the ice-covered St. Lawrence to the town of Lévis, curling bonspiels, a dog-sled derby, skating and skiing, parades with elaborate floats, masked balls, and participation by both locals and visitors, most of whom appear to be high school and college students in absolutely massive quantity. Hotels and restaurants are mob scenes, with service at its worst, and the charm of the city is almost 100 per cent absent. For most visitors, especially first-time adults, non-Carnival Quebec is to be preferred at any time of year, including winter, when there are skiing, skating, and tobogganing right in the heart of town and throughout the region.

Environs of Quebec City: The region in the vicinity of the capital is not to be overlooked. Consider an excursion to—or a stay at —*Lac Beauport* for golf and swimming in summer, for skiing (excellent facilities and special activities during the Quebec Winter Carnival period) in winter, for relaxation at any time. Earmark a day—or at least part of a day—for a drive to and through *Île d'Orléans*—an enchanting bit of Old Quebec which has made but grudging recognition of the twentieth century—wonderful old country churches and farms whose houses reflect the architecture of earlier eras. *The Shrine of Sainte-Anne-de-Beaupré* draws some two million visitors a year, many of them pilgrims come to be healed of illness. Sainte Anne has attracted the faithful since the middle of the seventeenth century. The present enormous basilica, under construction since 1922, is distinguished more by its great size than the aesthetics of its design. It, a much older chapel near it, and St. Joachim Church (a few miles east)—a fine early French-Canadian specimen of religious architecture—are the principal points of interest. All about the basilica are various commercial enterprises, which add no charm to a visit there. Easily seen en route are *Montmorency Falls,* higher (273 feet) but much smaller and less impressive than Niagara.

Murray Bay (La Malbaie), Tadoussac, and the Saguenay River: You will not, if you look at a map, find Murray Bay on it; there's no such town and there's no such bay. English-speaking Canadians have given this name to the area around the town of *La Malbaie*. It is on the north shore of the St. Lawrence, and was long noted as the site of a baronial-style resort hotel, the Manoir Richelieu. Not far north of Murray Bay is the town of *Tadoussac,* site of a somewhat less elaborate resort, Hôtel Tadoussac, and at the point where the Saguenay River connects with the St. Lawrence. The Saguenay flows through some of the most spectacular river scenery in the Western Hemisphere. It is flanked by great cliffs and enormous granite capes which extend as high as 1,800 feet. Cruise ships covering eastern Canadian waters often sail up the St. Lawrence into the Saguenay, stopping at the principal towns. It's a lovely way to take in the area, if the frequent summer fogs do not interfere.

The Gaspé Peninsula is Quebec at its most other-world. Geography has kept this protrusion into the Gulf of St. Lawrence as nearly a part of the past as any inhabited region of North America, north of Mexico. Because of the still-traditional village life engendered by its remoteness, and because of its natural beauty, the Gaspé has become a tourist classic in recent decades. It has a paved highway that skirts its shores for a distance of 550 miles, and with comfortable accommodations along the way. The traveler considering a Gaspé tour requires a bit of time. The minimum required to get around the peninsula, after having arrived at it, is two days—and that should be stretched to three or four, if at all possible. En route north to it by car, the motorist will pass through two towns of some importance just before reaching the peninsula. *Rivière du Loup,* a town of about fourteen thousand, is a busy transport terminus. Amenities are good, and the area is attractive to vacationers, with good swimming, golf, and tennis. *Rimouski,* a bit larger than Rivière du Loup, which is some sixty miles distant, is a largely industrial city (saw milling is the principal industry) with modern facilities for the visitor and a dramatically situated lighthouse. *Mont Joli* is the town at which the Gaspé Peninsula Highway actually begins, and to where both trains and planes fly from Montreal and Quebec. From here one either drives about the peninsula or traverses it by means of a tour bus. Gaspé—particularly its northern and northeastern shores—is beautiful, with rocky cliffs extending right into the sea. In many of the villages and farms life is lived much as it has been for many generations. There are roadside shrines and high-steepled churches in the settled areas, beret-topped youngsters helping their parents in the fields, fishermen mending their nets on the beaches. *Matane* is the largest town; it, like Mont Joli, has both train and air connections with Montreal and Quebec. Smaller *Cap Chat* affords lovely bay views. From Rivière à Claude, one can take off—by jeep or shoe leather—for an ascent of the peninsula's highest peak, Mont Jacques Cartier (4,160 feet). There are other villages—*Gros Morne,* with its towering cliffs, ancient *Rivière la Madeleine, Rivière au Renard,* its harbor filled with fishing craft. *Gaspé Town,* site of the only deep-water harbor on the peninsula, is where Cartier first went ashore in Canada, in 1534, and the site of the Catholic Cathédrale du Christ-Roi (1969) that has to be the handsomest and most striking contemporary wood-frame church extant; and *Percé,* the peninsula's most noted destination. Here is the reputed Percé Rock—a great obelisk rising from the water. The Centre d'Art de Percé in a restored 1780 Norman-style structure is at once art-gallery-craft-shop-theatre, snack-bar, and after-dark-café-cum-entertainment. Percé offers the widest choice of accommodation on the peninsula, deep-sea fishing, excursions to a number of scenic points, and trips by boat to Île Bonaventure—just a few miles offshore, and the site of a remarkable, provincially operated sanctuary for countless thousands of birds, many species of which I guarantee you've never seen before. Just north and east of Gaspé Town is Forillon National Park—a historic first for Quebec, which was for long the only province without a national park (it preferred running its own provincial parks) until this one was created in 1970. The territory is the beautiful Forillon Peninsula, on the Gulf of St. Lawrence. There's an interpretive program, as well as nature walks, swimming and deep-sea fishing.

Sept-Îles is the entry-town for the far north. It has grown from a minuscule fishing settlement into a substantial community. Located near the entrance to the St. Lawrence—north of the northern shore of the Gaspé Peninsula—Sept-Îles' success story is attributable to the role it plays as a port for iron ore, brought to its harbor by means of the railway leading north—more than 360 miles—to the mines at Schefferville, Labrador. HUNTERS AND ANGLERS NOTE: package tours to the tundra of the far northern regions of the area now known as New Quebec, take off from Sept-Îles. Especially popular with the dedicated sportsman are the September fly-in safaris for caribou, to the Ungava Bay region, north of the 50th Parallel.

Provincial parks in Quebec, aside from those already mentioned: *La Vérendrye,* the largest in the province, is of especial interest to fishermen—speckled trout, northern pike, walleye, gray trout. Big and beautiful, it is also a bit out of the way, in the western part of the province. *Laurentides Park* embraces some 3,600 square miles in the Laurentians; it, too, is mainly an angler's domain.

SHOPPING

Montreal ranks with Toronto as a great Canadian shopping center, indeed as one of the finest in North America. The downtown section, essentially grid-patterned, is relatively compact and agreeable to walk about. Rue Sainte-Catherine is the principal business thoroughfare with the major department stores as its landmark. Two blocks north, parallel with Sainte-Catherine, is Rue Sherbrooke, easily distinguished because of the McGill University campus facing onto it. This is one of the city's smarter shopping streets along with Rue Crescent, running perpendicular to it, with the Musée des Beaux-Arts, on Sherbrooke at Crescent, an easy-to-remember Rue Crescent locator. Now then, going south from Rue Sainte-Catherine, the next principal east-west thoroughfare is Boulevard Dorchester, onto which face Place du Canada-Dominion Square, and such landmarks as the domed Cathédrale Marie-Reine-du-Monde, Le Reine Élizabeth-Queen Elizabeth Hotel, and adjacent Gare Centrale, with the tower of the Hôtels Château Champlain and Bonaventure to the south. Beneath this area one finds the vast Place Ville-Marie and Place Bonaventure shopping complexes—the core of Montreal's earlier-described underground city.

Now, given one's bearings ever so concisely, here are some shopping specifics. Start with handicrafts. To the great credit of the Quebec provincial government, the region's handicraft tradition is officially encouraged. Provincial officials estimate that there are some 12,000 artisans working at traditional crafts, so that one can count on finding the charming carved wood *habitant* figures, hand-woven textiles and tapestries, handsome pottery, enamel work, and jewelry, as Indian and Eskimo crafts. The provincially operated *Centrale d'Artisanat du Québec* (Quebec Handicraft

Centre) is a first-rate source; it is at 1450 Rue Saint-Denis. Also good, with very high-quality, high-priced articles, is *Guilde Canadienne des Métiers d'Art Québec* and the adjoining *Galerie d'Art Esquimau* (2025 Rue Peel); look for hooked and braided rugs, traditional wrought-iron work and country-style pine furniture among the specialties here. Other handicrafts shops include *Le Viaduc* and *Madame de Bellefeuille,* both in the Place Bonaventure shopping centre with the latter also located in Place Ville-Marie; *Labyrinth* at 46 Rue Sainte-Catherine ouest, *Le Rouite,* 3411 Rue Saint-Denis, and the *Château de Ramezay Museum, Vieux Montréal.* ART GALLERIES are many. Earlier described, eminently browsable *Dominion Gallery* (1438 Rue Sherbrooke ouest) is the biggest and among the best, but there are others of note. *Galerie Moos* (1430 Rue Sherbrooke ouest) is among these. *Robert Slatkoff* (1455 Rue Crescent) specializes in limited series editions of Canadian prints. *Marlborough Godard* (1490 Rue Sherbrooke ouest) sells works of internationally known artists. *Waddington Galleries* (1456 Rue Sherbrooke ouest) is another leader. And *Eaton's* department store's Foyer des Arts (9th floor) features Canadian works. *Jacoby's* (480 Rue Saint-François-Xavier) is an art-antiques auction house, and advertises its sales regularly in the press. DEPARTMENT STORES are a major Montreal asset. The Rue Sainte-Catherine quartet are all worth knowing. *Eaton's,* at Rue Université, is the biggest of the lot, a nine-story giant covering an entire city block. There is a Canadiana souvenir department on main, along with a bakery that's convenient for shopper-sustenance, and a good book department. There are a variety of restaurants (of which more later) with the fanciest on nine, others on five and the basement. Housewares is on four, and the Adam men's boutique—one of Canada's smartest—is worth a visit; on two. *Hudson's Bay Company*—simply *La Baie* or *The Bay* to Montrealers—fronts Place Phillips. Its first-rate Canadiana shop is on main, and its also-excellent china and housewares are on four. There are restaurants, about which more later, on six (the best), seven (a cafeteria), five, and the basement, with its *casse-croûte,* or snack bar. That same lower floor is the site of a rather super *super-marché. Simpson's,* at Rue Metcalfe, has a Canadiana shop on main, along with tempting food, bakery, and candy departments for hungry shoppers. Housewares, including what is reputed to be the biggest English china selection in town, is on five. There are places to eat, as well, including the convenient Petit Café, a counter place, in the basement. *Ogilvy's,* at Rue Montagne, is a lovely old-fashioned place, all crystal chandeliers and marble columns—at least on main. It goes back to 1866, remains essentially conservative in its merchandising. Check souvenirs on main, housewares on four, and note that there are a post office and *casse-croûte* in the basement, not to mention the first-rate Tartan Room Restaurant on four. Ogilvy's imports clothing and accessories, both men's and women's from both England and France, to keep both Francophone and Anglophone locals happy, not to mention us visitors. *Dupuis Frères* is probably the least-frequented of the department stores, at least by visitors. It's a venerable French-Canadian firm, now in contemporary quarters at the Place Dupuis complex, on Rue Sainte-Catherine est—away from the center of downtown. China, gifts, and souvenirs are on the mezzanine along with books—mostly French language—and a worth-knowing-about pharmacy. Dupuis Frères' restaurant when it was in its old quarters, was the only alcohol-licensed department store eatery in town. That is no longer the case, but the restaurant —on main in the current quarters—remains very good. That same floor has *casse-croûte,* candy, and bakery departments. Several other heart-of-town Rue Sainte-Catherine stores are of visitor interest. *W. H. Smith & Son,* the British booksellers, have a big shop, with an excellent Canadiana department, on Sainte-Catherine at Metcalfe. *Birks,* the jewelry firm one encounters all across Canada, has its main store—and it's a big one—on Sainte-Catherine at Rue Union. *A. Dionne & Sons* (Sainte-Catherine at Drummond) is a long-time and distinguished fancy-grocery, dear to the hearts of Montreal gourmets; have a look around and you'll see why. *Régie des Alcools,* the provincial liquor-store operation, has among its many outlets convenient ones in Place Ville-Marie and Place Bonaventure, as well as a *Maison des Vins*—with wines the specialty—at 600 Avenue du Président Kennedy (corner of Rue Union). *Holt, Renfrew,* as smart and high-styled a specialty-shop chain—both women's and men's clothing and accessories; gifts, too—as to be found in Canada, has a lovely store on Rue Sherbrooke at Mountain, and a Place Ville-Marie shop, too. Take the Métro out to Place Alexis Nihon to note its bold, futuristic architecture and shops—none especially distinguished—then walk over to the adjacent Place Westmount whose architect was the same Mies van der Rohe of New York's Seagram Building fame (and a lot else, as well). Place Westmount's shops are noteworthy, too, and include Pierre Cardin, Lanvin, Hermès, Yves St. Laurent-Rive Gauche (men's and women's) and Bally shoes—among the well-known European names—and such posh local stores as *Lily Simon* (with Courrèges imports and men's wear), *Lucas* (jewelry), and *Henry Marks* (men's wear); restaurants and cafés, too. Back downtown, now, and a few specifics on earlier-recommended *Rue Crescent—Carol* (men's and women's custom shirts) at 2077, *Synonyme,* with Cacharel women's clothes (2070); *Neville & Burge*—antiques (2130); *Artisanat Hongrois*—Hungarian needlework gifts (2140); Félix Simon—men's wear (2170); and the *Old Vic Pine Shop*—antique Quebec furniture (2190).

Quebec City: The headquarters in the capital of the earlier-recommended *Centrale d'Artisanat du Québec* is at 2700 Boulevard Laurier in the Place Laurier shopping complex; recommended as your first stop for a wide variety of quality crafts, from jewelry to weaving, with especially good carved-wood articles. In Place Royale, in the Lower Town, *La Rédoute* is to be recommended—handsome hand-knit shawls, pottery, jewelry, silver, woodwork. In this same area is *Boutique Sous-le-Fort* (55 Rue Sous-le-Fort), and it's good for enamel work and contemporary-design jewelry. The Lower Town's Rue Saint-Paul is dotted with antiques shops. Ceramics are a specialty at *L'Atelier de Céramique Julien* (17 Rue des Jardins); interesting tapestries here, too. *L'Atelier* (44 Côte de la Montagne) specializes in Eskimo soapstone carvings and prints, Indian and Quebec crafts. *Librairie Carneau* (47 Rue Buade and 34 Rue Sainte-Anne) vends books in both the French and English languages, with Canadiana a special subject. *Holt, Renfrew,* the estimable men's and women's specialty store chain, is in Quebec at the Place Hôtel-de-Ville (Rue Buade), and the Place Sainte-Foy shopping center, with a smaller branch in the Château Frontenac. *Place Québec* is a super-modern shopping complex beneath the Québec Hilton, and its shops include *Bulle*—for handicrafts. Place Sainte-Foy is considerably away from the center of town, but is a shopping center of enormous size and variety, and includes as well the earlier-mentioned *Holt, Renfrew* and an excellent branch of *Eaton's* department store. The **Gaspé Peninsula,** so long isolated from the rest of the province, has retained its handicraft traditions, and offers the visitor a wide selection—unusual jewelry, wooden toys, quilts and woven work, lovely hand-carved sea gulls and other birds perched on bits of driftwood. A provincial body, Dévelopement des Métiers d'Art dans l'Est du Québec, promotes craft production in the Gaspé and the lower St. Lawrence region, and operates a number of retail shops in this area. In **Gaspé Town** the outlet is *Compagnie des Artisans de Gaspé,* and in **Percé,** the shop is called simply *"e"*—the symbol of the regional craft organization. Other sources of local handicrafts and souvenirs in Percé are the boutique of *le Centre d'Art de Percé,* and *Au Bon Secours.* Other sources in Gaspé Town are *Magasins Continental* and *Ardenlee Gift Shop.*

CREATURE COMFORTS

No North American city has a finer hotel plant than Montreal. Quebec City, for so long a one-luxury-hotel town, now has a quartet of top-category hotels; no similar medium-size Canadian city is any better equipped. If the Laurentians have not appreciably improved in recent years, they hold their own, and so do most other areas of visitor-interest in the province. As for the inner man, well, Montreal remains a world leader. And one eats well throughout the province, for the French heritage extends, happily, to gastronomic as well as to other manifestations of *la culture Québecois.* Despite the dominance of the French language, staffs of hotels and motels of any substance, provincewide, are bilingual, or at least the members of those staffs coming into contact with guests. So there need be no linguistic anxiety on the part of the out-of-province visitor. My selection of hotels follows.

Montreal: *Le Reine Élizabeth-The Queen Elizabeth* (900 Dorchester Boulevard ouest) continues year in year out—so far as I am concerned—as the most remarkably well run hotel of its size with which I am all that familiar. When one considers that it has more than 1,100 rooms and suites, the skill with which it is managed is remarkable. Service, by and large, is first rate and kindly, from reception desk through coffee-shop cashier. There are a range of restaurants, of which more later, one of the city's top boîtes, and direct connection to Canadian National's Gare Centrale, Place Ville-Marie (where the hotel operates a number of restaurants) and from it to the other areas of the vast, earlier-described underground city. A Canadian National hotel, operated by Hilton Canada. *Le Château Champlain* (Place du Canada) remains as beautiful and as beautifully run as when I covered its official opening in the mid-sixties. Its façade—a slim tower with crescent-shaped windows that have become its trademark—is among the more distinctive in town. Its standard twins (the bulk of the 612 rooms and suites) are spacious and quietly luxurious. Its 35th-floor suites are exceptional, and not only the David Williams-decorated Royal Suite, one of whose more recent inhabitants was indeed a royal—Queen Mother Elizabeth. The restaurants are the best—and by that I mean best-tasting—of any in the CP Hotels chain. But that is not surprising, this being the most meticulously operated of that estimable organization's hotels. The *Ritz-Carlton* (1228 Rue Sherbrooke ouest) was a leader even before it spent several million dollars in the early seventies to refurbish one of the most beautiful of North America's hotels. It remains elegant and traditional style as before, but with even more panache. Bedrooms and suites are capacious and flawlessly equipped. The public spaces—there are a quartet of restaurants—are the subject of more space later on. Most important is the low room count. With just under 250 rooms and suites, the Ritz can give personal service. And does. The *Constellation Hotel* (3407 Rue Peel at Sherbrooke) is very contemporary and, like the Ritz, small enough (162 rooms) to be able to give personal attention to guests. There's a congenial bar, good restaurant, and the Club 21, an amusing rooftop boîte. The *Hotel Bonaventure* occupies the upper floors of the Place Bonaventure complex, which means that to reach its lobby one must wait for one of the passenger elevators from the street level. At times this can take quite a while, but once gained the hotel proper is attractive and well operated, with a big lobby, off of which is a landscaped outdoor swimming pool that is heated in winter, and rarely without customers at any season. The bedrooms (there are 612) are well designed and comfortable, and there are a variety of places to eat, drink, and be entertained, one of which is later discussed; Western International. The *Sheraton-Mt. Royal* (1455 Rue Peel) has an enviable heart-of-everything location. It's an elderly, traditional-style house with more than a thousand rooms, some much nicer than others. The lobby is high-ceilinged and humming, and there are a variety of wine-dine spots. *Le Quatre Saisons* (rues Sherbrooke and Peel) is the Montreal outlet of the Four Seasons Inn on the Park chain, whose properties run from London's Inn on the Park to Calgary's Four Seasons. This is an eminently luxurious, full-facility house with 320 handsome rooms and suites with motifs embracing soft leather, raw silk, and marble; a posh restaurant, lobby, cocktail lounge, evening entertainment, as well as indoor pool and sauna. *Hotel Meridien Montréal* is the first North American outpost of the Air France-related Meridien chain, whose Paris hotel I know and like. This one has 616 rooms and suites, and a delightful assortment of places to dine, drink, and dance. *Loews La Cité Hôtel* (*Cité Concordia*) is an architecturally striking 500-room house adjacent to Mount Royal Park. It's Loews' second Canadian hotel, after Le Concorde in Quebec City, and is a part of the Cité Concordia office building-shopping-arcade-apartment-house complex. Bedrooms feature pairs of double or king-size beds. There are a pair of handsome restaurants, a bar-lounge, and a health club that includes pool, saunas, whirlpools, squash, and handball courts. And all those Cité Concordia shops in connection. *La Régence Hyatt* (doesn't Hyatt Regency sound nice in French?) is a sleek 800-room house on Place Victoria, the third such in the Big Three Canadian cities, with sister-Regency Hyatts in Vancouver and Toronto. This one has a trio of restaurants and as many bar-lounges, as well as a roof-top boîte, with a health club among its other amenities. *Holiday Inns* require a directory of their own in Montreal. The old established *Holiday Inn Centre-Ville* (420 Rue Sherbrooke ouest) is full-facility, with a range of restaurants and lounges, pool, and sauna. *Holiday Inn Place Dupuis* is newer, smart looking, and with a handsome restaurant and equally inviting bar-lounge. Then there is *Holiday Inn Dominion Square,* 38 stories and 868 rooms, and the flagship of the global chain of more than 1,500 hotels, with a full range of amenities. There are a pair of *Ramada Inns: Ramada Inn Centre Ville* is an agreeable, 205-room, well-equipped house at 1005 Rue Guy, while *Ramada Inn East* (5500

Rue Sherbrooke est) is larger (249 rooms) but with slightly lower tabs. *Quality Hotel Montreal* (410 Rue Sherbrooke ouest) has 183 modern rooms, restaurant, bar. *Hôtel Berkeley* (1188 Rue Sherbrooke ouest) has the distinction of being next door to the Ritz-Carlton, but is modest, a nice house in its own right, with an enclosed sidewalk café that's fun for breakfast, an Austrian restaurant within, and bar-lounge. *Hôtel Château Versailles* (1659 Rue Sherbrooke ouest) is hardly in the image of the castle whose name it bears, but can be nice for budget travelers, if you can have one of its rooms with bath (the majority of the total 79 are so equipped). There is no full-service restaurant, just a breakfast room. *The Montréal Aéroport Hilton* (Dorval Airport) embraces its original circular building with more than 300 rooms, as well as an addition with 174 rooms that was part of a $6 million refurbishing program completed in 1975. There's a big pool-centered garden that summer guests enjoy, and public rooms—Au Coin de Feu Restaurant, La Discauto discothèque, cocktail lounge, coffee shop—that guests enjoy year-round. This hotel, more than any other airport inn I know, in any country, has charm and ambience. Bravo, Hilton Canada. *Château Mirabel* (Mirabel Airport) is a 350-room hotel with a full range of facilities, in the new-as-tomorrow Mirabel Airport complex. A CP Hotel. **The Laurentians** run a wide gamut and, like any popular resort area close to a major population center, can disappoint if one is not careful with hotel selection. *Mont Tremblant Lodge* is a 6,000-acre complex housing guests in several pavilions, including the main building as well as cottages. Public areas are understated as regards décor, but eminently comfortable. Facilities for every season are remarkable —summer swimming through winter skiing. Mont Tremblant sets a delicious table, and there are congenial quarters for leisurely drinks. All in all: top-rank. *Gray Rocks Inn* is another long-time Lac Tremblant leader—a lovely, traditional-style country resort, in a pretty setting, with full facilities for both summer and winter-sports vacationers, and an activity-packed schedule for guests who like to keep busy. *Le Château,* near the main Gray Rocks cluster, is a kind of inn-within-the-inn complex, with its own restaurant and pool. *La Sapinière* **(Val David)** is understated, in the manner of larger Mont Tremblant, but very smart indeed, with comfortable accommodations, activities, and amenities for both winter and summer diversion, and—this is worth knowing—a restaurant that is probably the most reputed in the region, and with good reason. *Alpine Inn* **(Sainte-Marguerite Station)** is a charmer, a bit of the Tyrol transplanted to the Laurentians, but not cornily. There's an inviting multistory lobby with handsome restaurant and bar-lounge on the upper level. Rooms (there are 88, some in chalets) are wood-paneled, plaid-accented, and welcoming. There are indoor and outdoor pools, golf and tennis, curling and skating rinks, and a kitchen that is one of the most prestigious in the Laurentians. *Mont Gabriel Lodge* **(Sainte-Adèle)** is large and rambling, with accommodations in the main house and a pair of extended wings, as well as in cottages. Facilities are wide ranging and adequate if without style, charm, or any special kind of ambience. **Eastern Townships (Cantons de l'Est)—Sherbrooke:** *Le Baron Motor Hotel* (Highway 1) is a low-slung modern complex with 126 rooms and suites, attractive public areas, that include lobby and inner-court-garden-cum-swimming pool. Le Chavelier Restaurant is a winner, and there's a cocktail lounge with entertainment. CP Hotels. *Wellington Hotel* (68 Wellington Street, downtown) has more than 80 rooms, restaurant and cocktail lounge, with entertainment. **Granby:** *Le Castel Motel-Hotel* (Highway 1) has 138 rooms (some with kitchens), swimming pool, restaurant, cocktail lounge. **North Hatley:** *Hovey Manor's* main building is an atmospheric turn-of-century house. The location is lakefront, with swimming, tennis and other summer diversions; ski packages in winter. Accommodation is in the main house and a group of cottages, and there are both restaurant and cocktail lounge. *Hatley Inn* occupies an elderly house, too; smaller than the Manor, but nice. **Magog:** *Hotel Cheribourg* has two dozen modern rooms with bath, and a good restaurant and bar. *Cabana Lodge* is long on the scene; it's lakefront, with 30-plus rooms, good restaurant, cocktail lounge. **Saint-Marc-sur-Richelieu:** *Auberge Handfield*—a charmer of a country house in a lovely garden; rooms are Old Quebec style, and the fine restaurant is, too; *L'Escale,* a summer showboat-theatre in the Richelieu River, is a near-neighbor. **Hull:** *Sheraton Le Marquis Hotel* is a 10-story, 133-room Sheraton franchise, with a good restaurant, coffee shop, popular bar-lounge with nightly entertainment, and comfortable rooms, some with rather super views of the Ottawa skyline, across the river. **Montebello:**

Château Montebello was for long a private club for rich—very rich men—which the rest of us heard about but couldn't visit, except as personal guests of members. For some seasons now, the Château has been operated as a year-round resort by CP Hotels. The bucolic setting is beautiful and so is the plant, most especially the lobby-lounge—log-beamed and 4 stories high, with a central flagstone fireplace extending to the ceiling—that in itself makes a visit worthwhile. There's a great high-ceilinged dining room, congenial drinking parlors, and the rooms are nice, too, and there's golf, tennis, fishing, and riding—during the warm-weather months; curling, cross-country skiing, and other winter-sports. The country house of Quebec patriot Louis-Joseph Papineau, on the grounds, is used for private parties, but otherwise open to inspection. Montebello lies between Montreal and Ottawa from where it draws most of its clientele. It deserves to be better known beyond those cities. **Trois-Rivières:** *Le Baron Motor Hotel* (Route 2), has more than a hundred modern rooms, in an extended U-shaped structure with the Salle Laviolette Restaurant, coffee shop, and cocktail lounge (with entertainment), off the lobby of the main-entrance building. There's a nice outdoor pool. *Auberge des Gouverneurs* (975 Rue Hart, downtown) is an attractive link of the Quebec Gouverneurs chain. There are nearly 130 rooms, restaurant, coffee shop, cocktail lounge. *Motel Montclair* (Highway 2) has 50-odd modern rooms, restaurant, cocktail lounge. **Quebec City:** Talk about transition! As regards its hotel plant, Quebec City's is the most dramatic in Canada over the last decade. For something like three quarters of a century, this had been a one-hotel—one top-rank hotel—town, with all of the advantages and disadvantages thereunto pertaining. The sole advantage lay in the fact that the one hotel was one of the continent's great ones and that if you wanted No. 1, you had no agonizing decisions to make. The disadvantages were that the hotel—as who could blame its management, with no major competition?—coasted on its laurels and its architecture and allowed plant, service, and cuisine all to deteriorate. The hotel is *Château-Frontenac*. It's a towering mock-French castle—and marvelous mock-French at that—with a strategic location on Dufferin Terrace high above the Lower Town and the St. Lawrence. Since it opened in 1893 it has been a magnet for visitors—celebrated and otherwise—and its registers reveal names like

Roosevelt and Churchill (during the World War II Quebec Conference), Elizabeth II and Philip (during the period when the sovereign could enter the province without excess concern over security). In recent years, when the competition started building, good
old CP Hotels saw the handwriting on the wall and plunked down
something like $10 million to restore and refurbish the Great Old
Lady. All of the approximately 600 rooms and suites were remod-
eled and brightened up. Public areas were carefully—and faithfully
—restored, rather than obliterated, with attention to the old original materials—wood paneling, tapestries, chandeliers, fireplaces,
marble, brick, and stone. The most striking aspect of the project is
Le Village—a terrace-level complex that is a replica of an early
Quebec settlement and embraces a restaurant with open-hearth
cooking, a boîte-cum-entertainment, and a terrace-café-cum-view.
There are, as well, a new main dining room-lounge, tea room, and
an expanded shopping mall. Bravo, CP Hotels! Now for the competition, whose appearance on the scene has changed Quebec from
a provincial backwater into a cosmopolitan center. *The Québec
Hilton* is a star-component of the ultra-mod Place Québec
complex—offices, movies, restaurants, three-tiered shopping area
and thousand-car garage and convention center—just next door to
Parliament. There's a mod-look lobby, 600 spiffy rooms and suites,
an elevated swimming pool and sun deck, a coffee shop—Café de
la Place—that draws lots of locals (always a good sign) the smart
Rotisserie Villeray, and the roof-top Toit de Québec, for casual
buffet lunch and dinner-dancing, whose views of town and river
are unsurpassed. Via remote control, the Hilton operates a dis-
cothèque, Le Boulet, occupying a seventeenth-century house in
the Place Royale. *Loews Le Concorde* (Place Montcalm) is the
capital's most striking contemporary structure. Québecois architect Dimitri Dimakopoulos' 450-room 30-story beauty is a startler
even as one regards its irregular façade—with one side a dramatic
45-degree angle—leading upward to the dome-topped Astral Restaurant. Interiors—lobby, spacious bedrooms and suites, engag-
ingly titled restaurants (Le Boueuf Charolais, L'Oenothèque, Aux
Fine Herbes—this last the coffee shop), bars, cabaret, pool—are
among the most imaginative of any contemporary-design hotel in
Canada. And I know quite a few. Loews' first Canadian hotel—it
preceded the Montreal house—is at once elegant and amusing and

convenient. *Auberge des Gouverneurs* (Boulevard Saint-Cyrille)—
a link of a province-wide chain of similarly titled hotels—occupies
9 floors of a 25-story building. There are 400 well-equipped rooms
and suites, a main restaurant—Le Talemeller—coffee shop, cocktail
lounges, swimming pool. Location is super. Like the Québec Hilton, the Auberge is linked to Place Québec, with shops, convention center, and garage. *Holiday Inn* (395 Rue de la Couronne) is
a full-facility of this round-the-world chain, facing Place Jacques-
Cartier, with 243 rooms and suites, nice places to eat, drink, and
relax. *Hôtel Clarendon* (57 Rue Sainte-Anne) is a long-time
heart-of-town favorite, with a nice traditional—if not grand-luxe—
ambience. There are a hundred-plus rooms, many of them most
agreeable, an atmospheric dark-beamed restaurant that's one of
the best in town, and a comfortable cocktail lounge often populated by locals. *Motel-Hôtel Le Voyageur* (2250 Boulevard
Sainte-Anne) is actually more of the former than the latter; a horizontal, 2-story complex centered around a pool, with spacious
rooms, restaurant, cocktail lounge with entertainment, and a location not far from downtown. *Hôtel Château de Pierre* (17 Avenue
Sainte-Geneviève) is small—just over a dozen rooms—but central
—in the shadow of the Château-Frontenac—and in a nice old
house. All rooms have bath, and the management includes continental breakfast, there being no restaurant or bar. *Hôtel Château
Fleur de Lys* (15 Avenue Sainte-Geneviève) is still another centrally situated small place—15 rooms and suites with bath, some
with kitchen, in an elderly house; no restaurant or bar. *Hôtel
Château Laurier* (695 Est Grande-Allée), though no relation to
the establishment of that name in Ottawa, is a smallish (54 room)
house; all units have bath, and the restaurant—rather bravely retaining its long-time title—Georges V—in this most anti-monarchial
of the provincial capitals—is one of the best in town. Away from
the center, places worth knowing about include: *Quality Inn*
(Boulevard Laurier in Sainte-Foy)—200 rooms, restaurant, coffee
shop, bar-lounge, pool. *Auberage Nouvelle-Orleans* (Boulevard
Laurier 1300, Sainte-Foy) is a Ramada Inn with 100 modern
rooms, pool, cocktail lounge with entertainment, and Le Vivier—a
locally reputed seafood restaurant; *Holiday Inn Sainte-Foy* (Rond
Point, Sainte-Foy) reliable, full-facility, 350 rooms; *Auberge des
Gouverneurs* (Boulevard Laurier 3030, Sainte-Foy)—236 attrac-

tive rooms, pool, restaurant, cocktail lounge. **Lac Beauport** (north of Quebec City): *Hotel Manoir Saint-Castin* is an excellently appointed, extensively equipped, lakeside resort hotel open the year round and with facilities ranging from skiing to swimming, including an 18-hole golf course, and—not to be taken lightly—one of the better restaurants in the province. A lovely spot. **La Malbaie** (Murray Bay): Unless and/or until baronial 350-room *Manoir Richelieu*—for many years one of the continent's premier resorts—reopens, the recommendation here is for infinitely smaller, simpler *Motel Chez Pierre,* with half a hundred comfortable rooms, restaurant, and cocktail lounge with entertainment. **Tadoussac's** *Hôtel Tadoussac* is an elongated, 142-room white-frame house, an old-school charmer of a complete summer resort, with a wooded setting at the confluence of the St. Lawrence and Saguenay rivers, facilities for golf, fishing, tennis, and pool-swimming, congenial after-dark activity. On the grounds are a pair of antique structures —a mini-stockade put up in 1600, and a charmer of a mid-eighteenth-century white-frame chapel. And, oh, that Saguenay scenery! **Arvida:** *Hôtel Manoir du Saguenay* is a traditional-style, 86-room resort hotel in a bucolic setting, with fishing, golf and other diversions, restaurant, and cocktail lounge. **Rivière-du-Loup's** long-time favorite *St. Louis Motor Inn* remains inviting—85 nice rooms and one of the best restaurants in the region. **Rimouski:** *Auberge des Gouverneurs* (Highway 132) is a winner—nearly a hundred pleasant rooms, pool, very good restaurant, and cocktail lounge with entertainment; a link of the chain of the same name. *Hôtel Saint-Louis* (214 Rue Saint-Edmond) is at once central and comfortable with 100 rooms with bath, and a restaurant so good that it draws the locals as well as in-the-know visitors. **Matane:** *Hôtel-Motel Belle Plage* remains a pleasure, on the St. Lawrence River, with 45 main house and motel rooms, beach, and, best news, exceptional river-view restaurant whose seafood is among the best in the Gaspé. **Gaspé Town:** *Baker Hôtel-Motel* is on an in-town eminence that allows its visitors splendid views of town and water. There is a rambling frame house and a newer motel addition, with rooms in both; harbor-view restaurant, cocktail lounge. **Percé:** *La Normandie Hôtel* is a lovely ocean-front establishment, with a welcoming and capacious lobby, a first-rate restaurant with good views as well as good food (bouillabaisse is a specialty), cozy cocktail lounge, and 53 comfortable rooms. *Au Pic de l'Aurore* is brilliantly situated, named for the cliff on which it is perched (which translates as Peak of Dawn). This is a cluster of a couple of dozen fireplace-equipped log cabins, and as many motel rooms. There's a restaurant and cocktail lounge, too; views are the most sublime in the neighborhood. *L'Auberge du Gargantua* is another hilltop establishment. The dozen-plus motel-type rooms are routine and minimally comfortable, but the restaurant has achieved a considerable local reputation, well deserved for its local seafood as well as classic French dishes, but disproportionately costly. **Sept-Îles:** *Auberge des Gouverneurs* (666 Avenue Laure) is an outpost of the provincewide chain of this name—and a good one, with 124 nicely outfitted rooms, pool, restaurant, cocktail lounge with entertainment, and central situation. *Hôtel-Motel Sept-Îles* (451 Rue Arnaud) is at once central, and with a fine view of the Gulf of St. Lawrence with the newer 75 of its 175 rooms the ones to aim for. Very good restaurant and cocktail lounge.

Dining in Montreal: This is one of the great restaurant cities but because most short-term visitors have other things to do than eat I have forced myself to recommend in this book only a limited selection of interesting places in a variety of categories for all budgets. FRENCH-CANADIAN: *Restaurant au Quinquet* (354 Boulevard Saint-Joseph) is for traditional regional dishes like cod's tongues, pea soup, other hearty specialties. *Auberge Le Vieux Saint-Gabriel* (426 Rue Saint-Gabriel) is a showplace of Vieux Montréal— a splendidly restored multistory house that goes back to the seventeenth century. Main dining rooms and bar are on the ground floor, with private rooms—popular for groups—above. If the food is not distinguished, the ambience more than compensates. *Les Filles du Roy* (415 Rue Saint-Paul est) is another perfectly beautiful restored Vieux Montréal house, with both traditional Québecois and French dishes, charmingly costumed waitresses, eye-filling décor. FRENCH: *Les Halles* (1450 Crescent Street) is first-class French dining at its very best. Atmosphere is animated and attractive, staff is professional, and the food is unsurpassed in Montreal; consider the quenelles de brochet, the duck with pears and wine sauce, the gâteau Paris-Brest. *Chez Bardet* (591 Boulevard Henri-Bourassa est) is a longish taxi or a Métro ride (to the door) from downtown, but well worth the trip, for this is one of the best classic-French restaurants in North America, elegant to look upon, with skilled service, and most important, superlative cuisine, whether you choose among the beef, veal, chicken, or fish dishes, remembering as you go along to stay in shape for the house's Grand Marnier soufflé. *Hélène de Champlain* (Île Sainte-Hélène) is La Ville de Montréal putting its best foot forward, a municipal operation of finesse and charm. Not expensive either and—note well—with one of the best wine-cellars in a city full of same. *Le Navire* and *le Petit Havre* are near—but unrelated—neighbors on Rue Saint-Vincent in Vieux Montréal, the former at No. 427, the latter at No. 443. Each occupies a lovingly restored old house, each is good looking, and each has middle-tab delicious French dishes. *L'Amphitryon* (320 Rue Notre-Dame est) is another Vieux Montréal pleaser in a lovely antique of a house. The menu is authentic French, and there are well-priced daily lunch specials, a different group each day. And wines: they come from fifteen countries. *Café Martin* (2175 Rue de la Montagne) occupies a very grand late-nineteenth-century town house, and you want to go for a leisurely dinner; the experience is like visiting affluent friends. Service is deft, ambience luxurious, and the food classic French and not overly costly. *Saint-Amable* (188 Rue Saint-Amable) is a Vieux Montréal landmark, in a great Place Jacques-Cartier house, with a cuisine that does it justice. There are dining rooms on both main and upper floors, and although you can't go wrong, regardless of selection, do consider the Tournedos Opéra. Moderately expensive. *Le Vert Gallant* (1425 Rue Crescent) is very smart, with a stylish look and a distinguished cuisine, mostly classic French. Though not cheap, the prix-fixe dinners are very good buys. Festive. *L'Escargot* (Place Ville-Marie) is an always-buzzing, mid-category restaurant that is one of a number operated by Hilton Canada in Place Ville-Marie. Specialties are snails in a variety of styles, but there is other good bistro-style French food, as well. Deservedly popular. HOTELS: You rarely go wrong in any Montreal hotel. But some hotel restaurants stand out. The *Ritz-Carlton* distinguishes itself in every one of its dining rooms. Start in the basement, with the Ritz Café. Can there be a smarter breakfast locale anywhere in North America? (Lunch and dinner, too.) On that same level is the intimate Maritime Bar, with seafood the favored choice at lunch and dinner both. Then ascend to the main floor, to the Café de Paris. This is the main dining room and one of Montreal's most important. Begin with a drink in the adjacent lounge, then move in to the Café for lunch or dinner, making a switch, in summer, to the garden restaurant out back—with ducks paddling about in its pond. The *Château Champlain* offers a tempting choice, too. The lobby-floor Neufchatel is elegantly paneled and chandeliered, eighteenth-century style; the menu is classic French, the service flawless. Le Tournebroche is on the same floor, more country-bistro in ambience, with open-hearth kitchen and bread bakery both in full view; good roasts, steaks. L'Escapade, up on the roof, specializes in buffets, hot and cold (lunch is a better buy); dancing in the evening. And then there's Le Caf'Conc—an absolutely marvelous theatre-style cabaret, of the type you went to on your first visit to Paris. *Le Reine Élizabeth-The Queen Elizabeth Hotel's* Beaver Club is its leading restaurant. The look of the place is Early-Quebec-Trappers. Rich trappers, that is. This is a long-popular choice for Montrealers who want to impress visiting *bombardiers* and was the basis for a newer western-Canada counterpart—with a lumberman's theme—in the same chain's Hotel Vancouver. The lamb, beef, and fish specialties are noteworthy. *Hotel Bonaventure:* Dining with a view from on high can mean the substitution of a view for a tasty meal. Not so in Le Castillion. And the view here—in this hotel whose lobby is up in the air—is of the off-lobby garden, centered with a swimming pool. Expensive, but the flourishes are no compensation for the fare. SEAFOOD: Montreal surprises with an abundance of really good seafood restaurants. No city in North America does better in this respect, not even San Francisco, much less New York. *Desjardins* (1175 Rue Mackay) is an old-timer, on the scene since 1892, with honestly prepared, nicely presented fish in infinite variety. Family-managed, which means nice service, with the prices middle category. *La Marée* (404 Place Jacques-Cartier) is a splendid Vieux Montréal mansion, with food to match—a lobster bisque, for example or moules marinière for mussels fans. More prosaic fish, too. Fine wines, lovely service. Fairly expensive. *La Tortue* (adjacent to La Crêpe Bretonne on Rue Saint-François-Xavier in Vieux Montréal) is a charmer, with the look of a seaside tavern, an open-to-view grill and oven, and scrumptious food; the fish soup and the broiled Arctic char are indicated. STEAKS are everywhere to be had, in Montreal as elsewhere. Still this pair of sources are worth knowing about. *Gibby's* (in a well-restored and charmingly furnished old house at 298 Place d'Youville) and *The Cleaver* (1219A Rue Université) are two good choices. SWISS: *William Tell* (2055 Rue Stanley) looks Swiss, feels Swiss, tastes deliciously Swiss—fondue, of course, but the great potato preparation known as rosti and wonderful Swiss veal dishes. Not expensive. ITALIAN: *Porto Fino* (2040 Rue de la Montagne) serves a range of pasta dishes, and northern specialties as well. Salads crisp and delicious as only the Italians can make them. Desserts include a luscious Zuppa Inglese. Medium-priced. *Fenice* (6877 Rue Saint-Hubert): variations on a theme of fettucine. HUNGARIAN: *Paprika* (330 Avenue Victoria) is the genuine article—goulash, strudel, and a range of other Hungarian specialties. CHINESE: *Sun-Sun* (1023 Rue Clark) for very good Cantonese. DELI: *Ben's* (900 Boulevard Maisonneuve ouest) is for corned beef and pastrami sandwich specialties. CRÊPES: *À la Crepe Bretonne* (2080 Rue de la Montagne and several other locations) serves Brittany-style pancakes in nearly 100 ways, both savory and sweet. COFFEE, APERITIFS, SNACKS, PLATS DU JOUR: *Casa Pedro* (Crescent at Maisonneuve) is a major see-and-be-seen congregating spot; go for a cup of cappucino or a meal. BUDGET: *Dupont & Smith* (1454 Rue Peel) is as agreeable a place as you'll find for an inexpensive, nicely served, full-course dinner in an attractive setting. Very good value. Lunch, too. *Le Languedoc* (425 Rue McGill) is known mostly to Montrealers anxious for a leisurely and uncostly dinner (lunchtime is busier). The fare is French with a good choice of fish, meat and poultry entrées, sprightly service, and reasonable prix-fixe tabs. *Café de la Promenade* (in the Bourse—or Stock Exchange—Place Victoria) is a good, cheap place to know about for lunch, or even a simple dinner. *Chez Loulou les Bacchantes* (2070 Rue de la Montagne) is shortened to "Le Bistro" by locals. This is an amusing Montreal version of a Paris bistro out of the twenties, with sandwiches-baguettes—on elongated pieces of French bread—a specialty. Fun. *Thursday's* (1449 Rue Crescent) is imaginatively got-up, with simple things like soups and hamburgers. *Sir Winston Churchill's* (1455 Rue Crescent) is pubby and popular, with daily specials and sandwiches, and nice vibes. DEPARTMENT-STORE EAT-

ING: *Hudson's Bay Company* (La Baie) offers nourishment in a number of locations, most interestingly in the Regency Room, far more stylish looking than so inexpensive a place deserves to be; waitress service of hot and cold plates, sandwiches, and salads, with the roast beef a specialty. The Bay's La Soupière offers a different hearty soup each day, served as a package with bread and butter, dessert, and beverage—and reasonably. There's a cafeteria, too. *Eaton's* has a choice of eateries, but its ballroom-sized ninth-floor restaurant is the grandest, unlicensed though it is. The ladies love it for afternoon tea (the pastries are good), but you may go for prix-fixe or à-la-carte lunches or dinners on evenings the store is open. *St. Lawrence Cafeteria* (Place Ville-Marie) is the least glamorous of the slew of Hilton-operated restaurants in "La Place"—but it's good to know about for inexpensive breakfasts, snacks, and meals.

Quebec City restaurants: Of course you will want to have a meal at Château Frontenac, where *Le Village* complex is moderate-priced and fun for a meal or a drink; consider also the Château's *Champlain Room,* its elegant main restaurant. *Le Boeuf Charolais* is authentic French-accented and attractive—in Loews le Concorde Hôtel. And *Le Villeray* of the Québec Hilton is likewise. The *Clarendon Hotel Restaurant* is very good, too. *Chalet Suisse* (26 Rue Sainte-Anne) is beloved of both Québecois and visitors, thanks to good value. Swiss fondues, of course, but other dishes, too, including lobster. *Chez Guido* (73 Rue Sainte-Anne) is a long-time leader, in a lovely old house. The menu runs a wide gamut, at once French, Italian, and Québecois. *La Traite du Roy* (25¼ Rue Notre-Dame) is an atmospheric old Place Royale house with a fine French kitchen. *Le Café de L'Estoc* (next to Château Frontenac) is agreeable in summer for hamburgers and drinks on its terrace. *Georges V* is the restaurant of the earlier-recommended Hôtel Château Laurier (695 Grande-Allée est). *Le Continental* (23 Rue Saint-Louis) is an old reliable, for moderate-priced lunches and dinners, French style. *La Chaumière* (22 Rue Couillard) occupies the cellar of an ancient house, serves good steaks, seafood, and salads, is a super choice for dinner. *L'Ancêtre* is another Rue Couillard (No. 17) favorite; smallish but good restaurant. *Café de la Cour,* on the Rue Saint-Jean, is inviting, and understandably so, for dinner (Rue Saint-Jean is restaurant-filled and dotted with café-terraces; it's fun to stroll after dinner and pop in for a drink or two along the way). Two other suggestions, one for pastry, the other for beer. The first is *Patisserie Kerhulu* (Rue de la Fabrique); the second is *Brasserie Le Gaulois* (Rue Buade), a big three-floor establishment, lively on summer evenings, and with a good albeit simple menu embracing soups, steaks, and sandwiches.

Saskatchewan

LA SASKATCHEWAN

Best times for a visit: *Summer is the ideal season, with hot, sunny days, and cooler evenings. Winter is snowy and can be very cold, with below-zero days not uncommon. Regina's average minimum during the coldest month is eight below; its*

average maximum for the warmest month is seventy-nine. Spring comes late, generally in May, and is short-lived, as is autumn, which embraces late September and October. **Transportation:** *Highways, particularly in the southern part of the province, are excellent; they are less developed in the sparsely settled north. The Trans-Canada Highway runs 408 miles, from Moosomin in the east, to Maple Creek in the west; it passes through Regina; major north–south routes lead into it. Most of the bus service is provided by Saskatchewan Transportation Co., a Crown Corporation which covers the province, often carrying mail, and upon occasion blood plasma and medical supplies, on its more remote routes. Air Canada links Saskatchewan with the rest of Canada and foreign points. TransAir flies between Regina, Saskatoon, and Prince Albert, as well as to points in Manitoba and Alberta. Saskair serves the northern region of the province, and there are a number of charter airlines catering to northern fish and game camps. Both major railroads serve Saskatchewan. Canadian Pacific has been on the scene since 1882, when its first train to the region brought settlers to farm free homesteads. CP and Canadian National now have a total of some 8,700 miles of track in the province. CP's transcontinental trains pass through Regina, Moose Jaw, and Swift Current. CN's trans-Canada line runs north of CP's, with Saskatoon its major stop. There also are north–south services.* **Having a drink:** *Licensed dining rooms, cocktail rooms, and beverage rooms; beverage rooms in hotels sell bottled beer to take out; certain restaurant rooms are licensed to serve wine and beer only. Liquor and beer by the bottle are sold at provincial liquor stores, and in certain rural areas, in other kinds of stores licensed as "special liquor vendor agencies."* **Further information:** *Department of Tourism and Renewable Resources, Regina; Agent General of Saskatchewan, 14/16 Cockspur Street, London; Canadian Government Office of Tourism, Ottawa, and branches.*

INTRODUCING SASKATCHEWAN

The most loyal son of Saskatchewan would be the first to admit that his province does not rank among Canada's most scenic, and what with Alberta and British Columbia directly west, this is one of the crosses he must bear. But Saskatchewan has a great deal to otherwise recommend it, aside from its intriguing and difficult-to-spell name, which is a derivative of the Cree word, *kisiskatchewan,* meaning "swift-flowing river."

This almost perfect oblong of a province—the most regularly delineated of any in Canada—is hardly a new settlement, if one takes the long view of things. Its first known residents were Paleo Indians, big-game hunters who made the great trek from Asia at the time of the last Ice Age. Eons later, when the Europeans trod the territory in the late seventeenth century, they found it populated by diverse Indian tribes—aggressive Blackfoot, Assiniboines, and Cree among them. The land they discovered was a vast region—the north (part of the Canadian Shield) rocky, swampy, game-filled, and lake-dotted; the south a mass of billowy grass prairie land and home to great herds of buffalo.

Traders and trappers: It was not until 1794 that Saskatchewan saw its first permanent settlement erected at Cumberland House by Samuel Hearne. By that time traders and trappers had been moving through the area for some decades, bedding down at temporary trading posts along the canoe routes during the rivalry for control of the fur trade between the Hudson's Bay and North West companies. With the merger of those two firms, the area became more settled. It remained part of Hudson's Bay's own domain until 1870, when rights were sold to the Canadian Government. In 1874 the first Mounties—officers of what was then known as the North-West Mounted Police (and wearing caps resembling those of modern hotel bellmen)—took over law enforcement from Hudson's Bay agents. Most of the settlers at that time were métis—people of mixed Indian and French blood.

But in 1882 the Canadian Pacific Railway reached the area. More settlers from the east arrived, and towns were born along the track—Regina, Moose Jaw, and Swift Current among them. Saskatoon was founded by members of a temperance society, British artisans settled near Moosomin, a pair of Jewish communities were created near Moose Mountain, and crofters from Scotland made their homes near Wapella. Non-English-speaking groups were to follow—Mennonites from Germany, Scandinavians, Hungarians, Ukrainians, Russians.

End of the buffalo herds: The region's population was following the pattern of Canadian—and North American—settlement. But there were problems. In 1883 a severe crop failure caused tremendous hardship, not only for the newer settler-farmers but for the old-timers—Indian and métis trappers. The buffalo herds—from which they had obtained food, clothing, and shelter—had been indiscriminately slaughtered. Their way of life and, indeed, their livelihoods, were destroyed. And so they banded together under one of their number, Louis Riel—a locally born hunter of French-métis parentage—to win self-government. Their original efforts—peaceful ones—met with no success, and violence followed. Their final battle, known in the history books as Riel's Rebellion, was at Batoche in 1885, and led to defeat, with Riel executed the following year in Regina.

But, oddly enough, Riel's Rebellion did Saskatchewan no lasting harm; on the contrary, it brought attention to Indian-métis problems and attracted new settlers, for many of the soldiers brought from the east to fight the Riel forces liked what they saw and returned with their families. The Canadian Government's free land grants attracted them and others as well. True, they went at farming too rapidly, not considering the wisest use of their land. Too much soil was plowed under that should have been left covered. But this was realized much later. At the time, the area that now constitutes Saskatchewan was progressing to the point where it was deemed ready to become a province on its own. In 1905 the districts of Saskatchewan, Assiniboia, and Athabaska were detached from the Northwest Territories to constitute the Province of Saskatchewan.

Wheat and the Depression: Progress continued to be the password. Settlement increased, the rich prairie soil yielded great crops of wheat, to the exclusion of other crops. And there was virtually no industry. In 1929, when the Great Depression swept the globe, it came close to sweeping Saskatchewan all the way under. The province suffered, aside from economic setbacks, the worst drought it had ever known. Crop prices plummeted. Many thousands were without means of income. Saskatchewan had the dubious distinction of being a major Dust Bowl area—drab, gray, dust-darkened skies blanketed its vast, flat terrain.

Recovery from the Depression was gradual, and with it came the realization that the province could not rely solely on agriculture if it was to thrive. Farming (principally wheat) remains the major money earner. About a quarter of the populace still live on farms, some 75,000 of them occupying some 65 million acres. Saskatchewan grows more than half of all of Canada's wheat, most of its oats and rye, and a good deal of its barley and flax. Of all the cultivated land in Canada 40 per cent is in Saskatchewan, and much of that province's grain makes its way to distant countries.

But industry—particularly the development of mineral resources —is coming to the fore. Some 6,600 wells pump 214,000 barrels of oil per day in southern Saskatchewan. In the northwestern part of the province, uranium is being produced, and in the southwest, helium. Nearly a score of mining companies are developing what promises to be one of the most important sources of high-grade potash in the world. Concurrent with the development of the mines has come the establishment of plants and mills to service them, and all manner of auxiliary industries.

Two socialist decades: Saskatchewan's provincial government has played a great role in its destiny, particularly in recent decades. Indeed, its government has been one of its most interesting features, for Saskatchewan had the first democratic socialist government in North America. Its Cooperative Commonwealth Federation Party (later renamed the New Democratic Party) was in power for two pioneering decades, 1944–64, much of that time under a single premier—T. C. Donalds. The socialists were out of office from 1964 until 1971, when under Premier Allan Blakeney, they regained power; Mr. Blakeney's party retained its leadership in the 1975 elections. The socialists championed the co-operative movement for both farmer and consumer, and with considerable success. They established government-owned businesses—telephones, buses, utilities. They were the force behind the South Saskatchewan River project, an eight-year program to create dams on the South Saskatchewan River—and a 140-mile-long reservoir, to irrigate some two hundred thousand acres of land.

Through its Saskatchewan Power Corporation, the province has been able to bring electrification to 99 per cent of its farms; before it was formed in 1949, only a relative handful had electricity. The provincial telephone company owns nearly 400,000 of the approximately 440,000 phones in the province. Through consolidated schools, many thousands of pupils have been taken from one-room schoolhouses into modern centralized plants with diversified curricula. Besides the University of Saskatchewan and its expanded campus at Regina, there are a novel program for the education of children in the sparsely settled north, and a challenging adult-education program. There has been an imaginative social welfare program, running a wide gamut—children's services, vocational rehabilitation of the physically handicapped, homes for the aged, work with unmarried mothers. The co-operatives are best exemplified by the Saskatchewan Wheat Pool, which dates from 1924 and is the world's largest grain-elevator concern. But there are other co-ops—wholesale, retail, marketing; co-operative insurance companies, a co-op oil refinery, others that operate community buildings such as meeting halls, skating, and curling rinks. Altogether, the province has nine hundred thousand co-op memberships, coming from the towns as well as the farms; most recent is in the north where métis, Indians, and whites have joined forces to market their produce and provide themselves with goods and services. Indeed, there are, in Saskatchewan, more co-ops in relation to the population than in any other part of Canada.

The government medical program: But it is not co-ops, power plants, or social welfare programs or even a government telephone company that has most distinguished Saskatchewan. What did make people sit up and take notice, insofar as Saskatchewan is concerned, was its leadership in the field of medicine. For it is this province that in 1962 inaugurated the first comprehensive, government-controlled medical insurance plan on the continent, after an initial period that saw protesters at the Legislative Building in Regina, locked doctors' offices, midnight conferences of medicos, excited press coverage throughout the land—and abroad, as well; and just about every kind of dire prediction from the plan's opponents except, perhaps, the end of the world. The plan succeeded, however, to the point where it has been implemented in 1968 by covering an eye examination by medical doctors as well as optometrists; later in 1973 with a novel hearing-aid plan, and in 1974 with an innovative children's dental-care plan.

Province of joiners: The people of the province are fiercely devoted to blowing its horn. The province has produced more than its share of distinguished local sons; some say it leads in the export of brains and talent to Toronto, Ottawa, Montreal, and Vancouver, in the fields of government (ex-Prime Minister John Diefenbaker is a good example), journalism, television, and sports. The Saskatchewan man or woman who is not a member of at least a handful of organizations—political, religious, professional/occupational, athletic—is hard to come by. Life in the small places revolves around the curling rink, lodge, and church. And country people—not unlike those of plains areas like, say, Kansas—think nothing of a hundred-mile excursion of an evening for an event of interest in a not terribly nearby city.

There is a love of history—provincial and local history, for the most part—and although the fondness for things material does not perhaps exceed that of other peoples in other provinces, it at times appears to, in Saskatchewan. The emphasis on bigness and firstest-with-the-mostest is strong.

No matter, Saskatchewan has learned through its own bitter experience how to take care of itself, how to give a good break to all of its citizens. A bit of squareness can be forgiven a province whose people—the descendants of pioneers—have themselves had the guts to pioneer with government programs bolder than any undertaken by their neighbors on what is the world's most progressive continent.

YOUR VISIT TO SASKATCHEWAN

There is no need at this stage to belabor the point, but to give you an idea of Canada's vastness simply note that Saskatchewan, only No. 5 in size (as well as population) among the provinces, is decidedly larger in area (251,700 square miles) than France (212,659 square miles). With less than a million inhabitants (compared to France's 47 million), it should be apparent that the province is anything but cramped for breathing space. Many first-time visitors find it difficult to adjust to the fact that Saskatchewan is not all wheat fields. Indeed, most of it is taken up with the aforementioned forests, lakes, and rocky, scrubby terrain of the north (two thirds), with only the lower third prairies.

The bulk of the population lives in the south. There are but two important cities, but there are fifteen provincial parks, one noted national park, a trio of national historic parks, four-score-plus regional parks, more than two hundred campgrounds—and more lakes per capita than any other province. It is the lakes and woods that are the chief lure for visitors, most of whom are fishermen and hunters from neighboring American states. (Fishing—especially for trout, northern pike, and Arctic grayling—is exceptional, and there are a number of popular fly-in fishing camps.)

The kind of attractions that draw so many tourists to provinces like Alberta, British Columbia, and eastern regions are not found in Saskatchewan. Families on budget holidays do enjoy the parks, though. And the compulsive tourist—the kind who doesn't like to miss a province when he's in the neighborhood—will surely find at least a brief stopover worthwhile, particularly if he is from an area devoid of prairies. For it must be admitted that to behold golden wheat billowing in the wind for as far as the eye can see—with the steeplelike silhouettes of the grain elevators offering the only contrast—is a memorable western Canada souvenir.

Regina is Saskatchewan's capital and chief city, and I would hope that its residents and their descendants will remain eternally grateful to the late Princess Louise, wife of the Marquis of Lorne—who was Canada's Governor-General for part of the late nineteenth century. For it was Princess Louise who selected the city's present name—the Latin for queen—in honor of her mother, Victoria. Regina's original name was Pile o' Bones, an accurate if not particularly pleasant description of what it was when settlers took it over from the Indians, who had assiduously amassed great collections of buffalo bones on its site, in the belief that an open display of remains of the vanished buffalo would cause it to return. The bones have, to be sure, long since been swept away, for it was in 1882—the year the Canadian Pacific reached the area—that Regina was designated the capital of the Northwest Territories, of which it was then a part.

The first habitations were tents. They began to be replaced by wooden buildings as settlers trickled in. The Mounties arrived in 1883 to make their headquarters in Regina, and although their topmost brass are now in Ottawa, they remain very much on the scene. In 1905 Saskatchewan was detached from the Northwest Territories to become a province, and Regina was transformed into *its* capital. There were then but a few thousand residents, but the surrounding prairies were attracting wheat farmers and the town experienced its first boom. By 1911 it boasted thirty thousand residents, but the following year a disastrous tornado almost completely destroyed the place. Only after World War I was there any substantial recovery, and that was vitiated by the Depression of the thirties. Since World War II, Regina—whose economic vicissitudes have been much like all Saskatchewan's—has made a rather startling comeback.

Regina is neither a Winnipeg nor an Edmonton. There is still a prairies feel to it—much more so than in neighboring capitals—and it has not the natural advantage of the South Saskatchewan River that helps make nearby Saskatoon so attractive. Still, recent developments have seen Regina become increasingly sophisticated, more zippy, and less hostile to the kind of amenities that North Americans have come to expect in their cities.

For the visitor, the city is at its most inventive with the Wascana Centre—a 2,000-acre, heart-of-town complex, unique in North America, and embodying the Legislative Building, university campus, arts centre, natural history museum, and wildlife sanctuary.

The Legislative Building is not a great deal unlike many of the American state capitols, nor those of neighboring Manitoba and Alberta, for that matter. It has a 188-foot dome, under which are quantities of elaborate rooms employing some thirty varieties of marble in their décor, including the Legislative Assembly, the Lieutenant Governor's Room, the Executive Council Chamber (with walls decorated in silk tapestry), the Premier's Office; and the Legislative Library. More impressive than the interior of the building (whose esthetics are as heavy-going as one might imagine, considering that it was built during the "heavy" period, 1908–12) is its setting—nearly 170 acres of beautifully landscaped grounds and formal gardens along the banks of Lake Wascana, the core of Wascana Centre.

Far newer than the Legislative Building is the Saskatchewan Museum of Natural History, a product of the mid-fifties, in which a couple of dozen startlingly realistic habitat groups are on display, which indicate the variety of the province's terrain and animal life, going in sequence through five regions—grasslands in the south through to the subarctic north. You'll see elk on the Saskatchewan River, moose in Bronson Forest, pelicans at Last Mountain Lake, even the buffalo of old on the plains.

No longer the national headquarters of the Mounties (these have been in Ottawa since 1920), the RCMP's Regina Barracks is primarily a training college for the force, the larger of two in the country. Recruits study judo, boxing, swimming, marching, and the federal statutes and criminal code of Canada. The training college is open to the public, and one of the treats of Regina is to see the Mounties' famous musical parade. The elderly chapel is lovely, but there is more: Queen Elizabeth II visited Regina in 1973 to dedicate a handsome new museum at the Regina Barracks of the Royal Canadian Mounted Police. It tells the Mounties' story from their founding—there is memorabilia dating back to the early Indian-and-trapper period—through to a 1973 thank-you note from the Queen's secretary (written from Holyrood House in Edinburgh) to the RCMP's commandant, upon her return from Regina.

The Saskatchewan Centre of the Arts is a beauty, and contains both the 2,000-seat Jubilee Theatre and Haybridge Hall for meeting and banquet use. The restored boyhood home of Prime Minister John Diefenbaker—brought from the town of Borden—operates as a museum. The constantly expanding Regina campus of the University of Saskatchewan includes the Provincial Archives and—perhaps most important for most visitors—the Norman Mackenzie Art Gallery, with a smallish but choice permanent collection of paintings, changing special shows, and a vitality and dynamism far out of proportion to its size. There is still another art museum—the Dunlop Art Gallery—in the Regina Public Library; mostly displays by local artists.

Saskatchewan House, long the official residence of the province's Lieutenant Governors, now sees summer service as the site of a play dramatizing the trial for treason in 1885 of métis leader Louis Riel.

Saskatoon, unlike Regina, whose beauty is man-made, is perched on the pretty, uncommercialized banks of the South Saskatchewan River. Named for a delicious berry that grows wild in the region, the city's two sectors are joined by half a dozen bridges. Though smaller than Regina, in terms of population, Saskatoon is growing; the competition between the two cities is so keen that you take sides at your own risk.

Saskatoon has come a long way since 1882, when it was settled by eastern teetotalers who were members of the Ontario Temperance Society. They were not able to make a boom town out of the place, but it eked along into the twentieth century—just barely. The population in 1901 was a bit over one hundred, but before long more settlers came—a good many of them from across the border in the United States. Today, Saskatoon is over the one hundred thousand mark. Just outside of town in the splendid graystone structured campus of the University of Saskatchewan (with a $15-million Medical College and hospital the highlights). Within the city, the parks along the banks of the river are uncommonly attractive, with the château-like towers of the Bessborough Hotel towering over their green lawns and gardens.

The first-rate Western Development Museum exhibits all manner of historic *objets*. Other museums include the offbeat Museums of Ukrainian Arts and Crafts, and of Ukrainian Culture; the university's Marquis Hall Art Gallery and Fraser Herbarium; the Memorial Art Gallery, with an especially good Canadian collection; and the Mendel Art Gallery, also strong on Canadian works. The big summer bash is called Pioneer Days, an event-packed July week in which the whole town participates.

North Battleford and Battleford are a pair of towns on the North Saskatchewan River not far north of Saskatoon. The former —newer and larger of the two—is visit-worthy for three reasons: Battleford National Historic Park—with five restored structures from a nineteenth-century Mountie post on the site; the Western Development Museum—a counterpart of the one in Saskatoon— that's a whole village full of turn-of-the-century houses and shops; and Battleford Historical Museum—housed in a lovely old church. Nearby Battleford was one of the first settlements in the prairies and the original headquarters—preceding Regina—of the North-West Mounted Police, who were on the scene there as early as

1876. In 1878 Battleford became headquarters for the North Western Territorial Council, and it was there, in 1885, that the Riel
Rebellion ceased when the rebels, under Louis Riel, surrendered
to the Mounties.

Batoche, not far northeast of Saskatoon, is the site of Batoche
National Historic Site. The place to head for is the rectory of little
Saint-Antoine-de-Padoue Church, which is now a museum telling
the story of an 1885 battle between Louis Riel's métis forces and
the government's militia, during the métis' abortive efforts to make
their independent métis state viable.

Prince Albert City and Prince Albert National Park are separated by thirty-six miles. The town through which you will pass en
route to the park to the north, is quite literally the gateway to
northern Saskatchewan, one of the province's oldest communities,
and its fourth largest city. Originally settled in 1776 by a trapper
named Peter Pond, who built a trading post on the north side of
the North Saskatchewan River, it had a rebirth some nine decades
later, on the river's other shore, when the Reverend James Nesbitt
brought some settlers from the south. To visit: the ex-church in
Bryant Park that is now the town's historical museum; and Lund's
Wildlife Exhibit—800 Canadian animal, bird, and fish specimens.

Waskesiu ("red deer" in the Cree language) is the summer
resort that is the headquarters of *Prince Albert National Park*—a
splendid, 1,500-square-mile region of lakes by the hundred, and
green forests that had for centuries been happy hunting grounds
for the Cree. Highly elevated for Saskatchewan (close to 2,000
feet), Prince Albert offers trees in profusion—spruce, pine, poplar,
birch; a variety of animals—deer, moose, elk, black bear, muskrat,
beaver, fox; swimming at the beach on Lake Waskesiu, and facilities, as well, for boating, fishing, riding, tennis, and even an
18-hole golf course. There's a little museum designed to give visitors a picture of the flora and fauna of the region, and places to
stay and to eat. Canoeing, incidentally, is excellent in the park for
many of the lakes are linked with each other.

Lac La Ronge: You're not quite in the extreme north of
Saskatchewan when you arrive at Lac La Ronge—but you're close
enough. One hundred eighty miles north of Prince Albert, Lac La
Ronge, with the network of lakes that surround it, is a fishing
mecca of no little consequence. There is charter air service from

the south (planes can fly you directly to your camp or lodge), and a road from Prince Albert. The town of La Ronge is small, but the basic amenities are there, including fishing and hunting equipment stores, a museum, and an Indian Handicrafts center and shop. The fish bite unceasingly—pickerel, lake trout, pike, for example—and the countryside, just beneath the rocky expanse of the vast Canadian Shield, is thick with evergreens—fir, pine, spruce—muskeg swamps, and deep, cold lakes.

Moose Jaw (forty miles west of Regina) is Saskatchewan's fourth largest city but is distinctive principally because of its memorable name, the fact that it was home to an industrious band of bootleggers during the American Prohibition period, and several attractions: a five-hundred-acre Wild Animal Park with a great variety of species and a children's zoo; the red-brick Victoria School, built in 1889 and still in service; and a pair of museums. The Museum of Saskatchewan's Prairie Pioneer Village comprises restored turn-of-the-century structures of varied types. The Centennial Museum in lovely Crescent Park features paintings by Saskatchewan and other Canadian artists, and some Indian exhibits.

Fort Qu'Appelle (just east of Regina) originally a Hudson's Bay post, and a onetime Mountie base as well, now is home to an important regional historic museum, the Hansen-Ross Pottery School, and a Sioux reserve, with Katepwa and Echo Valley Provincial Parks nearby.

Gravelbourg, southwest of Moose Jaw, is an unexpected enclave of French Canadians, several Catholic institutions, including a cathedral, seminary, and convent.

Saskatchewan provincial parks, operated by the Department of Tourism and Renewable Resources, extend from Lac La Ronge in the north to Cyprus Hills and Moose Mountain in the south. There are fishing, boating, and picnic grounds at all of them. Briefly, here's the rundown: *Moose Mountain* is on Kenosee Lake near the North Dakota border, is one of the largest of the lot, and boasts an 18-hole golf course, as well as swimming, boating, and a lodge. *Cypress Hills,* in the southwest just thirty-five miles north of the U.S. frontier, is a big-game refuge, and features golf, a heated swimming pool, saddle horses, a lodge and restaurant, cabins, and a tent camp. *Greenwater* is fine for pike and pickerel fishing;

there's dancing at night, a playground for the kids, restaurant, cabins, trailer and tent camps. *Goodspirit*—swimming, camping, varied accommodations. *Pike Lake*—ideal for outings from Saskatoon. *Echo Valley*—mostly for swimming and picnics. *Duck Mountain*—the works, from boating to dancing; ditto for *Greenwater Lake. Rowan's Ravine,* on Lost Mountain Lake, offers a small bay for boatmen, and modern picnicking and camping installations. *The Battlefords* is a good stopover point for visitors to the historic sites in that region. Others: *Katepwa, Buffalo Pound, Nipawin.* There are, as well, more than eighty *regional parks*—operated jointly by the provincial and municipal governments. All have picnic grounds and many provide swimming, fishing, golf, and other facilities.

SHOPPING

Shops for crafts—wares made by Saskatchewan Indians as well as products from throughout Canada, Indian, Eskimo, and otherwise—are scattered about the province. **Regina:** *Canadian Craft Shop* (Regina Inn Mall) has a good selection of handmade jewelry, ceramics, Indian artifacts, Eskimo soapstone, whalebone and ivory carvings, and other crafts from all over Canada. *Smith's Prairie Rock Shop* (2222 Wallace Street) abounds in minerals. *Saskatchewan Council for Crippled Children and Adults' Shop* (825 McDonald Street) sells ceramics and other wares made by disabled artisans. Eleventh Avenue is the main shopping street downtown. *Simpson's* department store has a small Canadiana shop on its main floor where one also finds paperback books, candy, tobacco; there's a cafeteria and post office in the basement. *Hudson's Bay Co.* has Canadiana on main, also, along with groceries, baked goods, candy, and a pharmacy, with an attractive buffet-style restaurant in the basement. The modern *Golden Mile Shopping Center* is on the south side of town near Vagabond Motor Inn. **Saskatoon:** *The Trading Post* (255 Second Avenue South) carries a range of handicrafts from throughout Canada. *Rock Cellar* (320 Ninth Street East) specializes in local minerals but sells handicrafts, too. *Saskatchewan Council for Crippled Children and Adults' Shop* (1410 Kilburn Avenue) vends ceramics crafted by the disabled; other gifts. **North Battleford:** *Battleford Native Handicrafts Co-op* sells locally produced Indian wares. *Battleford Sheltered Workshop Handcraft Centre* sells a variety of hand-produced things—silkscreen prints, objects in wood, needlework. *Lesser's Rock Shop,* over in Battleford, sells rocks and Indian crafts. **Lac La Ronge's** *Northern Handicraft Co-Op* is a provincial crafts pioneer, long noted for its Cree-produced articles, including moccasins, jackets, mokluks, and jewelry. **Fort Qu'Appelle's** *Hansen-Ross Pottery* (Bay Avenue at Fifth Street) is a reputed center for the production of handcrafted ceramics from local clays; interesting stone jewelry, too.

CREATURE COMFORTS

If Saskatchewan is without an overabundance of memorable hotels—its most distinctive is the château-style, riverside Bessborough in Saskatoon—it holds its own, as regards modernity and comfort. **Regina:** The centrally located, 15-story *Regina Inn* is modern, well-equipped, and nicely run. Both bedrooms and suites are comfortable, the lobby is capacious, there's a beamed, pubby main restaurant, coffee shop, cocktail lounge, good meeting and convention facilities, an adjacent shopping arcade, and a heated pool. In case you are wondering, given the name and the similarly named Calgary Inn and Winnipeg Inn: The Regina Inn is *not* a part of the Western International chain. *The Hotel Saskatchewan,* CP Hotels' long-time Regina outpost, had when I last sampled it, seen better days. At least if you were in an ordinary room. The Royal Suite, especially designed and furnished for the 1973 visit of Queen Elizabeth II is nothing less than the most exquisite—and tasteful—such apartment I've seen in any city on the continent. And there was, when I last checked, a floor or two of refurbished regular-size twins and singles. But, unless this has been extended to the rest of the hotel—which is the plan—don't expect the uniformly high-standard that is the general norm for CP hotels. Restaurant and cocktail lounge, but no coffee shop. *Landmark Golden West Inn* (4150 Albert Street) is modern, low-slung, and comfortable, with a steak restaurant, coffee shop, cocktail lounge, and pool. *Vagabond Motor Inn* (4177 Albert Street) is not dissimilar from the

Landmark—contemporary motor-inn décor—with restaurant, cocktail lounge, coffee shop, and well-equipped rooms. The 12-story, 209 room *Sheraton Centre Motor Inn* is centrally located (Victoria Avenue at Broad Street) with a pair of pools (one for kids), sauna, game room, restaurant, sensibly big coffee shop, cocktail lounge, and high-ceilinged lobby. EATING IN REGINA: *L'Habitant* (2169 Lorne Street) is Québecois-owned, small, attractive, and inviting, with the eastern province's famed pea soup and steaks the specialties. *Golf's* (1945 Victoria Avenue) is an exceptionally good-looking steak house, with a capacious cocktail lounge, professional staff, and reliable fare. It's a newer branch of the Golf's in Saskatoon. *The Blade & Barrel,* Landmark Inn, is good for steaks, and the *Steak House* of the Regina Inn is good, too. Agreeable late-hours drinks spots include the *Pig & Whistle* and its next-door neighbor, the *Red Fox,* lounge-restaurant in the *Bell City Motel*. **Saskatoon:** For long a star of the Canadian National chain—it was CN-designed in the château style of the twenties—the *Bessborough* is now an independent operation, but still a one-of-a-kind beauty that a city as small as Saskatoon is lucky to have. There are 260 rooms with bath, and the attractive public rooms include a restaurant, coffee shop, cocktail lounge, and heated pool. *Sheraton Cavalier Motor Inn* is attractive and full-facility, with nearly 200 rooms with bath, restaurant, lounge-cum-entertainment, outdoor pool, barber and beauty shops. *Imperial 400 Motel* (610 Idylwyld Drive South) has 150 rooms with bath plus 300 kitchen-equipped units, as well as a heated pool, sauna, restaurant, and cocktail lounge. Saskatoon's *Holiday Inn* (22nd Street and First Avenue) has nearly 200 cheery rooms, restaurant, coffee shop, cocktail lounge, pool. **Prince Albert:** *Sheraton-Marlboro Motor Inn* has 120 contemporary rooms and a range of pleasant places to eat, drink, and be entertained. *Imperial 400 Motel* offers 100 rooms with bath plus 20 kitchen-equipped units; pool, too. **Lac La Ronge:** *La Ronge Motor Inn* has half a hundred rooms, restaurant, cocktail lounge. A variety of other types of facilities—camps, simpler cabins, as well. **Moose Jaw:** *Harwood's Moose Jaw Inn* has varied accommodations with 100 rooms all told, restaurant, and cocktail lounge. *Matador Inn* has a couple of dozen rooms, restaurant, and cocktail lounge, heated pool. **Fort Qu'Appelle:** *Fort Hotel* has nearly 30 rooms, some nicer than others, restaurant, cocktail lounge. **Waskesiu (Prince Albert National Park):** *Lakeview Hotel* has more than a dozen units of varying types, restaurant, cocktail lounge. *Manville's Waskesiu Bungalows* and *Armstrong Hillcrest Cabins* both have considerable cabins and rooms of varying degrees of comfort; the former has both restaurant and store. Certain **provincial parks** offer accommodations and eating facilities. These include *Cypress Hills* (cabins, restaurant), *Duck Mountain* (cabins, restaurant), and *Greenwater Lake* (cabins, and a simple café).

Yukon Territory

LE TERRITOIRE DU YUKON

Best times for a visit: *Unless you're a polar bear, no doubt about it—June through September, when the days are warm and sunny (seventies and eighties, but occasionally the nineties) and nights are pleasantly cool. Winter is* really cold,

*with below-zero temperatures the rule, and when I say below
zero I mean as low as sixty below. The autumn—through October—is coolish. Spring thaws—April, May, and possibly late
March—make car travel difficult during that season.* **Transportation:** *The famed Alaska Highway—with all due respects
to the forty-ninth American state—is misnamed, for 1,221
of its 1,523 miles lie within Canada, 580 of them in the
Yukon. The highway begins in Dawson Creek, British Columbia, and terminates in Fairbanks, Alaska. Not to be confused with the Trans-Canada Highway, the largely unpaved
Alaska Highway is an all-weather gravel road with a 50
m.p.h. speed limit, which can be dusty in dry periods, occasionally muddy, and along which pesky mosquitoes and black
flies may, at times, be encountered. (Don't travel without a
bug bomb!) There are compensations, though, for the road
follows one of the most spectacularly beautiful routes on the
North American continent, and it is well maintained. Accommodations, stores, places to eat, and service stations are to be
found at convenient points, and thanks to the latitude, there
are as many as twenty hours of light per day during the summer. From the Alaska Highway, there are roads—also of
gravel—that branch off to Dawson City and Mayo, both in the
Yukon; and to the port of Haines, Alaska (from Haines
Junction, Yukon). The Sixty Mile Road goes from Dawson
City northwest to the Alaska border. Buses of Canadian
Coachways make daily summer runs to southern Canada and
into Alaska. There is summer bus service, too, between
Whitehorse and Dawson City. CP Air maintains service between Vancouver and Whitehorse. Northward Airlines connects Whitehorse with Mayo and Dawson City, and a number
of charter services are utilized for trips to minor communities
and for fishing and hunting parties. Wien Air Alaska links
Whitehorse with Juneau and Fairbanks; and there is air service as well to the Northwest Territories. The only rail route in
the Yukon is one of the continent's most scenic, and of especial tourist interest: the White Pass & Yukon Railway traverses the same route followed during the Gold Rush between
the Pacific port of Skagway, Alaska—over 110 miles of
mountainous, narrow-gauge track—and Whitehorse. Skagway*

*is served by ships, including luxury liners on the Califor-
nia-Alaska run.* **Having a drink:** *Licensed restaurants and
hotel dining rooms, cocktail lounges, beer parlors (also called
taverns) for men only, at major towns, along with government liquor stores. Liquor may be bought by the bottle at
cocktail lounges and beer parlors, which are open as late as
2* A.M. **Further information:** *Department of Travel and Information, Government of Yukon Territory, Whitehorse,
Yukon; Canadian Government Office of Tourism, Ottawa
and branches.*

INTRODUCING THE YUKON

Make no mistake about it: The Yukon *continues* to cast its
spell. Its name—even to the countless Americans (*and* Canadians)
who are not quite sure precisely where it is, or just *what* it is—still
evokes images of great space and snowy peaks and panning for
gold in the Klondike and tales of Robert W. Service and bearded
prospectors. The Yukon is all of these things, but it is at the same
time a surprisingly progressive chunk of Canada with a tiny but
no-nonsense populace—hospitable but hard-working—that is determined to spur its development regardless of the obstacles that have
been an impediment during its relatively brief history.

For, as history goes—even in new countries like the United
States and Canada—the Yukon is spanking new. It did not know
the white man until 1842, when Robert Campbell of the Hudson's
Bay Company explored parts of it while opening it up to the fur
trade. A scattering of trading posts were opened in ensuing years,
and gradually—very gradually—a handful of prospectors trickled in
to pan for gold. But the Yukon's history really began on August
17, 1896. On that day, a prospector named George Washington
Carmacks and two Indian friends—one known as Skookum Jim, the
other at first called Tagish Charlie and later Dawson Charlie—discovered gold on Bonanza Creek, a tributary of the Klondike River.
They made their strike on the basis of a tip provided by still another prospector, Robert Henderson, who had asked them to let
him know what they found. The Yukon, at that time, was every-
man-for-himself country. Carmacks and his associates were so busy

getting rich on their strike that they never got around to passing the word to Henderson, and the man who was indirectly responsible for the Gold Rush never heard about Bonanza Creek until after it had been entirely staked out.

The Gold Rush: But the outer world got the message. (It is a measure of the continuing isolation of the Yukon that to this day points without the territory are still known as "The Outside.") They started coming in 1897, but it was during the following year that they came by the thousands—overcoming floods, deep snows, frigid temperatures, and at times non-existent facilities. Within a few years, the tent-settlement they used as their headquarters—named Dawson City for a noted archaeologist—had mushroomed into a hardly insubstantial town with a population nearing thirty thousand. And villages sprang up at other gold-producing tributaries of the Klondike River. Within eight years, $100 million worth of gold had been mined, the peak year being 1900, with production valued at $22 million.

But Dawson City's glory was short-lived. By 1911, the Gold Rush having ebbed, the population was down to five thousand. And ever since then—even though Dawson was the capital of the territory until 1953—it has continued to shrink in size, until now it has less than a thousand inhabitants. (But Yukoners do not forget that August 17—the date of the Bonanza discovery—is Discovery Day, a territorial holiday.) Mining—silver, lead, and zinc—continued, and communications and transport were improved. Still, during the Depression years in the 1930s, economic activity was at enough of a standstill to have led the Federal Government to consider making the territory a part of the province of British Columbia. But Yukoners—small in number but vocal in their protests to Ottawa—were successful in their opposition.

The Alaska Highway: The territory's second great boom came as a result of World War II, when the Canadian and American governments concluded that a road, linking Alaska to British Columbia and the United States, would be of strategic desirability and importance. And so construction began on the Alaska Highway—then called the Alcan (Alaska-Canada) Highway—in March 1942. Thousands of construction workers—mostly military—were sent to the Yukon to build the road, and the then tiny town of Whitehorse became the hub of the operation. The project they undertook—and it was largely the accomplishment of black U.S. battalions, for the American army still was racially segregated—did more than develop Whitehorse. It made the community so much more important and convenient—as a transport and commercial terminus—that in 1953 Whitehorse took over as territorial capital from Dawson City. The highway brought the Yukon more into contact with its neighbors than had ever before been the case. The amenities of modern life went north. Educational facilities mushroomed. Mining activity has once again come to the fore. (Much of Canada's silver comes from the Yukon, and gold, lead, zinc, copper, platinum, and other minerals are still being mined.)

Fur trapping continues as the mainstay occupation of the Indian populace. And fishing, forestry, and farming are developing along with the newest industry—currently booming tourism.

Progress in self-government: Meanwhile, the Yukoner takes his situation in stride. The territory, still with a tiny population, is considerably behind the ten provinces insofar as self-government is concerned. Its chief executive, the Territorial Commissioner, is federally appointed. Its Territorial Council of seven members is elective, and so is the territory's sole member of the House of Commons in Ottawa. But the Council has nothing like the power of a provincial legislature, and Yukoners still consider themselves colonials and work for the day when the Yukon will have the same status as the ten provinces to the south.

YOUR VISIT TO THE YUKON

Glance at a map and you'll see that the Yukon covers but a fraction of the area occupied by the staggeringly vast Northwest Territories, of which it had once been a part. And it is less than half as big as Alaska. But do not underestimate its size. Occupying some 207,000 square miles, it is larger than all of New England, double the size of the British Isles, two and a half times the area of Texas, and it occupies as much space as all of the Maritime Provinces combined. Named for an Indian word translated variously as "clear waters" and "big river," it is a land of more than a dozen *major* rivers, the longest of which—the Yukon—extends for nearly two thousand miles. Kluane, its foremost lake, exceeds 150 square miles in breadth and gives its name to Kluane National Park, established in 1972 and embracing such peaks as 19,850-foot Mt. Logan of the magnificent St. Elias range—Canada's highest. The Arctic Circle runs through the Yukon's northern tip (the Midnight Sun shines round the clock during June and July in the north, but even in the south there is light during that period for most of the day!). The Arctic Ocean delineates the Yukon's northern frontier; Alaska is to the west, and the Northwest Territories fringe the east, with more of Alaska and British Columbia to the south.

The wonder is not that so few people have come to live in this remote section of the world, but that so many have. Still, upon examination, the touristic drawing power of the territory becomes eminently understandable, despite the lack of luxurious accommodation. For make no mistake about it: this is still frontierland. Only in the capital will you find facilities that approximate those of other major Canadian cities and resorts. The paved road is still a rarity. The only skyscrapers are the mountains. The cost of living is higher than on the "Outside" because everything must be transported great distances. But the Yukon remains one of the most exciting areas of Canada—dynamic, uninhibited, splendid in its beauty and its vastness; populated by young-minded, friendly folk who *must* know what it means to be neighborly in order to survive.

The essentials of a Yukon holiday? I would consider as requisites Whitehorse, the capital; Dawson City, the onetime Gold Rush boom town; and the Haines Junction-Kluane Lake-St. Elias Mountains area. For the angler, hunter, and camper, there are limitless destinations, including more than a score of government-operated camping grounds, lakes teeming with lake and rainbow trout, arctic grayling, northern pike, and whitefish; woods and slopes populated with moose, caribou, mountain sheep, and black, brown, and grizzly bears.

There are a trio of circle routes worth one's consideration. The first is via the Alaska Highway to Whitehorse, north to Dawson City, west into Alaska, back into the Yukon past the St. Elias Mountains. The second takes one from Whitehorse south to Carcross and its scenic environs, with a return to Whitehorse. And the third begins in Haines, Alaska, continues by road to the Haines Junction region of the Yukon, proceeds to Whitehorse, and takes one over the White Pass and Yukon Railway to Skagway, Alaska, and, presumably, a waiting ship bound for Vancouver, Seattle, San Francisco or Los Angeles. The hurry-up traveler should be happy to settle for flights from Vancouver to Whitehorse and Dawson City and an excursion to Haines Junction before returning by air to British Columbia.

Whitehorse, not unlike Dawson City, has had its ups and downs. From a pre-World War II settlement of some eight hundred persons, it turned into a boom town—during the construction of the Alaska Highway—with a populace close to forty thousand. But by 1945, when the Highway was finished, the figure dropped to under four thousand. Now Whitehorse—stable and with a modern façade—hovers around the thirteen-thousand mark, as the Yukon's biggest city, its seat of government, a transport hub of the northwestern tip of North America, and Canada's westernmost capital—even more westerly than Victoria, B.C. Occupying a flattish valley encircled by mountains—from which one gains a striking view—the city retains a good bit of its historical façade. One wants to see the contemporary-design City Hall and the Yukon Regional Library, with its great central stone fireplace, the handsome Vocational School, the modern Federal Building, and the attractive residential neighborhoods—possibly even the Lions Club's open-to-the-public heated swimming pool.

But time must be allotted for a leisurely perusal of Yukoniana lovingly collected in the Yukon Historical Society's McBride Museum, which moved from its original log structure to next-door larger quarters in 1967. The Anglicans' charming Old Log Church is in sharp contrast to its modern successor—one of the smallest Anglican cathedrals extant. (There is a Roman Catholic cathedral —Sacred Heart—as well.) There remains the cabin of Sam McGee and the log houses of other old-timers. The paddle-wheel steamer moored in the Yukon River is a reminder of not-far-distant Klondike days, and is now a museum with National Historic Site cachet. There is an old Indian cemetery, and there is the log-cabin-style railway station of the White Pass & Yukon Route; watching the narrow-gauge train come in each afternoon is a favorite local pastime. But even better is going aboard the train for the 110-mile mountain journey to amusing Skagway, Alaska, remaining overnight in that handsome port, and returning to

Whitehorse the following day. The route follows for some miles the Gold Rush trail of 1898, and at times chugs along at altitudes approaching twenty-nine hundred feet.

Outside of town is Miles Canyon on the Yukon River, where Jack London acquired a tidy little fortune guiding boats through its rocky walls, at twenty-five dollars per craft, and through which passed thousands of prospectors in Gold Rush days. Today, a suspension bridge spans the canyon, to the delight of sight-seers. And the modern M.V. *Schwatka* makes three-hour excursion trips out of Whitehorse—through the canyon and up the river. The fantastically powerful Whitehorse Rapids—now dammed—and also just out of the city, are another worthwhile destination. (It was in the rapids that Chief Whitehorse—for whom the city and river are named—drowned.) Whitehorse is pleasant for in-town strolls and drives into the surrounding hills. A summer requisite is a performance of the Klondike-flavor Frantic Follies, while—all through February—Whitehorse celebrates with the Sourdough Rendezvous, and varied special events. Recent years have seen Main Street shops augmented by those of the modern Qwanlin Mall on Fourth Avenue.

Dawson City is, at first glance, sad. One cannot help but be unhappy at the near demise of what had been a lusty, lively, wealthy boom town only as recently as the first decade of this century. But the Dawson with a populace of some thirty thousand is now ancient history. Today, with a nucleus population of some eight hundred, it has made a comeback as a remarkably popular tourist destination. The visitor to the Yukon who misses Dawson misses a dramatic chunk of North American history. Still to be seen are the cabin where Jack London and Robert Service lived, recently restored; the Palace Grand Theatre—now proudly designated a National Historic Site and where the must-see *Gaslight Follies* is performed nightly in summer; the original post office, Diamond Tooth Gertie's Saloon—with gambling and can-can dancers; the paddle-wheeler *Keno,* still moored in the river and now doing duty as a museum of the Gold Rush era and a National Historic Site.

The one-time Government Administration Building (built in 1901) is now the Dawson City Museum—full of historic exhibits. And before you leave, ascend the mountain known with affection as Midnight Dome (ideal for a night view in midsummer, but for a dusk or daylight view at *any* time). It affords a vista of the town, the Klondike River, and the surrounding mountains which is one of the most memorable in all Canada. Drive over to Bonanza Creek, where the original strike was made. Talk with the old-timers still resident in Dawson; some have never left the region. The Klondike—named after the Indian "trondiuck" meaning "hammer water"—is more than a river. To this day, it evokes one of the most romantic and derring-do eras of North American history. And one relives it by means of as little as twenty-four hours on the spot in Dawson City. Ideally, that visit should be made the weekend of Discovery Day, August 17, when the town and its many visitors celebrate with anything but reserve or decorum. But Dawson, at any time during the summer, is a Yukon requisite.

Haines Junction is the little settlement (population about two hundred) on the fringe of Kluane National Park that is smack in the midst of what I can describe only as the Yukon's greatest natural splendor. It is there, in the Shakwak Valley, that one gains access to a view of the magnificent St. Elias Mountains. The highest in Canada, this range includes sixteen peaks taller than the tallest of the Rockies. In the area, too, is the Yukon's biggest and loveliest lake, Kluane—forty-six miles long and fringed by a rim of snowy peaks which reflect themselves in its waters. To be seen too are beautiful Kloo and Kathleen lakes, Tatshenshini Falls, the Klukshu Indian village, and the little Catholic church that is a regional landmark. Nearby is the 10,000-square mile Kluane Game Reserve, the Canadian Government Agricultural Experiment Station—whose experiments in Far North farming are of interest even to non-farmers, Bear Creek Summit, one of the highest (3,204 feet) on the Alaska Highway, and Boutillier's Summit—at 3,280 feet the highest point between Fairbanks and Whitehorse, from which is afforded a glorious view of Kluane Lake. Not far distant is Soldiers' Summit, at which the Alaska Highway was formally dedicated in 1942 by Canadian and American officials and a quartet of American soldiers, two of them black and representing the black battalions that played a major role in the highway's construction.

Carcross (a contraction of Caribou Crossing) is the hamlet on the Tagish-Carcross Highway, from which George W. Carmacks and his Indian associates departed on their successful search for gold in Bonanza Creek. Now a tiny settlement, it is situated in an area of scenic mountain splendor, and there remains a number of frame structures dating back to '98 days. It was at Carcross—just north of the Alaska border and due south of Whitehorse—that the last spike of the White Pass & Yukon Railway was driven in 1900—signaling the completion of the rail route between the Yukon and Skagway, Alaska. To see are pioneers' graves in the cemetery, an old White Pass & Yukon stagecoach, and an also-aged paddle boat and train locomotive. Tagish Lake is a local beauty spot and the trout fishing is superb.

Mayo, southeast of Dawson City, is known for its silver mines, which are Canada's richest. It is not without reminders of the Old Days—sod houses and the lake, but it has a modern façade, as well, and not far off is Keno Mountain, from whose 6,200-foot peak one gains a brilliant regional view.

Watson Lake is the easternmost of the Yukon's major communities, and the first Yukon town on the Alaska Highway as it enters the territory from British Columbia—just a few miles distant. It is set in a pleasant wooded area, and a unique tourist attraction: a collection of "milepost" signs (indicating distances from Watson Lake to points throughout the planet) begun by Alaska Highway workers in 1942 and added to each season by visitors unofficially representing the Chamber of Commerce of their home towns; there are well over a thousand.

SHOPPING

There are native-mined gems, rocks, and minerals of great variety on sale in shops throughout the territory, and they're made up into rings, bracelets, and brooches. One also finds sealskins made up into parkas and other furs. In **Whitehorse,** *Murdoch's* (207 Main Street) is an old reliable source for these and other souvenirs. *Yukon Ivory Shop* (309 Main Street) is another outlet. *Igloo Sporting Goods* (205A Main Street) is worth knowing about for camping, fishing, and hunting gear. *Yukon Indian Craft* (102 Main Street) specializes in Indian wares. *Mac's News Stand* (203 Main Street) is big on regional books. There's a *Woolworth's* at Qwanlin Mall, and *Hougen's* (305 Main Street) is the leading department store. In **Dawson City:** *Dawson Artscraft* has fur parkas and a selection of curios.

CREATURE COMFORTS

No Canadian provincial or territorial capital has had a more dramatic increase in accommodation facilities over the last decade than the Yukon's. **Whitehorse's** leader is the ultra-modern, centrally located *Travelodge* (Second and Wood) with 90 rooms, a licensed dining room, lounge, and coffee shop, not to mention the territory's most complete meeting and convention facilities. All rooms have TV, radio, and television and, of course, bath. Also good, and also modern, is the *Sandman Motor Inn* (2288 Second Avenue) with 42 well-equipped rooms, licensed restaurant and lounge, barber shop, and beauty salon. Nice, too, is *Ben-Elle Motel* (411 Main) with 38 rooms, attractive licensed restaurant, and lounge. *The Yukon Inn,* formerly rather oddly named the Tourists' Services Motor Hotel, is a 47-room house, with a wide range of facilities and an adjacent shopping center; there are licensed restaurant, lounge, and coffee shop, and a tavern. Leading WHITEHORSE RESTAURANTS include the *Golden Garter*—with Gold Rush décor, a lively ambience and good steaks and seafood; the *Cellar,* in the Edgewater Hotel (First and Main), with Alaska King crab and lobster tails, as well as roast beef and steaks; and the *202 Club,* with seafood specialties. **Dawson City's** leaders include the *Eldorado Hotel* (Third Avenue and Princess Street)— all rooms with bath, phones, radio, and TV, and with a licensed restaurant and lounge; and the *Gold City Motor Hotel* (Fifth Street at Harper), with 58 rooms, all with bath, licensed restaurant and lounge, and adjacent campgrounds, trailer park, and laundromat. **Haines Junction:** *The Kluane Park Inn* has modern rooms, all with private bath and a licensed restaurant that's open around the clock during the summer months. Cocktail lounge, too. **Watson Lake:** the *Belvedere Motor Hotel* has 51 well-equipped units, all with private bath and phone; a licensed restaurant and lounge, barber shop, and bank branch. **Alaska Highway** accommodations include the *Alas/Kon Border Lodge* (Mile 1202) with nearly 80 comfortable rooms with bath, licensed restaurant, lounge, and gas station; *Burwash Lodge* (Mile 1093), with 25 rooms, licensed restaurant and lounge, gas station, and a management happy to arrange fishing and hunting expeditions in the neighborhood; *Marsh Lake Resort* (Mile 888.3), with accommodations in lakeside cabins as well as rooms, licensed restaurant and lounge, groceries and curios, fishing guides and boats, and an adjacent trailer park-cum-laundromat; and the *Rancheria Hotel,* with a couple of dozen units, licensed restaurant-lounge, and gas station.

Acknowledgments

Many friends and colleagues on both sides of the border—some of whom I first came to know in connection with research for this book's First Edition—have been helpful in connection with the Revised Edition, for which I undertook half a dozen trips to and through Canada, from the Atlantic to the Pacific. Dan Wallace and Alex Carman of the Canadian Government Office of Tourism in Ottawa were as wonderfully supportive with this edition as with its predecessor, and I am most appreciative. Frank Galipeau, of the CGOT's New York office, has never been too busy to offer assistance in any number of ways, *et à lui, et ses collègues, je dis: merci bien.*

I want also to thank, alphabetically, for their personal kindness and professional co-operation: Ted Balderson, Patricia and Gary Bannerman, Susan Baumgartner, Georgia Beach, Benoît Bélanger, Lucien Bergeron, Joyce Berto, William Black, Anne Marie Bolger, Lis Brewer, Eileen Burford, A. H. Calvert, Emile Cochand, Dick Colby, Dorothy Cook, Antoine Corinthios, Karl Crosby, George Davidson, Elaine Deck, Ed Douglas, Harvey Dryden, Manny Ellenis, Janice Farrar, Louis Finamore, Ralph Gallup, John Gow, Denis Gosselin, Christopher Gowers, Marc Hamel, Frank Healy, Valerie Hynd, Pamela Jackson, Shirley Jones, Bill Kilfoil, Cory Kilvert, Gerry Krisch, Denis Lachapelle, Pierre Laliberté, Barry Lavelley, Keith Lawrence, Brian Lilley, Ann Lodge, Evan Lloyd, Ken MacKell, Colin McDonald, Jim McGregor, John McLeod,

George Marsh, Anita Marshall, Glen Moore, Maureen Mowbray, Wilf Organ, Bill Ozard, Verne Prior, Cecil Ravenswood, Max Reichardt, Meredyth Rochman, Phil Shea, Eugène Simon, Gordon Traynor, Pierre Valiquette, Al Venn, Gérard Viau, Dalton Waller and Charles Weatherup.

Larry Ashmead, my editor during the course of the last six A to Zs, left Doubleday to accept a challenging new post before this revised edition of this book was published. But he was very helpful in its preparation, and I thank him, as well as editor Betty Corson at Doubleday Canada, in Toronto. Louise Fisher typed the final draft of the manuscript with her usual expertise, and copy editor Marie Haller's eagle eye and blue pencil are both appreciated. Whatever errors crop up are mine, as are, of course, the opinions expressed.

R.S.K.

Index

Note: Page references for topics of greatest importance are in **boldface**.

Aberhart, William "Bible Bill," 42–43
Acadia, 127–29, 139, 175, 176, 185, 249
Aerial tramway, 55
Agassiz (B.C.), 88
Airlines, 22, 33–34; *see also* Transportation *under each province*
Aklavik (N.W.T.), 168
Alaska Highway, 22, 33, 34, 40, 67, 86, 325, 327–28, 329, 330, 332, 333, 334–35
Alberta, 39–65
  climate, 39
  creature comforts in, 58–65
  further information, 40
  having a drink, 40
  history of, 6, 41–44, 47–48, 163
  shopping in, 56–58
  transportation, 40
Alberta Game Farm (Alta.), 48
Alcan Highway, *see* Alaska Highway
Alcohol, *see* Having a drink *under each province*
Alexander, Lincoln, 11
Alma (N.B.), *see* Fundy National Park
American Revolution, 5, 180; *see also* Loyalists
American Society of Travel Agents (ASTA), 31
Amherst, Lord Jeffrey, 146, 186
Amherst (N.S.), 176–86, 192, 195
Amtrak, 32, 262
Annapolis Royal (Port Royal) (N.S.), 4, 174, 184–86, 194, 265
Antigonish (N.S.), 187–88, 192, 195
Appalachian region, 2
Aquarium, 274
Arboretum, 82
Architecture, 16; *see also* Historical museums and buildings
Arctic Ocean, 329
Area of Canada, 1–2
Argentia (Newf.), 155
Armdale (N.S.), 193
Arnolds Cove (Newf.), 157
Art, *see* Painting; Sculpture
Arvida (Que.), 300
Astor, John Jacob, 70
Atlantic Provinces, 2, 10; *see also* New Brunswick; Newfoundland; Nova Scotia; Prince Edward Island
Aulac (N.B.), 126
Aulnay de Charnisay, d', 128
Auto rental, 34
Avalon Peninsula (Newf.), 144, 152–53

Baddeck (N.S.), 190, 192, 196
Baffin Island, 163, 168
Baldwin, Robert, 204
Ballet, 14, 102, 111, 222, 278

Banff National Park (Alta.), 33, 46, 50–53, 57–58, 60–61, 64–65, 83
Barkerville (B.C.), 85–86
Barnard, George Henry, 79
Barrett, David, 73
Barrington (N.S.), 182n
Basque immigrants, 154
Bathurst Inlet (N.W.T.), 170
Batoche (Sask.), 310, 318
Battleford (Sask.), 317–18, 320
Bay of Fundy, 132, 137–38, 179, 184
Beaches (and swimming)
  Atlantic, 139, 153, 182, 183, 187
  Northwest Territories, 166
  Ontario, 213, 229
  Pacific, 75, 83
  Quebec, 285, 286
  Saskatchewan, 319, 320
Beaufort Sea, 167
Beaverbrook, Lord, 133–35, 138, 139
Belfast (P.E.I.), 254
Bell, Alexander Graham, 190
Belleville (Ont.), 235
Bennet, Bill, 73
Bennet, William Andrew Cecil, 73
Bird sanctuaries and museums, 137, 212, 255, 287
Black Duck (Newf.), 158
Black flies, 161, 325
Blacks in Canada, 11, 176, 227, 228
Blakeney, Allan, 311
Blanshard, Richard, 71
Borden (P.E.I.), 247
Borden (Sask.), 316
Border crossing, 26, 228
Botanical gardens, *see* Gardens
Bourassa, Robert, 267
Bracken, John, 44
Brandon (Man.), 108, 114–16, 121–22
Braynwyn, Frank, 108
Brigus (Newf.), 153, 157
British Columbia, 3, 32, 53, 66–99
  climate, 66
  creature comforts in, 90–99
  further information, 67
  having a drink, 67
  history of, 6, 68–73
  shopping in, 88–90
  transportation, 67
British Commonwealth of Nations, 6–7
British North America Act (1867), 5
Brochet (Man.), 119–20
Brock, Sir Isaac, 212
Brockville (Ont.), 213, 234
Bronson Forest (Sask.), 316
Brule, Etienne, 203
Buffalo herds, 48, 56, 114, 167, 316
Burlington (P.E.I.), 254

Bus service, *see* Transportation *under each province*
Button, Sir Thomas, 103
By, Col. John, 206, 212

Cable-car rides, 52, 53, 78
Cabot, John, 4, 145, 146, 150, 174
Cabot Trail (N.S.), 190, 191
Cajuns, 176
Calendar, Canadian, 35–38
Calgary (Alta.), 23, 26, 42, 45, 47, 48–50, 57, 59–60, 63–64, 78, 108
Campbell, Robert, 326
Campbell, Sir William, 219
Campbell River (B.C.), 94
Camp Gagetown (N.B.), 129, 133
Camping, 35
Campobello Island (N.B.), 137, 139, 141
Canada Council, 12
Canada East, 266
Canadian Broadcasting Corporation, 16
Canadian Cordillera, 3
Canadian Government Office of Tourism, 22, 31–32, 35
  branches of, 23–25
Canadian Press, 14
Canadian Rockies, 3, 44, 55, 73
  ice fields in, 53–54
Canadian Shield, 2–3, 41, 119, 162, 204, 319
Canadian–U.S. border, 3, 26, 228
Canoeing, 35
Cantons de l'Est (Que.), 279–80, 296
Cape Breton Highlands National Park (N.S.), 190, 191
Cape Breton Island (N.S.), 145, 175–76, 177, 179, 187, 188–91
Cape Tormentine (N.B.), 126, 247
Capp, Al, 118
Caraquet (N.B.), 139
Carcross (Yukon), 329, 332–33
Careless, J. M. S., 1
Cariboo Country (B.C.), 71, 85–86
Caribou (N.S.), 187, 247
Carillon towers, 80, 207
Carmacks, George Washington, 326, 332
Car rental, 34
Cartier, Jacques, 4, 127, 248–49, 265, 271, 281
Cavendish (P.E.I.), 253, 254, 257
Ceramics, 16, 221, 284, 319
Champlain, Samuel de, 127, 131, 174, 175, 185, 186, 203, 214, 229, 249, 265, 271, 281
Champlain Park (Ont.), 230
Changing of the Guard, 208, 284
Charlottetown (P.E.I.), 15, 249, 250–53, 256–57, 258–59
Chatham (N.B.), 139
Chatham (Ont.), 227, 240
Chester (N.S.), 183, 192, 194
Chéticamp (N.S.), 191, 192, 196
Chinese immigrants, 72
Churches, cathedrals, and shrines
  Alberta, 47
  British Columbia, 77, 81–82
  Manitoba, 109, 112–13, 117

New Brunswick, 133, 136, 137
Newfoundland, 150
Northwest Territories, 167
Nova Scotia, 180–81, 183, 187–88, 191
Ontario, 209, 210–11, 215, 218, 223, 225, 229
Prince Edward Island, 251–52, 254, 255
Quebec, 272–75, 277–78, 281, 283–85, 287
Yukon, 330, 332
Churchill, Sir Winston, 119, 147
Churchill (Man.), 117, 119, 122
Churchill Falls (Labrador), 144, 155
Churchill River, 2
Clarenville (Newf.), 158
Clearwater Provincial Park (Man.), 118, 122
Climate of Canada, 29–30; *see also* Climate *under each province*
Clothing for Canada, 30
Coastal ships
  Atlantic, 32, 126, 144, 155, 172–73
  Pacific, 32, 68, 87, 330
Coast range, 3
Cold Lake, 44
Columbia River, 2
Colville Lake (N.W.T.), 167, 169
Commercial fishing, 72–73, 102, 105, 145, 147, 154, 177–78
Conservatives, *see* Progressive Conservative party
Consulates, U.S., 26
Cook, Capt. James, 70
Cooperation Commonwealth Federation Party, 311
Coppermine River, 163
Corner Bank (Newf.), 154, 157, 158
Cornwall (Ont.), 212, 234
Cornwallis, Lord, 179
Corte Real, Gaspar, 145–46
Courtenay (B.C.), 82, 83
Covered bridges, 130, 135
Cranberry Portage (Man.), 118
CTV (network), 16
Cuehesnay Falls (Ont.), 230
Cunard, Joseph, 139
Currency, Canadian, 28
Customs (at border), Canadian and American, 26–27
Cuyler, Abraham, 189
Cypress Hills Provincial Park (Sask.), 319, 323

Dalvey Beach (P.E.I.), 257
Dance, 112; *see also* Ballet
Da Roza, Gustavo, 110
Dartmouth (N.S.), 194
Dauphin (Man.), 122
Dawson City (Yukon), 325, 327, 328, 331–32, 334
Dawson Creek (B.C.), 33, 40, 67, 86, 95
Deer Island (N.B.), 137, 141
Deer Lake (Newf.), 158
Deighton, Gassy Jack, 78
Diefenbaker, John, 9, 313, 316
Digby (N.S.), 186, 194–95
Donalds, T. C., 311

Dorchester (N.B.), **138**
Douglas, Maj. Clifford Hugh, 43
Douglas, Sir James, 71, 87
Drake, Sir Francis, 69
Drapeau, Jean, 279
Drumheller (Alta.), **56**, **63**
Duck Mountain Provincial Park (Sask.), **320**, **323**
Du Guast, Pierre, *see* Monts, Sieur de
Duncan (B.C.), **83**, **94**
Dunn, Lady (second Lady Beaverbrook), 134
Duplessis, Maurice, 267

Eastern Townships (Que.), **279–80**, **296**
Eaton, Cyrus, 187
Echo Valley Provincial Park (Sask.), **319**, **320**
Edmonton (Alta.), 13, 16, 40, **45–48**, **56–57**, **58–59**, 78, 108
Edmundston (N.B.), **135**, **139**, **140–41**
Elections, 9
Elizabeth II (Queen of Canada), 8, 47, 208, 252, 264, 316
Elizabeth (wife of King George VI), 8, 91, 209, 264
Elk Falls (B.C.), 82, **83**
Elk Island National Park (Alta.), **48**
Ellesmere Island, **162–63**
English language, **19**, 149
Erickson, Arthur, 76, 77
Ericson, Leif, 4, 174
Ernest Manning Provincial Park (B.C.), **88**
Eskimos, 10, 16, 155, **164–68**
  museums of, 47, 50, 119, 167, 221, 253, 276
Etienne, Georges, 108
Experimental Farm (Man.), 115
Exploits River, 154
Expo 67, 275, 278

Family Compact group, 204
Ferryland (Newf.), **156–57**
Fertilizer manufacture, 86
Films, **16**, 212
Fishing, **34–35**
  Alberta, 55
  Manitoba, 114, 116, 118
  New Brunswick, 130
  Newfoundland, 154, 156
  Northwest Territories, 167
  Nova Scotia, 187
  Ontario, 213, 229, 230
  Saskatchewan, 314, 319, 320
  Yukon, 333
  See also Commercial fishing
Flag of Canada, **12**
Flin Flon (Man.), **118**, **122**
Football Hall of Fame, 223
Forillon National Park (Que.), **287**
Fort Anne National Historic Park (N.S.), **185**
Fort Beauséjour National Historic Park (N.B.), **139**
Fort Cipewyan (Alta.), 41
Fort Frederick (N.B.), 128

Fort Garry (Man.), 104, 107; *see also* Winnipeg
Fort George Park (B.C.), **86**
Fort Henry (Ont.), 206, **214**
Fort Langley National Historic Park (B.C.), **87**
Fort McLeod (B.C.), 70
Fort Nelson (B.C.), **87**, **95**
Fort Qu'Appelle (Sask.), **319**, **321**, **322–23**
Fortress of Louisbourg National Historic Park (N.S.), 179, **189–90**, **192**, **196**
Fort Sainte Marie I (Ont.), 203
Fort St. John (B.C.), **86–87**, **95**
Fort Smith (N.W.T.), 56, 163, **167**, **169**
Fortune (Newf.), 144, **159**
Fort Wellington National Historic Park (Ont.), **213**
Fox, Luke, 103
Franklin, Sir John, 163
Fraser, Simon, 70, 86
Fraser River, 2, 71, 74, **87–88**
Fredericton (N.B.), 128, 131, **133–35**, **139**, **140**
French language, 11, **19**, 112, 113, 129, 135–36, 138, 191, 212, **263**, **268–69**, 280, 282
Frobisher, Sir Martin, 163
Frobisher Bay (N.W.T.), **168**, **169**
Fundy National Park (N.B.), **137–38**, **139**, **141**
Fur industry, 105, 328

Gagetown (N.B.), **133**, **140**
Gander (Newf.), **153–54**, **158**
Garde, Charles, 108
Gardens
  Alberta, 56
  British Columbia, 77, 82
  Manitoba, 115–16
  Nova Scotia, 181
  Ontario, 223, 228
  Quebec, 274
Gaspé Peninsula (Que.), 4, 265, **286–87**, **292**, **300**
Gatineau Park (Que.), 280
George VI (King of Canada), 8, 91, 209
Georgetown (P.E.I.), 254
Georgian Bay (Ont.), **229**, **240**
German immigrants, 42, 105, 176, 180, 183, 310
Gilbert, Sir Humphrey, 146, 150
Glacier National Park (B.C.), 83, 85, **94–95**
Glacier National Park (Montana), 55
Gold, 71, 72, 85
  See also Klondike Gold Rush
Gomes, Estevão, 127
Goodspirit Provincial Park (Sask.), **320**
Goose Bay (Labrador), 144, **155**
Government of Canada, **7–10**, **208–10**
Governor-General, **8–9**, 15, 208, **209–10**, 252, 284
Granby (Que.), **280**, **296**
Grandes Ballets Canadiens, Les, 14, 111, 278
Grand Falls (N.B.), **135**, **140**
Grand Falls (Newf.), **154**, **158**
Grand Manan (N.B.), **137**, **141**
Grand Pré (N.S.), **185**, **192**

Gravelbourg (Sask.), **319**
Great Bear Lake, 2, 167, **169**
Great Depression (1930s), 42–43, 147, 310–11, 315
Great Slave Lake, 2, 34, 162, 166, 167, 169
Greenwater Lake Provincial Park (Sask.), 319–20, 323
Grimshaw (Alta.), 33, 161
Gros Morne (Newf.), 153
Group of Seven, **13**, 46, 75, 80, 110, 227
Guelph (Ont.), **225, 239**
Guy, John, 153

Haines Junction (Yukon), 329, **332, 334**
Halifax (N.S.), 13, 15, 26, 172, 178, **179–82**, 192, 193, **196–97**
Hamilton (Ont.), 11, **223, 235**
Handicrafts, **16–17;** *see also* Shopping *under each province*
Happy Valley (Labrador), **159**
Harbour Grace (Newf.), 153
Harrison Hot Springs (B.C.), **88, 96**
Hartland (N.B.), 130, **135**
Hay River (N.W.T.), **167, 169**
Hearne, Samuel, 163, 309
Heceta and Quadra Expedition, 70
Henday, Anthony, 41
Henderson, Robert, 326–27
High Commissioners, 210
Highways, 22, **33–34;** *see also* Alaska Highway; Trans-Canada Highway; *and also* Transportation *under each province*
Hilton of Canada, 32
Historical museums and buildings
Alberta, 47, 48, 52, 55, 56
British Columbia, 76, 80–81, 83
Manitoba, 109–11, 113, 114, 119
New Brunswick, 131–33, 135, 137–39
Newfoundland, 150–52
Northwest Territories, 166
Nova Scotia, 180–81, 182, 184–87, 189–90
Ontario, 205–12, **214**, 215, 217–20, 223, 225–28, 230, 231
Prince Edward Island, 250–51, 254, 255
Quebec, 273–74, 277, 281, 283–84
Saskatchewan, 316–19
Yukon, 330, 331
History of Canada, **4–7**
Hockey Hall of Fame, 221
Holidays, Canadian, **35–38**
Holloway, Godfrey, 79
Hotels, 22, 32, 33; *see also* Creature Comforts *under each province*
Honey Harbour (Ont.), **229**
Houlton (N.B.), 247
House of Commons, **9**, 202, 207–8
Howe, Joseph, 177
Hudson, Henry, 103, 163
Hudson Bay, 2, 103, 105–7
Hudson's Bay Company, 5, 17, **18**
in Alberta, 41, 45, 58
in British Columbia, 70–71, 82, 87
in Manitoba, **103–4**, 111, 113–14, 117, 120
in Northwest Territories, 163, 167
in Saskatchewan, 309, 319
in the Yukon, 326

Hull (Que.), 207, 212, **245**, 280, **296**
Hungarian immigrants, 310
Hunting, 22, **34–35;** *see also* Wild animals

Ice-Field Highway (Alta.), **53–54, 62**
Icelandic immigrants, 105, 117
Imperial gallon, 31
Indian (East Indian) immigrants, **72**
Indian-Eskimo Association of Canada, 10
Indians, 119, 164, 167, 230, 328, 332
history of, 17, 41–42, 103, 127, 202–3, 248, 309
Indians, museums of
Alberta, 47, 49, 52
British Columbia, 77, 83, 87
Manitoba, 109, 114, 117
Newfoundland, 152
Northwest Territories, 167
Nova Scotia, 187
Ontario, 221, 227, 229
Prince Edward Island, 255
Quebec, 276
Saskatchewan, 319
Ingonish Beach (N.S.), **196**
Interior Plains, 3
International Peace Garden (Man.–N.Dak.), **115–16**
Inuvik (N.W.T.), 163, **167–68, 169**
Irish immigrants, 103, 176, 203
Irving, K. C., 134

James Bay (Ont.), 230
Japanese immigrants, 72
Jasper National Park (Alta.), 32, **54–55, 62–63,** 65
Jewish immigrants, 310
Johnson, Lyndon B., 137
Johnson, Philip, 46

Kamloops (B.C.), **85, 95**
Katepwa Provincial Park (Sask.), 319, 320
Kaufmann, Walter, 111
Keewatin, District of (N.W.T.), 163
Kelowna (B.C.), 95
Kelsey Bay (B.C.), **82,** 83
Kenora (Ont.), **231, 241**
Kentville (N.S.), 185, **192, 194**
King, William Lyon Mackenzie, 44, 212, 214, 217, 226, 280
Kingston (Ont.), 206, 213, **214–15, 234–35**
Kitchener (Ont.), **226, 235**
Klondike Gold Rush, 45, 48, **326–27, 331–32**
Kluane National Park (Yukon), 328–29, 332
Knight, Capt. James, 119
Kokanee Glacier Provincial Park (B.C.), 86
Kootenay country (B.C.), **72,** 86
Kootenay National Park (B.C.), 83, **84, 94**
Kouchibouguac National Park (N.B.), 137

Labrador, 32, 144, 147, **155,** 287
Lac Beauport (Que.), **285, 300**
Lac du Bonnet, **116**
Lac La Ronge, 318–19, **321, 322**
Ladysmith (B.C.), **82**
Lake Asotin, 48
Lake Athabasca, 44

Lakehead (Ont.), **230–31**
Lake Louise, 33, **52–53, 61–62,** 83
Lake Manitoba, 107
Lake Nipissing, **229–30**
Lake of the Woods, 231
Lake Simcoe, 229
Lake Winnipeg, 2, 107, **116–17**
Lake Winnipegosis, 107
La Malbaie (Que.), **285, 300**
La Ronge (Sask.), **319, 321, 322**
Last Mountain Lake, 316
La Tour, Charles de, 128
Laurentian Mountains, **279, 295–96**
Laurentides Park (Que.), **288**
Laurier, Sir Wilfred, 6, 212
Laval, Bishop, 282, 284
La Vérendrye, Sieur de, 103, 112, 116
La Vérendrye Provincial Park (Que.), **288**
Leacock, Stephen, 229
League of Nations, 6
Lebensold, Fred, 211, 276
Léger, Jules, 8
Lery, Baron de, 175
Lesser Slave Lake, 44
Lethbridge (Alta.), **55–56, 63**
Lévis (Que.), 261, 281
Lewisporte (Newf.), 155
Liberal party, 9–10, 129, 148, 178, 267
Lieutenant Governors, 9
Literature, **15,** 184, 227, 254; *see also* Poets
Liverpool (N.S.), 182*n*
London, Jack, 331
London (Ont.), **227, 239–40**
Longfellow, Henry Wadsworth, 176, 185
Longheed, Peter, 44
Lorne, Marquis of, 42, 314
Louisbourg, *see* Fortress of Louisbourg Na-
  tional Historic Park
Lower Canada, 203–4, 206, 266
Lower Fort Garry (Man.), **113–14**
Lower Post (B.C.), 87
Lowrer, A. R. M., 21
Loyalists, 5, 128, 133, 134, 136, 176, 214,
  216, 280
Lunenberg (N.S.), 176, **183, 192, 194**
Lusby, Vernon, 111
Lynch, Charles, 106

McCord, David Ross, 277
McCrae, John, 225
MacDonald, Brian, 111
Macdonald, Sir John A., 5, 17, 109, 210, 215
MacDonnell, Miles, 104
McDougall, George, 45
McInnis, Edgar, 1
McKay, Thomas, 209
Mackenzie, Sir Alexander, 70, 87, 163
Mackenzie, William Lyon, 204, 217
Mackenzie Highway, 33–34, 40, 161, 165
Mackenzie Mountains, 3, 162
Mackenzie River, 2, 162, 163
Mactaquac Provincial Park (N.B.), **135**
Magazines (periodicals), **14**
Magnetic Hill (N.B.), **138**
Magog (Que.), **280, 296**
Magog River, 280

Mahone Bay (N.S.), 183, **192**
Mail, **27–28**
Maine–Nova Scotia ferry, 32, 173
Maisonneuve, Sieur de, 271–72, 274
Maitland (N.S.), 182*n*
Mallorytown (Ont.), 213
Malpeque (P.E.I.), **254,** 258
Mance, Jeanne, 272
Manitoba, 19, **100–24**
  climate, 100
  creature comforts in, **120–24**
  further information, 101
  having a drink, 101
  history of, 6, 44, **103–6,** 163
  shopping in, **120**
  transportation, 101
Manning, Ernest, 43–44
Marconi, Guglielmo, 150
Margaree River Valley, **190–91**
Maritime Provinces, *see* New Brunswick;
  Nova Scotia; Prince Edward Island
Marystown (Newf.), **159**
Massey, Vincent, 8
Matane (Que.), 286, **300**
Mayo (Yukon), 325, **333**
Medical insurance, 312–13
Medicine Hat (Alta.), **56, 63**
Mennonites, 105, 106, 310
Métis, 104, 112–13, 309, 310, 316
Michener, Roland, 8
Midland (Ont.), 203, **229**
Midnight Sun, 329
Milk River, 44
Milltown Cross (P.E.I.), **255**
Minerals, 3, 73, 86, 105, 118, 155, 166, 202,
  311, 327, 328
Miramichi Bay (N.B.), 127
Monck, Viscount, 209
Moncton (N.B.), 135, **138, 141–42**
Montague (P.E.I.), 254
Montcalm, Marquis de, 5, 265, 282
Montebello (Ont.), **296–97**
Mont Joli (Que.), 286
Montreal (Que.), 13–16, 23, 26, 262, 266–70,
  270–76, 301–5
  hotels in, 32, **292–95**
Monts, Sieur de (Pierre du Guast), 127, 174,
  175, 185
Moore, Harvey, 255
Moore, Henry J., 115
Moores, Frank, 148
Moose Jaw (Sask.), 309, **319, 322**
Moose Mountain (Sask.), 310, 319
Moosomin (Sask.), 310
Morrisburg (Ont.), 206, 212
Mosques, 47, 187
Mosquitoes, 161, 325
Mount Assiniboine, 51
Mount Golden Hind (B.C.), 82, 83
Mounties, *see* Royal Canadian Mounted
  Police
Mount Logan, 3, 329
Mount Revelstoke National Park (B.C.),
  83, 84, **94–95**
Mount Stephen, Lord, 32

Mount Tremblant Provincial Park (Que.), 279
Mount Uniacke (N.S.), 182*n*, 184
Mount Whitehorn, 53
Museums
  airplanes, 212
  anthropology, 76, 80, 212
  archaeology, 281
  art, *see* Painting
  automobiles, 215
  brewery, 227
  decorative arts, 276, 277
  dinosaurs, 49, 56
  Eskimos, 47, 50, 119, 167, 221, 253, 276
  films, 212
  firefighters, 186
  forestry, 82, 83, 231, 280
  furniture, 221, 283
  historical, *see* Historical museums and buildings
  Indians, *see* Indians, museums of
  maritime, 76, 79–81, 152, 219, 255, 274
  military, 152, 212, 214, 215, 274
  natural history, 52, 76, 80, 212, 316, 318
  old glass, 254
  oriental, 80, 220
  postal, 212
  prisons, 215
  R.C.M.P., 316
  religious, 274, 281
  science and technology, 212, 222
  scouting, 212
  sports, 221, 223
  toys, 113, 221
  Ukrainian, 109
  villages, 49, 77, 139, 212–13, 219, 227, 279, 319
Music, 115; *see also* Symphony orchestras
Muskeg, 3
Muskoka Lakes, 229, 240

Nahanni National Park (N.W.T.), 167
Nanaimo (B.C.), 82–83, 94
National anthem, 12
National Ballet of Canada, 14, 222
National Film Board of Canada, 16
National motto, 12
National parks, 22–23
Natural gas, 41
Nelson (B.C.), 86
Nelson River, 2, 103
Nesbitt, Rev. James, 318
New Brunswick, 19, 32, 33, 125–42
  climate, 125
  creature comforts in, 140–42
  further information, 126
  having a drink, 126
  history of, 6, 127–29
  shopping in, 139–40
  transportation, 126
Newcastle (N.B.), 138–39
New Democratic Party, 10, 73, 105, 311
Newfoundland, 19, 32, 143–59
  climate, 143
  creature comforts in, 157–59
  further information, 145

having a drink, 144–45
  history of, 6, 145–48, 150
  shopping in, 156–57
  transportation, 144
New France, 5
New Glasgow (N.S.), 195
New Quebec, 287
Newspapers, 14–15
New Westminster (B.C.), 74
Niagara Falls, 205, 224–25, 238–39
Niagara-on-the-Lake (Ont.), 15, 225, 239
Nootka (B.C.), 70
North Battleford (Sask.), 317–18, 320, 321
North Bay (Ont.), 200, 229–30, 240–41
Northcliffe, Lord, 154
North Hatley (Que.), 280, 296
North West Arm (N.S.), 182
North West Company, 5, 70–71, 86, 104, 163, 230, 272, 309
Northwest Territories, 17, 42, 56, 160–70
  climate, 160
  creature comforts in, 168–70
  further information, 161
  having a drink, 161
  history of, 162–64, 310, 314–15
  shopping in, 168
  transportation, 161
Norway House (Man.), 120
Nova Scotia, 19, 32, 171–97
  climate, 171
  creature comforts in, 191, 192–97
  further information, 173
  having a drink, 173
  history of, 4, 6, 127, 128, 145, 174–77, 249
  shopping in, 178, 191–92
  transportation, 172–73
Novelists, 15, 184

Oakes, Sir Harry, 225
Odell, Jonathan, 133
Oil industry, 41, 48, 105, 311
Okanagan Valley (B.C.), 67, 86
Old Fort Henry (Ont.), 206, 214
Ontario, 17, 19, 199–245
  climate, 199–200
  creature comforts in, 233–45
  further information, 201
  having a drink, 201
  history of, 6, 163, 202–4, 206–9, 212–14, 216–17, 266
  Quebec compared to, 202
  shopping in, 231–33
  transportation, 201–2
Opera, 14, 50, 78, 112, 222, 278
Order of the Good Time, 174
Orillia (Ont.), 229, 240
Oromocto (N.B.), 133, 140
Oshawa (Ont.), 215
Ottawa (Ont.), 8, 13, 16, 26, 200, 206–12, 233, 244–45, 315
  hotels of, 209, 233–34
Ottawa River, 203, 280
Outaouais, the, 280
Owen Sound (Ont.), 13

Pacific Rim National Park (B.C.), 83

Painting, 12–13
Alberta, 46–47, 49, 50
British Columbia, 75–76, 80
Manitoba, 109, 110
New Brunswick, 133–34, 136
Nova Scotia, 181, 184
Ontario, 211, 219–20, 221, 223, 226–28
Prince Edward Island, 252–53
Quebec, 275–77, 280, 284
Saskatchewan, 316, 317, 319
Paper mills, 154
Papineau, Louis Joseph, 266
Parks, national, 22–23
Parksville (B.C.), 94
Peace of Paris (1763), 103, 203, 265
Peace River, 44, 86
Pearson, Lester B., 9, 12, 137, 212, 268
Peggy's Cove (N.S.), 182–83
Pelatt, Sir Henry M., 218
Penticton (B.C.), 86, 95
Percé (Que.), 287, 292, 300–1
Perez, Juan, 70
Peterborough (Ont.), 223, 238
Petitcodiac River, 138
Philip, Price, 79
Phipps, Sir William, 282
Pictou (N.S.), 187, 192
Pike Lake Provincial Park (Sask.), 320
Placentia (Newf.), 146, 147, 153, 155
Plains of Abraham (Que.), 5, 265, 282,
283–84
Planetariums, 47, 76–77, 110
Poets, 15, 135, 225
Point Escuminac (N.B.), 127
Point Pelee National Park (Ont.), 228
Point Pleasant (N.S.), 182
Police, 17–18; *see also* Royal Canadian
Mounted Police
Poole, Ernest R., 46
Population of Canada, 1
Port-aux-Basques (Newf.), 144, 154–55, 158,
172
Port de Grave (Newf.), 153
Port Hill (P.E.I.), 255
Port Moody (B.C.), 33
Port Nelson (Man.), 103
Port Royal (N.S.), *see* Annapolis Royal
Pre-Cambrian Shield, *see* Canadian Shield
Prime Minister, 9–10, 208, 210, 252
Prince Albert (Sask.), 318, 322
Prince Albert National Park (Sask.), 318,
323
Prince Edward Island, 6, 32, 103, 126, 174,
246–59
climate, 246–47
creature comforts in, 256–59
further information, 247
having a drink, 247
history of, 6, 127, 248–50
shopping in, 255–56
transportation, 247
Prince Edward Island National Park
(P.E.I.), 253, 257
Prince George (B.C.), 86, 87, 95
Prince Rupert (B.C.), 87, 95–96

Progressive Conservative party, 9–10, 44,
105, 129, 148, 178, 204
Provencher, Bishop, 112
Pugwash (N.S.), 187

Quebec, 17, 19, 260–306
climate, 260–61
creature comforts in, 292–306
further information, 262–63
having a drink, 262
history of, 4–6, 163, 264–68, 271–72, 281–
82
Ontario compared to, 202
separatism in, 11–12, 264, 267–68
shopping in, 288–92
transportation, 261–62
Quebec City (Que.), 4, 8, 14, 15, 26, 165,
208, 281–85, 291–92, 305–6
hotels in, 33, 297–300
Queen of Canada, 8, 202, 210
Quesnel (B.C.), 85

Radio, 16
Radium Hot Springs (B.C.), 84
Rae (N.W.T.), 166–67
Railroads, 6, 22, 32–33, 86, 109, 155; *see
also* Transportation *under each prov-
ince*
Rattenbury, Francis M., 79
Red Deer River, 44
Red River, 103, 105
Regan, Gerald A., 178
Regatta, 224
Regina (Sask.), 17, 42, 108, 307–10, 312,
314–16, 320, 321–22
Religions in Canada, 19; *see also* Churches,
cathedrals, and shrines; Mosques
Restaurants, *see* Creature Comforts *under
each province*
Revelstoke, *see* Mount Revelstoke National
Park
Rideau Canal, 206, 209
Riding Mountain National Park (Man.),
114, 121
Riel, Louis, 104, 113, 114, 310, 316, 318
Rimouski (Que.), 286, 300
Rivière du Loup (Que.), 286, 300
Robichaud, Louis J., 129
Rockies, *see* Canadian Rockies
Rockport (Ont.), 214
Rocky Point (P.E.I.), 255
Rodeo, 55
Rogers Pass (B.C.), 83, 85
Rondeau Provincial Park (Ont.), 227
Roosevelt, Franklin D., 137, 147, 214
Roseneath (P.E.I.), 257–58
Rothermere, Lord, 154
Rowan's Ravine Provincial Park (Sask.),
320
Royal Canadian Mounted Police (Mount-
ies), 17–18, 42, 50, 76, 161, 167, 208,
309, 315
show by, 115
training college for, 316
Royal Winnipeg Ballet, 14, 102, 111
Rupert's Land, 42, 103

Russian immigrants, 310
Rustico (P.E.I.), **254**

Sackville (N.B.), **139**
Saguenay River, 286
St. Andrews (N.B.), **136–37, 139, 141**
St. Boniface (Man.), **112–13,** 123
St. Catherines (Ont.), **223–24, 235**
Saint Croix River, 127
Sainte-Adèle (Que.), **296**
St. Elias Mountains, 3, 329, 332
Sainte-Marguerite Station (Que.), 296
Saint John (N.B.), 127, 128–29, **131–32,**
    134–35, 139, **140,** 150
Saint John River, 127, 132, 133, **135–36**
St. John's (Newf.), 16, 26, 131, 146, **149–52,**
    155, **156, 157–58**
St. Laurent, Louis, 148
St. Lawrence Islands National Park (Ont.),
    213–14
St. Lawrence Lowlands, 2
St. Lawrence River (Seaway), 2, 180, 202,
    212, **223,** 273, 281, 285, 286
Saint-Marc-sur-Richelieu (Que.), 296
St. Mary River, 44
Saint-Pierre and Miquelon, 144, 146, 172,
    197–98
St. Stephen (N.B.), **136,** 141
Samuel, Sigmond, 221
San Juan Island, 72
Saskatchewan, 42, 44, 108, **307–23**
    climate, 307–8
    creature comforts in, **321–23**
    further information, 308
    having a drink, 308
    history of, 6, 104, 163, **309–13**
    shopping in, **320–21**
    transportation, 308
Saskatchewan River, 2, 44, 316
Saskatoon (Sask.), 108, 309–10, **317, 320–21,**
    322
Sault Ste. Marie (Ont.), 200, **230**
Scandinavian immigrants, 310
Schefferville (Labrador), 155, 287
Schreyer, Ed, 105
Scotch immigrants, 103, 106, 177, 187, 203,
    249, 310
Sculpture, 47, 110, 220, 230; *see also* Eski-
    mos—museums of
Selkirk, Lord, 103–4, 107, 112, 249, 254
Selkirk (Man.), 116
Semple, Robert, 104
Senate, Canadian, 9, 207–8
Sept-Iles (Que.), 155, **287, 301**
Service, Robert W., 326, 331
Seven Oaks, Battle of (1816), 104
Shaughnessy, Lord, 32
Shediac (N.B.), **139**
Shelburne (N.S.), 182*n*
Sherbrooke (N.S.), 182*n*
Sherbrooke (Que.), **280**
Ships, *see* Coastal ships; Museums—mari-
    time
Shopping in Canada, 29; *see also* Shopping
    under each province
Simpson, George, 113

Sixty Mile Road, 325
Skagway (Alaska), 330, 333
Skiing, 52, 55, 86, 274, 280, 285
Skin-diving, 116
Smallwood, Joseph, 148
Social Credit Party, 10, 43, 73
South Dildo (Newf.), 157
South Saskatchewan River, **311–12,** 315, 317
Sparks, Nicholas, 106
Spohr, Arnold, 111
Sports, 221, 223
Stampedes, 48, 56, 85
Stanhope Beach (P.E.I.), **257**
Starrs Point (N.S.), 182*n*, 185
Statute of Westminster, 6
Steele, Sir Samuel, 109
Stephenville (Newf.), **158**
Stikine Mountains, 3
Stirling, Earl of, 175
Stowe, Harriet Beecher, *Uncle Tom,* 227
Stratford Festival, 15, 205, **226–27,** 235
Strathcona, Lord, 60
Strathcona Provincial Park (B.C.), **83**
Strathgartney (P.E.I.), **255**
Stuart, David, 70
Sulphur Mountain, 51, 52
Summerside (P.E.I.), **253, 258**
Swan River (Man.), 122
Swift Current (Sask.), 309
Swimming, *see* Beaches
Swiss immigrants, 183
Sydney (N.S.), 144, 172, **188–89 192, 195–**
    96, 198
Symphony orchestras, 14, 78, 111, 223

Tadoussac (Que.), **285–86, 300**
Tagish Lake (Yukon), 333
Takakkaw Falls (B.C.), 84
Television, 16
Terra Nova (Newf.), 153
Theatre, **15–16**
    British Columbia, 16, 78
    Manitoba, 16, 110–12, 113
    New Brunswick, 133
    Nova Scotia, 15, 178
    Ontario, 15, 216, 225, **226–27**
    Prince Edward Island, 15, 252, 254
    Quebec, 15–16, 274, 275, 278, 284
The Pas (Man.), **117–18, 122**
Thompson (Man.), **118, 122**
Thompson River, 71
Thousand Islands, **213–14, 234**
Thunder Bay (Ont.), 200, **230–31, 241**
Timber industry, 72, 105, 129
    museums of, 82, 83, 231, 280
Time zones in Canada, 2
Timmins (Ont.), **230, 241**
Tipping, Canadian attitude to, 28
Topsail (Newf.), 153
Toronto (Ont.), 14, 16, 23, 26, 105, 200,
    201, 203, 205, **215–23, 231–33, 241–44**
    hotels in, 33, **235–38**
Tourism in Canada, 21–22; *see also* Further
    information *under each province*
Tours in Canada, **31, 34**

Trans-Canada Highway, 22, **33–34**, 40, 67, 101, 126, 144, 148, 154, 172, 200, 230, 247, 261, 281, 308
   Canso Causeway of, 187, 190
   Rogers Pass section of, 83, 85
Trappers' Festival, 117–18
Travel Agent, The (journal), 22
Traytown (Newf.), **158**
Trois-Rivières (Que.), **280–81, 297**
Trotsky, Leon, 180
Troupe, Capt. J. W., 79
Trudeau, Pierre Elliott, 10, 268
Truro (N.S.), **187, 192, 195**
Tundra, 107
Tunnel, longest, 85

Ukrainians, 42, 47, 97–98, 106, 109, 310, 317
Uncle Tom (Stowe), 227
Ungava Bay, 287
Uniacke, James B., 177
United Empire Loyalists, *see* Loyalists
United Farmers Party, 43
United Nations, 7
United Press International, 14
Universities and colleges
   Alberta, 47, 51, 55
   British Columbia, 76, 77
   Manitoba, 106, 109, 113, 114
   New Brunswick, 134, 136, 138, 139, 177
   Newfoundland, 152
   Nova Scotia, 177, 178, 181, 184, 185, 187, 188
   Ontario, 209, 215, 217–18, 223, 226–28, 231
   Prince Edward Island, 253
   Quebec, 269, 275, 276, 280, 283
   Saskatchewan, 312, 316, 317
Upper Canada, 203–4, 206, 214–16
Upper Canada Village (Ont.), 206, 212–13
U.S.–Canadian border, 3, 26, 228
U.S. consulates in Canada, 26

Val David (Que.), 295–96
Vancouver, Capt. George, 70, 80
Vancouver (B.C.), 13, 14, 16, 23, 26, 32, 67, **74–78, 88–89, 96–98**
   hotels in, 32, **90–93, 96**
Vancouver Island (B.C.), 73, **82–83, 94**
Van Horne, Sir William, 32
Vanier, Maj. Gen. Georges P., 8, 9
Vernon (B.C.), **95**
Verrazano, Giovanni da, 175
Versailles Peace Conference, 6
Victoria (Queen of England), 206–7
Victoria (B.C.), 13, 16, 67, 71, **78–82, 89–90, 99**
   hotels in, 33, 79, **93–94, 98–99**
Victoria Island (N.W.T.), **169–70**
Vikings, 4, 117, 145, 174
Vimont, Bartholémy, 272

Wabush (Labrador), **155, 159**

Walter, John, 47
Wapella (Sask.), 310
War of 1812, 5, 212–14, 216
Wasaga (Ont.), **229**
Wasagaming (Man.), 114
Waskesiu (Sask.), **318, 323**
Water-skiing, 116
Waterton Lakes National Park (Alta.), **55, 63**
Watson Lake (Yukon), **333, 334**
Wawa (Ont.), 230
Weaving, **16**
Wells Gray Provincial Park (B.C.), 85
Whales, 119
Whitehorse (Yukon), 327–28, 329, **330–31, 333–34**
Whiteshell Provincial Park (Man.), **116, 122**
Wild animals, 48, 53, 84, 130, 155, 156, 316, 318, 319, 329, 332
   See also Buffalo herds; Zoos
Williams Lake (B.C.), 85, **95**
Windsor (N.S.), **184–85, 194**
Windsor (Ont.), **228, 240**
Wine festival, 224
Winnipeg (Man.), 14, 16, 23, 26, 78, 101, 103–6, **107–12, 120–21, 122–24**
Wolfe, Gen. James, 5, 265, 282
Wolfville (N.S.), **185**
Wood Buffalo National Park (Alta.– N.W.T.), 56, 167
Wood Islands (P.E.I.), 187, 247
Woodstock (N.B.), **135**
World War I, 6, 108, 151, 180, 208
World War II, 7, 43, 147, 148–49, 154–55, 178, 180, 212, 264, 327, 332

Yarmouth (N.S.), **186, 192, 195**
Yellowknife (N.W.T.), 17, 161, 163, 164, **166, 168–69**
Yoho National Park (B.C.), 53, **83–84, 94**
York (Ont.), *see* Toronto (Ont.)
York (P.E.I.), **254–55**
Yukon River, 2, 331
Yukon Territory, 3, 17, 86, **324–35**
   climate, 324–25
   creature comforts in, **334–35**
   further information, 326
   having a drink, 326
   history of, 326–28
   shopping in, **333–34**
   transportation, 325–26
   See also Klondike Gold Rush

Zoos
   Alberta, 47, 49
   British Columbia, 75
   Manitoba, 109
   Ontario, 222, 227
   Quebec, 274, 280
   Saskatchewan, 319

R